Diary of a Contraband
THE CIVIL WAR PASSAGE OF A BLACK SAILOR

Diary of a

Contraband

THE CIVIL WAR PASSAGE

OF A BLACK SAILOR

William B. Gould IV

STANFORD UNIVERSITY PRESS
STANFORD, CALIFORNIA

Stanford University Press
Stanford, California

Printed in the United States of America on acid-free, archival-quality paper.

Frontispiece: William B. Gould in his veteran's hat

Dedication page photograph: William Benjamin Gould III (1902–1983),
July 11, 1942, at Wilmette Harbor, Wilmette, Illinois

Library of Congress Cataloging-in-Publication Data
Gould, William Benjamin.
  Diary of a contraband : the Civil War passage of a Black sailor /
[edited by] William B. Gould IV.
    p.   cm.
  Includes index.
  ISBN 0-8047-4640-0 (cloth : alk. paper)—ISBN 0-8047-4708-3 (pbk. : alk. paper)
  1. Gould, William Benjamin, 1837–1923—Diaries.   2. United States—History—
Civil War, 1861–1865—Personal narratives.   3. United States—History—Civil War,
1861–1865—Participation, African American.   4. United States—History—Civil War,
1861–1865—Naval operations.   5. African American sailors—Diaries.   6. Sailors—
United States—Diaries.   7. Gould family.   8. Dedham (Mass.)—Genealogy.
9. Wilmington (N.C.)—Biography.   I. Gould, William B.   II. Title.
E591 .g68   2002
973.7'415—dc21   2002009238

Original Printing 2002
Last figure below indicates year of this printing:
11   10   09   08   07   06   05   04

Designed by James P. Brommer
Typeset in 11/16 Bulmer

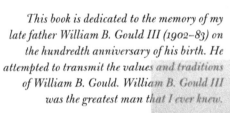

This book is dedicated to the memory of my late father William B. Gould III (1902–83) on the hundredth anniversary of his birth. He attempted to transmit the values and traditions of William B. Gould. William B. Gould III was the greatest man that I ever knew.

Contents

Plates appear after pages 6, 84, and 274

Maps

Foreword

MARK O. HATFIELD

United States Senator, 1967–1997

With *Diary of a Contraband: The Civil War Passage of a Black Sailor*, William B. Gould IV has delivered something both inspirational and of real consequence to the world of American history. Through years of hard work and determination, the author has created an insightful and thought-provoking book in which he uncovers countless treasures of family history that will no doubt cause descendants of the first and the fourth William B. Gould to read this volume with tremendous pride. Equally certain is the fact that the serious literary and historic value of this work will be appreciated far beyond the Gould family. With the author's helpful assistance, the reader is able to look back over 140 years and view the life of a slave who seized his freedom and embarked on a journey rich in historical significance and overflowing with personal drama and danger.

We can only imagine how a twenty-four-year-old William B. Gould felt on that rainy night in 1862 as he and seven other slaves escaped and braved twenty-eight miles of the Cape Fear River in hopes of reaching the Atlantic and joining the Union Navy. The daring plan worked and all eight "contrabands" were taken aboard the U.S.S. *Cambridge*, a Union ship participating in the North Atlantic Blockading Squadron. Although the coincidence is striking, the eight could not have known that within an hour and a half of their first encounter with the Union Navy near Fort Caswell, North Carolina, President Lincoln would convene a Cabinet meeting at which his intent to issue the Emancipation Proclamation was finalized.

Gould had risked all and had won his freedom from slavery. As a free man, he took an active and, we learn, a very satisfying role as a member of the Union Navy in bringing about the demise of the centuries-old institution from which he had just escaped. One imagines that echoing in the ears of young Gould were the words uttered by President Lincoln in 1860: "Let us have faith that right makes might."

Gould's civil war naval diary, which is the heart of *Diary of a Contraband*, allows the reader to watch through Gould's eyes as his ship hunts down vessels attempting to break the Union's naval blockade. The author's painstaking research allows the reader to view the full context and significance of these events, while at the same time experiencing some part of the exhilaration Gould must have felt as he became a paid member of the crew—a sailor who was free to come and go as he pleased, and who frequently did just that.

Diary of a Contraband provides a wonderful complement to the *Slave Narrative Collection* housed at the Library of Congress. The *Slave Narrative Collection* is a fascinating compilation of interviews of former slaves conducted from 1936 to 1939 by participants in the Federal Writers Project. Because these interviews took place so many years after the conclusion of the Civil War, when the interviewees were advanced in years, and were recorded by interviewers of varying abilities, historians have at times discounted the reliability of these personal accounts (see Norman R. Yetman, "Ex-Slave Interviews and the Historiography of Slavery," *American Quarterly*, 36.2 [Summer 1984]: 181–210). *Diary of a Contraband* offers much firmer footing for the serious historian, as young William B. Gould appears to have recorded the significant events of the day in his own hand at or soon after the time they took place.

Gould was among a small number of slaves in the Antebellum South who were able to read and write. One of the many mysteries surrounding this man is how he came to possess his impressive literary skills. Regardless of how he gained them, the reader benefits from the vibrant detail in his account. As the author reveals, Gould's contributions to this nation did not end with his service in the Union Navy. His outstanding life, in Dedham, Massachusetts, following the war, exemplifies American citizenship at its best—citizenship that burned brightly because our nation transcended the inhumanity of slavery.

Preface

This book is about my great-grandfather William B. Gould and focuses, in particular, upon the diary he kept between 1862 and 1865, years in which he was in service to "Uncle Samuel," as he liked to call our Uncle Sam. But it is impossible for me to write about William B. Gould without setting forth some memories of his descendants, particularly those I knew as a child.

Some of my most vivid childhood memories are of the Dedham, Massachusetts, funerals of the great-uncles in the 1940s and 1950s. Each funeral and the festive meals prepared thereafter by my Aunt Isabel Gould at her Dedham house represented not only a child's first awareness of death, but also the gathering of all the Massachusetts Goulds from whom we were separated by the long driving distance from our home in Long Branch, New Jersey. The public viewing of those open caskets is forever seared into my consciousness. And with each burial, the proud past and legacy provided by William B. Gould became more distant and difficult to recapture.

Inevitably, my own recollections as a child and my hour of trial and peril as Chairman of the National Labor Relations Board in Washington, D.C., play into my great-grandfather's Civil War story because, in my view, during those years I was in combat with people who supported many of the same policies and principles of the defeated Confederacy against which William B. Gould fought.

In the last third of the previous century, Massachusetts and North Carolina—the states of William Benjamin Gould's birth and most of his adult residence—loomed large in the body politic. The names of President John F. Kennedy, the sponsor of 1960s civil rights legislation, and Senator Edward M. Kennedy have dominated Massachusetts, just as now-retiring Senator Jesse Helms and former Senator Lauch Faircloth have come to symbolize aspects of politics and attitudes in North Carolina's modern era. William B. Gould left North Carolina for Massachusetts—though he obviously retained an involvement and interest in the former, particularly with so many friends in responsible positions in North Carolina Reconstruction.

That political figures from those two states in particular have had so great a hand in my Washington career has made me reflect anew on the role of both Massachusetts and North Carolina in my own life. Issues akin to those about which war was fought in the 1860s were played out again on the stage of 1990s politics. The volatility and polarization in both eras is in no small respect mirrored by the political realignment that took place in both parties. As Robert William Fogel has noted in *The Fourth Great Awakening* (2000), "It is the political realignment of the 1850s that is most similar to the political realignment of the 1990s."

Support during my NLRB tenure came from both parties, especially by the "Radical" Republican from Oregon, Mark Hatfield, a lineal descendant of some of the most prominent of the Confederacy's adversaries in the Republican Party between 1861 and 1865. Senator Hatfield was my best friend and most influential supporter in the Congress during my tenure. And without Massachusetts' Ted Kennedy's leadership in the confirmation process, I could not have served in Washington.

In August 2001, I had a chance to return again to Boston, Massachusetts, the place where I was born. And as I walked its streets I could see in my mind's eye my father's description of hundreds of Civil War veterans marching down its grand avenues. While in Washington from 1994 to 1998, I visited Massachusetts and North Carolina on a number of occasions and was able to walk in the paths established by the first William B. Gould more than a century ago. His memory and the stories I heard about him from my father while I was a young and middle-aged man gave me the strength to stand firm against the conservative Republicans' withering assault upon the New Deal legislation of Franklin D. Roosevelt —the legal instruments that promote the Emancipation Proclamation and the Thirteenth Amendment's prohibition against involuntary servitude, and thus build on what William B. Gould and his comrades accomplished in 1865.

As I have previously written, the visits to Appomattox, Gettysburg, Antietam, the Wilderness, Fredericksburg, and Manassas while I resided in Washington all served some of the same purposes and renewed my sense of purpose rooted in the sacrifice that he and succeeding generations made for me and my children.

In a profound sense, the results obtained in 1865 for which William B. Gould and so many others struggled valiantly have come under attack with the rise of right-wing conservatives like Newt Gingrich, Tom DeLay, and especially former Senate Majority Leader Trent Lott of Mississippi, who openly consorted with segregationist and white supremacist forces in his home state in the 104th and 105th Congresses. The fight against these men and what they stand for reminds us again of the retreat sounded since William B. Gould's celebration of victory in 1865.

I owe principal inspiration for this work to the William B. Goulds who went before me—particularly my father—as well as to my mother, Leah F. Gould. I am well aware that I could not have enjoyed the career I have had were it not for the sacrifices that all my Gould forebears made, in one war or another.

﹏

A number of dedicated and capable people made substantial contributions to the completion of this book. I could not have completed it without the exceptional research and organizational skills of Sarah Preston, my assistant at Stanford Law School. Scarcely a day went by when she did not present something new and original or exciting. More than just a research assistant, she was an editor who critiqued my written words and reminded me of matters that I had overlooked or forgotten, organized the footnotes, and then typed the manuscript as well. Not least, she created both the Glossary of Naval Terms and the table of William B. Gould's correspondents in the Appendixes. Her abilities in all of these areas are superlative. In short, I could not have completed this work without her help.

Among the many others I am grateful to, I must mention my oldest son, William B. Gould V, who provided the first typescript version of parts of the diary—it was transcribed by Sally Palepoi; and Mary Ann Sawyer, my outstanding confidential assistant at the National Labor Relations Board, who typed a second and complete version of the diary on her own time at home. I shall never forget her unqualified loyalty and devotion to me. Along with my Chief Counsel William R. Stewart, she was the nerve center of the NLRB in the 1990s.

I am also grateful to Diana Buttu of Stanford Law School, who was the first to begin to identify many of William B. Gould's correspondents. Her valuable research and organization of the diary—she was the first to arrange for its typing exactly as it was written, misspellings and all—helped me and alerted me to many avenues of research.

I am particularly indebted to Professor John Hope Franklin of Duke University who, when here at Stanford Law School as Phleger Professor of Law, read the entire diary and submitted a memorandum to me about it. This served the twofold purpose of highlighting passages that I had not paid sufficient attention to and guiding me in future research. I am especially grateful to Professor Franklin.

Others were most helpful as research assistants—Roger Davidson, Learie Luke, Jennifer Schniedwind, Sally Gordon, Deborah Ho, Anna Giske, Scott Heald, and Jim C. Harper II. The Stanford Research Opportunities Department provided me with financial assistance to pursue certain lines of research, for which I am deeply grateful.

I am most fortunate to have the resources of the Stanford Law School Library to draw on. The library has responded to so many of my requests and has provided valuable help to me on this book. In particular, I am grateful to Erika Wayne for her resourcefulness, intelligence, and indefatigable good cheer.

David Woodbury did the valuable map work, and I am very grateful to him. I would like to thank Candis Griggs, who took many photographs for me of various objects that belonged to William B. Gould. Similarly, I thank Stephen Gladfelter, of the Stanford University Visual Art Services, who photographed the diary and my great-grandfather's medals. I am also grateful to Mark Hayes of the Old Navy Department at the Naval Historical Center in Washington, D.C., for attempting to educate me about naval terms and institutional practices. I am especially appreciative of the work done for me in Dedham by my friend former Administrative Law Judge for the NLRB, George F. McInery; and for the assistance of Father John Fesq and Father Edward Kienzle of that city's Church of the Good Shepherd.

Particularly worthy of mention are Beverly Tetterton, a specialist in local history and genealogy at the New Hanover County (N.C.) Public Library; Peg Bradner, a library volunteer at the Dedham Historical Society; and Morris Rabinowitz, former director of the Dedham Public Library. They provided me with much information about William B. Gould in both places and also provided me with background information about both Wilmington and Dedham. Beverly Tetterton arranged for me to speak in Wilmington in 1998 and provided me with useful contacts, notably, George Stevenson, Private Manuscripts Archivist at the North Carolina Department of Cultural Resources; Jonathan Noffke, former curator of the Bellamy Mansion in Wilmington; Professor David Cecelski of the University of North Carolina; and Professor Chris Fonvielle of UNC Wilmington. In Wilmington, Michael Murchison, a former NLRB lawyer, graciously hosted me on one of my early visits to that city and provided me with relevant background material. I am grateful to him for his help and hospitality.

Helen Seager of the Friends of the African Meeting House introduced me again to Nantucket during my three visits there in the 1990s—I had not been to Nantucket since I was a child. She provided me with valuable information about the island, and she discovered a series of newspaper articles from the 1850s about my great-grandmother's purchase out of slavery. Ms. Seager arranged for me to speak in Nantucket on Memorial Day, 1998. I am grateful to her for all of her help.

I am also grateful to Professor Joseph Reidy of Howard University and Rebecca Livingston of the National Archives in Washington, D.C. I had the privilege to serve with them on the Advisory Committee of Howard University's African American Civil War Sailors Project, which did pioneer research on black sailors in the War of the Rebellion.

I would like to thank Jaime Martínez García, director of the Office of Tourism in La Coruña, Spain, who helped me trace WBG's path on the *Niagara* in La Coruña and El Ferrol.

Presentations that I made at the Research Institute of Comparative Studies in Race and Ethnicity and the African and African American Studies Department at Stanford University in 2001 helped me organize my thoughts about this work.

The penultimate draft of this work was read by Professor William Andrews, Chairman of the History Department, University of North Carolina; Professor Barbara Allen Babcock, Judge John Crown Professor of Law at Stanford Law School; Professor Michael Klarman, James Monroe Professor of Law, Albert C. Tate, Jr., Research Professor, and Professor of History at the University of Virginia; Beverly Tetterton; and Peg Bradner. I thank all of them for the time, effort, and expertise they so generously gave to me.

I could not have completed this work without the help of any of these people. Of course, I take full responsibility for any errors or deficiencies in it.

Finally, during these past three decades, the patience and understanding of my family—my wife, Hilda Elizabeth, and my three sons, William Benjamin V, Timothy Samuel, and Edward Blair—were essential, and I am grateful to all of them.

My hope is that this book will help tell the story of this most extraordinary individual who struggled on behalf of the Flag of Right and Equality, as he called it, and accomplished so much in the time given to him—William B. Gould of Wilmington, North Carolina, and Dedham, Massachusetts.

Dramatis Personae

The Other Seven Contrabands

Joseph Hall.   His part in the dramatic escape from Wilmington on September 20, 1862, is chronicled in *The Anglo-African*, as is his relationship with Lucilla Moseley. He and his wife settle down in Old Port Comfort, Va.

George Price.   He left Wilmington to join the *Cambridge*, but may have deserted thereafter. Nonetheless, he plays an active role in North Carolina politics during Reconstruction. He represents New Hanover County in the state House of Representatives and Senate. In 1881, he heads a delegation that meets with President James A. Garfield to protest against the unfair distribution of federal offices in North Carolina.

Andrew Hall.   The brother of Joseph Hall. He settles in Cambridge, Mass., after the war and apparently has some contact with WBG thereafter.

John Mackey.   He corresponds with WBG during the war and passes news to him about Wilmington.

Charles Giles.   Corresponds with WBG.

Nothing is known of the two other men—**John Mitchell** and **William Chanse**—beyond the fact that they were in the group of eight picked up by the *Cambridge*.

Friends and Acquaintances

Henry Smith.   A shipmate of WBG's on the U.S.S. *Niagara*. He is placed
in irons for some infraction, but makes several interesting and provocative
contributions to *The Anglo-African* about the ship's European voyage.

Robert Hamilton.   The editor of *The Anglo-African*, the major black
abolitionist newspaper in New York City, whose offices WBG frequently
visits. He and WBG correspond, and he must have reviewed or edited some
of WBG's articles and letters to the editor.

Abraham Galloway.   The Scarlet Pimpernel of North Carolina, he escapes
in 1857 and returns to the South as a spy for the Union forces during the war.
He apparently knew WBG in North Carolina before the war. They get
together in New York City in the spring of 1864 shortly after Galloway meets
with President Lincoln in Washington. He serves in the North Carolina
Legislature after the war.

Immediate Family

Elizabeth "Betsy" Moore.   WBG's mother. She is born in Wilmington,
N.C., where she is a slave. She dies on March 13, 1865.

Alexander Gould.   WBG's father. He is born in England and lives in
Granville County, N.C.

Eliza Mabson.   WBG's sister. She lives in Wilmington and is the mother of
five children, two of whom, George Lawrence Mabson and William Mabson,
are involved in Republican Party politics during Reconstruction. She
corresponds with WBG while he is at sea in 1865.

Cornelia Williams Read (1837–1906).   WBG's wife. Born into slavery in
Charleston, S.C., she is the daughter of Diana Williams and William Read.
She is brought by her owner to Wilmington and apparently meets WBG
there. She is bought out of slavery in 1858 and taken north to Nantucket. She
and WBG are married at the African Baptist Church there. In Dedham, she is
active in the work of the Episcopal Church of the Good Shepherd as well as
Grand Army of the Republic activities.

Diana S. Williams (d. 1860).   Cornelia's mother. She is born in Charleston, S.C., where she is a slave. Her sisters, Ann and Julia, reside in Nantucket and Boston, respectively. Ann's husband, the prominent Baptist minister James E. Crawford, orchestrates the purchase of Diana and Cornelia out of slavery in 1857 and 1858.

William Read.   Cornelia's father. He is born in Charleston, S.C. Nothing more is known about him.

Medora Williams Gould (1866–1944).   She is the oldest of WBG's children and is born in Nantucket. She works at home and never marries. She is a well-read woman, and some of her books are handed down through the generations.

William B. Gould Jr. (1869–1931).   He is WBG's second child and is born at Taunton, Mass. He works as a clerk for the Hawley, Folsom Company in Boston. He is a vestryman of the Church of the Good Shepherd in Dedham and serves as a sergeant in the 6th Massachusetts Regiment, Company L, during the Spanish-American War. He marries Hannah Jane Jordan of Cambridge, Mass., in 1901. He is the only one of WBG's eight sons and daughters to have children: William B. Gould III, Ernest, Robert, and Marjorie.

Frederick Crawford Gould (1872–1949).   He is born in Dedham and never marries. He works as a machinist and is a veteran of World War I.

Luetta Ball Gould (1873–1967).   She is born in Hyde Park and never marries. She moves to New York, where she works as a stenographer, and separates herself from the rest of the Gould family.

Lawrence Wheeler Gould (1875–1958).   He is born in Hyde Park and never marries. He is a veteran of World War I. He alone carries on WBG's work as a plasterer and mason, though two of WBG's other sons, Herbert and Frederick, briefly try their hand at this physically demanding trade. On his death, the diary is discovered among his possessions.

Herbert Richardson Gould (1878–1957).   He is born in Dedham and works as a government inspector in Massachusetts. In World War I, he serves as a first lieutenant in the 367th Infantry. He marries Agnes Gould of Gouldtown, N.J., a distant relative of William B. Gould III's wife, Leah Felts Gould.

Ernest Moore Gould (1880–1945).   A twin son of WBG's, born in Dedham. He is a faculty member of the Howard University Dental School in Washington, D.C. In World War I, he is a first lieutenant in the 350th Field Artillery. He is survived by his wife, Fannie Butler, of Washington, D.C.

James Edward Gould (1880–1963).   Ernest Gould's twin brother. He works as a draftsman and serves as a first lieutenant in World War I in the 367th Infantry, the same regiment as his brother Herbert. He is the last of WBG's six sons to die. He is survived by his wife, Isabel Hurling, of South Carolina.

Other Family Members

George Lawrence Mabson.   He is the mulatto son of WBG's sister, Eliza Moore, and George W. Mabson, a prominent white man in Wilmington, N.C. He provides one of the first links between Wilmington and Boston, where he goes to school in the 1850s. A frequent correspondent of WBG's during the war, he serves in both the U.S. Navy and the 5th Massachusetts Cavalry. After the war, he earns a law degree at Howard Law School in 1871. He becomes the first black lawyer in the state of North Carolina. He serves in the state House of Representatives and Senate, and represents New Hanover County at the Constitutional Convention of 1875. He makes an unsuccessful run for a U.S. House seat in 1870.

Thomas H. Jones.   A member of the family through marriage. He flees from Wilmington to New York in 1843. In the North, he is active in abolitionist circles and after a brief flight to Canada when his freedom seemed in jeopardy, he lives variously in Boston and New York. He becomes known as the central figure in a book published in 1854, *The Experience of Thomas H. Jones Who Was a Slave for Forty-Three Years*. The Jones family appears to have provided WBG with ties to the abolitionist communities in both New York and Boston. They, like Mabson, provide a connection to the North and probably influence WBG's decision to settle near Boston after the war.

Mary Moore (Aunt Jones).   She is the aunt WBG meets with in Boston in the spring of 1863. She is a sister of his mother, Elizabeth. Her husband, Thomas H. Jones, and she are the parents of the Jones cousins who exchange many letters with WBG while he is at sea.

Julia Ward Williams (1811–70).   One of Cornelia Read's aunts. She is born
in Charleston, S.C., but comes to Boston at an early age. She is a teacher
and is involved in a number of efforts to aid the freedmen. She marries the
Reverend Henry Highland Garnet in 1841.

Henry Highland Garnet.   Cornelia Williams Read's uncle by marriage, he
is a prominent black preacher and the man who triggers the series of events
that leads to her purchase out of slavery. He becomes a major opponent of
Frederick Douglass on issues relating to exhortations to slaves, the black
press, and (until he has a change of heart after the war) colonization.

James E. Crawford.   He is a well-known minister of the African Baptist
Church on Nantucket who is married to Cornelia Williams Read's Aunt Ann.
He arranges for the purchase of both Cornelia and her mother out of slavery
in 1857 and 1858. The Goulds are married by him at his church in Nantucket
in 1865.

Diary of a Contraband

THE CIVIL WAR PASSAGE OF A BLACK SAILOR

Prologue

William Benjamin Gould (1837–1923) was an extraordinary man by any measure: a slave, a contraband who served in the U.S. Navy during the Civil War, literate at a time when few blacks had access to formal education, and most important for the historian, a diarist and published writer. For these reasons alone, his story should be preserved. But I have another reason for writing this book, and it is not simply because I am his great-grandson. The diary, with its manner of expression as well as the values articulated therein, put me in mind of my father, William Benjamin Gould III.

Now, nearly twenty years after his death, the memories of my father are as strong as ever. His characteristics, as I recollect them, were those of compassion, wisdom, and an intelligent thoughtfulness. He was possessed of a passion for equality and fairness. And he was a man who loved his family, church, and country—and, above all, life itself. The diary of the first William B. Gould and his related writings give me the same sense of this man. Thus, what I observed as child is inseparable from what I have read about and by the first William B. Gould.

I well recall seeing my father read the diary in our living room in New Jersey and discussing it with him. My impression was that this written work gave my father a new and more profound appreciation for the greatness of William B. Gould and his achievements under the most difficult of circumstances.

This book, containing WBG's Civil War diary from 1862 to 1865, has been three decades in the making. I have made the decision to publish the diary in its entirety, albeit with annotations, because (1) of its historical significance—I am aware of only two other Civil War diaries by black sailors, and none from any naval veteran who emerged from slavery;[1] (2) I came to the conclusion that the

1

humdrum and tedious aspects of his life in the United States Navy were as important as the military conflicts, his more eloquent passages, and his commentary on the events of the day, including the state of race relations in the United States and in the navy. I also thought it important to publish the diary as it was actually written, including misspellings (common amongst literate people at that time) and grammatical errors.

The diary is not introspective in the sense that one gets a real sense of WBG's feelings. It was written with the expectation that it would be read by others. William B. Gould was a man of action and the diary describes the life of a sailor in action between 1862 and 1865.

In the main, WBG holds his deepest emotions within him, though, on occasion, his loneliness cries out, particularly when he has not heard for some period of time from his wife to be, Cornelia Williams Read, or at the time of his mother's death. For instance, as he returns to Massachusetts at the war's conclusion, and he hopes that he will soon hear "the cry of *Land ho*," he expresses restive frustration over his ship's slow movement across the Atlantic: "A painted ship apon A painted Oceon."[2] And then only a few weeks later, he says: "The Moon shone forth in its splendor and one could sit for hours and medetate apon the works of nature. Myself I devideed my thoughts between Nature and the loved ones at Home and longs for the hour of our meeting wich we all cincerely hope will be soon."[3]

Similarly, emotion bubbles to the surface when the progress of the War of the Rebellion is set forth—for instance, outrage at the Fort Pillow massacre and the government's failure to retaliate against the Confederate execution of black soldiers and a carefully contained jubilation upon hearing the news of Appomattox and the "invincible" Grant's victory there. Nonetheless, on the written page he possesses a tough inner fiber, a quality that is quite similar to that which I observed in the behavior of my own father, William B. Gould III. Though WBG's views are expressed and indignation on behalf of others is articulated, there is no display of personal hurt or victimization in the diary or his other writings.

A word about how I came by the diary and about the work itself. No one in my immediate family in New Jersey had heard of this diary until 1958, when my great-uncle Lawrence Gould died and bequeathed his property to my father. On arriving in Dedham, Massachusetts, the Boston suburb where many family members have lived since WBG chose it as his home, my father discovered that many papers and books were being thrown out. It was at this point that my father found the diary in the attic at 303 Milton Street.

The diary chronicles WBG's daily life in the navy from September 27, 1862, to his discharge three years later, on September 29, 1865. There are only two major hiatuses, one for the period May–October 1863, when he is hospitalized with the measles, and the other for the late September 1864–early February 1865 period, which appears to be a section that was somehow lost.

The extant material consists of two books plus some forty unbound pages that appear to have once been part of another book. Today the book's bindings and pages are fragile. The edges of the unbound pages relating to early 1865 have fallen away, thus disrupting some of the narratives set forth here.

The first book is approximately 8" by 6" and ¾" deep. Its compressed cardboard cover is covered in decorative paper that has faded to a mottled green-and-black color. Both the sewn binding and leather spine are fragile but intact. The book is divided into two sections. The first forty-five pages cover the end of WBG's service, from May 27, 1865, to his discharge on September 29, 1865. The last fifty pages begin with his first entry on September 27, 1862, when his first ship, the U.S.S. *Cambridge* is coaling at Beaufort, North Carolina, and end with May 3, 1863, at which point he enters the Chelsea Naval Hospital. The two sections of the diary are separated by a number of blank pages. Immediately following the September 29, 1865, entry there are two pages of trade instructions relating to formulas for mixing types of cement, clay, etc.; these are written in a fainter pen than the entries. In the middle of the book, surrounded by many blank pages, WBG inserted two undated entries, "Notes by WBG" and "The Negro his Friends and Foes." Those items, also in a fainter pen, are written from the bottom line of the diary to the top, or upside down. Although their placement in the diary makes dating these items difficult, I have thought that WBG wrote them before the war. Inserted in the book before the first page are an August 2, 1907, letter from E. L. Mason, Special Examiner of the Department of the Interior, Bureau of Pensions, to WBG arranging an appointment and, with this letter, a portion of an old newspaper with mathematical calculations on it.

The second book is approximately 7¾" by 6" and is ½" deep. The cover is made of compressed cardboard covered in black decorative paper. The sewn binding is now coming apart, and the leather that used to cover the spine has deteriorated significantly. On the first page of the book WBG wrote:

Journal of W. B. Gould's
cruise in the U.S.
Frigate Niagara
Commencing
October 13th /63

On the front inside cover he inscribed the names of the Confederate ships that were captured or destroyed by the *Cambridge* and the *Niagara*:

Emma Tuttle   )
Wens. Dec. 3rd   ) 62
Briliant   )
J. C. Roker   )
Time, Jan. 23rd 63
Georgia, Aug. 12th 64

The entries in this book proceed continuously from October 13, 1863, the day he is transferred from the Chelsea Naval Hospital to the receiving ship *Ohio* and then to the *Niagara*, to September 5, 1864. At the end of the September 5, 1864, entry, WBG writes: "End of book No. 3."[4] The facing page contains a sketch of what appears to be the C.S.S. *Stonewall*, the Confederate ship the *Niagara* confronts in Spain and Portugal but ultimately does not fight.

The unbound pages begin with an apparent continuation of a February 4, 1865, entry. (This partial entry—the first part is nowhere to be found—induced my father to believe that someone had destroyed the earlier portions of the diary covering late 1864 and early 1865.) When I received the diary, these loose pages were placed inside the front cover of the first book, where they fit chronologically. However, the size and physical attributes of the pages suggest that they may have once been part of another book. The unbound pages were originally approximately 8" by 6½", somewhat larger than the pages in the other books. They are in the most fragile condition and have deteriorated by as much as ¾" around the edges, so that some of the text has been lost. The paper appears to have been damaged by water. As in the rest of the diary, the unbound pages are lined and contain writing on both sides. However, unlike the pages in the two bound books, these have a double-lined 1¼" left-hand margin, where WBG wrote the date of each entry.[5]

Notwithstanding the diary's complicated chronological order in the original, this book commences with the September 27, 1862, entry and moves day by day until the last entry on September 29, 1865. To retain the precise order of pages as contained in the original would have been both confusing and disruptive.

Except for the photos of the diary itself, there is another aspect of the diary that cannot be replicated in this book. This is WBG's elegant penmanship, an art that has been lost for more than one generation. His handwriting puts educated contemporaries to shame. Those who will want to view it in its entirety may do so by visiting the website established by the Stanford Law Library at www.law.stanford.edu/library/goulddiary.

Elegance—a word that I have used in connection with WBG's craftsmanship as well as his handwriting—is a word that suits well his manner of expression and use of language, both of which are frequently understated and sardonic. Sometimes these features are not visible because of the necessarily hurried nature of his disciplined daily entries, made from time to time immediately before and after naval battles in both North Carolina and Europe. But these features are obvious from portions of the diary, as well as his published writings in *The Anglo-African*. In the minutes he kept for the Hancock Mutual Relief Association, which I discovered in my mother's home in April 2001, WBG makes the most boring and monotonous meetings come alive with a facile and easy pen.

Finally, a couple of notes on conventions. WBG routinely refers to people by initials in his entries, and to have annotated each occurrence of the ones who can be identified seemed to me excessive. Readers will find whatever information I have on them in Appendix B, the table of correspondents. I suspect many readers will not have encountered the word *contraband* as used in the title and throughout the text. The dictionary definition of "contraband of war" is "goods that a neutral nation cannot supply to a belligerent nation except at the risk of seizure and confiscation."[6] As noted in Chapter Three, General Benjamin Butler of Massachusetts was the first to refer to a group of escaped slaves, whose owners demanded their return, as "contraband of war." This practice signified the North's ambivalence about the slavery issue, and the term came to be taken up by WBG's contemporaries. The U.S.S. *Cambridge* log, for example, characterized him as one of eight "contrabands" who came on board. Accordingly, it is exactly the right word for this book. One of the dictionary definitions of *contraband* is in fact "a Negro slave who escaped to or was brought within the Union lines."[7]

The first book of William B. Gould's diary, covering both the beginning of his service from September 27, 1862, to May 3, 1863, and the end of his service from May 27, 1865, to September 29, 1865. (Photograph by Steve Gladfelter, Stanford Visual Art Services)

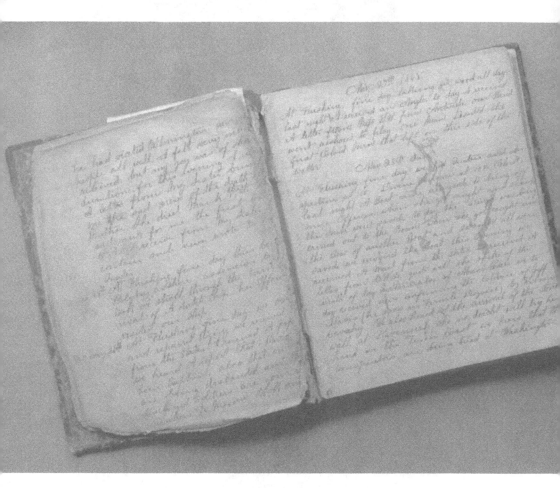

The last page of the unbound portion of the diary that was originally in another book ending with May 26, 1865, inserted next to the entry for May 27, 1865, which begins the first book. (Photograph by Steve Gladfelter, Stanford Visual Art Services)

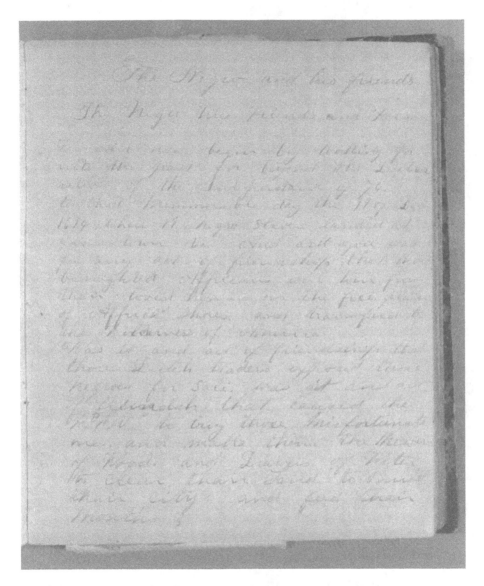

This entry, "The Negro his Friends and Foes," appears in the middle of the first book surrounded by blank pages. It may have been written before the war. (Photograph by Steve Gladfelter, Stanford Visual Art Services)

The second book of the diary, which covers WBG's service from October 13, 1863, to September 5, 1864. (Photograph by Steve Gladfelter, Stanford Visual Art Services)

This sketch, which WBG made opposite the entry for September 5, 1865, in the first book, appears to represent the Confederate *Stonewall*, the ironclad that his ship stalked in Europe.

These unbound pages contain WBG's April 15, 1865 entry: " . . . in the Harbor of Cadiz . . . On my return on board I heard the Glad Tidings that the Stars and Stripe[s] had been planted over the Capital of the D—nd Confedercy by the invincible Grant.

l. 14th anchor and stood down the River ... day.
At Sea fine weather we are runni... ...ved
to the Westward verry fine indeed. ...and.
l. 15th At Sea fine weather took A Pilot a...
8 bells ran in the Harbor of Cadi...
we anchord of Quarentien. we were
visited by the health surgeon, our pa...
pers were not properly signd we were
quarentiend untill about 9 Oclock
when we were allowd to visite the
citty — I was among the luckey ones th...
went on shore I found Cadis to be qu...
clean but the streets are verry narrow and
the citty must be very hot in conse
quences on my return on board I heard
the glad tidings that the Stars and Strip...
had been planted over the capital of th...
Sum ... Confidercy. by the invincible ...
Grant while we honor the living sol—
diers who have done so much we must
not forget to whisper for fear of de... ...her
sturbeing the Glorious sleep of the m... ...the
who have fallen. Mayrters to th... ...
of Right and Equality.

While we honor the living soldiers who have done so much we must not forget to whisper for fear of desturbeing the Glorious sleep of the ma[ny] who have fallen. Mayrters to the cau[se] of Right and Equality." (Photograph by Steve Gladfelter, Stanford Visual Art Services)

The diary as it appeared on ABC's "Nightline" on July 3, 2001. The text pointed to by the author is WBG's reference to the Emancipation Proclamation. (Courtesy of ABC News)

ONE

An Introduction to William B. Gould:
In the Service of 'Uncle Samuel'

Sunday night, September 21, 1862,[1] in Wilmington, North Carolina ... The evening is both dark and rainy when eight black men take possession of a boat and embark on the Cape Fear River, four blocks from where William B. Gould resides on Chestnut Street. It is twenty-eight nautical miles from Orange Street to the mouth of the river as it flows into the Atlantic Ocean. And ahead lies heavily armed Fort Caswell, where the Confederate presence denies the U.S. Navy access to Wilmington's busy harbor.

As the boat silently sets out from Orange Street, the men know that they must move quickly in the cover of darkness, for the alarm will soon be sounded for eight missing slaves. The word will go out promptly to the sentries posted along the Cape Fear River to be on the watch for these fugitives.

Down the river they descend southward toward the Atlantic, bending ever so slightly to the west at Smithville before the final dash down toward the cape itself. Though their boat possesses a sail, they dare not hoist it until they are in the Atlantic's swell. Thus, the eight men must take turns at the oars on this journey to "leave the land of chivalry and seek protection under the banner of the free."[2] It will take the entire night of September 21–22 to proceed beyond the river and to avoid inevitable detection at daybreak.

On September 22, with their sail set high to catch the ocean's breezes, they are spotted by both the U.S.S. *Cambridge* and the U.S.S. *State of Georgia*, part of the North Atlantic Blockading Squadron. In her September 22 log, the *State of Georgia*, operating close enough to Fort Caswell to see it at 8:00 A.M., says: "At 10 saw a boat . . . and at 10:10 *Cambridge* made signals . . . and started in chase of boat. At 11:20 the stmr *Cambridge* sent a boat and reported picking up a boat with eight contrabands on board. Ship lying too off the Fort [Caswell]." And

This map of the Cape Fear River as it flows from Wilmington to the Atlantic Ocean in the 1860s shows the route WBG and the seven other contrabands took that evening of September 21. (Courtesy of New Hanover Public Library)

here is what the *Cambridge* log said after she "spoke" to the *State of Georgia* at 9:50: "Saw a sail S.W.S. and signaled same to other vessels. Stood for strange sail and at 10:30 picked up a boat with 8 contrabands from Wilmington, NC."[3] Two other boatloads of WGB's friends are picked up by other ships.

Simultaneously another drama unfolds in Washington, D.C. The day before the escape from Wilmington, President Abraham Lincoln returns to the White House on Saturday to prepare for a Monday meeting with his cabinet about his intent to promulgate an emancipation proclamation. On Sunday morning, September 21, he rewrites the document, "the culmination of months of work and worry."[4] On Monday, almost simultaneous with the time at which WBG and the seven others are picked up by the *Cambridge*, the President announces his intent to fashion a preliminary proclamation through which the slaves held by those in rebellion will be freed on January 1 by virtue of the President's military authority.

On September 27, five days after William B. Gould boards the *Cambridge*, he begins a diary. It makes clear his complete disgust with, as he is to term it later, "things in Dixie."[5] In an undated entry titled "Notes by WBG," he writes:

> Slavery existed in England previous to and at the time of the settlement of the Plymouth colony. Scotch Prisoners taken at the battle of Dunbar were sent to Boston and sold before and up to 1650.

> When Affrican slavery were introduced: but it did not come with the Winthrops Company. . . . Sam Maverick, the owner of three (3) slaves who probably was brought from the West Indies in a ship that arrived in that year.

> A cargo of Negroes arrived at Boston in 1645. The sale was forbiden and the Negroes sent back at the expense of the Colony. Slavery did not increase until after 1700 and that was by the encouragement given by the Mother Country. As the Massachusetts Colony could not prohibit the importation or sale of slaves there was nothing left for them to do but to regulate the status of the children of slaves born in the Colony. In the Boddy of Liberties addopted in 1646, slavery was one of the topics treated, but no allusions were made to Race or color.[6]

He pursues the historical theme in an another undated entry, "The Negro and his Friends and Foes":

> We will now begin by looking far into the past far beyond the Declarration of Independence of 76 to that memmorable day the 11 of Dec. 1614 when 11 Negro

slaves landed at Jamestown Va. And ask you was [it] for any act of friendship that those benighted Affricans were torn from their loved homes on the free plains of Affrica's shores and transferred to the Wilderness of America. Was it and act of friendship that those Dutch traders exposed those Negros for sale. Was it and act of friendship that caused the F.F.V.'s to buy those misfortunate ones and make them the Hewers of the Wood and Drawers of Water to clear thair Land, to Build thair Cittys and feed thair Mouths?

And from the doings of that eventful day spring all of the evils of slavery in this country. From that day's work spring the . . . [7]

Here the passage is incomplete.

⤻

The first William Benjamin Gould (henceforth WBG) spends most of his adult life in Dedham, Massachusetts. But he is born on November 18, 1837, in Wilmington, North Carolina, the place from which he escapes in that perilous journey that could be dared and endured by only the young. Gould is a skilled tradesman, a plasterer and mason, or brick mason, who knows how to work with his hands and, ultimately, works as a contractor in Dedham, where he settles in 1871. But it is apparent that he is also a literate man who is widely read and is able to express himself on paper fluently and, at times, with an elegance peculiarly suited to what today seems to be the somewhat florid language and style of the nineteenth century.

The writings he has left to our own and future generations, and, indeed, his chance in life, are triggered by the Civil War (or the War of the Rebellion, as it is officially called). That prolonged and bloody conflict commences with the firing on Fort Sumter by Confederate rebels and secessionists as they seek to displace all federal authority in the seceding states. The war is at once a struggle over the preservation of the United States as a nation and, after an eighteen-month fitful and unsuccessful military struggle with the South, it is also about the question of whether slavery can be maintained, as Lincoln had earlier put it, in a "house divided." This is what WBG calls the quest for both "Liberty and Union."[8]

It is the slaves themselves who take the first step in bringing about this change in war aims by enlisting, first in the U.S. Navy, and later in the U.S. Army. Ambivalence about the policy toward freedom prompts federal officials to characterize such black recruits as "contraband," or seized property. But this effort brings down the plantation and caste system that had prevailed in the United States and expands the authority of the national government. As James McPherson notes, in describing a letter that President Lincoln writes to Horace Greeley on August 22, 1862, concerning slavery and the war:

> Lincoln spoke of the union nine times and the nation not at all. But in the Gettysburg address fifteen months later, he did not refer to the union at all but used the word *nation* five times. And in the second inaugural address, looking back over the past four years, Lincoln spoke of one side's seeking to dissolve the union in 1861 and the other side's accepting the challenge of war to preserve the nation.[9]

WBG is part of this effort to make the War of the Rebellion a war against slavery and to realize the new Republican Party's policy of free labor enterprise capitalism. The recruitment of blacks into the military, in the words of General Ulysses S. Grant, is to make it "terrible" for the enemy. Again in the words of McPherson, "Arms in the hands of slaves constituted the South's ultimate revolutionary nightmare. After initial hesitation, Lincoln embraced this revolution as well."[10]

It is that change of heart by the President that leads to WBG's entry into the service of "Uncle Samuel." In response to Lincoln's call, in 1861, for a blockade of southern ports, the Secretary of the Navy, Gideon Welles, organizes the Blockade Strategy Board, which begins to meet at Washington's Smithsonian Institution that summer. The board recommends the capture of Southern ports along the Atlantic coast as part of the blockade policy. Writes Robert Browning: "Seizing ports denied their use to privateers and blockade-runners and would serve the navy's logistical needs. Following the board's recommendations, the department instructed Flag Officer Silas Stringham, the commander of the Atlantic Blockading Squadron, to assemble a fleet to capture Hatteras Inlet, North Carolina."[11]

The surrender of Confederate forts at the Hatteras Inlet in August 1861 produces the first Union victory of the war. The Burnside Expedition, commanded by Brig.-General Ambrose Burnside (in the spring of 1863 he visits WBG's U.S.S. *Cambridge* at Newport News[12]) capitalizes on that victory in February and March 1862, bringing Roanoke Island, Beaufort (a coaling station for the *Cambridge*), New Bern, Washington, and Plymouth under U.S. occupation. With that, the North Carolina sounds come under the control of the North Atlantic Blockading Squadron, which is then attempting to disrupt the flow of goods in and out of Wilmington.

This is the second front against the Confederates and what makes WBG's dash to freedom down the Cape Fear River possible. But this front, which aims to disrupt supplies to Confederate forces operating in Virginia and to divert their attention southward, soon becomes defensive in nature. Two factors are responsible for what becomes a holding operation off the North Carolina coast. The first is General George McClellan's Virginia Peninsula Campaign in March 1862. General Burnside is now not only deprived of reinforcements, but worse, forced to give up 8,000 troops stationed in New Bern. And North Carolina naval resources as well have to be sent to assist McClellan on the peninsula. But the death knell for a robust North Carolina offensive is sounded by other military developments in that summer of 1862. And they, in turn, directly relate to the broadening of the war's objectives to include the abolition of slavery.

Initially, Lincoln resists Congress's efforts to destroy Confederate property interests in blacks through the Confiscation Acts, and he rescinds the orders of Generals John Frémont and David Hunter to emancipate all blacks in their departments. The President pushes and prods the border states to accept a system of compensated emancipation, a course of conduct directly related to the White House's reticence about freedom. But for a year Lincoln's efforts go unanswered, and only when the late spring of 1862 produces no accommodation or concession from the border state congressional representatives does he turn toward the idea of freedom itself. That policy shift is prompted, in substantial part, by the fact that the Southerners' property interest in blacks translates into black labor that frees up manpower for the Confederate military. It also helps the United States to explain its war philosophy to Europe, and specifically to Great Britain, which has already prohibited slavery, notwithstanding its failure to embrace the North's democratic ideal.

Thus, on July 22, 1862, Lincoln brings a preliminary Emancipation Proclamation with him to a Cabinet meeting. Writes Bruce Catton:

> Ten days after he had his talk with the border state men [on compensated emancipation] the President held a Cabinet meeting. To this July 22 Cabinet meeting he presented a certain paper, saying that he did not want any advice

on the substance of it, because he had made up his mind; he just wanted his Cabinet members to know what was coming and he would hear any comments that they might have to make. The paper was a document which has come down in history as the preliminary Emancipation Proclamation.[13]

It is Secretary of State William Seward who advises Lincoln to wait for a victory. The United States has just emerged from a series of setbacks—twice at Manassas (Bull Run) and most recently in what comes to be called the Seven Days Campaign. It is through the demoralizing rout of Union General John Pope at Second Manassas that the battle is brought to the very outskirts of Washington. As Stephen Sears says, "With the exception of Fort Monroe and nearby Norfolk, nearly all of Virginia was, or was about to be, free from Yankee occupation. The promising Federal second front along the North Carolina coast went unexploited in favor of reinforcing Pope's operations."[14]

Secretary Seward reasons that a movement toward emancipation under such circumstances would be viewed as an act of desperation in an attempt to prevail in some form other than the field of battle. As the Union and Confederacy vie for public and foreign opinion in Europe, Lincoln agrees with this advice and thus the proposal, and the July 22 meeting itself, remain a secret.

A month later, in the wake of the Confederate victories in Seven Days and Second Manassas, an emboldened Robert E. Lee strikes out on a journey northward, the ultimate objective of which may have been to attack or threaten Philadelphia, Baltimore, and even Washington itself. Lee crosses the Potomac in an invasion of Maryland that he believes "might win for [the Confederacy] the foreign recognition" that is a prerequisite to a successful revolution.[15] Indeed, both Britain and France, deprived of the cotton that drives their economies, seek to mediate the dispute with a view toward dismembering the United States and, in the process, edge toward explicit recognition of the Confederacy. In 1862, both countries become less discreet about their hostility toward the United States and the democratic ideal;[16] both eagerly anticipate the next Confederate success and the inevitable division of the United States that will ensue.

This aspect of the drama is one that will affect WBG in its second act. For when he crosses the Atlantic on the U.S.S. *Niagara* in the last year of the war, the Confederate cruisers that he and his comrades pursue are being built and harbored by British and French citizens with some form of governmental sanction, despite pro-Union British working-class sympathies. This, as WBG notes in his writings, brings Great Britain and the United States to the brink of war itself. The actions of the two countries produce an abiding anger in many Union sailors who, long after the war is over, do not forget the comfort that Europe had provided to the Confederacy.

Now, however, in September 1862, Lee's bold dash for victory reaches its apex in the bloody cornfields of Antietam, where one battle takes place in three stages and where the soldiers in one of the many Federal charges are blasted with a volley that, in the words of an observer, "was like a scythe running through our line."[17] The result is that both sides suffer their bloodiest losses of the war, and indeed, more soldiers go to their deaths than in any one day anywhere. Lee retreats and, much to Lincoln's consternation, McClellan allows the Confederates to proceed across the Potomac unimpeded.

Thus no one wins at Antietam. But Lee's southward retreat means the end of his northern offensive, allowing the cautious and vain General McClellan to claim a victory of sorts. Shelby Foote writes that "for Lincoln it was something less [than a victory], and also something more. The battle had been fought on a Wednesday."[18] On Thursday, President Lincoln begins to polish the Emancipation document that has been under discussion and debate for so long. "At noon Monday, September 22, he assemble[s] at the White House all the members of his cabinet."[19] There he advises them that Antietam is the occasion he has been waiting for: it is time to announce his preliminary Emancipation Proclamation.

It is at this point that the eight contrabands make good their Cape Fear River escape and William Benjamin Gould's life takes its most important turn. The runaways are picked up by the *Cambridge* on September 22, 1862, five days after the bloody Union repulse of Lee at Antietam and the very day on which President Abraham Lincoln announces his intent to promulgate the Emancipation Proclamation. Within a matter of days, WBG and his comrades would join the U.S. Navy. It is unlikely that they know of Antietam so shortly after the battle. Most probably, they see themselves as striking out for freedom at the Union's lowest ebb. As described above, these eight "contrabands" approach the U.S.S. *Cambridge*, part of the North Atlantic Blockading Squadron, from the coast. The squadron's mission is to patrol the porous coast near the Cape Fear River and adjacent waterways, and to diminish the number of blockade runners that are able to replenish the Confederate South's resources.

Two years later, in recalling the event, WBG writes that he and his companions are "kindly received by officers and men."[20] They seem to have been lucky in happening on the *Cambridge* that day, for there appears to have been considerable concern about the number of contrabands reaching the ships of the North Atlantic fleet. As one commander writes to his superior in the Department of the Navy, "Fourteen contrabands have reached the *Monticello* and *Penobscot* and several the *Cambridge* within a few days, and as the vessels have not room for them, will you please direct what disposition shall be made of them?"[21] But William A. Parker, the commander of the *Cambridge*, does not share this concern. On the contrary, just five days before he picks up the eight runaways, he writes to the same official, Acting Rear-Admiral S. P. Lee, proposing to make use of any contrabands he might encounter. "I have the honor to enclose for your approval," he writes,

> a requisition for the following rates now vacant to fill up the original complement allowed to this vessel by the Navy Department and they are necessary to render the vessel efficient. These vacancies have been caused by desertions at Baltimore; and by several men being sent home on sick-tickets. Viz:—Two Seamen, Eight ordinary Seamen, Three Landsmen, one First Class Boy, one Corporal and Three Private Marines. Total 18 men.[22]

William Benjamin Gould is to fill one of those vacancies: he is assigned to the position of First Class Boy. He subsequently becomes a Landsman, and then a Ward Room Steward. He duly takes note of the event in his diary, which he has begun just a few days before, on September 27: "All of us shipped today [October 3] for three years, first taking the Oath of Allegiance to the Government of Uncle Samuel."

From those first entries onward, WBG's diary chronicles day-to-day life in the navy as he experienced it. He keeps the diary faithfully for three years. Only a long hospitalization for the measles (from May to October, 1863) keeps him from his record of daily events.

WBG's service career takes several forms. He begins, as noted, as a crewman on the U.S.S. *Cambridge*, part of the North Atlantic Blockading Squadron. The work in this assignment is often difficult (pursuing a number of sails that disappear as they proceed toward land or beyond the horizon) and downright boring. And it is also lonely work. Already by Christmas 1862, just three months into the job, he and his fellows all have the "blues."

Yet, paradoxically, this is a very exciting period—a "period of daring exploit"—because the *Cambridge* is frequently locked in combat with Confederate ships and takes some prizes in the process. No doubt WBG is thoroughly exhilarated when, in a matter of just five days, the *Cambridge* and two other ships capture four blockade-runners and chase a fifth ashore. On this assignment, he experiences the peril of combat and the actuality of losses—prisoners of war taken by the Confederates—as well as triumphs.

Then, in the wake of those encounters, his rather creaky ship moves north, first to Newport News and Hampton Roads, Virginia, and then on to New York and Boston, where he visits with friends. More important from the point of view of his writing, he calls in at the offices of *The Anglo-African* in New York, a strong black abolitionist paper that provides coverage and support for the fighting black soldiers and sailors in the war. *The Anglo-African* looms large in WBG's story. He is a financial organizer for it, an avid reader of its articles, and a contributor under a *nom de plume* as well. During his first leave from the *Cambridge*, in the spring of 1863, he renews acquaintanceships with family in Boston, including "Aunt Jones" and his Jones cousins, and goes to see his wife to be, Cornelia Williams Read, on Nantucket Island, to which she has traveled from Wilmington.

Then illness befalls William B. Gould, and the diary is interrupted. We next see him in October 1863 in Boston, transferring to the U.S.S. *Niagara*, which lies aport in Gloucester, Massachusetts, for a couple of months waiting to fill its full complement. Then suddenly in December, the wooden steamship races off to Nova Scotia in chase of the Confederate-hijacked *Chesapeake*, which has sailed up the Maine coast and entered British-protected Canadian waters in the hope of eluding the U.S. Navy. The *Chesapeake* is docked at Pubnico Harbor in Nova Scotia, and two navy ships, the *Ella and Anna* and the *Dacotah*, are already in hot pursuit. On December 10, Secretary of the Navy Gideon Welles instructs Commander Craven of the *Niagara* to join the pursuit. The position of the other pursuing Union vessels, as one writer puts it, is vastly improved with "the arrival of the crack frigate U.S.S. *Niagara*," which with its "over a dozen

one-hundred-pound rifled guns and twenty eleven-inch smoothbores" increases
the "U.S. Navy's firepower . . . substantially."[23]

Though the *Chesapeake* is recovered by the *Ella and Anna*, the pirates are
able to escape with the aid of Canadians, as we learn from WBG's December 19
diary entry. He describes how some of the local people shower "abuse" on the
ship's crew with "everry thing they could utter." Thus, WBG's first adventure
as a crewman on the *Niagara* takes place in 1863 in Canadian waters. Early 1864
brings the ship into a struggle with the elements, a story we will come to in
Chapter Two. But the major events from the middle of that year until well into
1865 involve the search for Confederate cruisers abroad, and in the early part of
1864, the U.S.S. *Niagara* is refitted and prepared for a lengthy stay in Europe.
When, in 1911, WBG's account of his wartime experiences was recorded by the
local veterans' society, he was quoted as saying:

> News of the progress of the work on [Confederate ironclad rams] reached
> the United States from time to time until finally it was known that they were
> launched. It was also reported that the Confederates were trying to get a fleet
> together of which these rams were to be the nucleus and that the Privateers
> "Georgia" and "Alabama" were on the way to Liverpool to be refitted. The
> American Minister, Charles Francis Adams, had notified the English Govern-
> ment that if these vessels were allowed to go to sea, it would be construed by
> the United States as a declaration of war. That was the situation June 1, 1864,
> when the "Niagara" sailed for the European station having been assigned to
> the Irish Fleet and ordered to keep a sharp lookout for these rams.[24]

Navy Secretary Welles instructs Commodore Craven to seek out the Confederate ship C.S.S. *Florida*, but the *Niagara* does not make contact with her.
Then, the *Niagara* receives news that the C.S.S. *Alabama* has been sunk five
days after the *Kearsarge* has done her work. The *Niagara* would have matched
up well with the *Alabama* and, indeed, posed a greater threat to her than did the
Kearsarge. Indeed, "Semmes [the *Alabama*'s commander] chose to fight because he feared the arrival of more Union warships,"[25] and the *Niagara* would
have been first among them. Though WBG and his comrades are disappointed
that they did not get "a shot" at the *Alabama*, the *Niagara* crew are "as delighted
and as proud of the deed as if they had done it themselves."[26]

In Europe, the *Niagara* has two major confrontations. The first is with the

Confederate vessel C.S.S. *Georgia*, which had been sold to a British purchaser but is taken by the *Niagara* in the Bay of Biscay anyway.[27] "[The] next cruise that she [the *Georgia*] makes will be for Uncle Samuel," WBG promises in his diary.[28] The fact that the vessel is under British ownership (WBG states that she is to be refitted as a cruiser[29]) leads to an outcry in England, lengthy legal and political discussions in the British press, and eventually litigation in the United States, culminating in a decision by the Supreme Court upholding the propriety of the seizure.[30]

In the *Alabama* arbitration that follows the war—the United States successfully obtaining compensation for the havoc, financial or otherwise, wrought by her raids upon American shipping—the *Georgia* is referred to as an enemy ship that had been paid for by the British: "Here, then, is the case of a vessel, clandestinely built, fraudulently leaving the port of her construction, taking Englishmen on board as her crew, and waging war against the United States, an ally of ours, without once having entered a port of the power the commission of which she bears, but being, for some time, the property of an English subject."[31] Thus, the *Georgia*, as well as the *Alabama* and other ships, is the object of protest and anger to Britain by the United States.[32] In early 1865, the *Niagara* stalks one of the South's last hopes, the Confederate ironclad C.S.S. *Stonewall*, chasing her through the waters off Spain and Portugal. But here the *Niagara* is unsuccessful, much to WBG's frustration and anger. Early on, he states "[i]t realy looks as if we are to have [a] fight of some kind,"[33] and on February 11, he speaks of a "fight certain." On February 12, he remarks that the *Stonewall* is as an "ugley customer to handle, but we will not be dismayed."

Subsequently, he writes that this is to be a "desperate engagement,"[34] and on February 17, he states that he hopes that "she [the *Stonewall*] will soon leave this Port so that we can try her spirit." "We are expecting to fight" he writes on February 23, " . . . but who will be the victors remains to be seen." By March 3, the crew is "almost tired [as it] waited for the Ram [the *Stonewall*] to come out." On March 13, simultaneous with the arrival of the Union ship *Sacramento*, he writes, "Th[ere] is something in the Wind."And a week later, the *Niagara* chases the *Stonewall* back into El Ferrol.[35] A few days later, WBG declares, "we expect a fight to morrow," but he then concludes by noting that the *Niagara* is lying "quietly" at anchor "why we know not."[36]

A refusal to fight the *Stonewall* in March 1865 and her subsequent escape from Lisbon—where the *Niagara* is fired upon by Portuguese troops—leads to the court martialing of Commodore Craven. Craven is to answer for his decision not to directly engage the enemy, but as the *New York Times* maintains, the fact that the *Niagara* had chased the *Stonewall* into Lisbon harbor "in part disproved" that charge.[37] And it is quite probable that Craven simply had wished to resolve all doubts in favor of protecting his crew against needless casualties as the North's final victory seemed only weeks away. In the end, Craven is convicted on some counts, but not to the Secretary of the Navy Welles's satisfaction. Thus Welles vacates the conviction, wiping the *Stonewall* slate clean.

In any case, as WBG makes clear in his diary, two local factors intervene that make the pursuit of the *Stonewall* difficult and troublesome. The first is the involvement of both Spanish and Portuguese authorities, who are bent on keeping the conflict as distant from their shores as possible. In Spain, WBG notes the visit that the *Niagara* receives from the Spanish military just before the *Stonewall*'s departure from El Ferrol. And in Portugal, as we saw, the *Niagara* is fired upon when the authorities mistakenly conclude that she is about to violate Portuguese neutrality. Both governments are a substantial impediment to the *Niagara*'s freedom of action.

In Spain, the two ships play a cat-and-mouse game with each other. Commander Craven offers battle to the Confederates when the water is rough and tumultuous, conditions that give the *Niagara* the advantage. Naturally, the Confederates, through their commander, Thomas Jefferson Page, do not accept. When the sea is calm, the roles are reversed: the *Stonewall* approaches, and the *Niagara* withdraws as the enemy now gains the advantage. Under these circumstances, Craven considers his wooden ship to be substantially inferior to his adversary's and advises his superiors that he needs the assistance of at least two other ships to confront her.[38]

For the period immediately before the encounter with the *Stonewall* until early February 1865, we have to rely on WBG's recollections in 1911; this is the period that is presumably covered in the missing section of the diary. Here is what he had to say some fifty years after the fact:

> From Dover [the *Niagara*] went to Flushing and from there to Antwerp. At the latter place it was learned that the Confederates had bought a ship in London

called the "Sea King" and that it was to stop at some one of the islands off the
coast. The "Niagara" immediately started on a search for it, returning to Dover.
There it was learned that another ship called the "Laurel" had left Liverpool
with men and stewards for the "Sea King." The "Niagara" cruised about for a
week but did not come across either vessel. On returning to Antwerp it was
learned from the London papers that the ships had met and the "Sea King" had
received into its crew, stewards and ammunition from the "Laurel" and had
then changed its name to the "Shenandoah" and had hoisted the Confederate
flag. The search was then abandoned and the "Niagara" continued her cruise
visiting most of the important ports of England, Ireland, France and Spain.[39]

Shortly thereafter, while in Cadiz, Spain, WBG hears of Appomattox. "This,"
he says, "although a great piece of good news, made no change in the plans of the
Commander of the 'Niagara' as the war was not ended officially so the cruising
was continued."[40] The *Niagara* is ordered to track Confederate ships that might
still be at large. One of the first ports of call is Queenstown (now Cobh), Ireland.
WBG considers it a "verry fine Harbor. We were amediately beseiged by any
number of Boats in true Irish style."[41] And three days later, on June 22, 1865,
he is still struck by the warmth of the welcome: "They are continualy passing
around the ship in steam Boats Cheering for the stars and stripes."

Finally, after calls at most of the European ports, the *Niagara* traverses the
Atlantic and returns to the Charlestown Naval Shipyard near Boston. There,
WBG receives his honorable discharge on September 29, thus ending three
years and nine days "in the serveace of Uncle Sam."

In addition to scrupulously keeping up his diary, WBG finds enough time at sea
to carry on a voluminous correspondence. None of the letters he sends or receives have survived, but he keeps careful note of them in his diary. Appendix B
lists all the correspondents he mentions; they include a host of people in North
Carolina, New York, and Massachusetts, relatives, fellow contrabands, old shipmates, and new friends and acquaintances. Among his many correspondents
are several men who become prominent in North Carolina politics after the war,
including one of the former slaves who had fled from Wilmington with him,
George Price.

WBG also corresponds with those who must have planned their escape in concert with his: Virgil Richardson and Ben Greer of the *Penobscot*, and Thomas Cowan, Charles Mallett, and Frank Clinton of the *Monticello*. Wartime Wilmington means disease, crime, downright bawdiness, and the threat of invasion, which prompts the inland migration of some slaveowners and thus diminished supervision of slaves. These men move toward freedom together in three different boats, and all of them board their respective ships within hours of WBG on September 22.[42]

And it is not only men to whom William B. Gould writes, but also to women, both young and old, in New York and Boston. In New York, he attends a concert and church with Mrs. Ann E. Hoagland and visits her frequently at her Brooklyn address. The same is true of Mrs. Matilda Culbreth of Brooklyn, as well as a Mrs. White who dies in 1864.

George Price, a fellow contraband and shipmate who becomes a frequent correspondent,[43] obtains "considerable influence in the Negro community following the war. In predominantly Republican Wilmington, Price represents New Hanover County in the North Carolina House of Representatives from 1869 through 1870 and serves in the North Carolina Senate from 1870–1872."[44] Known as a fine orator, he is asked to speak at numerous meetings and ceremonies in Wilmington and elsewhere in North Carolina. In 1881, he leads a black delegation to Washington to meet with President James A. Garfield to protest against the unfair distribution of federal offices in North Carolina.[45]

Another of his prominent correspondents is Abraham Galloway, a runaway slave from Wilmington and the son of a white father and black mother. Galloway leaves Wilmington in 1857 and becomes an important political leader in "contraband camps and seaports occupied by the Federal army,"[46] as well as a spy for the North in North Carolina. WBG meets Galloway in New York (the wording of his entries suggests that they already know each other[47]) and attends a meeting with him on North Carolina suffrage shortly after Galloway meets with President Lincoln as part of a five-man delegation. During this period, Galloway travels extensively to both Boston and New York, meeting with abolitionist leaders. Like Price, Galloway serves in the North Carolina Legislature after the war as part of Reconstruction. He captures a state Senate seat in 1868, but dies before his term is up, in 1870.

Another individual with whom WBG meets in New York is William McLaurin, also a navy veteran who becomes active in Republican Party politics in the Reconstruction era. He is to represent New Hanover County in the North Carolina House of Representatives from 1872 to 1874.

Perhaps the most interesting of all of WBG's correspondents is his nephew George Lawrence Mabson, the son of his sister Eliza and George W. Mabson, a "white 'gentleman who stood high in Wilmington society.'"[48] Five Mabson children are the product of this union, and George W. Mabson later conveys property to WBG's sister. Mabson is part of the Wilmington-to-Boston connection, having been sent to Boston to attend school at the age of eight. At the outbreak of the war, he joins the navy and is assigned to the U.S.S. *Colorado*. When his tour of duty ends, he enlists in the 5th Massachusetts Cavalry,[49] where he takes part in the capture of Petersburg and Richmond. The Mabson family also appears to provide WBG with a connection to Wilmington in the years following the war. The 1880 census lists a Mabson boy who had been born in North Carolina as a boarder and employee of WBG's in Dedham; he is almost certainly the son of either George L. or his brother William.

Like Price, Galloway, Mallett, and his own brother William, Mabson becomes a political activist in the state of his birth. He is appointed to the office of justice of the peace by Governor William W. Holden in 1868, but his ambitions soon take him to Howard Law School, where he earns his degree in 1871. On his graduation, he returns to North Carolina and is promptly admitted to the New Hanover County Bar. He is North Carolina's first black lawyer. Described in the *Wilmington Weekly Journal* as "tall and slender, straight and thin, presenting the ghostly appearance of a sage philosopher and statesman,"[50] Mabson serves in the North Carolina House of Representatives and the Senate in the next years. After an unsuccessful run for Congress in 1874, he is chosen to represent New Hanover County in the Constitutional Convention of 1875.

These men, all young and associates of the equally young WBG before the war, are sometimes in the same trade and sometimes the product of interracial unions. Many plan their self-liberation with WBG, and they are all strongly committed to the same objectives of racial equality as he. Perhaps as David Cecelski has noted about Galloway, their proximity to the white world sharpened their sense of grievance and wrong in both slavery and discrimination.[51]

Unlike this circle of North Carolina friends, WBG chooses to stay in the

North after his discharge from the navy. Apparently, he gives some thought to returning to Wilmington, for he speaks with interest of a "fair chance of success [in] my business" when he returns to the city briefly at the end of the war.[52] But the pull to Massachusetts is considerable, and the magnet is of course Cornelia Williams Read. She is WBG's most frequent correspondent during the war years.

How is it that William B. Gould, a slave from North Carolina, has friends in New York and both friends and family in Boston? The connection is probably attributable in part to men like Mabson and Galloway, who live for some period of time in the North. But there is probably another, more basic connection. WBG speaks of meeting his aunt, Mary, in 1863, and we later learn that this is "Aunt Jones (No. 2 Sears Place Boston Mass)."[53] That would be, according to the Boston Directory for that year, Mrs. Thomas H. Jones. She is the second wife of Thomas Jones, and she and her husband play a very important role in WBG's life, as we will see. Born Mary R. Moore, she is WBG's mother's sister. She and Thomas marry in the 1830s, when both are slaves in Wilmington. The couple have children (WBG often speaks of his Jones cousins), and apparently are freed in North Carolina but live in constant fear of re-enslavement. Consequently, Jones sends his wife and all his children except one to New York in 1849 and joins them shortly thereafter. In New York, he becomes involved in the antislavery movement, and it is almost assuredly through him that WBG makes so many friends there, people he goes to church, concerts, and meetings with, and visits regularly in their homes.

A self-taught, literate man, Jones begins to lecture in both Connecticut and Massachusetts and becomes a staunch supporter of the great Massachusetts abolitionist William Lloyd Garrison. Presumably his activities bring him to the attention of the slave-catchers, causing him to seek refuge in St. John in the Maritime Provinces of Canada for a time. In 1853, he returns to Boston, where the narrative about his personal experiences in slavery is taken down. Published the next year as *The Experience of Thomas H. Jones*, the book dramatically tells of the degradation involved with slavery and the inability to choose freely. Jones subsequently moves from Boston, to live in both Worcester and New Bedford.

Meanwhile, his wife "Aunt Jones," Mary Moore, and their children stay on in Boston, and that is how WBG comes to meet them in 1863. He is in touch with his cousins in Boston, one of whom comes to see him during the time he is ill with measles. He corresponds with his cousin A. A. Jones (A.A.J.), as well as Aunt Jones, beginning at least in August 1864. This consanguinity, along with the fact that Cornelia is in Nantucket, obviously influences his move to Massachusetts—and the Jones connection is probably responsible for his decision to reside in Dedham. Dedham borders on Boston, and although WBG's family is just one of two black families there,[54] he no doubt sees the proximity of Boston and the Jones connection as a good environment in which to settle down. The road from Wilmington to Boston and thus Dedham had been previously taken, first by Jones, and then Mabson and perhaps others.

But judging by the diary, no exchange of letters comes close to matching the flow between WBG and his wife to be. Their correspondence is first noted in the diary on March 25, 1863, when the *Cambridge* is off Long Island en route to Boston. While his ship is docked in Boston, he writes: "I visited Nantucket. Meet Miss C.W.R. also had quite A good time in Boston and vicinety. Saw many of my aquaintances."[55] Their relationship seems to have flowered once WBG is transferred to the U.S.S. *Niagara* in the fall of that year. As he anticipates, this duty is much more stimulating work than the occasionally explosive but sometimes dull, dreary duty of the North Atlantic Blockade.

After the diary's hiatus that summer, it resumes in the fall, and we learn that he mails a letter to C.W.R. on October 15. The first letter that he acknowledges receiving from her is dated a week later, October 22, when his ship is at anchor off Gloucester. On October 29, he sends a picture to "C.W.R." and he receives a letter from her on November 2. Sometimes, as on November 16, he receives a letter and sends one back to her on the same day. The entries indicate that they exchange at least sixty letters.

But long days at sea on the U.S.S. *Cambridge* could be, in his words, "lonesome"—and probably even more so, his distancing from her for European duty aboard the U.S.S. *Niagara*. Here are a few of the many entries that reflect that mood:

> January 2, 1864, New York: "It is a shame to the country that we laying in the Harbor of New York and have been three days without A mail. Such is the regulation of uncle sam to his children. Oh for A mail, A mail. A Kingdom for A Mail."

Again at the Navy Yard in New York, January 10: "Indulge all day in thoughts of those far away and sigh for A letter. I hope some kind friend will send me one."

At Antwerp, Belgium, July 24, 1864: "A small Mail from the states but nary [a] letter have I."

At Cadiz, April 18, 1865: "[No] news except by Telegraph. Oh for [a] mail."

Again in Cadiz, August 24, 1865: "We received A Mail but not A line did I receive. No one favord me with A rememberance."

Note especially this entry for July 12, 1865, while he was in the North Sea at Flushing: "Oh C. why do you not write."

Similarly, emotions come to the surface when he learns of the death of his mother, Elizabeth Moore, which occurs just before the liberation of Wilmington: "I re[ceived] A letter from J.M. [John Mackey] _____ he had visited Wilmington. Saw m[any] people all well. I felt verry much releived but my joy was of short duration, for this evening [May 24,1865] I recei[ved] A letter from my Sister bring[ing] me the sad news of the death of Mother. She died March the 13ᵗʰ. _____ sad news for me. The first lett[er] that I receive from my Sister s[hould] contain such news."

↪

Not much is known about WBG's wife Cornelia, who predeceases him by many years. As the voluminous correspondence between WBG and Cornelia testifies, she is clearly a literate person. Like WBG, the way in which she was educated is a mystery.

My father could recall WBG well, but he was only four years old at the time of Cornelia's death, in 1906.[56] Cornelia Williams Read is born in Charleston, South Carolina, on May 30, 1837, which makes her about a half year older than WBG. In one of his applications for a veteran's pension, WBG states: "I knew her from childhood."[57] That statement is one of the many puzzlements about Cornelia. At first blush, it is hard to imagine how the two of them could possibly know each other as children when he lives in Wilmington, and she a considerable distance away in Charleston (especially given the transportation difficulties of their time). To answer that means to dip into a very complicated story indeed. It begins with the matter of how she comes into the possession of her last owner, John Newland Maffitt of Wilmington. Maffitt, a navy man who gains some fame before the war fighting the African slave trade, marries the widow of a naval friend, James Withers Read, from Charleston—Caroline Laurens.

Caroline Laurens of Charleston appears to have owned Cornelia as part of her first marriage to Read. When Maffitt and Caroline Laurens marry in 1852, subsequent to Read's death, they either move to Wilmington or return from time to time, but Cornelia is already fifteen years old. Thus, when WBG meets her at this point she is considerably older than the child that he speaks of in his pension application. The only real possibility of Cornelia and WBG meeting as children is that at some point while James Read is still alive, he and Caroline, on a visit to their friend Maffitt in Wilmington, take the child Cornelia with them.

Another unsolved question is whether Cornelia's parents are originally owned by Caroline Laurens's family or by James Read. Caroline Laurens is a descendant of the much-chronicled Ball family of Charleston through both her mother and her father.[58] Do Cornelia and William give their daughter Luetta the middle name Ball to signify that she is part of the Ball "family"? Possibly, for one or both of Cornelia's parents may have originally belonged to Caroline's parents, the John Ball Laurens, but the matter is unclear; they might also have belonged to James Read's parents, as the last name Read suggests.

So far as concerns Cornelia's emancipation and move to the North, the picture is much clearer, thanks to several articles in the Nantucket and New Bedford newspapers. The series of events that leads to her emancipation is triggered by Cornelia's aunt, Julia Ward Williams, and her husband, Henry Highland Garnet. As soon as Garnet learns that John Maffitt is planning to sell both Cornelia and her mother Diana, he alerts the Reverend James E. Crawford, who is married to another of Cornelia's aunts, to the imminent sale and possible separation of the two.

A black preacher and leading political figure who jousts with Frederick Douglass for leadership in the black community, Garnet is an early editor of *The Anglo-African.* But his influence wanes in later years because of his support for black emigration from the United States,[59] and he loses his position at the newspaper before WBG becomes involved with it.

Curiously, both Garnet the abolitionist and Maffitt the slaveowner later figure, if only tangentially, in WBG's life. WBG goes to hear Garnet preach in Brooklyn (though there is no hint that he tells Garnet of his relationship to Cornelia).[60] And Maffitt becomes a prominent Confederate naval commander, presiding over the C.S.S. *Florida*, which plies its marauding trade against American ships in Europe, Latin America, and Africa. Indeed, the *Florida* is one of the Confederate vessels with which WBG's U.S.S. *Niagara* is concerned when it departs New York for Europe in June 1864.

Garnet is in Jamaica when he learns of Cornelia and Diana's plight. According to the Nantucket *Weekly Mirror*'s account of their release from slavery, "[A gentleman] informed [Mrs. Garnet] of the sad condition of her youngest sister, Diana, and her daughter Cornelia, who had fallen into the hands of one John N. Maffit, of schooner Galveston, in the American Coast Survey, and had offered them for sale."[61] As soon as Garnet informs the Reverend Crawford of the situation, the minister springs into action:

One kind gentleman in this place [Nantucket] volunteered his services to negotiate for Mr. Crawford. He wrote and received a reply from Mr. Maffit, that "nothing would give him greater pleasure than to confer upon them the blessings of liberty, provided the Rev. gentleman (Mr. Crawford) would pay $1900 at sight"; but as he had no money nor means to raise it, Mr. ——— was obliged to suspend operations, and the matter assumed an entire new face. In December, however, another letter came to Mr. ———, in his behalf, informing him that he had *this day* closed a bargain for Cornelia, and contemplated selling Diana the first of January next. This was a new shock to them. How that family wept! How each member prayed earnestly to God to remove them, ere morning, from this wretched land! But a ray of hope was in store. The next day, a gentleman from this place entered into negotiations so that funds were raised and the deed is now accomplished. The mother was bought for $700, with ninety days privilege, which privilege was given to Mr. Crawford and his friends. A letter was written by him to Rev. H. H. Garnet of Jamaica (W.I.), apprising him of the fact, who used his influence with distinguished friends of England, members of the Friends' Society, Henry and Anne Ritcherson [sic], Newcastle-upon-Tyne, Dr. Somerville, Scotland, and Mrs. Hildrige of Shrewsbury, who immediately forwarded $500 to Mr. Lewis Tappan. . . . After securing his sister, his next steps were to release his niece, who could be bought for $1000. Letters were written to England by gentlemen of this town, which were answered by other letters containing £50. The balance was raised by Mr. Crawford, through the kindness of . . . members of the Society of Friends, who raised between $80 and $90 for him.[62]

Another source takes the story back earlier, to detail how the Reverend J. E. Crawford, who had ministered to the Pleasant St. Baptist Church for three years without "fee or reward" and "has supported himself and his family by his own labor, collected $700 and secured the freedom of his wife's sister [Diana]." The article goes on to describe his efforts to raise the sum required for Cornelia's emancipation: "He has now [July 1, 1857] relinquished his ministerial connection and his business here, and will soon engage in an effort to raise $1000 to purchase the liberty of a niece; the daughter of the sister-in-law who was rescued from slavery by his zealous labors. Such a man is deserving of encouragement; his industry, intelligence, ministerial devotion, and uprightness as a citizen, justly commended to favorable considerations."[63]

In a more detailed subsequent article titled "A Card," "J.E. Crawford and Family" express "their deep gratitude to all who have aided in accomplishing an end [her 'ransom'] so long and fervently desired by many anxious hearts." The writer states that "the amount demanded and paid was $1,000" and goes on to name each and every one of the benefactors, among them contributors from Great Britain: "nearly one-half . . . was raised in England by the subscription and efforts of Henry and Anne Richardson, members of the Society of Friends in Newcastle-on-Tyne, and a Miss Hilditch, of Shrewsbury."[64] The article thanks Mr. Christopher Hussey of Nantucket, who commences the correspondence with Mrs. Richardson that leads to the payment of $500 as well as an additional $481 obtained through Mr. Lewis Tappan, the prominent abolitionist of New York.

The *New Bedford Mercury*, which gives the best description of the actual trip to North Carolina to purchase Cornelia's freedom, remarks that Crawford "trembled for his safety in North Carolina, as free negroes are at a discount there, and Mr. Crawford is a free negro."[65] Crawford himself volunteered the information that when they boarded the train, Cornelia was not allowed to travel in the first class car but was placed in the baggage car. But it all comes out all right in the end, and as the *New Bedford Mercury* reports on February 26, 1858, "On Sunday last, the same girl was in one of our churches among her friends, and the subject of the warmest congratulations by reason of her escape from the land of captivity, even if she was purchased for so much gold."[66]

Cornelia's exodus to the North is thus almost as dramatic and perilous as WBG's. Here is how Anna H. Richardson describes her in an 1860 pamphlet chronicling various antislavery efforts:

> The next person to be referred to is Cornelia Williams, a bright young niece of our friend, Henry H. Garnet's, whom many of our friends kindly assisted to redeem from slavery in North Carolina about three years since. We rejoice to say this dear girl is going on very satisfactorily. She has been diligently pursuing her studies in a school at Nantucket, and appears to be much esteemed by all who know her. She kindly sends us a little letter now and then, again returning her glowing thanks to all who assisted in procuring her freedom. Her mother, Diana Williams (also a slave a few years since, and redeemed in part by the surplus of the "Wiems Ransom Fund"), has married an estimable Baptist minister within the last year, and Cornelia resides under their roof.[67]

As for WBG's early life, we know from his death certificate that his father, Alexander Gould, is a white man born in England, and his mother, Elizabeth Moore, is a black woman from Wilmington, North Carolina. The 1820 census shows Alexander living in Granville County, North Carolina. The *Niagara* muster rolls, which give WBG's height as 5' 5½", sometimes refer to him as "mulatto," and sometimes as "Negro."

We also know that WBG works as a plasterer and mason. This trade is clearly learned in North Carolina. He, in all probability, resides at the quarters maintained by Nicholas Nixon and works on such projects as the renowned Bellamy Mansion on Market Street, which is built between 1859 and 1861. His initials—in his handwriting—along with those of other workmen, are inscribed in the plaster of the mansion, which is one of the most prominent and distinguished antebellum structures in the whole of the South. The Bellamy Mansion craftsmanship is elegant and tasteful; it is a precursor of the kind of artful work that allows WBG to become a successful contractor and entrepreneur in Massachusetts.

Other than that, the only source we have for WBG's Wilmington years is the set of pension papers he files with the Department of the Interior, dated 1888, 1912, 1913, and 1915. In his 1913 submission, he states that he has no birth certificate:

I was born Nov. 18, 1837, at Wilmington, N.C. There is no official record of my birth and the only proof I can furnish is my marriage record, which is attached hereto and shows that I was 28 years old in November 1865. We had a Family Bible which was burned during the Civil War when our family home was destroyed. I have seen the record of my birth in that Bible many times just as I have given it above, and as I have always given it when required. I was mustered into the United States service Oct. 1, 1862 and gave my age as 24 years. On the 18th of November 1862 (the following month) I was 25 years old.

We can say with almost certainty that WBG is a slave. For one thing, his pension papers refer to him as a "contraband." More tellingly, the *Cambridge*'s log not only identifies him as such but identifies his owner—Nicholas Nixon. Nicholas Nixon is a peanut farmer, slaveholder, and member of Saint John's Episcopal Church in Wilmington. In his inventory of slaves in the North Carolina State Archives (Raleigh), he does not identify any of them by name. The slave schedule of 1850, which is part of the census for Wilmington (recall that the Constitution gave the slave states three-fifths representation for slaves), does not give personal names either, but it provides strong support for WBG's slave status. Among the sixty-nine slaves that Nixon owns, there is a twelve-year-old black youngster. WBG turns thirteen in November 1850.

Perhaps the most convincing evidence of all comes from WBG himself. As his ship, the U.S.S. *Cambridge*, comes near the shore of North Carolina in Rich Inlet in February 1863, he writes: "Took a good look at the place that I left in (62)."[68] It is apparent that he is looking at the Porter's Neck area, where the Nixon plantation is located.

The diary is clearly the work of a literate man, one who shows every sign of having received something more than an elementary education, since he has some knowledge of Shakespeare and French, as well as Spanish expressions. If WBG is a slave, and that seems in little doubt, how is it that he becomes literate at all, since masters are forbidden to teach slaves to read and write in North Carolina—or indeed in any of the Confederate states? Only in the border states that remain in the Union, like Maryland and Kentucky, is that a possibility.[69] As Kenneth Stampp writes, "The average bondsman, it would appear, lived more or less aimlessly in a bleak and narrow world. He lived in a world without schools, without books, without learned men."[70]

But WBG is far from being the "average bondsman," and he does somehow break out of what Stampp calls the "monotonous sameness of all [the average slave's] days." The best guess is that he is schooled at either the Front Street Methodist Church near Nicholas Nixon's slave quarters in Wilmington (some blacks are known to have been taught there) or Saint John's Episcopal Church in Wilmington.

Despite some evidence to the contrary, the Episcopal church is a substantial possibility. In this instance, at least, we might discount Stampp's claim that "the decorous Episcopalians [in the South] were ineffectual in their missionary work; even masters who adhered to this [faith] seldom managed to convert their own slaves."[71] For blacks in Wilmington are known to have frequently attended the church of their masters.[72] To be sure, WBG and Cornelia are married in the African Baptist Church in Nantucket, but that is probably out of deference to James Crawford, who is its pastor and who brings her out of the South. In sum, it is quite possible that WBG is an adherent of the church before he leaves North Carolina. And since John Maffitt is also a staunch Episcopalian, it is possible that Cornelia too is an Episcopalian before she comes north. On the other hand, it is only in Dedham that they both are baptized and then confirmed in the Church of the Good Shepherd, in 1878 and 1879. But whatever the origin of their allegiance to the Episcopal Church, it takes hold in the Gould family, and is passed down from one generation to another.

Closely aligned to WBG's religion is his philosophy and set of values and beliefs in the world. My father's favorite portion of the Episcopal Church Mass, or Eucharist—and thus mine as well—was the Comfortable Words of Christ: "Come unto me all ye that travail and are heavy laden and I will refresh you." It is this same concern for the masses and his fellow man that prompts WBG to speak about "Right and Equality" and the "Flag of Right" in his diary.[73] We return to this philosophy or worldview in Chapter Three.

TWO

William B. Gould's Worlds: Wilmington, Dedham, and the Intervening War

$\mathcal{T}$he stages for any discussion of William B. Gould are Dedham, Massachusetts, and Wilmington, North Carolina. They are only 664 miles apart. Today, that seems a relatively small distance. It is one and a half times the distance between San Francisco and Los Angeles. It is twice the long car journey on which my parents took my sister and myself on countless occasions from New Jersey to Boston. And yet when the first William B. Gould resided in both areas, the two centers were, in the most fundamental sense, worlds apart, and the distance had nothing at all to do with the difficulties of travel or geography.

Massachusetts was the most radically antislavery state in the Union. It was the home of America's most well-known abolitionist, William Lloyd Garrison, and was to boast one of the leading antislavery members of the U.S. Senate, Charles Sumner. North Carolina, albeit somewhat belatedly, was an integral part of the Confederacy.

When William Benjamin Gould was born in Wilmington on November 18, 1837, the city was the most important in North Carolina. Located on the Cape Fear River, which flows into the Atlantic Ocean, it was the seat of New Hanover County and was the state's largest city, port, and railroad center. During the War of the Rebellion, Wilmington was the Confederacy's major outlet to Europe and the blockade-runners that supplied Lee's Army of Northern Virginia.

At the end of the Civil War, black freedmen and freemen became influential in the Reconstruction government that flourished in New Hanover County. The party of Lincoln, the Republican Party, gained political control. Blacks constituted approximately 57 percent of the population.

But by the time of Reconstruction, WBG had long departed, having fled from

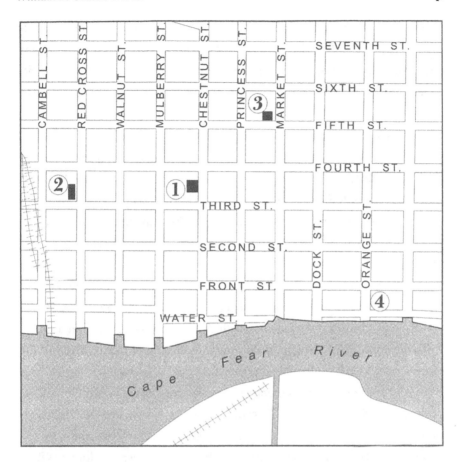

Downtown Wilmington, North Carolina. (1) William B. Gould's presumed residence at Nicholas Nixon's downtown property on Chestnut Street; (2) Saint John's Episcopal Church, where WBG may have received his schooling; (3) Bellamy Mansion on Market Street, where WBG did some of the masonry work; (4) foot of Orange Street at the Cape Fear River, where he and seven others commenced their escape from Wilmington. (Adapted by David Woodbury from *The Official Military Atlas of the Civil War*, Plate XXV, no. 5.)

Wilmington in 1862. And in the century to follow, Wilmington became less important, pushed to one side by the new rising metropolises of Piedmont (textiles and tobacco), Charlotte (textiles), Raleigh, Greensboro, and High Point (furniture), and Winston Salem, and into the shadow of university towns like Durham and Chapel Hill. Even today, it is not uncommon to encounter North Carolinians who have never been to Wilmington.

In 1990, the city underwent something of a revival when the final segment of

Interstate 40 in central North Carolina was completed, linking, in the words of a news reporter, "California with coastal North Carolina at the city of Wilmington."[1] Today, as the visitor wanders down toward the Cape Fear River, the city seems more complex and congenial than it was during its preeminence as a bastion of the Confederacy. As one moves toward the downtown business district, one encounters a plaque to a famous local resident, Captain John Winslow, whose *Kearsarge* sank the marauding rebel cruiser C.S.S. *Alabama*. Notwithstanding his disappointment in failing to get a shot at the *Alabama*, WBG was to say: "All honor to Captain Winslow and his brave crew."[2]

Proceeding beyond Princess Street to the banks of the river itself, the World War II battleship U.S.S. *North Carolina* is ever so prominently ensconced only a stone's throw from the trendy shops and restaurants, some of which are near the foot of Orange Street, whence WBG and the other seven contrabands set off in 1862. And lovely park benches in that area provide a view attractive enough to deflect the visitor's preoccupation with Wilmington's extreme humidity.

To the north of Wilmington is the gated community of Figure Eight Island, where former Vice President Al Gore sometimes stayed on vacation. Beyond that is Porters Neck and the contemporary tourist attraction of the Poplar Grove Plantation, the land on which WBG's owner, Nicholas Nixon, and the Foy family made their wealth in peanuts. And still farther north are Morehead City and Beaufort. All of these places were visited by the U.S.S. *Cambridge* during WBG's tour of duty with the blockade squadron.

To the south of the city is Fort Fisher, with which the *Cambridge* exchanged gunfire. It was a major Confederate stronghold until shortly before Wilmington was liberated by Union troops in 1865. Down the Cape Fear River to the south is another fort, Fort Caswell, near where WBG was picked up by the *Cambridge*.

Both localities—the city of Wilmington where WBG was born and the town of Dedham where he settled in 1871, half a dozen years beyond his service in the Civil War—enjoy prominence in the Revolutionary War against Great Britain. Indeed, Wilmington boasts that its armed rebellion against the stamp tax antedates the Boston Tea Party. Dedham, which is adjacent to the southern border of Boston, received its grant as a town from the Massachusetts Bay Colony in 1636, making it one of the oldest communities in the "land of the blue hills." In 1886, WBG, now a quarter of a century removed from Wilmington and one of

Dedham's leading citizens, served on the General Staff that commemorated and celebrated the 250th anniversary of Dedham's incorporation.[3]

Today, Dedham is an attractive bedroom suburb to the immediate south of Boston. Still known throughout the country and the world as the site of both the notorious Sacco-Vanzetti trial of 1921 and the oldest house in the country, the Fairbanks House, it is a smart, sophisticated, and relatively prosperous community, not anything like the small, sleepy town that WBG knew. (My sister Dorothy and I often dreaded some of the many visits to Dedham because we thought that it was dry and unexciting for youngsters. My great-uncles were, we thought, so clipped and Calvin Coolidge–like in their demeanor and speech as to be uninspiring. Dedham should be spelled Deadham, we often said.)

When WBG began to reside in Dedham in 1871, the town was dominated by Irish and German immigrants. The Goulds were one of just two black families there.[4] Aside from his house on Milton Street, WBG's wealth at his death in 1923 could be measured in mere hundreds of dollars. But the masonry skills he had acquired in North Carolina made him a respected and valued tradesman in his adopted home, enough so that he was awarded the contract for the important job of plastering Saint Mary's Roman Catholic church.

Said the *Dedham Transcript* in 1883, three years before his recognition as a leading citizen at the 250th anniversary celebration: "The plastering of the new catholic church is nearly finished, the windows put in place, and everything betokens an early occupancy of the basement."[5]

As noted, William B. Gould also did the exquisite plastering work in one of the grand antebellum mansions of Wilmington, the Bellamy Mansion. It is likely that he was one of the twenty individuals held by Nicholas Nixon, staunch Episcopalian and peanut plantation owner, in the town of Wilmington (most of his slaves in 1860 were in Rocky Point, 136 in total) at Chestnut Street, four blocks north of Orange Street. The Bellamy Mansion on Market Street was but a short walk from the Nixon establishment on Chestnut between Third and Fourth, about two and a half blocks from WBG's residence.

Much of what defined William B. Gould occurred in his adult years in Dedham. Here he became a respected craftsman and contractor in the plastering or brick mason trade. Here he would be a founding member of the Episcopal Church of the Good Shepherd. And here also he displayed activism and in-

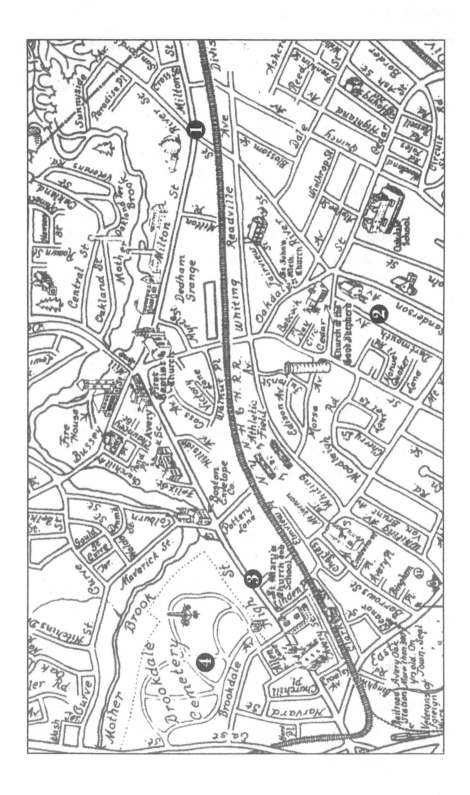

volvement in the GAR (Grand Army of the Republic) veterans' matters, serving as commander of the town's Charles W. Carroll Post 144 in 1900 and 1901. And most important of all, here six of his and Cornelia's eight children were born. Only the two oldest ones, Medora Williams (b. 1866) and William Benjamin Jr. (b. 1869), were born elsewhere, in Nantucket and Taunton, Massachusetts, respectively. Their siblings were Frederick Crawford (b. 1872), Luetta Ball (b. 1873), Lawrence Wheeler (b. 1875), Herbert Richardson (b. 1878), and the babies of the family, the twins James Edward and Ernest Moore (b. 1880)—who in a poem about the Dedham football team, were remembered as the "Gould boys," who "laid the line low" and played at each end for the club. Curiously, only one of the six boys, Lawrence, chose to carry on WBG's trade.

The middle names of the children showed that memories of North Carolina were not forgotten, at least on Cornelia's part; all but one were drawn from her own family or people who were close to her. Medora Williams bore Cornelia's mother's maiden name. Luetta Ball, as noted earlier, possessed the name of the South Carolina family who owned Cornelia and took her to North Carolina. Frederick Crawford was named for James Crawford, the Nantucket minister who brought Cornelia to Massachusetts in 1858 after she had been purchased out of slavery. Herbert Richardson was apparently named for Anna Richardson, who contributed and assisted in raising funds in England for the purchase and who took notice of Cornelia in subsequent writings.[6] WBG's side of the family was represented only in Ernest's middle name, Moore, the surname of WBG's mother.

In contrast to the relatively placid life Dedham offered as the turn of the century approached, WBG's home town of Wilmington moved in a very different direction after Reconstruction ended, with the institution of "Jim Crow" rule throughout the South, enforced by the Ku Klux Klan and blessed by the U.S. Supreme Court's "separate but equal" decision in 1896. In 1898, just as William

(opposite) A portion of Dedham, Massachusetts. (1) The Gould residences at 303 and 307 Milton Street near the Boston boundary line; (2) the Episcopal Church of the Good Shepherd, of which WBG was a founder; (3) St. Mary's Roman Catholic Church on High Street, where WBG did the plastering in the 1880s; (4) Brookdale Cemetery, where WBG, WBG Jr., and WBG III are buried. (Courtesy of Dedham Historical Society)

B. Gould Jr. was serving his country in the Spanish-American War, Wilmington saw a particularly bloody brutalization of blacks, resulting in both death and political intimidation.[7]

We do not know what contacts WBG maintained in Wilmington, though it is clear that he returned there at least once shortly after his discharge in 1865; and that one of the Mabson family lived with him in Dedham. But whether or not he continued his Wilmington connection, he was plainly not forgotten in that city. On December 16, 1917, the *Wilmington Dispatch* published a Sunday feature article, "Six Sons Serving," which recognized the wartime contributions of WBG and his sons:

> The current issue of The Crisis, a publication for negroes [i.e., of the NAACP], carries a full page picture of William B. Gould and his six sons, all of whom are in the service of the United States. The father is a veteran of the Civil War and was born in Wilmington, going to Dedham Mass. about 50 years ago. Three of the sons are first lieutenants, one a major in the reserve corps and two privates in the Regular Army.[8]

Note that the writer did not state why and how WBG left Wilmington for Dedham. The article simply mentioned that WBG served in the Civil War, without giving any hint that he was able to do so only because he had fled with seven other contrabands and had found refuge on a Union ship helping to blockade the city of Wilmington.

It is interesting to compare this piece with the news articles about WBG and his sons that were appearing in Dedham at the same time. Consider, for example, the relatively more respectful and warm tone of the following article, captioned "Three Soldier Boys Home": "Our well known fellow townsman, William B. Gould, Adjutant of Chas. W. Carroll Post 144, G.A.R., was an especially happy father Sunday in the fact that his three sons who are in the service spent the day at home. Herbert R. and James Edward are in the 367th Infantry at Camp Upton, while Ernest M. is in the 350th Field Artillery at Camp Dix. All three are first lieutenants."[9]

A week later, the same newspaper carried an article headlined "Dedham Patrons in the Limelight on Patriot Night," which gave the Goulds separate treatment under the subhead "Veteran Gould and His Three Chips Off the Old Block":

William B. Gould, a naval veteran of the Civil War, was given an ovation welcome. He told of his war-time experiences, the battles in southern waters and the chasing of Rebel privateers in European waters. He compared conditions in Civil War times with those of the present day and pointed out that "the big fighting machines of the now were simply improvements of the smaller fighting machines of the then." His father's tribute to his three boys in the service, two "over there" and the other momentarily expecting to go, was a splendid one, just such as an American father should pay to red-blooded sons ready to do and die for the honor of their country and flag. "I have ever tried to set them a good example," he said in closing, "and I expect to hear some good things from those boys."[10]

As noted, by the time WBG begins to serve his country in the War of the Rebellion, the conflict has become a struggle for freedom.[11] September 22, 1862, the day the U.S.S. *Cambridge* logs him in with the seven other contrabands, is the day that President Lincoln proclaims his intention to promulgate the Emancipation Proclamation. Issued in the wake of the bloodiest one-day battle ever, Antietam, the announcement becomes a beacon of hope for proponents of freedom and equality, not only in the United States, but throughout the world. Indeed in Europe, where the forces of reform and equality have been in retreat with the defeat administered to them in 1848, there is not a single republic left, prompting Lincoln's comment that the struggle for the Republic in the United States makes the United States the "last, best hope of earth."[12]

WBG's diary tells us that, for him, these are the real goals and objectives of the war. Consider this comment in 1864: "[H]eard of the departure of one battalion of the 5th Regiment Massachusetts Cavalry from Camp Meigs for Washington, D.C. May God protect them while defending the holiest of all causes, Liberty and Union."[13] On occasion, his commitment to the cause of war brings him to heights of eloquence—most of all, perhaps, when he learns of the surrender at Appomattox:

> On my return on board I heard the Glad Tidings that the Stars and Stripe[s] had been planted over the Capital of the D—nd Confedercy by the invincible Grant. While we honor the living soldiers who have done so much we must not forget to whisper for fear of desturbeing the Glorious sleep of the ma[ny] who have fallen. Mayrters to the cau[se] of Right and Equality.[14]

When the U.S.S. *Niagara* captures the *Georgia*, he writes:

[W]e boarded her and found her to be the Rebel Privateer "Georgia" from
Liverpool on her way to refit as A cruiseer, but the next cruise that she makes
will be for Uncle Samuel. . . . This capture makes our Crew feel verry
proud. . . . They [the crew of the *Georgia*] said that they ship'd in her to
go to the Coast of Affricca but they made A short voyage. . . . That is one
good deed for the "Niagara" and we hope that she will do many more before
the cruise is up. . . . We will now take A look for some of the other cruiseers
of would be King Jeff.[15]

As the war comes to a conclusion in 1865, he hopes that the "Conspiretors"
being tried in Washington "shall reap thair reward," and is gratified to hear that
"Davis [had] been carried to Washington to be tried by court martial on the indictment of treason. We hope that the sour apple tree is all ready."[16]

He is understandably dismayed and alarmed, then, to hear that the Confederates are being pardoned very quickly. From the tone of his statements on the
Confederacy in general, he clearly feels that the rebels are guilty of treachery,
and that it is unseemly to deal with traitors in an excessively lenient manner.[17]

His passion for the Union cause is well reflected in his complaint about the
army's inaction in the face of the massacre at Fort Pillow: "To day [April 16,
1864] we also heard of the capture of Fort Pillow by the Rebels and the Mascare
of all the troops, both White and Colard. Still the Govermet do not Retaileate."
We may suppose he is equally if not more chagrined some ten days later, when
he hears of a similar massacre in North Carolina: "Heard of the capture of Plymouth N.C. by the Rebels and a report of the Mascare of both White and colard soldiers belonging to North Carolina."[18]

Similarly, while sailing the Atlantic in search of Confederate cruisers, he seems
hardly to have been able to contain himself at the proposal making headway in
some circles to colonize blacks outside the country. In one of the most passionate statements we ever hear from him, he speaks with vigor of his opposition to
any such policy: "We see by the papers that the President in A speech intimates
Colinization for the colard people of the United States. This move of his must
and shall be resisted. We were born under the Flag of the Union and we never
will know no other. My sentement is the sentement of the people of the States."[19]

Ironically, this puts WBG at odds with Henry Highland Garnet, the promi-

nent black minister and onetime editor of *The Anglo-African* who sets in motion the series of events that lead to the freedom of WBG's wife to be, Cornelia.

More often, WBG is prone to understatement, particularly during the period
when he is still assigned to blockade duties aboard the U.S.S. *Cambridge*. Of the
shots coming from Fort Fisher on the shore of North Carolina, he says merely
that they are "too close to us to be at all agreeable"[20] In a similar vein, his only
comment on the fire his ship takes from the fort a few days earlier is that the rebels had "done some verry close shooting. Show'd that they knew thair work."[21]
When, in mid-November, the *Cambridge* happens on a Confederate ship, he la-
conically writes, "we told them good morning in the shape of a shot."[22] And he
notes of a later engagement that they "[b]ore down and sent our respects from
our Parrott [ship's gun]."[23]

WBG tends to pass off other things lightly, too—or at least to give the appearance of so doing. For instance, when his ship runs into heavy weather on
November 20, 1862, where the log of the U.S.S. *Cambridge* reports "Thunder
& Lightening with heavy rains & squalls," WBG says only that "the weather is
verry unsettled."

But surely the most memorable of all his understatements is his observation
about the Emancipation Proclamation upon first reading it: "Read [a]lso the
Proclamation of Emancipation. Verry good."[24]

There is one point, however, on which WBG is not understated: the mis-
treatment of black servicemen. He expresses great outrage, for example, at the
way some black soldiers who had been brought aboard his ship are treated:

> Yesterday about 300 men of the Maryland (colard) Regiment came on board
> (they being transfer to the Navy) and took dinner then departed for Ports-
> mouth N.H. They were treated verry rough by the crew. They refused to let
> them eat off the mess pans and calld them all kinds of names, one man his
> watch stolen from him by these scoundrels in all they was treated shamefully.[25]

⤺

William B. Gould is actively involved in the affairs of *The Anglo-African*, both
financially and intellectually. He visits the paper's offices frequently while he is
in New York and keeps in touch with the editor, Robert Hamilton, while the
Niagara is in Europe. In Hamilton, he meets one of the "leading black jour-

nalists of the Civil War era" who, though best known for his *Anglo* activities, "earned renown during the 1840s and 1850s as an articulate spokesman for black concerns."[26]

During his *Niagara* tour of duty, WBG organizes at least two subscriptions for the *Anglo*'s support. We know of these subscriptions both from his diary and from the newspaper itself, which runs two letters it receives from the crewmen of the *Niagara*. Although WBG is only one of several signatories to these letters, we can be sure he is a prime mover, if not the only force, behind those efforts.

On March 30, 1864, while en route to New York, he writes: "I took up A subscription to assist in sending A News Paper (The Anglo Affrican) to the colard soldiers of the Army of the United States." Then, on April 9, 1864, shortly after he notes visiting the *Anglo*'s New York office, the *Anglo* acknowledges this subscription under the headline "Three Cheers for the Boys of the Niagara!" Here the paper applauds the fifteen black crew members who sent the money and prints this letter from them:

> We, a part of the colored men on board of the U.S. steam frigate Niagara, seeing your appeal for assistance to furnish your very valuable paper to the colored soldiers of the army of the United States, and believing it will be of great good to them and the cause in which we are engaged, we subscribe the following amounts to assist to send your paper (The Anglo African) to the army without respect to regiment.

The letter then goes on to list the names of the fifteen crew members and the amount donated by each.[27] WBG is the last man listed.

On September 24, 1865, after his long journey across the Atlantic to Boston, WBG speaks of a second contribution to the *Anglo*: "received A Letter from . . . Mr. Robt. Hamilton [the paper's editor]. The Money sent to him in May last was received and acknowledged in the Issue of July 26." This contribution is in fact acknowledged on July 29, 1865, in a letter published under the title "Our Noble Tars Speak":

> Mr. Editor: While we are roaming around, watching the interests of Uncle Sam, we cannot but see the necessities of thousands of our own people liberated by the victorious march of the armies of the Union throughout the would be Confederacy. In order to assist in relieving the sufferings of our people we have taken up by subscription on board of this ship the amount enclosed. . . .

We receive the *Anglo* as regularly as our movements will permit, and right glad are we to receive it. It relieves the dullness of the long tedious hours passed at sea, and keeps us fully posted of what is being done at home. Continue in the good work and never cease until the top is reached. We hope soon to be where we too may lend a helping hand to this most glorious cause.

With deep sorrow we heard of the death of our beloved President, and the news has cast a gloom over all. We being, when the doleful news arrived, in the port of Lisbon, Portugal, displayed our colors at half-mast and fired a national salute of minute guns, and the Portuguese and English ships in port joined in paying this last tribute of respect to a just and good man, of whom the American people will ever be proud.[28]

Like several other contributions to *The Anglo-African*, this one is written by "Oley." Though the evidence for WBG as Oley is circumstantial, the coincidences are too many to believe that they are not one and the same. First of all, Oley is someone who has intimate knowledge of the escape of the eight contrabands from North Carolina. He cannot be one of the other seven (or anyone they may have told the story to), for WBG alone among them is familiar with the *Niagara*'s activities as well as the *Cambridge*'s. None of the seven others become members of the *Niagara*.

Second, certain turns of phrase point clearly in that direction. Compare, for instance, the reference to "would be King Jeff" in the diary and the reference to the "would be Confederacy" in the just-cited letter in *The Anglo-African*. Moreover, there are numerous instances in the Oley articles of the kind of droll understatement that is so common in the diary. For example, Oley's remark that "when the people of Wilmington expected Burnside to pay them a visit [the] Secessionists, not liking to fall before this General, removed from Wilmington into the interior of the State," has something of the same feel as WBG's wry statement, after the *Niagara* captures the *Georgia*, that the "next cruise that she makes will be for Uncle Samuel."[29]

Third, WBG records his attendance at a number of events in New York that are simultaneously reported on in the *Anglo*—for instance, the previously noted meeting on suffrage in North Carolina that he and Abraham Galloway go to in the spring of 1864.

Fourth, and perhaps the most important evidence of all, is the similarity between WBG's and Oley's accounts of the escape of Lucilla Moseley, the woman who is to become the wife of one of the eight contrabands, Joseph Hall. Here is WBG's account:

> The Mystic returnd from the shoals with the Mails of the Fleet. She exchanged Boats with us. One of our Lieuts went Pasenger in her. She had also thirteen Rebel deserters and several colard Reffugees among them several of My Aquaintances. Heard from my people. Mrs. L.M—ly was among the many that I saw. She saild about sun set for Hampton Roads.[30]

Oley, in reporting this episode, used exactly the same form of Lucilla Mosley's name as WBG: L.M—ly. Moreover, like WBG, he boarded the *Mystic* from the *Cambridge*:

> The writer of this article went aboard of the Mystic to carry our mail from the C—bridge, when I was surprised to see her [Mrs. L.M—ly] on board of that ship. I returned on board of my ship and related the fact to H., who was more than surprised. Our heroine went to Fortress Monroe and found a home with the home of the Provost-Marshall. Not long after the departure of the Mystic the C—bridge was ordered North. We arrived safely at Hampton Roads, where the lovers met again, and were happily married on the 20th of December, 1862. The lady now lives in Baltimore, Md., and her husband is on board of the gunboat W—na, off Charleston, S.C.[31]

Finally, there is another thing that weighs in on the side of WBG as Oley: the fact that WBG is in correspondence with Joseph Hall (as well as his wife Lucilla) even after he leaves the *Cambridge*. This places him extremely close to the central figures in the "interesting romance" that Oley is describing.

Another consideration, though it does not relate directly to the question of whether WBG is Oley, is that the story Oley tells jibes not only with what is in WBG's diary but also with the log of the U.S.S. *Genessee*, the ship that transfers Mosley to the *Mystic*. The October 28, 1862, log states that "eight men and one woman came alongside from shore. Eight came on board, reportedly escaped from Wilmington." And on November 2, the log notes that Lucilla Mosley is transferred to the *Mystic*.

According to Oley, Mrs. L. M., upon reaching Wilmington in male disguise, "again resumed her male attire, and, in company with four men [the log says eight men], procured a boat and made the attempt to run the gauntlet, in which they were successful, and arrived safely on board of the Genesee without her sex being discovered. She finally made it known to the Captain, who transferred her to the steamer Mystic, then going North for repairs."[32]

It is interesting, in this connection, that the *Anglo* runs an article describing the "Shameful Treatment" of colored soldiers on board the *Niagara*, a title reminiscent of WBG's pronouncement that those soldiers were "treated shamefully."[33] That article is submitted to the *Anglo* from the *Niagara*, not by Oley, but by someone named "Trumps." Whoever he is, he graphically recounts the indignities to which the soldiers had been subjected:

> On Tuesday afternoon last there came alongside of this ship a steamer from Baltimore, containing colored troops from the army. They were a fine looking set of men.
>
> Their commander came aboard to request our Commodore to furnish the men with food, as they had not had anything to eat for two days.
>
> Our Commodore gave his consent, and the soldiers came aboard and were mustered on the quarter-deck, where they had to wait one hour and a half before they could get a mouthful of victuals. The order was given to the cooks to spread their mess-cloths for the men, but, to the astonishment of all the officers, the crew got indignant and hid their mess-pans, spoons and cups, and the men were obliged to do the best they could with their fingers. Nor was this all. They were knocked and beat around the ship like so many dogs, and quids of tobacco were thrown in their faces.
>
> Now, Mr. Editor, what do you think of this? We rally to the defence of our imperilled country—we freely offer our lives in its defence—the government acknowledges the value of our services, and yet our brave fellows are permitted to be treated in this shameful manner.
>
> Will no service or sacrifice satisfy this horrible monster, prejudice?[34]

WBG may well be Trumps, but the case for that is far less certain than the one for him as Oley. One argument for his being Trumps is fairly strong, though: the fact that all of Oley's contributions occur after Trumps's description of the Maryland incident. Perhaps WBG writes under the name Trumps and then under the *nom de plume* Oley thereafter.

On the whole, WBG reserves his sardonic and understated writing style for serious subjects, and these he takes up throughout his diary. But he often covers lighter matters, too, and here he tends to write more or less straightforwardly. For instance, he matter-of-factly notes visits to the *Niagara* by "ladies" and "visitors on board." He speaks of dancing and gaiety while a shipmate in correspondence speaks of "Ladies . . . of rather doubtful character."[35] And as the *Niagara* leaves Spain, he "bid adue to Castiele and thair dark Eyed Beauties."[36]

Still another example of his remarks in this area pertains to the crew's hijinks in New York City:

> I returnd about 12 Oclock to find quite A number of Ladies assembled and Danceing goin on. We now made preperation for the Luncheon wich pass'd off finely when Danceing was again resumed wich lasted til four when the Band left. The Company remaind later and the last did not get away until about five. So end our trouble of to day.[37]

Of a drunken revel at a farmer's fair in Flushing, he writes: "Seem'd to be the Rule for every boddy to drink as much Gin as they could stand under and many both Male and Female could not stand but A verry short time."[38]

WBG reports some things that strike him as funny. For example, off New Inlet in North Carolina, the ship "[l]ost several Barrells of Potatos over board. All the Cooks were driven out of the Galley by A shower of spuds down the Galley skylight."[39] But he quite obviously finds his initiation into the duties of wardroom cook something less than that:

> All the men haveing less than three months to serve were transfered to the North Carolina [just before the European departure]. Among them was Charles E. Profs and Charles H. Scott, Ward Room Serveants and Hutcheson Allen Ward Room Cook. Here we was left without A Cook but I attempted to get the dinner ready amid the greatest confusion immaginable. . . . To night feeling very tired from my new occupation that I must leave off. Hopeing that on the morrow will bring some one to fill the place made vacant by the transfer of H. Allen.[40]

Other times he speaks in a self-deprecating manner, as when he describes one accident he had, an incident that must have been terribly uncomfortable, if not frightening, as a "bath":

> This Morning [March 16, 1864] I went to the supply store and got our stores then came down to the ward to return on board here. I took an unintentional

bath. The Ladder that we had placed alongside of the warf for our conveineance of geting in and out of our boats the Ladder had become coated with Ice and as I descended the Ladder to the boat I slip'd from the Ladder into the River. I was rescued by the boats crew. It was verry cold and my face and clothes becamed coated with Ice. I soon got on board and changed my clothes. In the Evening I felt quite unwell from the effect of my bath.

Always ready for new experiences, WBG, to paraphrase him, avails himself of the opportunity to see Europe and observe what surrounds him. In Spain, he notes: "It looks verry strange that in this country where Nature have lavished her riches that there should be so many Poor People."[41] As his ship passes up the river from Antwerp, he remarks that "the Country presents beautiful scenery. . . . beautiful Cottages, and Farms looking verry Beautiful."[42] He is further impressed by the riches that made Antwerp so important in this period: "We commence seeing Gold and Silver wich is good for our Eyes."[43] A few days later, he describes the *Niagara*'s response to the grand reception she received in Belgium: "We fired a salute of 17 Guns and one of Nine. We Drilld one of our Guns Crewe to show them how we handled our Parrott Carragees. We fire off one of our 150 lbs. Rifles twice to see how they liked the noise."[44]

And hear what WBG has to say about Antwerp on a day that is full of sadness and adventuresome activity: "Morning Rainy. Lost my Port Monnie. Went on shore. Had a fine time generaly. Went up to the top of the Tower of the Cathedral by ascending six hundred and sixteen steps (616). F[o]und every boddy verry kind."[45]

The diary of William B. Gould is both eloquent and methodical. His work as a United States Navy man is undoubtedly sometimes "tedious," the word that appears in the letter to *The Anglo-African*. The log of the ship frequently says: "nothing unusual has transpired," "nothing transpired worthy of note," "nothing important occurs," "all hands painting, cleaning." And yet, just as one is lulled with the sense that hardly anything ever comes along to break the tedium, suddenly some reference to an event on the ship or a significant turn in the war sneaks in. His diary requires careful attention even in the midst of tedium.

Finally, it seems clear that WBG either had some prior exposure to the sea before he is assigned to the *Cambridge* or is a quick study once in the U.S. Navy. Listen to his comments of March 29, 1864, while out on the Atlantic:

All last night we went before the gale. . . . The Gale still blows fresh and the seas running verry high. We Ship'd several through the night and one sea fill'd the Ward Room with Water. I have got duck'd awfully last night. It was worth something to be apon the Deck, although thare is so much danger in A storm thare is something verry sublime in one, to hear the roar of the storm, the hissing of the Waves, the whistling of the Rigging and the Cannon like report of the torn sail and above all this the stern word of Command and the shrill sound of the Boatswain's Pipe all adds to the granduer of the scene, for thare is something grand in A storm. All night with eager eyes both Offercers and Men pace'd the Deck watching our Foretopsail feeling in A measure secure as long as we could carry Sail at all, it has stood through the night. Thare is no sign of the storm abateing, all the Galley fire is out, and nothing to Eat is the cry, and almost nothing to wear on account of the Water. Shine out fair sun and smote the Waves that we may proceed on our course and all be saved.

The calm he displays in the teeth of the grandeur of the storm is particularly remarkable, given the fierce conditions described in the *New York Times*:

The *Niagara* again experienced a severe storm of hail, rain and sleet, and an intensely violent gale, but for having a fair wind it would have been more terrible than the one above described; the vessel shipped heavy seas over her gangways, and the violence of the waves were such that some of her ports were stove in; nearly all her sails were literally torn in shreds, and flying at the mercy of the winds; at this time the vessel had all canvas spread, was running before the wind.[46]

The *Times* speaks of the ship being delivered from the "very jaws of death."

Similarly, although WBG acknowledges that he himself feels ill at sea, he speaks in an avuncular and almost dismissive fashion about those who are seasick and seem to have less experience than he possesses. "The greater portion of our Crew being Landsmen's on thair first cruise thare is A large number of them sea sick. You can see them trying to get forward by crawling and helping each other. They do not like thair first feelings of A seafareing."[47] Still, even the most seasoned sailor might feel a bit queasy when, as the *New York Times* reports, the whole of the day is

. . . exceedingly rough; a severe rain-storm and a heavy gale. About 11 P.M., the storm increased, and the gale assumed still greater violence; the waves were mountains high, the ship rolled frantically and labored heavily. In the middle watch the scene on this vessel beggars description; cutlasses, mess-chests, muskets, and, in fact, every movable thing were tossing about the decks promiscuously, and it required much courage to pass from one part of the ship to the other.[48]

But, as with other perils at sea, not least the Confederate enemy and discrimination, William B. Gould is to persevere and to return to Massachusetts at the conclusion of the war.

THREE

The Democratic Impulse and the Navy: Two Influences Shaping William B. Gould's Wartime Experiences

$\mathcal{T}$he great democratic reforms of the modern era have emerged from the United States, particularly those emanating from the war that was fought between 1861 and 1865. The New World's central political and social achievements sprang from the Emancipation Proclamation, issued initially by President Abraham Lincoln on September 22, 1862, and formally proclaimed on January 1, 1863. The central vision of the American system of government rests in the ideas of democracy and the rights of all people embodied in it, and in the post–Civil War constitutional amendments, ideas that stand in sharp contrast to the years when the United States was in the grip of the slave economy, with all that this meant for the repression of equality.[1] They stem from those fateful years of which William B. Gould was a part—years in which British and French leaders, in particular, watched the bitter struggle overseas in anticipation, hoping against hope that the new democratic system on the other side of the Atlantic would be defeated or badly splintered.

Once it became clear that the War of the Rebellion was a war against slavery, public opinion in Europe began to support the Union, even though it was known that Britain and France had made it clear to Washington that they "had a basic contempt for the American socio-political system and regarded the American sectional conflict as the consequence of an excess of democracy and the inability of the American people to elect 'natural leaders' from among the 'best men' in the nation."[2]

The bloody struggles of Antietam and Gettysburg, the extraordinary loss of life and limb at so many other battlefields and at sea as well—and the surrender and peace signed at Appomattox—produced the great Civil War amendments that reversed the infamous *Dred Scott* decision, in which the Supreme Court declared blacks to be property even in the free territories.[3] That reversal, in turn, provided the United States with the historical framework for both the Supreme Court's historic landmark *Brown v. Board of Education* ruling of 1954, which condemned "separate but equal" as a denial of equal protection under the Constitution,[4] and the civil rights legislation of the 1960s. Title VII of the Civil Rights Act of 1964, our most comprehensive legislation on discrimination in the workplace, is in some respects a lineal descendant of these nineteenth-century developments.

So is the National Labor Relations Act of 1935, in the sense that it purports to fashion a code of conduct and establish an administrative agency to resolve disputes and promote compliance with the law. The NLRA provides all workers with the right to engage in the collective bargaining process and to deal autonomously with employers through their designated representatives.[5] It is a modern adaptation of the philosophy articulated by the Supreme Court in 1911, namely, that the United States is committed "to make labor free but prohibiting that control by which the personal service of one man is disposed of or coerced for another's benefit."[6]

For the world, the southern rebellion was seen to have its roots in opposition to the "free soil movement," whose adherents stressed the dignity of free labor and work. Those views were espoused by President Lincoln himself before the armed conflict. During the presidential campaign of 1860, he made a particularly revealing statement, in light of how future events unfolded:

> When one starts poor, as most do in the race of life, free society is such that he knows he can better his condition; he knows that there is no fixed condition of labor for his whole life. . . . I want every man to have the chance—and I believe a black man is entitled to it—in which he *can* better his condition—when he may look forward and hope to be a hired laborer this year and the next, work for himself afterward, and finally to hire men to work for him! That is the true system.[7]

When one examines Lincoln's views and modern legislation on the same or comparable subject matter, it is important to consider such speeches as those that he gave to the New York Workingmen's Democratic Republican Association on March 21, 1864, where he said: "The strongest bond of human sympathy, outside of the family relation, should be on uniting all working people, of all nations, and tongues and kindreds."[8] He took a similar tack in his first annual message to Congress, and his words resonate with us today. Said the President: "Capital is only the fruit of labor and could never have existed if labor had not first existed."[9] Indeed, he saw economic democracy as an integral part of political democracy.

Lincoln also supported the right of workers to withhold their labor and to strike. It bears noting that, in this, he ran against the tide of laissez-faire thinking that predominated in the nineteenth century, and that swept through the country again toward the close of the twentieth century. He made his views clear as early as 1860 by openly supporting a well-organized strike conducted by the boot and shoe workers of New England. Lincoln regarded the right of free laborers to strike as a "virtue, not a failing, of free society," as G. S. Boritt has written in *Lincoln and the Economics of the American Dream*.[10]

Boritt also notes that during the Civil War, several delegations of strikers from the Machinists and Blacksmiths Union of New York visited the White House to speak with the President about their position. According to him, the

> labor representatives took great comfort from their interview, reasoning that although their employers refused to deal with them, Lincoln received them. "If any man should again say that combinations of working men are not good," they concluded, "let them point to the Chief Magistrate." They even quoted the President as saying "I know that in almost every case of strikes, the men have just cause for complaint." It is rather likely that the union men quoted Lincoln correctly.[11]

Of course, Lincoln's view of labor was closely related to his view of slavery. Again, in 1860, he asserted: "'Owned labor' would compete with free labor so as to 'degrade' the latter." And, in an earlier and lengthy speech to the Wisconsin State Agricultural Society in Milwaukee on September 30, 1859, he noted that, according to the so-called "mud-sill" theory, a hired laborer was "fatally fixed in that condition for life" and thus his condition was the same as that of a slave.[12]

But as Lincoln noted, this theory proceeded on the assumption that labor and education were incompatible, and that one could not improve oneself and one's family through free labor. Lincoln's view was antithetical to all of this. He firmly believed that workers should be able to rise to new horizons.

Because of that conviction, Lincoln, unlike other proponents of the rights of labor, did not see the working class as a well-defined unit. To some extent, Boritt says, Lincoln shared the view that there was a harmony between capital and labor, and that it ought to be promoted so as to increase the ability of workers to rise out of their class—an idea consistent with those propagated today both by collective bargaining and by proponents of employee participation.

Lincoln succeeded in making his argument against people being "fatally fixed" the prevailing philosophy in the Union from the Civil War onward through the enactment of the Thirteenth Amendment, which he sponsored before his assassination.[13] (The possibility of personal mobility was a view that was assuredly an abiding principle for William B. Gould, whose very life, as he rose from servitude to employee and then employer and owner of capital, was vivid testimony to that proposition.) The idea that employers and employees have harmonious rather than conflicting objectives was closely connected. Eric Foner has written of some of the tensions between the early Republican Party's ideology of free labor (an ideology to which William B. Gould also undoubtedly subscribed) and later laws guaranteeing a worker's right to engage in collective bargaining and strikes.[14] As Foner says:

> Those Republicans, like Lincoln, who endorsed the right to strike usually meant that laborers should be free to leave their jobs and take others, rather than that they should shut down the establishments of their employers. . . . The basic Republican answer to the problem of urban poverty was neither charity, public work, nor strikes, but westward migration of the poor, aided by a homestead act.[15]

Foner stresses the anti-interventionist position of the Republicans on matters relating to labor conditions, even hours of work. WBG seemed to endorse that approach when, in an undated document decrying a policy of discrimination and the "wholesale deportation of the Negro," he stated: "The black American is very seldom mixed up in the labor troubles that are now shaking the foundations of our government. Does the Negro love his country? He has *ever* been loyal to this country even when denied the rights of citizenship."[16] He went on to set out three essential characteristics that he considered prerequisite to "good citizenship": "(1) intelligence; (2) 'ability to acquire wealth'; (3) love of country." His was truly, in Foner's words, a "middle-class perception of the social order."[17]

WBG's views were conservative in the sense that he apparently had little sympathy for "the labor trouble" of the day. His idea of free labor was the notion that a person could rise as far as his talents would allow him. Yet he also seemed to harbor some of the early Republican Party's suspicions regarding accumulated wealth—particularly when it interfered with the equality of opportunity and promoted a fixed station in life for those who did not start with advantage. In the words of Benjamin Brewster, my father's boyhood and lifelong friend, "He was a conservative man. The Goulds of Dedham were a conservative family."

Another pillar of WBG's philosophy, which some today would characterize as conservative, was his belief in a strong military as the only protection for individual liberty and equality. That central part of his thought is what brought him, and all his sons after him, to enlist in the service of the United States.

$\backsim$

The period immediately preceding the War of the Rebellion saw enormous changes in warfare throughout the world, and especially in naval warfare. In the wake of Napoleon's defeat at Waterloo in 1815 came a host of important scientific discoveries, the most important of all being the improved steam engine devised by James Watt. Great Britain was the first of the world's countries to benefit from his invention, and her navy was to dominate the seas and commercial trade in coming years.

But as the events of the 1860s drew nigh, the matter of the defense of the United States at sea seemed to get little attention from the nation's leaders and opinion makers. The navy played a role in the Mexican War of 1846–48, but, for the most part, that war was the army's show. The new technological advances appeared to bypass the U.S. Navy. States William M. Fowler:

> Contemporary European commentators are apt to write off the American Navy because of both its small size and lack of modern ships and weapons. In the 1850s, for example, paddle wheels were still popular in the American Navy, though it had become clear how vulnerable they were to enemy fire. One British observer remarked that the American Navy was the last one still planning to sail into battle in side-wheelers. Even the more modern screw-propelled steamers in the fleet—*Merrimack, Roanoke,* and *Minnesota*—were criticized by sophisticated foreign observers. One British reviewer noted that

the screw-frigate *Niagara* [WBG's second ship during the Civil War] had "no beauty to recommend her." Beauty or not, though, the steam frigates at least were a far step ahead of side-wheelers and sailing frigates.[18]

For the Union at the beginning of the war, it was not simply a question of a failure to keep pace technologically. The U.S. Navy lacked competent and experienced officers, given the large number of those who had hailed from the South. Somewhere between one-sixth and one-quarter of the Naval Officer Corps had "gone South" with the commencement of hostilities in 1861, though "a number of Southern officers remained loyal to the Union, such as Captain John Winslow of North Carolina, Stephen Lee a Virginian and cousin of Robert E. Lee and the South Carolinian Percival Drayton and the Tennessean David Farragut, who does become the first Vice and full Admiral of the US Navy."[19]

Notwithstanding all of these problems, the navy becomes an important part of the war effort. This much was made clear in President Lincoln's early proclamation of the blockade of southern ports. Before that, as Ivan Musicant has said, the U.S. Navy was "a drowsy, moth-eaten organization":

The Civil War caught the United States Navy at the nadir of one of its periodic "dark ages." Less than half of its ninety wooden ships were in commission, and these were spread around the globe in little flag-showing squadrons, more for the sake of national prestige than strategic purpose.

The navy's institutional memory reached to its last great endeavor, the War of 1812, in which several senior captains of 1861 had fought as child midshipmen. . . . The victorious Mexican War of fifteen years past gave some experience in blockade, shore bombardment, and amphibious operations in support of the army. But on the waters there were no contests, for Mexico had no navy.

The two decades prior to the Civil War witnessed revolutionary changes in war at sea with the advent of steam navigation, shell-firing guns, and iron-armored vessels, and the U.S. Navy had participated, more or less, in these new industrial age technologies. [In 1860, however], fully thirty-four of the navy's serviceable ships were powered by sail only, and tentative experiments in armor plate had borne no fruit.[20]

The country simply had not understood the nature or importance of the advances in naval technology. And as Frank Merli has said:

Although a number of Americans had made important contributions to various phases of the emerging technology—Robert Fulton, Matthew C. Perry, John M. Brooke, and John A. Dahlgren, to name only a few—the Union navy had done little to prepare itself for the new direction in sea war. This was so for a number of reasons: for one thing, many naval officers, especially in the higher echelons of officers, had outlived their usefulness but remained in rank, a bulwark against reform. . . . Little wonder that when its greatest challenge came, the Federal navy found itself decrepit, disorganized, and demoralized, in a condition that was made very much worse by the lethargic response of James Buchanan's administration to the impending crisis: when Lincoln proclaimed his blockade of nearly 4,000 miles of enemy coast, he had about forty ships to implement it.[21]

As Stephen Wise has noted, the navy was nonetheless well equipped with ordnance. The artillery it possessed, the Dahlgren gun, "was one of the world's finest cannon and was capable of firing round cast iron shot and shell, some weighing up to 440 pounds."[22] WBG, as we have seen, several times mentioned the rifled Parrott gun, "a high velocity weapon that fired a bullet-like projectile," which "had a longer range and was more accurate than the Dahlgren, but . . . was not as durable."[23]

The blockade, initiated on April 19, 1861, and extended to North Carolina and Virginia subsequent to their secession on April 27, was a direct response to Confederate President Jefferson Davis's call for privateers to attack the property of the United States and capture northern Merchant Marine ships at sea. Aside from inflicting harm and damage to the United States, the idea was to so disrupt northern commerce that affected European nations like Great Britain and France would intervene on the side of the South. And, of course, it was hoped that this action would so preoccupy the North as to take away ships that were otherwise needed to implement the blockade. This blockade policy, perhaps the most important of the Union's war initiatives, was associated with the "Anaconda" strategy of economic strangulation of the South advocated by General Winfield Scott. As noted in Chapter One, it was facilitated in North Carolina by the occupation of cities like New Bern and Beaufort, as well as Hatteras Inlet and Roanoke Island. WBG spends some considerable time at Beaufort as his ship, the U.S.S. *Cambridge*, comes in to coal.

It is clear from both the blockade and other naval engagements that steam power facilitated the naval bombardment of forts—a fact that became particularly important in North Carolina. The *Cambridge* exchanged gunfire with Fort Fisher, guarding the mouth of the Cape Fear River. And notwithstanding the navy's somnolent state, both sides quickly learned the lessons of the Crimean War, in which the Russians' "ironclads" destroyed the Turkish naval vessels.

The Civil War made the United States a world-class sea power. The success of the *Monitor* in confronting the *Merrimack* at Hampton Roads meant that the Union would go down a path of greater reliance upon new ironclads.[24] But even before this battle, Secretary of the Navy Gideon Welles saw clearly that the so-called Wabash-class steam frigate, of which the navy had approximately a half-dozen, was not well suited to blockade operations in the shallow waters off the southern coast. (The U.S.S. *Niagara*, on which WBG served in European waters in 1864–65, was one of these half-dozen vessels.) Some 500 ships participated in patrolling 4,000 miles of coastline from the Potomac to the Rio Grande. By 1864, the Union navy had 45,000 enlisted men and 6,000 officers; and approximately 670 ships, including more than 300 steamers and 65 ironclads.

The navy was vital to the land invasion of North Carolina and the capture of Beaufort and New Bern, as well as Morehead City and Fort Macon, cities that WBG's *Cambridge* helped to blockade until 1862, when General McClellan ordered General Burnside to "launch an inland attack" from his base at Hatteras Inlet. Burnside's assignment was to seize Beaufort and Goldsborough in North Carolina and to simultaneously mount a strike at the Wilmington and Weldon railroad. The objective, as earlier noted, was to cut off supplies going to General Lee's army in Virginia, an effort that would provide a different dimension to Anaconda, or strangulation. In order to carry out this ambitious policy, the navy fleet doubled within the first four months of the blockade, and more ships were steadily added in the next half year, by which time the number had increased sixfold.

William Fowler finds it lamentable that "the nation remembered the Federal soldiers, as it did not remember its sailors. . . . The navy deserves to be remembered for without its notable contributions, the North could not have won the war."[25] But President Lincoln did not overlook the navy's role. In assessing the state of the war effort after Vicksburg and Gettysburg, he credited, in almost poetic terms, what he called "Uncle Sam's web feet" for the achievements obtained: "Nor must Uncle Sam's web feet be forgotten," he declared. "At all the watery margins they have been present. Not only on the deep sea, the broad bay, and the rapid river, but also up the narrow, muddy bayou, and wherever the ground was a little damp, they have been, and made their tracks."[26]

When WBG joined the navy in September 1862, he was one of the earliest blacks to join in the North's war at sea. The policy toward the recruitment of blacks by the U.S. Navy evolved in fits and starts. Indeed, each war in the nineteenth century was considerably different from that in the century to follow, where a southern-dominated navy relegated blacks to menial positions, explicitly excluding them from naval commissions altogether.

In the nineteenth century, the roles of the respective services were reversed. The navy had in fact been relatively integrated since the 1790s. The "first significant enlistment of African American sailors occurred during the Revolutionary War, when blacks served in all of America's navies."[27] But though the navy never out and out barred blacks, regulations from the 1840s onward limited their number to about 5 percent of the enlisted force. Still, manpower shortages often eroded racial barriers. The army, by contrast, from the adoption of the Federal Militia Act in 1792 onward, had prohibited blacks from serving altogether. It was only to relent and allow blacks into its ranks during the Civil War after the navy had done so.

As Benjamin Quarles has noted in *The Negro in the Civil War*, accepting blacks into the services was the most "insistent" problem the Lincoln administration faced in 1861 and 1862.[28] It emerged, according to him, after the Union defeat at Bull Run, which was attributable "in part to the Confederate military defenses constructed by slaves."[29] General Benjamin Butler of Massachusetts was the first to devise a solution to the problem that accommodated the ambivalence of northern policy toward the issue of slavery—an ambivalence that grew out of Lincoln's desire not to offend the Border States and their powerful slaveholders, particularly given the strategic position of some of those states. As Lincoln had said, "I hope I have God on our side. But I must have Kentucky." Keeping Maryland in the Union was also crucial. Both states were of immense strategic importance, Kentucky because of its navigable waterways, and Maryland because of its close proximity to the capital.

Thus, the policy of ambivalence was embraced by General Butler, and the Union was to characterize escaped or fugitive slaves as "contraband." That policy was similar to Congress's enactment of legislation in 1861 providing for the forfeiture of all slaves whose masters had permitted them to be used in the military or naval service of the Confederacy. Quarles notes that this legislation "strengthened the hand of the small band of Union officers who from the beginning had been in favor of freeing the slaves."[30] Among them were John C. Frémont, "The Pathfinder," and Major-General David Hunter, who on their own initiative ordered the freeing of slaves in their areas. Those orders, issued in July 1861 and the summer of 1862, respectively, were rescinded by Lincoln.

Under the 1861 legislation, the question of the contrabands' status as property or human beings was unresolved. The Confiscation Act of July 17, 1862, was the next step in the process. It declared that any slave belonging to someone who was in rebellion was a free person. This law had the effect of increasing the number of fugitives in whom the U.S. Navy had a particular interest (the army at this point was still all white). For the navy, the contrabands promised to be both a good source of information on enemy locations and movements and a pool of recruits to fulfill its manpower needs. As summer became fall, the problem became more "insistent."

In fact, the navy had acted well before Congress clarified the status of contrabands. As early as 1861, it had accepted many runaway slaves, and ultimately, black sailors accounted for 20 percent of the navy's total enlisted force, a proportion that was nearly double the representation of black soldiers in the army.[31]

Initially, as in the army, the policy differed depending upon the commander involved. Thomas Craven, the commander of the *Niagara* during WBG's assignment, returned over twenty blacks to southern whites in 1861.[32] But by July of that year, Secretary of Navy Gideon Welles was taking a fresh look at the reluctance of commanders like Craven to employ blacks who had succeeded in escaping from the southern states. Welles informed Flag Officer Stringham to enlist contrabands already on board but stated that naval officers were not to attempt to entice slaves from their masters. Two months later, Welles officially authorized the employment of blacks on all ships, but at a level no higher than "Boys" (recall that this was the first position WBG held), at a compensation of ten dollars a month. "By late 1862, many ships' crews soon featured one-quarter to one-half black sailors."[33] As Joseph P. Reidy has written:

During the first ninety days after Fort Sumter, when nearly three hundred black recruits enlisted, fifty-nine (20 percent) were veterans with an average of five years of prior naval service per man. Over succeeding months, the proportion of black men in the service increased rapidly. At the end of 1861, they made up roughly 6 percent of the crews of vessels. By the summer of 1862, the figure had climbed to nearly 15 percent.[34]

This policy was of course driven by a shortage of sailors. The number had climbed because squadron commanders had begun openly soliciting contraband recruits when Secretary Welles advised them that no more men could be sent to them because the pool of enlistments had run dry. By late 1862, "all of the squadron commanders in American waters were willingly employing Contrabands."[35]

According to Reidy, of the approximately 17,000 black sailors in the navy during the Civil War whose place of birth is known, some 7,800 came (like WBG) from one of the Confederate states.[36] "The firsthand experience these men had with slavery," Reidy contends, "distinguished them from their freeborn northern counterparts":

> Moreover, whereas northern freemen could enlist when they chose, men held in bondage often had to rely on the circumstances of war for the opportunity to do so. Not simply awaiting their fate, black men escaping from slavery helped create opportunities for the federal government to protect them and accept their offers of service.[37]

Although initially blacks could only be recruited as first-class boys, policy changes later in 1861 allowed them to come in at the higher grade of landsman. Later still, in 1862, all jobs were made open to them up to the position of petty officer. This ability to be promoted is what has prompted commentators like Herbert Aptheker to say that "there was a relative absence of segregation and discrimination of Negroes in the Civil War Federal fleet."[38] Ironically, the policies of that era compare favorably with the racially exclusionary practices of the U.S. Navy in the succeeding century.

All the same, the picture was not as rosy as Aptheker suggests. There was in fact a good deal of discrimination in the navy, though it was certainly not of the same dimensions as in the army. In the first place, restricting blacks to the lowest positions constituted the rankest kind of discrimination. WBG spent most of his naval career in the two lowest classifications, boy and landsman. As Reidy notes:

Although the Navy Department did not establish a formal system of racial separation during the Civil War, Secretary Welles's guidelines for recruiting and rating black sailors nearly accomplished exactly that. For wittingly or not, the policy reinforced the prejudices of recruiters, naval officers, and white enlisted men to the effect that black enlistees would contribute to the war effort as laborers and servants rather than as skilled seamen. Of the approximately 17,600 men whose base rating is recorded, more than 14,400 (or 82 percent) were rated as boy or landsman. This discounting of black men's seafaring skill at times plagued even the most experienced of men.[39]

Not only were there no black officers in the navy during the War of the Rebellion, there were none until World War II.[40] In this respect, the policies of the army and the navy in this period were uniform.[41]

In the second place, as we can see from WBG's diary, there was considerable racial discord aboard ship. He wrote, for example, that, while they were in New York, "there was A malee [melee] on Deck between the white and colard men."[42] And a year later, while the *Niagara* was in La Coruña, Spain, we hear that "four or fiv[e] white fellows beat Jerry Jones (co[lored]). He was stabd in his left shoulder. Verry bad."[43]

Third, black-face minstrel became, in the words of Michael J. Bennett, "convenient conduits through which Union sailors funneled and projected worries concerning their situational similarities [the lack of independence in confined quarters] with contraband sailors."[44] In respect to this, WBG wrote, "Our Minstrel Troup give one of thair entertainments this evening. I wish them success."[45] The following day he commented, "Last night the Minstrel Troup acquited themselves creditabley."[46] It is difficult to determine precisely what he meant, but apparently his view was that the minstrel on the *Niagara* was not as harmful as he had anticipated. As Reidy has noted: "Despite the demeaning character of the minstrel stereotypes, black sailors often experienced a degree of ambivalence toward minstrelsy, whose tunes and lyrics might strike sentimental rather than strictly demeaning chords."[47]

This view is confirmed by the only other published black naval diarist of the war, Charles Fisher, who noted that he, along with others, "went to rehearse our pieces" in a minstrel show, and that one of his fellow black sailors "brought down the house."[48] He confirmed the fact the he was one of the minstrels and stated that, on June 12, 1863, "the minstrels are gotten in for our amusement and to relieve the tediousness of [ship duty]."[49] Accordingly, it is difficult to ascribe racism to a program that black sailors found acceptable and enjoyable, and, in some instances, actually participated in.[50]

The problem of tedium during ship duty, to use the words of Fisher, could often give rise to discipline and disciplinary problems. A primary area of concern here was desertion, but as WBG noted, blacks appear to have been underrepresented among those who deserted.[51] The penalty for George Williams "was thirty days double Irons solitary confinement on bread and water except on every seventh day. Then he was to have full rations with the loss of three months pay."[52] Blacks were also underrepresented in connection with discipline arising out of violations of supervisory authority.

Theft, of course, was punished harshly: "Three men for stealing were sentanced to thirty days in Double Irons on bread and water and the loss of three months pay."[53] In another instance: "A man that was caught stealing was lash'd up in his Hammock for three nights. Then he was made to walk up and down the deck with A bag tied around him with a play card attached with the word theif apon it."[54] Similarly, double irons was the penalty for a refusal by some of his shipmates to obey orders.[55]

The discontinuation of the liquor ration on August 31, 1862, led to some of the problems. For instance, double irons for thirty days with bread and water and the loss of three months' pay was imposed for smuggling liquor on board.[56] It was thought—and a court martial was convened to this effect—that Henry Smith, the black author of articles about the *Niagara* in *The Anglo-African*, was "bringing on board Liquor to sell to the men."[57] WBG reports: "The Sentence of Henry Smith for the offence above stated were thirty days confinement in single Irons with the loss of two months pay."[58]

Sometimes the offenses were petty in nature.[59] Said WBG just two weeks before his discharge from the navy: "This Evening there was three Men caught (Playing Cards in the Fore Hold) by the First Lieut. They were put into the Brig."[60] Even WBG was punished for sewing in the pantry, which apparently constituted an offense.[61] But at no point did WBG suggest that there was a racially uneven or disparate impact of disciplinary sanctions.

Fourth, on some ships the eating facilities were segregated. The *Niagara* crew's "shameful treatment" of the black soldiers that WBG bemoaned and perhaps wrote about in *The Anglo-African* is suggestive; he seems to have considered the incident out of the ordinary or exceptional. To repeat the pertinent part of his account: "[The] 300 colored men of the Maryland Regiment [who] came on board. . . . were treated verry rough by the crew. They refused to let them eat of[f] the mess pans and calld them all kinds of names. . . . in all they was treated shamefully."[62]

These discriminatory and segregationist policies reflected the position the North had taken at the beginning of the Civil War, which was that the United States "was a white man's country and the whites would fight this war."[63] Nonetheless, the navy pursued a different policy. And we have already seen the reason for that: its policy was established out of purely practical considerations, not in the pursuit of racial equality or fairness. After all, as Valuska, Aptheker, and Bolster have chronicled, some numbers of blacks were seasoned sailors who had served in the navy in previous military conflicts.[64] More important, white enlistments became increasingly problematic as it became clear that the war would not conclude quickly. Initially, in the first four months of 1861, according to Aptheker, only 5.5 percent of total navy enlistments were black. But when the draft was instituted in 1863, the problem was exacerbated by the fact that naval enlistments did not count in the draft quotas for some areas. WBG's U.S.S. *Niagara* was in Gloucester, Massachusetts, for much of the fall of 1863 in a painstaking and difficult search for new recruits there.

The first black recruits were primarily free blacks, but as the months wore on, there was a "silent exodus of escaping slaves [who] sought the protection of Union lines."[65] Although initially in doubt about what to do with these refugees, who faced almost certain reprisal if they were returned to their masters, the Secretary of the Navy did not hesitate long. He authorized the employment of contrabands on ships of war on September 25, 1861.

Once parts of the South came under Union control, the navy worked diligently to sign up slaves who had fled from their masters. Though WBG was not a beneficiary of this policy, the U.S. Navy affirmatively recruited contrabands in his home state:

> The refugee camps that sprang up in Union-occupied areas . . . proved a
> rich source of recruits. In the camps of coastal North Carolina, for instance,
> recruiters from the North Atlantic Blockading Squadron displayed posters

promising good pay and other amenities and urging volunteers to "Come forward and serve your Country."[66]

But, again, though contrabands could go into the navy, discrimination was still recognized. Blacks admitted could proceed no higher than the level of Boy, the lowest classification. On April 30, 1862, this was changed so as to allow all jobs up to petty officer to be accessible to blacks who joined the navy. Much to his discomfort, WBG was made a wardroom steward in June 1864, and thus became one of the few blacks who was a petty officer "of the staff."[67] In this connection, Reidy's comments are once again illuminating:

> Approximately 8 percent of the black sailors (roughly 1,400 men) were rated as cooks and stewards over the course of the war. Cooks and stewards earned premium pay (twenty-five or thirty dollars a month), and they were technically petty officers, yet as petty officers of the staff they generally lacked the authority over other enlisted men that petty officers of the line possessed.[68]

Moreover, as noted, not one single black served in a command or officer position during the entire War of the Rebellion.

FOUR

William B. Gould's Other Writings

*S*ome of the selections in this chapter ran in *The Anglo-African* under the pen name Oley. They were almost certainly submitted by William B. Gould, for the reasons set out in Chapter Two. Obviously, the newspaper edited them for publication. Any errors in the original have been allowed to stand.

"An Interesting and Romantic Narrative"

This article was published in *The Anglo-African* on June 11, 1864, under the pen name Oley. The principals are WBG's fellow contraband Joseph Hall and his future wife, Lucilla Mosley.

There lived in the town of Wilmington, New Hanover Co. N.C., in the year of '62, a young man, a carpenter by trade. Although a slave, he was a finished workman. We will call his initials J.S.H.

There also lived in the town a young widow, Mrs. L.M—ly, of very fine appearance, also a slave, and owned by A.J. De R., a merchant of Wilmington, and one of the first Secessionists of the place. By the wily arts of Cupid these two persons, Mr. J.S.H. and Mrs. L.M., were enamoured of each other, and in due time had exchanged vows, and were looking forward to the time when they should become united.

All things went pleasantly with them until June, '62, when the people of Wilmington expected Burnside to pay them a visit. The Secessionists, not liking to fall before this General, removed from Wilmington into the interior of the State. Mr. A.J. De R. removed his family to the town of Hillsboro, Orange Co., N.C. and took his servant (Mrs. L.M.) with his family, thus separating the two lovers.

After thus being separated the young man became dissatisfied with things in

Dixie (although he kept up a regular correspondence with his lady love), and concluded that he would leave the land of chivalry and seek protection under the banner of the free. Accordingly, himself and seven others took possession of a boat and embarked from the foot of Orange street on Sunday night, September 20th, 1862. It being very dark and rainy, they descended the Cape Fear River in safety, and arrived the next day on board of the U.S. steamer C—bridge, then on blockade duty off Cape Fear. They were kindly received by officers and men.

We will now leave Mr. J.S.H. and companions amusing the crew of the steamer with tales of Dixie and return to Mrs. L.M. at Hillsboro. It only took two or three days for the news to reach Hillsboro that H. was missing. It was a severe blow to her; but supposing what direction he had gone to get into Federal lines, she at once formed a plan to follow him. She first disposed of all her effects, then she bought a through ticket for Wilmington. She was soon missed, and the telegraph being faster than the cars she was arrested at Goldsboro, 84 miles from Wilmington, and lodged in jail to await the coming of her owners.

She remained in jail three days and on the third night she escaped from jail, and being acquainted in the place, she soon found a friend in whom she could confide. She met a young musician from Wilmington who was the bugler in a guerilla band. We will call his initials J.J. She stated her case, and he, offering her his assistance, procured for her a rebel uniform, and she also passed as a musician.

They went boldly up to the office, bought tickets for Wilmington, and stepped aboard the train, she with her bugle slung at her side as boldly as if she was a genuine bugler. When they arrived at Warsaw, where they stopped for refreshments, she met face to face with one of her would be captors on his way to Goldsboro to get her from prison.

It was only a short time before they were again in motion, and arrived safely in Wilmington, where she had plenty of friends. She did not remain in Wilmington long, for, being determined to follow Mr. H., she again resumed her male attire, and, in company with four men, procured a boat and made the attempt to run the gauntlet, in which they were successful, and arrived safely on board of the Genesee without her sex being discovered. She finally made it known to the Captain, who transferred her to the Mystic, then going North for repairs.

The writer of this article went aboard of the Mystic to carry our mail from the C—bridge, when I was surprised to see her on board of that ship. I returned on board of my ship and related the fact to H., who was more than surprised. Our heroine went to Fortress Monroe and found a home with the home of the Provost Marshal. Not long after the departure of the Mystic the C—bridge was ordered North. We arrived safely at Hampton Roads, where the lovers met again, and were happily married on the 20th of December, 1862. The lady now lives in Baltimore, Md., and her husband is on board of the gunboat W—na, off Charleston, S.C.——OLEY

"Our Noble Tars Speak—How They Feel For the Freedmen"

William B. Gould was a passionate supporter of *The Anglo-African* and raised money for it among his crewmates. This letter, enclosing the funds amassed from one such effort, was published in the newspaper on July 29, 1865. WBG is listed among the contributors, but he is undoubtedly the one who composed the letter submitted by Oley.

U.S.S. Niagara

Mr. Editor:

While we are roaming around, watching the interests of Uncle Sam, we cannot but see the necessities of thousands of our own people liberated by the victorious march of the armies of the Union throughout the would be Confederacy. In order to assist in relieving the sufferings of our people we have taken up by subscription on board of this ship the amount enclosed, and below you will find the names of the donors. Wm. H. Belt, D.C., Wm. Briggs, N.Y., James H-g-e, N.Y., Jerry Jones, Pa., Peter Freeman, Mass., Wm. Harris, N.J., Geo. Swan, Mass., Chas. Johnson, P.R., Aaron Halsted, N.Y., Charles Wadkins, P.R., Richard Johnson, Md., Frank Walker, N.Y., George Brown, Pa., Jacob Tucker, N.S., $1 each. J.S. Ladue, N.Y., $2; Henry Taylor, Mass., $3; Peter Ferdinand, Port Byron, 50 cts; Jos. Prince, N.Y., Henry Smith, Va., A.F. Gomery, N.Y., $5 each; Mr. W.H.H., $3; Wm. B. Gould, N.C., $4; Friend, $3; Mr. W.A.C., 15f.; Mr. T.R.W., 20f.; A friend, 10f.; A friend, 3½ f.

We exchanged the gold for paper money, and are thus able to transmit to you sixty-five dollars and fifty cents ($65.50), which you will please dispose of for the best interest of those for whom it is sent.

We receive the Anglo as regularly as our movements will permit, and right glad are we to receive it. It relieves the dullness of the long tedious hours passed at sea, and keeps us fully posted of what is being done at home. Continue in the good work and never cease until the top is reached. We hope soon to be where we too may lend a helping hand to this most glorious cause.

With deep sorrow we heard of the death of our beloved President, and the news has cast a gloom over all. We being, when the doleful news arrived, in the port of Lisbon, Portugal, displayed our colors at half-mast and fired a national salute of minute guns, and the Portuguese and English ships in port joined in paying this last tribute of respect to a just and good man, of whom the American people will ever be proud.——OLEY

"A Portion of the Cruise of the U.S. Steam Frigate 'Niagara' in Foreign Waters Compiled from the Journal of Wm. B. Gould"

William B. Gould was a member and officer of the Charles W. Carroll Post, No. 144, Grand Army of the Republic, in Dedham, Massachusetts. In 1911, he recounted, presumably with his diary before him, some of his adventures overseas to a scribe at the post, who produced this "Supplemental War Sketch." That person, whoever he was, clearly wrote up the account in his own words, though he seems to have borrowed WBG's phraseology from time to time. The document is contained in a book of war sketches of GAR members in Dedham. It is housed at the Dedham Historical Society.

The "Niagara" arrived at New York from Halifax, N.S., on December 23, 1863. Here important changes and repairs were made in the vessel, twenty eleven inch guns being removed to reduce top heaviness.

After the fight of the Iron Clads at Hampton Roads, Va., March 8 and 9, 1862, the Confederates contracted with the Lairds Ship Building Co. of Liverpool, England, for two iron clad rams. News of the progress of the work on them reached the United States from time to time until finally it was known that they were launched. It was also reported that the Confederates were trying to get a fleet together of which these rams were to be the nucleus and that the Privateers "Georgia" and "Alabama" were on the way to Liverpool to be refitted. The American Minister, Charles Francis Adams, had notified the English Government that if these vessels were allowed to go to sea, it would be construed by the United States as a declaration of war. That was the situation June 1, 1864, when the "Niagara" sailed for the European Station, having been assigned to the Irish Sea and ordered to keep a sharp lookout for these rams. The U.S. Ship "Kearsarge" was already cruising in the English Channel intending to head off any vessel trying to make port. The "Wachusett" and the "Sacramento" were to follow the course of the Rebel ships.

The "Niagara" crossed the Atlantic leisurely heading for the Bay of Biscay. The men were drilled daily in gunnery as the only hope of being able to effect a capture lay in the amount of accuracy of fire, the "Niagara" being an old wooden ship, while those of the enemy were modern iron clads. The "Niagara" was armed with twelve two hundred pound Parrott rifles, four twelve pound Napoleon rifles, and four twenty-four pound Howitzers for close work. On June 24, an English pilot who came aboard off Lands End England brought the news that on Sunday, June 19, the "Kearsarge" had sunk the "Alabama." The crew were as delighted and as proud of the deed as if they had done it themselves. The "Niagara" continued its journey up the Channel, passed the Strait of Dover, and was piloted from Flushing up the River Scheldt to Antwerp where it anchored off the Hotel de la Crux Blanche. Mr. Crawford, the American Minister, came on board and the port was saluted with twenty-one guns. On the 29th the crew began to coal ship but were interrupted by a visit from the Governor and Minister of War, as it was necessary to salute them. The Commodore, Thomas T. Craven, who was in command of the "Niagara," with his staff, went to Brussels to visit the American Minister there, and later the visit was returned. Many other important persons came on board also. On July 2, the coaling continued all night until ten the next morning, when the ship was unmoored, weighed anchor, and started down the river. When passing the fort it was saluted by twenty-one guns. On July 6, it anchored at Cherbourg, France, where it found the "Sacramento" and "Kearsarge." The latter was being repaired. All hands on board the "Niagara" were mustered on deck to hear the Articles of War read. On the night of July 12, while cruising about the Strait of Dover, the "Niagara" had the misfortune to burst a cylinder head which was repaired at Flushing, and on July 16, it again anchored at Antwerp where numerous visitors continued to come aboard daily. On July 18, the "Sacramento" arrived at Antwerp also but left on the twenty-third. About this time there was a rumor that the King was to visit the vessel, but he did not.

On July 30, the "Niagara" again left Antwerp, and on August 2, she passed

Lands End, England, and entered St. Georges Channel, and continued up the coast of Wales, headed for Liverpool. On August 3, in Liverpool Harbor, she passed the two rams built for the Confederates, but they were still under the care of the English Government, and were guarded by the Royal Marines. At Liverpool, August 4, the "Niagara" saluted the Irish Flag and the English Commodore came aboard. The vessel was coaled and left Liverpool on the 5th, getting out to sea. Certain changes were now made in the masts, smoke stacks, etc., which were intended as a disguise. A white stripe was put all around about her hulk which gave her the appearance of an East Indianan. The cruise was continued to the Bay of Biscay, and on August 8, a steamer was sighted to which the "Niagara" gave chase, having first set all fore and aft sails, and put all lights out. This vessel was overtaken on the 9th and was found to be a Mediterranean mail steamer. On Wednesday, August 10, the "Niagara" found herself off the coast of Portugal, and on the 12th, after the national salute of twenty-one guns, entered the harbor of Lisbon. The Articles of War were again read, and the ship was coaled. On Sunday, the 14th the American Minister came aboard for a visit, after which she weighed anchor and left for the open sea.

On the 15th, while cruising about the coast of Portugal, she sighted a steamer about which there was some suspicion. The "Niagara" gave chase, and after keeping on her course for about five miles, she suddenly changed. The "Niagara" fired on her, and she displayed the English colors. After another shot she hove to, and an officer and boats crew from the "Niagara" were sent aboard and found her to be the Rebel steamer "Georgia" that had been repaired at Liverpool and was now on her way to be turned over to the Confederates for service as a privateer. Her crew of thirty-five men was transferred to the Niagara, and a prize crew was put in charge of her, and she was sent with several invalids, mail, and other things to the United States. She set sail at about noon of August 16, departing with the cheers and good wishes of the crew of the "Niagara."

After the "Georgia" had started on her course to the United States the "Niagara" followed keeping her in sight until the morning of the 17th when she had disappeared. The latter then changed her course, returning eastward, and entered the English Channel and anchored at Dover where the crew taken from the "Georgia" was put ashore, as they claimed to be English subjects. From Dover she went to Flushing and from there to Antwerp. At the latter place it was learned that the Confederates had bought a ship in London called the "Sea King" and that it was to stop at some one of the islands off the coast. The "Niagara" immediately started on in search for it, returning to Dover. There it was learned that another ship called the "Laurel" had left Liverpool with men and stores for the "Sea King." The "Niagara" cruised about for a week, but did not come across either vessel. On returning to Antwerp it was learned from the London papers that the ships had met, and the "Sea King" had received the crew, stores, and ammunition from the "Laurel" and had then changed its name to the "Shenandoah" and had hoisted the Confederate flag. The search was then abandoned and the "Niagara" continued her cruise visiting most of the important ports of England, Ireland, France, and Spain.

In February 1865, a search was undertaken for an ironclad which was reported that the Confederates had either bought or had built for them at Marseilles, France, called the "Stonewall." This vessel was discovered at Ferrol, Spain, where it was in dry dock. It was massive and heavily armed. The "Niagara" entered the harbor, which is a deep land-locked basin capable of accommodating a thousand ships in safety, and anchored close to a Spanish sloop of war. It saluted and displayed the colors, and the Confederates did the same. When some of the crew from the "Niagara" were given short leave they engaged in hand to hand encounter with some of the men from the "Stonewall" and came off the victors, bringing back a gray cap as a trophy. While the "Niagara" was in the harbor of Ferrol, the "Sacramento" arrived which was also cruising about. At noon the day following the arrival of the "Sacramento," it being Washington's Birthday, the Spanish flag was saluted with the National salute of twenty-one guns. The two vessels then put to sea and anchored next at Corunna where they coaled and exchanged courtesies. Afterwards they continued to cruise about watching for the "Stonewall" to leave the harbor of Ferrol. This was repeated on the 23rd of March, but on the next day, the 24th, a Spanish officer boarded the "Niagara," and while he was holding a consultation with Commodore Craven, the commander of the "Stonewall" which had been manoeuvering at the mouth of the harbor, came out into the bay and later in the day, sailed away. The "Niagara" had been forbidden by the Spanish officer to leave its anchorage and therefore, according to the rules of European nations, could not go in pursuit for twenty-four hours after the "Stonewall" had left. When the time expired the "Niagara" put to sea followed by the "Sacramento." The next harbor made was the port of Lisbon where the ram "Stonewall" was discovered. The "Niagara" anchored in such a position that the movements of the ram could be watched, but in spite of this precaution, the "Stonewall" got away to sea, and the "Niagara" was again detained for twenty-four hours. When about to go to sea the following day, and abreast of Fort Castle Belem, the "Niagara" was fired upon by the fort. The colors were dipped but the firing continued until she put about although no great damage was done. Later a government official went on board and offered an apology.

While in the harbor of Lisbon a blockade runner sailed, passing close to the "Niagara," flying both the Confederate and English flags. From Lisbon the cruise was continued to Cadiz, where on April 22, mail was received which announced the surrender of General Lee to General Grant. This although a great piece of good news, made no change in the plans of the commander of the "Niagara" as the war was not ended officially, so the cruising was continued. On May 7, upon entering the harbor of Lisbon, a number of important vessels were found there, among them the "Kearsarge," together with four English frigates, and one English ship of the line. The "Kearsarge" had just returned from the United States, and brought the news of the assassination of President Lincoln. This created great consternation with some loss of self-control among the crew and the next day they were mustered upon deck and the Articles of War were read. The ship was then put in mourning. The National salute of twenty-one minute guns was fired at sunrise, at noon, and at sunset. At sunrise the "Kearsarge" accompanied the "Niagara" in the salute, and all of the ships in the harbor displayed the American colors at half-mast. At noon when the Niagara again fired, she was accompanied by the English ship of the line and the four English frigates. And at sunset the firing was accompanied by all of the ships in the harbor and by the forts.

On the 10th of May a Russian fleet of four ships arrived in the harbor of Lisbon. This was the funeral of a Russian prince whose body was being borne from the Mediterranean to Russia. The "Niagara" and the "Kearsarge" were then waiting to join the procession as were the other vessels representing their respective governments. On the morning of May 12, the ships formed in order and went to sea, the Russian flag ship leading and the other Russian, English, French, Spanish, and Portuguese vessels followed according to their rank, making a procession several miles in length. The next objective point on the journey to Russia was Plymouth, England at which point the noted English vessels, "Black Prince" and "Achilles" joined the procession. Several ships were left at Plymouth, as they were not able to proceed further, and the journey was continued up the Channel, stopping at each important port. From time to time different vessels left, but the "Niagara" continued as far as Dover, being the last foreign vessel to leave the Russians. From Dover the Niagara went to Flushing and from there again to Antwerp.

"Items of Interest from Wilmington, N.C."

This is another submission from Oley. It was published in *The Anglo-African* on November 4, 1865. This may be the only return trip William B. Gould made to his hometown after the war. He appears to have thought momentarily of settling there but chose to remain in the North.

Dear Anglo,

We arrived hear safe after a rough though short passage. We found the old Town anything but what we left it. Her streets are entirely deserted. Her wharves that used to groan under a million of barrels and thousands of bales are entirely bare. Her stores are all closed with a few exceptions, and her workshops are silent. The river glides noiselessly by, and not a ship there to break the current. The grass is growing unmolested in her streets.

Yet with all this change for the worse, there is still a greater change for the better. You miss the Auction Block in Market Square where the traffic in human beings used to be carried on. Her Traders Jails are turned into military Guard Houses, where at any time you may see any number of the former Lords of the soil taking a view of the passer by from a commanding position. The nine O'clock Bell, too is silent, and when you walk out at night the demand for your Pass is not made, and upon the whole, Wilmington is changed.

I find several schools in full blast with a crowd of Scholars, and Teachers are in demand. The colored citizens are fully alive to the matter of dollars and cents, and are driving quite a trade among themselves, and hope, when the season fully opens, to do a fair share of the business of the Town.

Rain is wanted here very much. It is reported that there is quite a lot of produce waiting transportation, along the Rivers but cannot be brought to Market on account of the low state of the water. Vegetables, have suffered much from the drouth. The Rail Roads are in running order again, but they are shabby affairs when compared to what they once were.

I am very sorry to find our people so backward in regard to the most important questions of the day. They seem to be waiting the action of the State Convention now in session, or for the meeting of the Legislature, I do not know which, but they seem perfectly contented for the present.

They have two Union Leagues here but they are not doing any thing, meetings were called twice this week, but adjourned for want of a quorum. Some of the Freedmen are in a very bad condition for the coming winter, many others have returned to their former homes and entered into contracts, with the land-owners at fair wages. Several have leased farms on shares with the Government and the thrifty ones seem to be getting along with a fair prospect of success. Yet there are many who are supported by the public at large, mostly women and children, and it will tax our strength to the utmost to care for this class of persons.

Wages are very fair, and mechanics are in demand, the necesaries of life are high, but Clothing we find cheaper here, in proportion, than in New York City. We think as soon as it becomes a little colder and the sickness abates that these people will do a very fair business. The Small Pox is very bad, and they say that there is some four hundred cases at present in the town. Wilmington is garrisoned by the 37th and 39th Regiments of Colored Troops. The men are quiet and orderly, and the citizens are well satisfied with them, excepting the "secesh" who want them removed.

While the white Troops were here, there was a reign of terror. The 6th Connecticut never failed to uphold the honor of the State of Wooden Hams and Nutmegs. A man was not to be seen upon the street with a watch visible or it was immediately confiscated and they were not at all particular whether it was done in the manner prescribed by law or not. There was rejoicing among white and colored people the day they left.

In my business here there is a fair chance of success, and I hope in my next to be able to forward you an addition to your list of subscribers. The *Anglo-African* takes well. There was an agent here, but he did not meet with much success. There is to be published at Raleigh a paper devoted to the rights of the colored people, called the *Journal of Freedom*. Motto is "Universal Suffrage." In my next I will be more concise.——OLEY

Untitled and Undated Document

> This undated document can probably be attributed to William B. Gould.
> The handwriting suggests that it was prepared by the same person who
> recorded the "Personal War Sketch" cited above. This document turned
> up late in my research; I found it in my mother's home in 2001.

Mr. Speaker and members of the house,

I speak in opposition to the resolution. The persons under discussion are eight millions of American citizens. As this is a government in which each and every citizen does an equal share towards shaping the policy of the country, this wholesale deportations of the Negro cannot take place without his consent. He was brought here against his will but during a residence of 250 years and more he has grown somewhat stronger. Granted that we have the consent of these eight millions of people, at a very low estimate, the cost would be enormous. Has Uncle Sam so forgot his shrewdness as to be ready to waste hundreds of millions of dollars on a mere whim?

That the scheme is impractical is a self-evident fact. These 8,000,000 of people represent a large percentage of the wealth of the country. Not only wealth that can be counted in dollars and cents, but wealth that is represented by muscle. The commercial, agricultural, and manufacturing interests of the country are largely dependent on Negro labor. Why should the country seek to do away with that so essential to its welfare? Why should 8,000,000 of people who are more American (if residence in this country for generations counts in being and American) than 50% of the white population be sent out of it.

Mr. Speaker and members of the house, the answer to that question is that there is an unreasonable prejudice against the Negro. A prejudice that is so narrow and un-Christlike as scarcely to be believed existing in a Christian country. Does the color of a man's skin limit the quality of his mind and his ability? If so, the illustrious men of every country would be those of the blond type. Recollect that Hannibal was a black man. That Dumas had Negro blood in his veins. That Gen. Dodd one of the foremost officers in the French army today is a black man.

The chief argument advanced towards this scheme is that the Negro is an undesirable citizen. What are the essentials of good citizenship? First, intelligence; second, ability to acquire wealth; third, love of country. Is the Negro intelligent? History repeats itself, but the Negro is making history; for never in mediaeval or ancient history can we find a people who in so short a time have evinced the amount of intelligence and acquired learning, refinement and culture as can be found among the Negroes of the U.S. Has the Negro the ability to acquire wealth? In the state of Louisianna the amount of property owned by Negroes is 18,100,000; in Texas, 18,000,000; in Mississippi, 13,400,000; in South Carolina, 12,500,000; North Carolina, 11,000,000; in Georgia, 10,000,000; Tennessee, 10,000,000; Alabama, 9,000,000; Arkansas, 8,000,000; Florida, 7,900,000; Missouri, 6,600,000; Kentucky, 6,900,000; Virginia, 4,000,000. Surely such figures remove the charge of shiftlessness and improvidence. You will notice that these figures are given from the states that are most urgent in their demands to be rid of these people. It is very seldom that the Negro is an occupant of an almshouse; seldom that you find him begging.

The black American is very seldom mixed up in the labor trouble that are now shaking the foundations of our government. Does the Negro love his country? He has *ever* been loyal to this country even when denied the rights of citizenship. He was one of the first victims of the Revolutionary War, and did valient service in the war of 1812. Black men have always served in the Navy with great credit to themselves.

Of the 25 men at Harpers Ferry, 5 of them were black, and when Lincoln called for troops to stop the Rebellion, enough men here in Boston came forward to make a brigade but were told that there was no place for them. [They,] however, notwithstanding the insult, formed part of the 200,000 who risked their lives when this country was at the point of disruption.

I think that if people would allow themselves to be governed by *reason* and not by prejudice they would be willing to give the *black American citizen* the same chance that is accorded the outcasts of other nations who flock to our shores in such vast numbers.

Market Street, Wilmington, N.C., in the 1850s. (*Ballou's Pictorial Drawing-Room Companion*, p. 201, 1855; courtesy of New Hanover County Public Library)

Above, WBG's initials in the plaster of the Bellamy Mansion. This beautiful antebellum house in Wilmington was built between 1859 and 1861. (Courtesy of Bellamy Mansion Museum)

Right, the elegant and careful plastering work done on the Bellamy Mansion by WBG and others. The author first saw this building at a cocktail party in 1997, unaware that his great-grandfather had worked on it. (Courtesy of Bellamy Mansion Museum)

This scene of Wilmington in the 1860s shows the corner of South Front and Orange streets. It is at the foot of Orange Street at the Cape Fear River that WBG and seven other contrabands take a boat on September 21, 1862, and set off down the river for the Atlantic Ocean. ("Wilmington's Front Street, 1865," *Frank Leslie's Illustrated Newspaper*, March 1865; courtesy of New Hanover County Public Library)

8- Wind. At 9 spoke "State of Georgia"
9.50 Saw a sail S.W.b.S. and
signalized same to other vessels.
Stood for strange sail and at 10.30
picked up a boat with 8 Contrabands
from Wilmington N.C. Stood back
towards the Anchorage at 11.15
11.45 Anchored in 6½ fath water 6 faths chan
Fed. point bearing N.W.b, N½N.
Names of Contrabands and their Mast
Joseph Hall owned by Wm C Benticott
George Price   "   "   do
Andrew Hall   -   -   do
Wm B Gold   ..   Nicholas Nixon
John Mackey   - .   John Nash
Chas Giles   . .   Dan Russell
John Mitchell   . -   Kellam P Martin
Wm Gause   ..   Wm Robbins
                          H. W. Wells
                          Masters Mate
Wind - 4 PM As per cols
W C Odione, Masters Mate

The log of the U.S.S. (United States Steamer) *Cambridge* for September 22, 1862, which reports a "strange sail" at 9:50 a.m. and states that eight contrabands are picked up at 10:20. William B. Gould is one of them and corresponds with most of the other seven until the conclusion of the war. (Courtesy of National Archives)

Top, the log of the U.S.S. *State of Georgia* for September 22, which notes that it "saw a boat to leeward and at 10:10 *Cambridge* made signal . . . and started in chase of boat. At 11:20 the stmr *Cambridge* sent a boat and reported picking up a boat with eight contrabands on board. Ship lying too off the Fort [Caswell]."

Bottom, the U.S.S. *Cambridge*, on which WBG serves from September 1862 through the spring of 1863. (U.S. Naval Historical Center Photograph, NH 61565)

(a)

(b)

(c)

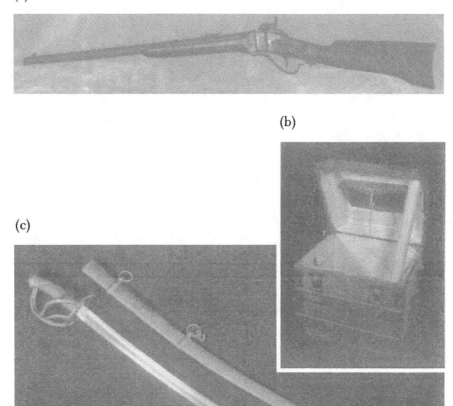

WBG's memorabilia. (a) WBG made good use of this rifle while firing at Fort Caswell when the *Cambridge* engaged gun batteries there in the fall of 1862. (b) The locker that WBG kept on board (note the fine pouch in which he undoubtedly kept his voluminous correspondence, both outgoing and incoming). (c) The cutlass he held aboard the U.S.S. *Niagara*, which, at least at the time of the *Stonewall encounter*, he was required to sharpen. He says on February 11, 1865: "The Crew were o[rdered] to sharpen their Cuttlasses an[d] we took up A plenty of shots." (d) The medals and commemorative coins that belonged to WBG. (e) The hat that he wore as a member of the C. W. Carroll Post 144 of the Grand Army of the Republic in Dedham, Mass. (f) A service medal given to WBG with Union naval vessels appearing on the back. (Photographs: [a] Robert O. Schrott; [b], [c], [e] Candis Griggs, Griggs Conservation; [d], [f] Steve Gladfelter, Stanford Visual Art Services)

(d)

(e)

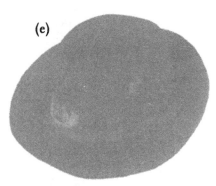

(f)

The second book open to December 31, 1863 where WBG writes: "This Morning two coal Bargees came alongside and we again commenced coaling. About 8 bells it commenced snowing quite hard. It snowd and raind alternately all day and night. We coald until 10 Oclock P.M. when we were obliged to Knock off and the account of the Storm, it blew verry hard from S.E. the Old year of (1863) went out Furiously as if it was angry with all the world because it had finished the time alloted to it. Sooner or lateer we must follow." (Photograph by Steve Gladfelter, Stanford Visual Art Services)

The Anglo-African.

NEW YORK, JUNE 11, 1864.

AN INTERESTING AND ROMANTIC NARRATIVE.

THERE lived in the town of Wilmington, New Hanover Co. N. C., in the year of '62, a young man, a carpenter by trade. Although a slave, he was a finished workman. We will call his initials J. S. H.

There also lived in the town a young widow, Mrs. L. M——ly, of very fine appearance, also a slave, and owned by A. J. De R., a merchant of Wilmington, and one of the first Secessionists of the place. By the wily arts of Cupid these two persons, Mr. J. S. H. and Mrs. L. M., were enamoured of each other, and in due time had exchanged vows, and were looking forward to the time when they should become united.

WBG raises money for and contributes articles to this prominent black newspaper. "An Interesting and Romantic Narrative" is one of the articles he submits to *The Anglo-African* under the pen name Oley.

Figurehead of the U.S. Steam "Frigate Niagara" built on the model of the yacht America that won the yacht race in England in 1851, by George Steers, of New York. The "Niagara" assisted in laying the first Atlantic cable to Europe

Top, in the fall of 1863, WBG joins the U.S.S. *Niagara*, which, after its involvement in the successful capture of the *Chesapeake* hijacked by the Confederates in December of that year, visits New York and Boston and embarks on a voyage to Europe in search of Confederate cruisers built by the British and French. This photograph shows the *Niagara* at the Boston Navy Yard , ca. 1863. The Bunker Hill Monument is in the background. (U.S. Naval Historical Center Photograph, NH 57980)

Bottom, the figurehead of the *Niagara*. The caption in WBG's handwriting reads: "Figurehead of the U.S. Steam Frigate "Niagara" built on the model of the yacht, *America*, that won the yacht race in England in 1851, by George Steers, of New York. The "Niagara" assisted in laying the first Atlantic cable to Europe."

The *Kearsarge* sinks the Confederate ship *Alabama* on June 19, 1864. WBG expresses his "disappointment" that the *Niagara*—at that point three weeks en route to Europe— did not get a shot at her, his ship being reputedly more formidable than the *Kearsarge*. (Edouard Manet, *Alabama and Kearsarge*, 1864, John G. Johnson Collection, Philadelphia Museum of Art)

Top, U.S.S. *Niagara* off Antwerp, a photograph given to WBG by one of his shipmates. The inscription reads: "U.S.S. Frigate 'Niagara' off Antwerp, July, 1864. To Comrade Gould from Shipmate James F. Hogan."

Bottom, The Confederate *Stonewall*. The bête noire of the *Niagara*, she eludes WBG's ship in Spain and Portugal without a fight. (Library of Congress, Prints & Photographs Division, Civil War Photographs, LC-B8171-7912)

La Coruña, Spain—where the *Niagara* sat offshore in an attempt to engage the iron-clad *Stonewall*—as it was in the nineteenth century. ("Vista y Puerto de La Coruña," from C. P. Vicenti, *El sepulcro de Moore*, 1857)

Top, The *Stonewall* was docked in El Ferrol, and in order to proceed to the Atlantic, she had to come from the Ría de El Ferrol in full view of the *Niagara* in La Coruña. However, on February 14, 1865, the *Niagara* proceeds down the passage to El Ferrol. WBG states: "The pasage is A verry narrow one bu[t] verry cold Watter." (Photograph by the author, 2000)

Middle, On February 14, 1865, WBG says about this section of the river: "The whole passage for A mile in length is one continued line of Fortifacations." The fortifications along both sides of the river remain to this day. (Photograph by the author, 2000)

Bottom, Belem Castle, Lisbon, Portugal. In pursuit of the *Stonewall* in Lisbon, the *Niagara* is fired upon from the Belem Castle for allegedly violating Portuguese neutrality law. The Portuguese government later apologizes for the incident. (Photograph by Katy Jonas, 2001)

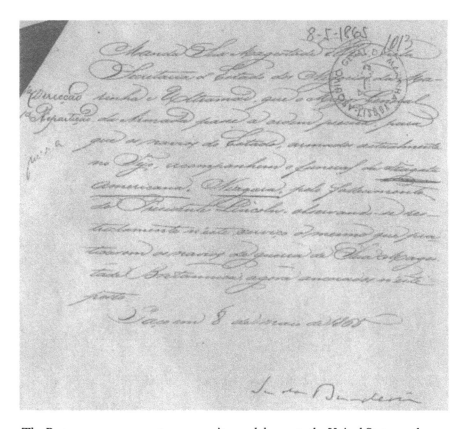

The Portuguese government expresses its condolences to the United States on the assassination of President Lincoln on May 8, and orders its fleet in Lisbon harbor to mark the occasion by accompanying the *Niagara*: "The Secretary of Affairs of the Portuguese Navy is to instruct the Major General of the Fleet to order the ships of the Navy, currently located in the Tejo, to follow the funeral rites for President Lincoln on the American Frigate *Niagara* by strictly observing the same procedures that are made by the Navy ships of her Britannic Majesty, now anchored in this harbor." (Courtesy of Biblioteca Central da Marinha, Lisbon; Translation by Osvaldo Agripino de Castro Jr., Visiting Scholar, Stanford Law School)

At the Charlestown (Massachusetts) Naval Shipyard, the building in which WBG receives his honorable discharge on September 29, 1865.

The Diary

Aboard the U.S.S. *Cambridge*

*O*n enlisting in the U.S. Navy in 1862, William B. Gould spent his first two years on the U.S.S. *Cambridge*, first as a Boy and then as a Landsman. That ship, an armed steamer, had been built in 1860 by Paul Curtis of Medford, Massachusetts. After Fort Sumter, the *Cambridge* was purchased at Boston on July 30, 1861, and commissioned on August 29, 1861, with Commander W. A. Parker in command.[1] Assigned to the North Atlantic Blockading Squadron from September 9, 1861, through October 5, 1864, she "helped tighten the stranglehold on the Confederacy as she cruised off the coasts of Virginia and North and South Carolina."[2]

The U.S.S. *Cambridge* was one of a number of ships that were chartered for this purpose. As Robert M. Browning, Jr., notes:

> Chartering vessels partially solved the navy's lack of warships and seemed economical because many believed the war would be short. . . . While charters temporarily solved the problem of acquiring vessels, it was by no means perfect. Many of the chartered vessels were old and worthless to their owners, but because of high demand, the navy renewed the leases or purchased them. Good examples in the squadron were *Monticello*, *Mount Vernon*, *Dawn* and *Cambridge*. Naval officers examining *Mount Vernon* and *Dawn* claimed they were "unfit for recharter." *Monticello* was in bad repair, and her commanders repeatedly complained about her during the war. At the beginning of the war, she leaked excessively, she was not coppered, she rolled badly, her boilers leaked, and she had numerous other problems. The machinery of *Cambridge* was so exposed that she was labeled "valueless for war purposes." Yet the navy eventually purchased all of them and they served during the entire war.[3]

William B. Gould began his diary on September 27, 1862, five days after being picked up by the *Cambridge*.

⤙

SUN. SEPT. 27TH

At Beaufort, N.C. We coald ship all night and until ten Oclock. We then up anchor hauld alongside of the Store Ship (Wm. Badger) for the purpose of takeing more Coal and stores on board.

MON. SEPT. 28TH

At Beaufort. Finishd Coaling to day. Took in stores. Fine day.

TUES. SEPT. 29TH

At Beaufort. Takeing in stores all day. Made preperation to convey some paroled prisoners to Wilmington.

WENS. SEPT. 30TH

At Beaufort. Finish'd takeing in stores. We were visited to day by Major General Foster and staff (Commander of the Department). Fine day.

> John G. Foster's forces, just two and a half weeks before this visit, had repulsed a Confederate attack on Washington, N.C., referred to frequently as "little Washington."[4] The *Cambridge* log for the 30th (hereafter just the "log") states: "Dressed ship with flags to receive Major General Foster, U.S.A. At 10:30 Gen'l F came on board and at 11:30 left the ship."

THURS. OCT. 1ST

At Beaufort. Fine day. Made preperation for Sea. About 1 Oclock A steamer came along side with Sixty seven Paroled Rebel Prisoners for us to take to Wilmington. We had them stowd on the Berth Deck and about 3 Oclock we up anchor and stood out to sea bound for our station off New Inlet N.C.

FRI. OCT. 2ND

Off New Inlet. We arrived last night about 11 Oclock. We came near being fired into by the Mystic mistakeen us for A Blockade-Runner. We learnt of the capture of the Sun Beam by the Mystic and State of Georgia. About 9 Oclock we hoisted A Flag of Truce and ran in lowerd A Boat and sent it to meet one from the shore. After consultation our Boat returnd and we anchord off Fort Fisher about 11 Oclock. About 1 Oclock A steamer came out from Wilmington anchord close to us. We soon transferd the Rebs and thair Baggage to the Steamer. We up Anchor and stood out to our Anchorage and the other steamer returnd to Wilmington By the By, the State of Georgia and the Mystic colli[d]ed last night damageing each other considerably. Made preperation for Painting.

SAT. OCT. 3RD

Off New Inlet. Got under way at five Oclock. Anchord about 9 Oclock. We painted ship. The State of Georgia Saild to day for the North. All of us ship'd to day for three years first takeing the Oath of Allegiance to the Goverment of Uncle Samuel.

SUN. OCT. 4TH

Off New Inlet. Got under way about 2 bells a.m. About 7 Oclock made out A Boat. Pickd her up. Containd four Men from Wilmington. About 8 bells we pickd up another Boat from Brunswick with four Men. At the same time A sail was reported. We gave chase. Proved to be the Yacht Hiawatha from Wilmington with twelve Men, heard from my people, all well.

> The log for Oct. 5, 1862, identified these twelve men and their owners as Edward Benticott, Abraham Price, and Simon Halsey (owner Wm. Benticott); David Betts (Richard Grant); Cyrus Hooper (Mrs. Myers); Abraham Ashe (Wm. Ashe); Marcus Giles (Wm. Giles); Joseph Hill (S. Waters); Theodore Broadley (Richard Broadly [sic]); Adam Smith (David Smith); David Jewett (Stephen Jewett); and John Savage (J. C. Savage). Some of these men must have known WBG's family.

MON. OCT. 5TH

Off New Inlet. Cruise as usual. Communicateed across the shoals. Sent home A coperal of Marienes, term expired.

TUES. OCT. 6TH

Off New Inlet. Cruise as usual. Sighnd accounts. The Blockade Runing Steamer. (Kate) is now lying under the Fort, formd an expadition to destroy her.

WENS. OCT. 7TH

Off New Inlet. Cruise as usual. Our Expedition did not leave last night on account of the weather.

THURS. OCT 8TH

Off New Inlet. Cruised as usual. Our Expedition faild to burn the steamer got lost in the fog, they will try again.

FRI. OCT. 10TH

Off New Inlet. Rained verry hard last night the expedition did not go. Cruised until 3 Oclock P.M. Cleard off. Made preperation to make another attempt at her. Wind strong, S.W.

SAT. OCT. 11TH

Off New Inlet. Cruised as usual. About 7 Oclock we got under way and ran in as near as we could to the shore, came to anchor. The Boats then left the ship (tow [two]in number) one in command of Lieut Strong of the Cambridge the Lieut Brannon of the Pennobscot. When approaching the steamer they were discoverd by the Batries when the expedition returnd but resolved to try again. I[t] began to Rain in the evening with light wind from the S.W. last night I kept Boat for the first time at Sea.

SUN. 12TH OCT.

Off New Inlet. Raining all night and all day. About 7 Oclock the "Mahaska" arrived with Recruits for the Squadron. After transfering our men on board she took on board all the Colard Men that came out along the Coast and saild for Hampton Roades about 4 Oclock P.M. the wind strong from the N.E. Sea Highly

MON. OCT. 13TH

Off New Inlet. Fine day. Cruised around as usual. Arriveal of the "Mount Vernon." We transferd Men to her for the "Penobscot." She saild for the mouth of the Cape Fear. Heard of the Battle Sheperdstown.

> The reference is to battles that took place on Sept. 20 and Sept. 25 of that year: "McClellan sent two divisions across the Potomac in a mild pursuit of Lee. Opposed by A. P. Hill, the Federals fell back and Lee's army withdrew to the

valley of Opequon Creek. The active part of the campaign had ended with fighting (on the 20th) near Shepherdstown, Hagerstown, Williamsport, and Ashby's Gap."[5] The 25th brought another confrontation: "In the east there was a Federal reconnaissance from Shepherdstown, western Va., and a Federal expedition from Centreville to Bristoe Station and Warrenton, Va."[6] This, of course, was the aftermath of the Sept. 17 battle of Antietam or Sharpsburg, one of the bloodiest of the war. The next day, Lee withdrew across the Potomac, with McClellan in rather tepid, or "mild," pursuit.

TUES. OCT. 14TH

Off New Inlet. Cloudy and windy, the "Mystic" communicateed across the shoals, braught us A Mail.

WENS. OCT. 15TH

Off New Inlet. Cloudy and windy, last night Raind and blow'd all night. "Mystic" saild for Beaufort.

THURS. OCT. 16TH

Off New Inlet. Cruised as usual, quite cool, we feel the approach of Winter. To day all hands were mustered to read the dismissial from the Navy of Com'dr Prebble for allowing the Rebel Privateer Florida (alias Oreta) passing through the fleet into Mobiele. Served out small stores.

> "Union commander George H. Preble of the *Oneida*, the senior naval officer off Mobile (on Sept. 4, 1862), ran his flagship out to meet the stranger (the *Oreto*), and signaled the *Winona* to join the interception. Commander John Newland Maffitt ordered his ship charged with explosives."[7] Preble failed to intercept the vessel, and the *Florida* was able to escape to the protection of the guns of Ft. Morgan.
>
> Four days later, Rear-Adm. D. G. Farragut, commander of the flagship *Hartford*, brought the incident to the attention of the Secretary of the Navy, Gideon Welles: "Sir: I regret to be again compelled to make another mortifying acknowledgement of apparent neglect, viz: the running of the blockade at Mobile by a ten-gun gunboat, supposed to be the 'Sands gunboat' from Captain Preble's report, herewith enclosed, that there was no want of vigilance. They saw her in good time but failed to sink or capture her. Why Captain Preble did not fire into her after she failed to stop or answer his hail, I cannot imagine. The commander of the 'Rachael Seaman' says, and I believe they all admit, that there never was a fairer opportunity for stopping a vessel until she passed them. Then, however, when it was too late, they commenced firing, the 'Oneida' first, the 'Winona' next and the 'Rachael Seaman' last."[8]
>
> Welles "excoriated" Preble for what he saw as inexcusable neglect, and

thought "an example must be made of him to encourage a more aggressive style of fighting by naval officers."[9] When the case was presented to President Lincoln, Preble was dismissed. The *Cambridge* log for Sept. 16 noted that, as navy regulations required, all hands had been mustered for a reading of the navy's General Order cashiering Preble and the Farragut report. As quoted in the log, the order stated that, effective Sept. 20, "Commander George Henry Preble, Senior Officer in command of the blockading force of Mobile, having been guilty of neglect of duty in permitting the armed steamer 'Oreto' to run the blockade, thereby not only disregarding Article 3rd, Section 10th, of the Articles of War, which requires an officer to 'do his utmost to overtake and capture or destroy every vessel which it is his duty to encounter' but omitting the plainest ordinary duty committed to an officer, is, by order of the President, dismissed from the Naval service from this date."

FRI. OCT. 17TH

Off New Inlet. Cruised as usual. Fine day. About 8 bells P.M. A sail was reported in the offing. We soon up Anchor and gave chase but night comeing on we lost sight of her and returnd to our anchorage about 7½ Oclock.

SAT. OCT. 18TH

Off New Inlet. Blowing verry hard from the Eastward. Bathurst (Boatswains Mate) was to day transferd to the "Mount Vernon" about 4 bell[s] we sent down Yards and Topmasts.

SUN. OCT. 19TH

Off New Inlet. Cruised all the Morning and [anch]ord about 8 bells. The weather have moderateed so much that mid day was quite pleasant. We had Muster and inspection at 4 bells.

MON. OCT. 20TH

Off New Inlet. Fine day. Painted the Main Deck. Rattled down Rigging. Make preperation for painting outside.

TUES. OCT. 21ST

Off New Inlet. Quite chilly. The Mystic arrived from Beaufort. We received A Mail. A sail reported at 4 bells. Mount Vernon overhaul her. A schooner of and from N.Y. for Port Royal.

WENS. OCT. 22ND

Off New Inlet. Quite cool and chilly. Painted the ship outside.

> According to the Oct. 22 log, the *Cambridge* "stood up the coast as far as the Masonborough Inlet and at sea turned and stood to the S.S.W."

THURS. OCT. 23RD

Off New Inlet. Got under way about 2 bells, discovered A sail gave chase, overhaul her. A prize to the Gulf Squadron bound north in charge of A prize crew.

FRI. OCT. 24TH

Off New Inlet. Got under way about 2 bells. About sun rise made out A sail. Overhauld her, the sloop Gaquet with stores to sell (sutters. After furnishing all the ships on this side she left for the mouth of the River. About five Oclock we made A sail, gave chase, it proved to be the Supply Steamer Massachusetts with supplies for the Squadron. We in company with the other ships of the fleet were soon buisey transfering our stores on board the ships. After supplying us she saild. Bound south. Verry fine day.

SAT. OCT. 25TH

Off New Inlet. Cruised as usual. Weather fine. Light winds from the southard.

SUN. OCT. 26TH

Off New Inlet. About midnight it come on to blow and Rain verry hard. Cleard of about 4 P.M. Wind from the west.

MON. OCT. 27TH

Off New Inlet. Cruised as usual. Blowing verry strong from the westward. Quite cold. Pea Jackets quite comfortable.

> Log entry for Oct. 27: "'Mt. Vernon' got under way to try the range of her 100 pdr. Parrott, fired three shots which were replied to by the batteries on Federal Point."

TUES. OCT. 28TH

Off New Inlet. Cruised as usual. Sent A mail across the shoals by the "Mystic." Sky overcast. Quite cool.

WENS. OCT. 29TH

Off New Inlet. Fine day. Cruised as usual. After supper we had Rifle Target Practice.

THURS. OCT. 30TH

Off New Inlet. Cruised as usual. Overhauld A Brig Bound to Beaufort. About 2 Oclock the "Daylight" arrived with A prize in tow, capturd on her way down. She braught us A Mail. I received two papers from my Nephew G.L.M. [George Lawrence Mabson].

FRI. OCT. 31ST

Off New Inlet. Cruised as usual. Weather fine. The "Mystic" communicated across the shoals to day. We learnt that thirteen Rebel soldiers that was on Picket came out and surrenderd to one of the vessels. To day we had Target Practice. In the evening we had A Boat Race between the Gig and Ranger, distance six miles Time Gig 37 Min. Ranger 39, the Gig wining by 2 Minutes.

> The details of the number of shots fired, the distance, and the kind of weapon are contained in the log for that day.

SAT. NOV. 1ST

Off New Inlet. Cruised as usual. Weather fine. All hands were mustered to hear the sentance of A man by the name of Hampleton to six years Hard Labor in A penetentiary for strik[ing] an Offercer of the Victoria with A Broom.

SUN. NOV. 2ND

Off New Inlet. Cruised as usual. Fine day. We had Devine Serveace at 4 bells. After serveace Read the Articles of War and inspection.

MON. NOV. 3RD

Off New Inlet. The "Mystic" saild for repairs being condemnd by A survey. Heard fireing this Evening, got under way, ran up to where it was, the steamer Daylight fireing apon some Rebel soldiers apon the Beach. Weather fine.

TUES. NOV. 4TH

Off New Inlet. The weather is becomeing quite cold. This Morning we heard fireing up the coast. Dispatched the "Mount Vernon" to ascertain what it was. The Daylight had driven A Barque asshore (the Sophia of and from Liverpool) and was destroying her. They (Mount Vernon and Daylight) boarded and capturd some of the Crew (the others escaped to the Shore) and braught them off. Then returnd to set the ship on fire. It then began to breeze up and soon the surf was rooling so high that they could not get off. They attempted several times but each time they were driveen asshore. Night comeing on the Gun Boats fired an ocasional shot to keep away the Jhonies.

| The Confederate soldiers and sailors were known as "Johnny Reb."

WENS. NOV. 5TH

Off New Inlet. We sent up our Life Boat and A lot of spare Rope to try and get the Men off but when Daylight dawn'd lo and behold the Rebs had nab them all and A Batry on shore sent the Boats word not to come near. There was 14 Men from the Daylight and 6 from the Mount Vernon. The Rebs sent out A Flag of truce to us informing us of the situation of our Men. We sent them (from the Daylight) thair clothes Bedding and some provissions. The Mystic returnd from the shoals with the Mails of the Fleet. She exchanged Boats with us. One of our Lieuts went Pasenger in her. She had also thirteen Rebel deserters and several colard Reffugees among them several of My Aquaintances. Heard from my people. Mrs. L.M—ly was among the many that I saw. She saild about sun set for Hampton Roads. Wind from the southard.

THURS. NOV. 6TH

Off New Inlet. About 4 Oclock all hands were calld to up anchor for Beaufort. The wind have changed to the Eastward. Quite fresh. Heavy sea. About dark we arrived off the Bar of Beaufort. No Pilot appearing. We came to anchor. Quite cold and Raining.

FRI. NOV. 7TH

Off Beaufort. About daylight the wind hauld to the West and cease'd Raining. We up Anchor and stood in about 7 Oclock took A Pilot. We Anchord in the Harbor about 9 Oclock. We Received A Mail from the "Montecella" who was just starting for the Cape Fear. In the Afternoon A coal Schooner came along side and we began to Coal Ship. Quite cold and rainy.

SAT. NOV. 8TH

At Beaufort. Verry disagreeable. Cold and Rainy. We had A snow storm to day wich lasted several hours. We Coald ship all Night.

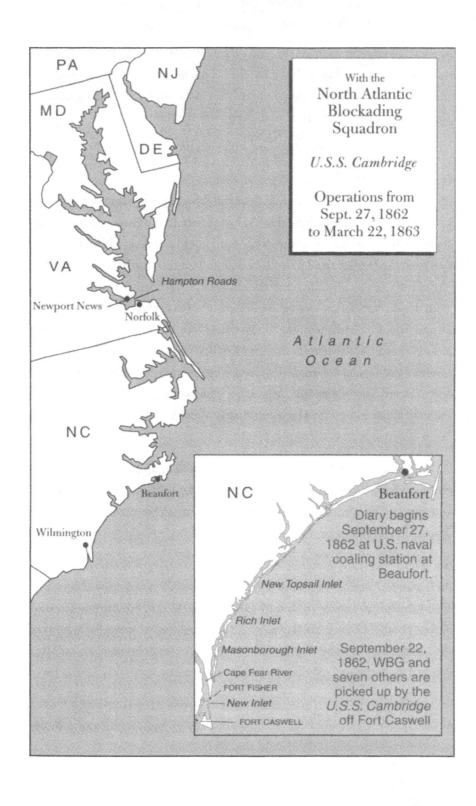

With the
**North Atlantic
Blockading
Squadron**

U.S.S. Cambridge

Operations from
Sept. 27, 1862
to March 22, 1863

PA

NJ

MD

DE

VA

Hampton Roads

Newport News

Norfolk

*Atlantic
Ocean*

NC

Beaufort

Wilmington

NC

Beaufort

Diary begins
September 27,
1862 at U.S. naval
coaling station at
Beaufort.

New Topsail Inlet

Rich Inlet

Masonborough Inlet

Cape Fear River

FORT FISHER

New Inlet

FORT CASWELL

September 22,
1862, WBG and
seven others are
picked up by the
U.S.S. Cambridge
off Fort Caswell

SUN. NOV. 9TH

At Beaufort. It cleard off during the Night. Much warmer. We finished coaling this Morning. Cleand ship. Arrival of the "Penobscott." Heard that the Union troops occupied Weldon.

> The rumor seems to have been untrue. Weldon, the northern terminus of the Wilmington and Weldon Railroad, provided supplies to Lee's army in Virginia, and was apparently not occupied until Wilmington itself was liberated, though the line was severed in August 1864.[10]

MONDAY NOV. 10TH

At Beaufort. Verry fine day. Went asshore to day. Three Men Deserted. One of them George P—e. I am verry sorry for it. Searched all Night for them but found them not.

> This may well be George Price, a North Carolina legislator during Reconstruction, who was picked up by the *Cambridge* with WBG on Sept. 22 and enlisted with him.

TUES. NOV. 11TH

At Beaufort. Fine day. About 7 Oclock a.m. we up Anchor and stood out for sea. Boun[d] to the Cape Fear. We arrived off our station at New Inlet about 5 Oclock. All well.

WENS. NOV. 12TH

Off New Inlet. Fine day. We communicated across the shoals. Sent the Mails of the other ships to them. One of our Men was transferd to the Daylight. Served out Cloathing.

THURS. NOV. 13TH

Off New Inlet. Cruised about until 8 Oclock. Anchord. Day verry fine. About 4 Oclock we got under way. Ran up to Masonboro Inlet. We had Target Practice.

FRI. NOV. 14TH

We remaind off Masonboro all night returnd to our anchorage this Morning. Fine day. Alls lovely.

SAT. 15 NOV.

Off New Inlet. Strong winds from the N.E. in the afternoon we sent down yards and Topmast. A heavy sea running. Lost several Barrells of Potatos over board. All the Cooks were driven out of the Galley by A shower of spuds down the Galley skylight. About 5 Oclock we got under way and ran out to sea. Blowing A Gale.

SUN. NOV. 16TH

The ship Rooling verry heavey. Still blowing A gale. Running hard. No sings [signs] of abateing.

MON. NOV. 17TH

About 7 Oclock last evening to began to Moderate and we stood in for the land. Came to Anchor in 7 fathoms of watter about 6 miles off of New Topsail Inlet. It ceased Raining about midnight and by 4 Oclock we were under way bound for the Inlet. The sun rose clear and tis now verry pleasant. About 1 bell A sail was reported close under the land right ahead. We gave chase. When within range of our Pet. we told them good morning in the shape of A shot for her to heave to. To this they took no notice. We sent another which fell under her stern. At this she about ship and stood for the Beach. Shot after shot was sent after her but they heeded not. She pill'd high and dry apon the Beach. We amediately Man'd the first Cutter and sent her in charge of Act Master Mace to board and destroy her. We also sent two other Boats to lend assistance. The first got into the Breakers and was capsized. Men and Boat was thrown apon the Beach. They boarded the Schooner and set her on fire, the crew haveing escaped to the shore. Now they wanted to come of[f] the surf being verry high their Boat could not get through. We attempted to float A line to them with Bouy's but that faild. Act. Masters Mate Wells attempted to swim in with A line but when he got into the surf he was obliged to cut the line. Then Act. Masters Mate Ordeorne took A line and was successfull in reaching the Beach. They got the Boat already to come out when A Boddy of Rebel Soldiers dash'd over the Hill at the double Quick and all were prisoners. We could see them plane from the ship marching off our Men and draging the Boats after them. We lost Eleven Men and three Offercers. Rather A Bad days work. We took on board our other Boats and started down the coast for our station where we arrived about four Oclock. Here the "Daylight" had drove A Brig asshore on Zeekes Island too near the Rebel works to board her.

The *Dictionary of American Naval Fighting Ships* characterizes this episode as one of the *Cambridge*'s "most daring exploits. (In it the) Cambridge's guns drove a schooner ashore near Masonboro Inlet, N.C. . . . . Boat parties rowed through boiling surf, which swamped one of the boats, to burn the schooner, only to be made prisoners themselves by a party of armed men who sprang out of the brush."[11] Cmdr. Parker filed a report of the incident with the senior officer off Wilmington the same day: "Sir: I have to report that at 8 o'clock this morning a schooner was observed near Masonboro Inlet. I immediately bore down upon her and fired my 30-pounder Parrott gun, at which the schooner ran ashore. A boat under the command of Acting Master W. H. Maies, with ten men, was sent to burn her, with instructions (as the surf was high) not to venture too near, and in case of doubt as to reaching the vessel safely to return. The boat, however, was swamped, yet the men with Mr. Maies reached the shore and fired the schooner, which is entirely destroyed. Two other boats, with Acting Master's Mates H. W. Wells and W. C. Odiorne, were sent to communicate and, if possible, give relief. Mr. Wells swam ashore with a line, but it having parted Mr. Odiorne followed with it and landed. Just at this juncture some thirty armed men came suddenly upon the party and all were taken prisoners."[12]

A couple of weeks later, on Dec. 3, Acting Master Maies sent his own report to the Secretary of the Navy. The pertinent passage reads: "Hon Sir: I respectfully make the following report concerning the capture of myself, Master's Mates Wells, Odiorne, and ten men, comprising petty officers and seamen, on the 17th November, 12 miles N.E. of Fort Fisher, N.C. while burning the British schooner *J. W. Pindar*, loaded with salt and attempting to run the blockade: on attempting to reach the schooner my boat was capsized, and with difficulty we reached the shore, but we effectually destroyed vessel and cargo. We made several unsuccessful attempts to gain our vessel, but failed. After remaining on the beach three hours, about twenty-five men of the Third North Carolina Cavalry came on us and made us prisoners."[13]

TUES. NOV. 18TH

Off New Inlet. Got under way at five Oclock. Cruised until 8. Come to Anchor at our usual anchorage. Arrival of the Mount Vernon. We received A Mail. I received three letters. Verry fine weather. We served out small stores.

WENS. NOV. 19TH

Off New Inlet. Cruised as usual. Morning cloudy. About 2 Oclock the "Massachusetts" arrived from the south. Our Gunner (Furgerson) took passage in her. He is orderd to the "St. Lawrence." Also A coperal of Marienes whose term has expired. The "Mount Vernon" fired at the Brig this Evening with hiting her. Raining lightly this Evening.

THURS. NOV. 20TH

Off New Inlet. Cruised as usual. The Mount Vernon fell in with A schooner that had run out. She was abandond. Took her in tow but it being verry rough she capsiz'd. She was loaded with naval stores. The weather is verry unsettled.

> The log described the weather in stronger terms: "Thunder & Lightening with heavy rains & squalls." That same day, Cmdr. Parker complied with a request for a complete list of the vessels the blockading squadron had destroyed off New Inlet thus far in November. By his account, there were six all together: one bargue ("Sophia"), by the *Daylight* and the *Mt. Vernon* in *Inlet* Masonboro on Nov. 4; one bargue and one schooner (names unknown) by the same two ships in the same place on Nov. 5; one schooner (name unknown) by the *Cambridge* near Masonboro Inlet on Nov. 17; one brig (English; name unknown) "Run Ashore between 'Fort Fisher' and 'Zeek's Island'" by the *Daylight* on Nov. 17; and one schooner (name unknown) southeast of Ft. Fisher by the *Mt. Vernon* on Nov. 20.[14]

FRI. NOV. 21ST

Off New Inlet. Cruised as usual. About four Oclock A sail was reported wich proved to be the Flag Ship ("Chicora") with Admiral Lee on board. She came to Anchor. Our Captain went on board and there remaind the most of the day. The "Daylight" saild for Beaufort. She took A mail from us. I sent three letters.

SAT. NOV. 22ND

Off New Inlet. Cruised as usual. About 8 Oclock the Admiral saild for Hampton Roads. Weather fine. Wind North West.

SUN. NOV. 23RD

Off New Inlet. Cruised as usual. The Mount Vernon pickd up A boat with two Men and one Woman (Refugees) from Wilmington. The "Maratanza" arrived this evening. She took our Mails and the Reffugees on board and saild about 5 Oclock for Beaufort. Weather verry fine.

MON. NOV. 24TH

Off New Inlet. Cruised as usual. About 5 Oclock we saw A sail close in shore. We tried to head her off but she being too close to the Fort she got in. Wind N.W.

TUES. NOV. 25TH

Off New Inlet. We cruised all day. We saw several the Brig. We fired three shots at them, when they all left, we had target practice. We anchord for the Night.

> Log entry for the day explains: "At 11 o'clock fired 3 shots from Parrot Gun at a Brig. ashore at a distance of 3½ miles. The shots were well lined but fell short about ½ mile."

WENS. NOV. 26TH

Off New Inlet. Cruised as usual. Blowing verry strong from S.W. Raind several hours this Morning, then cleard off. Cold.

THURS. NOV. 27TH

Off New Inlet. Cruised as usual. The "Daylight" arrived from Beaufort. She braught the news of the removeal of McClellan and the appointment of Burnside and that he was Marching on Richmond. Quite cold. Wind N.W.

> McClellan had in fact been replaced on Nov. 5: "At 11:30 P.M. (on Nov. 7) an officer from Washington appeared at McClellan's Rectortown, Va., headquarters with the orders of Nov. 5 removing him from command and turning the Army of the Potomac over to Ambrose E. Burnside. McClellan, surprised, stunned, hurt, wrote, 'I am sure that not the slightest expression of feeling was visible on my face.' He added, 'Poor Burnside feels dreadfully, almost crazy— I am sorry for him.' The military career of the most controversial general of the Civil War was ended. He was replaced by a competent, rather stodgy, and definitely uncertain officer who professed no desire for the command and who tried to turn it down."[15]

FRI. NOV. 28TH

Off New Inlet. Cruised as usual. Overhauld A sail, A schooner bound to Port Royal. Quite cold. Thick fog.

SAT. NOV. 29TH

Off New Inlet. Cruised as usual. Weather still verry unsettled and foggy.

SUN. NOV. 30TH

Off New Inlet. Cruised up the coast. Met the "Mount Vernon" with A Prize in tow, Capturd the evening before. She is loaded with salt and coffee, A schooner about 150 tons. Verry foggy.

MON. DEC. THE 1ST

Off New Inlet. Cruised as usual. Served out cloathing. The "Mount Vernon's" Prize saild for the North this Morning.

TUES. DEC. 2ND

Off New Inlet. Cruised as usual. Overhauld A sail. She was from New York for Port Royal. Quite cloudy and warm.

WENS. DEC. 3RD

Off New Inlet. Cruised as usual, about daylight we made A sail beating up close under Smith's Island. We amediately beat to Quaters. Ran down and tried [to] cut her off from the Inlet. They seeing this they made for Buzzards Bay and before we was near enough to prevent it she struck. Just as we were about to fire apon her another sail was reported out at sea. We gave chase. We spoke to her with our Darling when he hove to. We were soon along side in answer to our hail. The Captain said the schooner is yours. I tried to run in but could not. She was calld the Emma Tuttle of and from Nassau N.P. The "Mount Vernon" in the mean time was shelling the stranded schooner. About 10 Oclock we arrived at our anchorage with our Prize. Soon after the "Daylight" came in with A prize in tow, capturd this Morning after driveing one on shore at Masonboro. We then took the Prizes in tow and started for Beaufort. Blowing quite fresh and raining slightly.

> The first and best description of the events of Dec. 3 with the *Emma Tuttle* and *Brilliant* is in the report the *Mt. Vernon*'s Lt. James Trathen sent that day to Rear-Adm. S. P. Lee: "Sir: At daylight this morning I perceived a schooner close in shore making directly for New Inlet. The U.S.S. *Cambridge* and this ship immediately stood in chase. At 6:45 a.m. the 'Cambridge' fired a shot from her bow gun toward the schooner. At the same time observed another schooner bearing S. W. by S. *Cambridge* made signal to engage the schooner inshore, and stood in chase of the one to the southward and westward. We immediately commenced firing from the pivot gun; the schooner heading for the shore soon after grounded. After standing in as near as expedient, the wind being from the N. E., very fresh, with a heavy sea, we fired twelve 100-pounder shells, and observing that the schooner was fast filling with water and the sea making a complete breach over her, we hauled off and stood for the U.S.S. *Cambridge*, who had by this time overtaken the other schooner and had her in tow. The schooner proved to be the *Emma Tuttle* of Nassau. After communicating with the *Cambridge*, stood for the anchorage off New Inlet.

> At 10:40 observed a sail bearing N. E. by N. . . . Immediately stood in chase. At 11:30 discovered the U.S.S. *Daylight* in chase also; at 12:15 p.m. observed the *Daylight* board the stranger and take her in tow. At 12:30 p.m. passed within hail of the *Daylight* and discovered the schooner to be the *Brilliant* of Nassau. Stood back for the anchorage off Federal Point."[16] In his report of the incident, Cmdr. Parker of the *Cambridge* noted that he was running short of coal and was therefore going to head for Beaufort. He also felt compelled, he said, to "repeat my former statement; . . . we have not enough steamers on this side to maintain the blockade efficiently."[17]

THURS. DEC. 4TH

Last night about 11 Oclock we saw A sail. Gave chase and capturd the schoon J.C. Roker trying to run the Blockade. We took her in tow makeing three prizees. About four Oclock our Hawser parted. That deleyd us about four hours when we made all right again and started on our way. We arrived off Beaufort about 3 Oclock P.M. when we cast the Emma Tuttle loose. She proceeded on her way North in charge of Masters Mate Durgen. We stood in for Beaufort with the other two prizees in tow, passing the steamers "Guide" and "Marantanza" outward bound. We arrived safely in Port with our two Prizees. Wind N.N.E.

> This is the period the *Dictionary of American Naval Fighting Ships* speaks of when it says, "In a brief 5 days, she [the *Cambridge*] and two other ships in company took four blockade runners, and chased a fifth ashore."[18] Cmdr. Parker had another worry when he captured the schooners *Brilliant* and *J. C. Roker*. "I would beg to be informed," he wrote Rear-Adm. Lee, "of the course I shall pursue when a seized vessel is found to be unseaworthy, or containing cargo insufficient to defray legal adjudication, as in the present instance. I do not consider the *Roker* nor the *Brilliant* of sufficient value to hazard the lives of officers or men off stormy Hatteras, especially at this season, without a tow. . . . I would suggest that arrangements might be made at Beaufort to adjudicate upon such small unseaworthy craft as are mentioned above. It would certainly be advisable. . . . The *J. C. Roker* has a consular license, sealed and signed. I enclose the confession of the master, James S. Fields. The vessel was taken about 7 miles from New Topsail Inlet."[19]

FRI. DEC. 5TH

At Beaufort. Raining all day. We took A coal schooner alongside and began to coal ship. The wind hauld to south West blowing quite strong.

SAT. DEC. 6TH

At Beaufort. Coaling ship. Cleard off. Colder. Arrival of the John Adams and
Capital. Put in for coal.

SUN. DEC. 7TH

At Beaufort. We finished coaling ship about midnight. This is the coldest day
of the season. Salt watter freezed. We hear of the Battle of Fredicksburg, Va
and defeat of our troops.

> The error WBG makes here is inexplicable; the defeat at Fredericksburg was
> still six days off.[20]

MON. DEC. 8TH

At Beaufort. This Morning as we were geting up steam we found A leak in one
of the Boilers. We were obliged to take all the Coal out of one of the Bunkers
to repair the leak. A Frig braught us our stores. A little warmer. Two of our
Men attempted to desert from one of the Prizees but they was arrested and
braught back.

> On this day, Cmdr. Parker wrote to Maj.-Gen. J. G. Foster suggesting a coor-
> dinated effort for a direct assault on Wilmington.[21]

TUES. DEC. 9TH

At Beaufort. We repaird the leake in the Boiler and restowd the Coal. The
Capt. visited Fort Macon. Grog and Ration Money was served out. Make
preperation for Sea.

WENS. DEC. 10TH

About 8 Oclock this Morning all hands were calld to up Anchor and we were
soon plowing the Briney deep. On our way down another leak was found in
our Boiler. We arrived at or station about 7 Oclock P.M.

THURS. DEC. 11TH

Off New Inlet. We communicated across the shoals to day to send Capt. De
Haven to his ship "Pennobscot." He came A passenger with us. They held
A survey on our Boilers to day, they were condemn'd. Capt. Smith orderd us
to Hampton Roads. We arrived at our station about 9 Oclock P.M.

FRI. DEC. 12TH

Off New Inlet. Fine day. We transferd A part of our coal to the "Mount Vernon" and the "Daylight" and preperation for leaving the "M V" is to tow us up.

SAT. DEC. 13TH

About 9 Oclock last night we up Anchor and started for Hampton Roads in tow of the "M V." About 4 Oclock P.M. we made Cape Hatterass. Pass'd many sails bound south. Weather fine.

SUN. DEC. 14TH

About Nine Oclock we made cape Henry and at 1 Oclock we anchord off Fort Monroe. Our Capt. Reported to the Admiral. In the Road we found the Young Rover and Mystic and the English sloops Racer and Rinaldo. About 4 Oclock the "Colorado" arrived. She saluteed the Admiral.

MON. DEC. 15TH

This Morning we were visited by the Admiral and staff. We were surveyed and they concludeed to repair her here. Workmen went amediately to work apon the Boilers. To day our Dingy went up to Norfolk in tow of A steamer. In Backing out the steamer Back'd over the Dingy and the Coxswain Charles Bricknell was drownd.

TUES. DEC. 16TH

At Hampton Roads. Fine weather. Hard at work on our Boilers. Our Boat was braught back to day.

WENS. DEC. 17TH

At Hampton Roads. This Morning the workmen reported finished. We started fires but before we got up steam another leak opend and we were obliged to [put] out fires again and set the Workmen at work again. We were visited by Capt. Chase and staff. Cold and Raining.

> According to the log, Adm. Lee came aboard with Capt. Case, though WBG mentions only Case. But it is Admiral Lee to whom WBG refers on December 15.

THURS. DEC. 18TH

At Hampton Roads. Still at work apon our Boiler. Three Ensigns and two
Masters Mates joind us to day. Also Another Pilot. We took on board
Amunition and Arms. Arriveal of the Rhode Island. The English Ship
"Cadmus" went to sea. Quite cold.

FRI. DEC. 19TH

At Hampton Roads. The workmen compleeted thair work on the Boilers. We
got up steam. Took alongside A coal schooner and began to coal ship. The
"Cadmus" returnd to the Roads this Morning. She have been to the assistance
of A Barque asshore outside the cape there is A verry large fleet of transports
in the Roads. I have been asshore at New Port News several times. Clear and
cold. Wind North west.

SAT. DEC. 20TH

At Hampton Roads. Took on board several cords of wood. We finished
coaling about noon. Arrival of the "Ossepee" and "State of Georgia." Heard
of the sailing of the Banks Expedition.

SUN. DEC. 21ST

At Hampton Roads. Verry cold. Plenty of ice. In the Afternoon we ran in
alongside of the warf. Took on board A 30 lb. Parrott Gun for the Quarter
deck. In runing out we got onto A sand Bar but with the assistance of two
Tugs we soon got off and anchord in the stream. The "Montecella" arrived
from New York.

MON. DEC. 22ND

At Hampton Roads. About 9 Oclock we hauld alongside of the "Brandywine"
to take in stores. I went on board and took A good look at this old Majestic
ship. About three Oclock we finish takeing in stores. Musterd all hands. Got
under way and stood out for sea bound to our old station instead of the
North. Not so cold as on yesterday.

TUES. DEC. 23RD

At sea. We had A fine run with A light Breeze and smooth sea. About
5 Oclock we rounded Cape Hatrass. Pass'd several sails bound south.

The *Cambridge*'s departure from Hampton Roads—as well as that of the *Mount Vernon*—was noted in a communication from Rear-Adm. Lee aboard the U.S. flag-steamer *Philadelphia* in a report to Secretary of Navy Welles.[22]

WENS. DEC. 24TH

Off New Inlet. We arrived last night about 11 Oclock. In the confusion on our arrival the "Penobscott" and "Genesse" colli[d]ed but did not damage each other A great deal.

THURS. DEC. 25TH

Off New Inlet. This being Christmas I think of the Table at Home. Our Carpenter went on board of the "Penobscott" to repair damages. Fine day.

FRI. DEC. 26TH

Off New Inlet. Thick and misty. About 8 Oclock we pick'd up A Boat containing three Reffugee's one of my acquaintances, S—ge. After takeing them on board we ran up the coast opposite where S— lived and fired A Gun to let his people know that he was safe on board. They speak of verry hard times in Dixie.

> On this day Parker was again urging an attack upon Wilmington. This time, he urged Rear-Adm. Lee to bring the army in. Said Parker: "The heavy guns at both forts (Caswell and Fisher) as also at Wilmington point seaward and cannot be turned. General Whiting is in command of the Rebel forces here. Troops can be landed seven miles above Fort 'Fisher' and march to Wilmington without resistance saving a few pickets."[23] The view that the Union forces should immediately attack Wilmington was widely held.[24]

SAT. DEC. 27TH

Off New Inlet. Cruised around as usual. Fine weather but verry lonesom in the absence of news and we all have the Blues.

SUN. 28TH DEC.

Off New Inlet. Cruised around as usual. Sent one of the Refugees to the "Maratanza" and the other two to Beaufort. 5 Oclock P.M. got under way. Ran in close to the Land. Anchord for the Night.

MON. DEC. 29TH

Off New Inlet. Cruised as usual. About 8 Oclock A sail appaird. We ran out to hear A Morter Schooner for this station. About 4 Oclcok the Supply Steamer "Blackstone" arrived. After delivering our stores she saild for the South.

TUES. DEC. 30TH

Off New Inlet. Got under way about 2 bells. Stood up the coast. About 9½ Oclock we pick'd up A Boat containing six Men. They came out from Masonboro about 12 Oclock we spoke the "Penobscott." Sent three of the Men on board. We returnd to our station. Came to Anchor about 4 Oclock.

WENS. DEC. 31ST

Off New Inlet. At Anchor all day. Verry rough. Ship Rooling heavaly all day. Verry cloudy.

THURS. JAN. 1ST 1863

Off New Inlet. Got under way at 2 bells. Cruised up the Coast. About 11½ Oclock A sail reported. We overhauld her. A Morter schooner from Hampton Roads for this station we returnd to our station about about 5 Oclock P.M.

FRI. JAN. 2ND

Off New Inlet. Cruised as usual. About 6 bells A sail was reported the "Daylight" from Beaufort sent the other three Men on board of her. About 4 bells another sail ran out to her. A schooner. Capt. Chushing U.S.N. wanted volunteers to go on an expedition. Our Captain would not consent for any of our Men to go. Returnd to our station about 4 P.M.

SAT. JAN. 3RD

Off New Inlet. Cruised as usual. The "Genesee" arrived about 3½ Oclock from Beaufort, about 6 Oclock we ran close in shore and anchord for the night.

SUN. JAN. 4TH

Off New Inlet. We cruised up the coast, about 7 Oclock made A sail stood for it. The "Decotah" from Beaufort. Act. Ensign J. Frances came passenger in her. He came on board and reported for duty. We received orders to got to Beaufort. We saild amediately. About 5 Oclock we took A Pilot and by 6½ Oclcok we anchord in Beaufort harbor. We pass'd the "Montauk" asshore the Gun Boat "Miammi" and Transport "Thomas Freeborn" assisting to get her off we found in Port the "Pasaic" "James Adger" and "Columbia."

The log did not mention all the ships WBG refers to, but it did say there was a fleet of vessels off New Inlet that was "destined probably for an attack on Wilmington. Two of the ironclads are here 'Passaic' & 'Montauk.'"

MON. JAN. 5TH

At Beaufort. Began to coal ship. Verry cold and strong winds from the westward. Arriveal of the "Victorior."

TUES. JAN. 6TH

At Beaufort. Coaling ship. We began to take out the cargo of the Prize schooner "J.C. Roker" and we are to send it north in another vessel. The "Columbia" saild for New Inlet.

WENS. JAN. 7TH

At Beaufort. Coaling ship until about 9 Oclock. When we finish'd took in sea stores.

THURS. JAN. 8TH

At Beaufort. Takeing in stores. Fine day. I spent A part of the day asshore.

FRI, JAN. 9TH

At Beaufort. About 7½ Oclock we up Anchor and stood out for sea. About 8½ Oclock spoke the Rhode Island. Send A Boat to her. About 3 bells spoke the "Penobscott." Sent her Mail. About 2 bells P.M. spoke the "Columbia." Sent her mail. Came to anchor off New Inlet about 6 bells P.M.

SAT. JAN. 10TH

Off New Inlet. We got under way at 2 bells. Cruised along the coast. About 1 bell spoke the "Genesee." About 2 bells the Capt. of the Daylight came on board. Raining and blowing verry hard sea verry Rough.

SUN. JAN. 11TH

Off New Inlet. About 7 bells we got under way. Ran down to the shoals. Came to anchor. Sent three of the Montecella's crew around to her by Morter schooner No. 7. These Men had been on an Expedition with Capt. Chushing to Lockwoods Folly Inlet in wich they capturd (30) Muskets, after engageing and driving off the Rebs, they intended to have burnt two schooners that was up thare but on account of the Rebs having the advantage of ambushing his small force he returnd with A loss of two Men wounded. We up anchor about 5 bells. Ran down to our stations. Came to anchor for the night.

MON. JAN. 12TH

Off New Inlet. Cruised as usual. Anchord about six bells. All day we could see A large number of Workmen at work apon the Batries along the coast. We got under-way about 4 bells P.M. ran in close under the land. Anchord for the Night. About 8 bells we sent in A Boat in charge of Act. Ensign McGlenny to put down some Bouys in the Chanel. Boat returnd about 2 A.M.

TUES. JAN. 13TH

Off New Inlet. Cruised about until 6 bells anchord. A leak broke out in one of the Boilers. We blowd off steam to repair the leak, we were obliged to break out the coal in one of the Bunkers in order to repair the leak. All hand[s] were hard at work all day takeing out coal. Sent in A Boat in charge of Act. Ensign McGleney to pat down Bouys. About 1 Oclock we saw signals. Answered them. Supposed from our Boat.

WENS. JAN. 14TH

At Anchor. Off New Inlet repairing leak. Our Boat returnd about 4½ Oclock. About 5 bells A sail was reported. Sent the "Genesee" in chase at 12 Oclock. Fort Fisher fired A salute of (13) Guns, about 2 bells we sent in A Boat in charge of Act Ensign McGleney to put down some Bouy's and to see if the other Bouys were in thair places. The "Mount Vernon" convoyed the Boat when in about two miles of the Fort they oppend fire on the Boat with shell and shot and done some verry close shooting. Show'd that they knew thair work. The "Mount Vernon" returnd the fire. The "Gennesee" returnd from the chase reported the sail to be A sutters schooner bound to Port Royal from New York.

THURS. JAN. 15TH

At Anchor of[f] New Inlet. About 3.45 saw Rockets and signal lights along the Beach. We sent out A Boat on Picket duty about 9 Oclock. We completed the repairs on our Boiler so that we could get up steam. This Morning our Boat returnd about 8½ Oclock haveing been Pick'd up by the "Genesee." Blowing verry hard with drizzilling Rain. About 3 Oclock P.M. A Boat was reported by the look out Makeing for the ship. We sent our first Cutter and the Gig to thair assistance. The Boat was from "Columbia" which came for assistance, she haveing gone asshore on Masonboro Banks about six Oclock on Wensday Evening the 14th in A Gale of wind. The Boat left the "Columbia" at Eleven Oclock on the 14th but did not reach our ship until about 5 Oclock on the 15th. The Men were verry much used up haveing been rowing and exposed to wind and Rain for Eighteen hours. We amediately signalized to the "Genesee" but they did not notice us. We then up Anchor. Ran down to the "Mount Vernon" off the shoals to make them aquainted with the situation of affairs. After communicateing with the "Mount Vernon" about 7 Oclock we stood up the Beach. We arrived off Masonboro about 1 Oclock and came to anchor being impossible to find the wreck during the Night, it being verry Rough.

FRI. JAN. 16TH

We up anchor about 4 Oclock. Ran along the coast slowly. With the first streak of dawn came the sound of Artilery. We stood in for where we heard the fireing. There we found the "Penobscott" trying save the crew. The Rebels were fireing apon the wreck who had refused to hauld down the Flag of Right from the Mast. They also fired apon the Boats that were sent to pick of the crew if possible. The "Penobscott" succeeded in rescueing about 40 before we got up both ships ran in and opend fire on the Johnies, but it being verry rough we hauld off and came to Anchor.

SAT. JAN. 17TH

Off Masonboro Inlet. We had Breakfast at 6 bells then sent down Yards and Topmasts and otherwise cleard ship for action. We signalized to the "Penobscott" to do the same. About 8½ Oclock we up anchor, ran down and spoke the "Penobscott," then we both stood in for the wreck (it haveing calm'd down during the night the Rebs had boarded the wreck and took all prisoners. At day break we could see the boats plying to and from the ship with the booty) and open'd fire apon the same. The "Penobscott" got her 11 inch Gun disabled so that she was obliged to draw off. We kept up the fire for about 2 hours, when we discovered the wreck on fire we hauled off as we wanted to prevent the Rebs from geting any of her. The Rebels were repleying to us all the time from six Rifle'd field Peices which they handled with much skill and accrucy, though they did not hit us once many A shot pass'd too close to us to be at all agreeable. Just as we hauld off the "Genessee" came up but our captain sent her and the "Penobscott" down to the Inlet while we remaind and cool'd off for the Boys dander was up. The "Columbia" was A verry fine Iron steamer Brig Rig'd recently capturd of Charleston. Attemting to run the Blockade, she was fitted up as A Blockader. Carried A Batry of six 24 lbs. Howetzers and one 20 lb. Parrott Rifle. The Howetzers were thrown overboard and the Rifle spiked. So ends the cruise of the "Columbia" in ten days as A Blockader on the coast of North Carolina. The fault of her goin asshore said to be in the Leadsman giveing the wrong soundings.

> Of this day's action, the log said: "took in our anchor and in company with the 'Penobscott' stood in shore and opened fire on the wreck—The Rebels immediately fled for the shore—the Batteries on shore returned our fire many of their shells passing over but none striking us."

SUN. JAN. 18TH

Off Masonboro. We got under way about 7 bells. Stood down the coast. Came to anchor off New Inlet about 9½ Oclock. At ten we had Inspection and Muster. At anchor all day.

MON. JAN. 19TH

Off New Inlet. At anchor all day. About 8 bells A sail reported. Sent the "Penobscott" in chase.

TUES. JAN. 20TH

Off New Inlet. At anchor. Blowing verry hard. Verry heavy sea on. About 11 Oclock A sail reported. Sent the "Genesee" in chase. She sent in the schooner to us showing English collors. She anchord under out stern but her cable parted and she went to sea. It being so rough we could not board her.

WENS. JAN. 21ST

Off New Inlet. At anchor. Raining and blowing all day. About 2 bells A sail reported. Sent the "Penobscott" in chase. About 3 bells P.M. we up anchor. Ran in shore. Anchord for the night.

THURS. JAN. 22ND

Off New Inlet. About 2 bells we got under way and ran out to our anchorage where we remaind all day. Return of the "Genesee" from up the coast. About 3 bells P.M. got under way. Ran in shore. Anchord for the Night.

FRI. JAN. 23RD

Off New Inlet. Got under way about 1 bell. Ran up the coast. Returnd to our anchorage about 7 bells. About 2 bells the "Genesee" spoke us. About 6 bells A Boat was reported comeing off shore with A Flag of truce. Sent A Boat to receive the Flag. Our Boat return with the Boat in tow containing three Reffugees from Wilmington. The boat was one of the "Columbia's." About 4 Oclock A sail was reported. We gave chase and were soon alongside the schooner. Prooved to be the "Time" of and from "Nasau." To run the Blockade we took posession of her and put A Prize Crew on board and returnd to our anchorage about 10 Oclock P.M.

> The *Civil War Naval Chronology* states: "U.S.S. *Cambridge*, Commander William A. Parker, captured schooner *Time* off Cape Fear, North Carolina with cargo of salt, matches and shoes."[25] On the following day, Cmdr. Parker notified Adm. Lee of the capture of the *Time*: "Sir: The schooner *Time*, from Nassau, with an assorted cargo was taken as a prize by this vessel yesterday. . . . From the course the schooner was steering when discovered, the nonappearance upon her manifest of soda, matches, and shoes, already found in her, the contradictory statements of her master, and his apparent anxiety, I have no hesitation in considering the schooner a legal prize, and also that it is my opinion her master (Poland), now on board the *Cambridge*, will, if released, endeavor again to run the blockade."[26]

SAT. JAN. 24TH

Off New Inlet. Got under way about 4 bells. Cruised until 2 bells. Came to anchor about 4 bells. The "Genesee" spoke us. She took our Mail and the three Refugees. Also Act. Masters Mate Nickerson who have resignd on the account of ill health. We again got under way about 2 bells P.M. Ran in shore. Anchord for the Night.

SUN. JAN. 25TH

Off New Inlet. Got under way at 2 bells. Cruised until 8 bells. About four Bells we had Inspection and muster. Got under way about four bells P.M. ran in shore and Anchord for the Night. Weather fine.

MON. JAN. 26TH

Off New Inlet. Got under way at 4 bells. Cruised up the coast. About 10½ Oclock heard heavy fireing from the S.S.W. Came to Anchor about 3 bells P.M. about 7 bells two Boats in charge of Act. Ensigns Small and McGleney went in to attempt to burn A Brig that is anchord under the Fort.

TUES. JAN. 27TH

Off New Inlet. About 4 bells verry foggy. About 6 bells Mr. McGlenny returnd and about 4 bells Mr. Small returnd. They got lost in the Fog. They faild to accomplish thair object. About 6 bells we discoverd A leak in the Bottom of the Boiler. About 12 Oclock the "Daylight" saild for Beaufort for repairs. About 4 bells P.M. we got under way. Ran in shore and in anchord for the night. Heard of the departure of the Iron Clad fleet for Charleston.

WENS. JAN. 28TH

Off New Inlet. Got under way about 4 bells. Ran out. Came to anchor about 2 bells. Saw several vessels bearing S.E. about 6 bells got under way. Ran in shore. Anchord for the Night.

THURS. JAN. 29TH

Off New Inlet. At anchor all day. Fine weather. Heard of the sailing of the Expidition for Charleston. Got under way about 2 bells P.M. Ran in shore and anchord for the Night.

FRI. JAN. 30TH

Off New Inlet. We got under way about 2 bells. About 3 bells made A steamer under the land. We beat to Quaters. Bore down and sent our respects from our Parrott when she about ship and stood for us. The U.S. Transport steamer "Guide" loaded with troops for Charleston. Put them on thair coast about 8 bells P.M. A sail was reported. Bore down and spoke her. One of the Transports with troops for Port Royal. Returnd to our anchorage about 8 Oclock.

SAT. JAN. 31ST

Off New Inlet. Got under way about 2 bells. About four bells made several sails bound to the southard. Sent the "Penobscott" in chase. Saw A steamer in the River flying the English collars. We anchord about 8 bells. About 8 bells P.M. Fort Fisher fired A salute of 21 Guns. M. McGleney went in on Picket duty.

> Cmdr. Parker's report says that a "steamer was discovered near Ft. Fisher inside of New Inlet bearing the rebel flag at her main and the English flag at her fore. . . . She had apparently run the Blockade during the night. The weather was misty. I have, also, to report that Ft. Fisher fired a salute of Twenty One guns at 4 P.M. this day."[27]

SUN. FEB. 1ST

Off New Inlet. We got under way about 2 bells. About 4 bells pick'd up our Boat. We came to anchor about 2 bells. At 10 Oclock we had Inspection and Devine Serveace got under way at 2 bells P.M. Ran in shore. Anchord for the night.

MON. FEB. 2ND

Off New Inlet. Fine weather. We up Anchor about 2 bells and ran out and anchord about 2½ Oclock. About 3 bells P.M. we ran in and Anchord off Fort Fisher.

TUES. FEB. 3RD

Off New Inlet. Verry cold. The Decks coverd with Ice. We got under way at 2 bells. Cruised off shore. Returnd to our anchorage about 11 Oclock.

WENS. FEB. 4TH

Off New Inlet. Verry cold. At Anchor. There was A survey held on the Penobscott's Boilers to day. She was condemnd and will proceed north for repairs. Last night while the "Penobscott" was lying at Anchor she roold so heavaly that she roold over board A Parrott Rifle from her forecastle. Verry rough indeed.

THURS. FEB. 5TH

Off New Inlet. Raining and Blowing verry hard. About 7 bells A sail reported. A goverment schooner loaded with Beeves (she showd signals of distress) bound for New berne. She could not get an offing and came down before the wind. We took her in tow. About 4 bells P.M. the Hawser parted severely wounding Burham and Briggs Boatswains Mates. We came to anchor the schooner astern. She broke her Main-Boom. Towards the evening more moderate.

FRI. FEB. 6TH

Off New Inlet. We got under way about 1 bell. Quite calm with A thick fog. Could not see the schooner. About 7 bells we spoke the "Genesee." About 6 bells A.M. Fort Fisher open'd fire on us but did no harm. Sent our mail on board of the "Genesee." She saild for Beaufort. We anchord about 5 bells.

SAT. FEB. 7TH

Off New Inlet. Got under way about 3 bells. Ran up the coast. Met the Daylight about 8 bells. Comeing from Beaufort. We received A Mail. We returnd to our anchorage about 4 bells where we remain the rest of the day.

SUN. FEB. 8TH

Off New Inlet. We got under way at 4 bells. We had Inspection and Muster about 3 bells P.M. we got under way and ran in shore for the night.

MON. FEB. 9TH

Off New Inlet. We got under way at 4 bells ran out. Came to Anchor about 8 bells. A verry thick fog. About 4 bells cleard up. A sail reported gave chase another sail sent the Mount Vernon after one and we follow'd the other. They ran away from us. We returnd to our anchorage about 3 bells P.M.

TUES. FEB. 10TH

Off New Inlet. Got under way about 4 bells. Cruised up the coast. Verry foggy until about 10 Oclock when it cleard up A sail in sight. Stood for it. The sloop of War "Iroquois." Capt. Case who came to retrieve Capt. Parker. We received orders to go in for repairs. We also received 9 Men two of them being deserted from our ship, the 10th of Nov. 62 at Beaufort. About 3 bells got under way ran in shore. Anchord for the night.

WENS. 11TH

Off New Inlet. Got under way at 4 bells. Cruised along shore until 10 Oclock when we anchord. Got under way again about 5 bells. Ran in shore. Anchord for the night.

THURS. FEB. 12TH

Off New Inlet. We got under way about 4 bells. Cruised all day. Our pet squirrel got drownd. Came to anchor about 6 bells P.M.

FRI. FEB. 13TH

Off New Inlet. Fine day. Got under way about 7 bells A.M. ran out to the Gulf makeing 11 knots. Returnd to our Anchorage about 4 bells P.M.

SAT. FEB. 14TH

Off New Inlet. Fine day. Got under way about 8 bells [A.]M. Cruised until
2 bells P.M. Anchord for the night.

> Though, except for feelings of loneliness and the "Blues" at the previous Christ-
> mas, WBG does not express discontent with shipboard duty, Cmdr. Parker was
> apparently concerned about morale, reminding Adm. Lee "that the officers and
> crew of this vessel have been engaged in the Blockade for the last year and a half
> without any opportunity to visit their families and friends, or any relaxation
> from their arduous duties except a short time at Baltimore. Nearly every officer
> and man attached to this vessel are natives of the Northern States, and it is very
> desirable that they should be allowed the usual privileges of visiting their
> friends while the vessel is refitting for active service. This will be impossible if
> Norfolk or Baltimore be the Port selected in which to make the repairs. My ex-
> perience at Baltimore convinces me that the repairs can be made at the North
> cheaper, better and more expeditiously than will be possible, either at Balti-
> more or Norfolk. Besides, it is nothing more than common justice to allow the
> men a short leave of absence to visit their homes. I have not been absent a sin-
> gle day since I reported for duty on board in August, 1861, and this is the case
> of many others. The health of the men would be improved, and they would be
> more contented and happy by having this small indulgence."[28]

SUN. FEB. 15TH

Off New Inlet. We up anchor about 8 bells [A.]M. Cruised about until 2 bells.
Came to Anchor about 10 Oclock. Inspection and Muster Devine serveace,
about six bells. A sail was reported. We gave Chase. Returnd to our Anchorage about 4 bells. About five bells saw signals. Heard fireing. A thick fog. Beat
to Quaters. Slipd cable. The Daylight fire'd at A steamer trying to get out. We
cruised about until 10 Oclock. Came to Anchor.

MON. FEB. 16TH

Off New Inlet. We got under way about 4 bells. Received the Mail from the
Squadron and about 8 bells we saild for Beaufort. About 1 Oclock we pass'd
Rich Inlet. Verry close in shore. Took A good look at the place that I left in
(62). About 3 bells made A sail. Stood for it. The "Genesee" bound out
from Beaufort. We received A Mail. I received four letters and 3 papers.
About 7 bells we anchord of[f] Beaufort. Quite cold with strong winds from
the Westward.

> I went to the land next to Rich Inlet on Figure Eight Island in February 1997
> and looked back to the shore as he must have done that day. WBG was look-
> ing directly at the Nicholas Nixon Plantation at Porters Neck.

TUES. FEB. 17TH

We got under way about 4 bells. Stood in for the Bar. Took A Pilot about 8
bells. Ran in and anchord off the Rail Road Depot about 2 bells. Raining all
day. Maild A letter for N.Y., one for Boston.

WENS. FEB. 18TH

At Beaufort. Raining all day. About 8 bells the U.S.S. "Mercedeta" arrived on
her way north for repairs that she received in the engagement with the Reb
Iron Clads off Charleston S.C. Also arrived A French Transport in distress
from Verre Cruz for France. Coaling ship. About 4 bells were obliged to quit
coaling on account of the Rain. Quite cold.

> The attack WBG refers to occurred earlier, on Jan. 31, during which the U.S.S.
> *Mercedita* "was so severely damaged by ramming and shellfire that she sur-
> rendered, but later was able to get under way and escape. *Keystone State* was
> set afire, her boilers struck with ten or more shell. Other vessels were less seri-
> ously damaged. As usual, scalding steam caused most of the killed casualties,
> with four killed and three wounded on *Mercedita* and twenty killed and twenty
> wounded on *Keystone State*. The Confederate ironclads withdrew unhurt.
> The Confederates took the victory to mean a lifting of the blockade and so de-
> clared to foreign powers. But the blockade was not really broken, despite the
> temporary interruption."[29]

THURS. FEB. 19TH

At Beaufort. Cease'd raining. All hands calld about 8 bells to coal ship. Cleard
off about noon. The ship that is in the offing is the English ship Oseian
employed by the French as A transport her machinery is disabled. Day fine.

FRI. FEB. 20TH

At Beaufort. Coald ship all night. Finish'd this Morning. Served out Money.
Wash'd down Decks then A great rush for the sutters schooners. In the
Evening the steamer S.R. Spaulding came in put out stores and proceeded on
her way south. Weather verry fine.

SAT. FEB. 21ST

At Beaufort. About 4 bells all hands were call'd to make preperation for sea.
About 7 bells up anchor and stood out for sea. As we were goin out we pass'd

the steamer "Chicora" comeing in after dischargeing the Pilot. We put on the sail and were sendding along at A respectable rate for our station. Spoke the "Daylight" about 8 bells. Sent thair Mail. We reported to the Flag Ship about 2 bells. We then lowerd yards and Topmast and came to Anchor. Blowing quite fresh from N.E.

SUN. FEB. 22ND

Off New Inlet. We had A severe Hail storm. Hail fell as large as Peogeons Eggs. We got under way about 1 bell P.M. Cruised till dark. Came to anchor about 7 bells for the Night. Quite cold.

MON. FEB. 23RD

Off New Inlet. Got under way about 2 bells. Cruised about until 3 bells when we anchord. About 1 bell pick'd up A Boat containing three Colard Reffugees from Masonboro. About 6 bells A steamer reported. Slip'd cable gave chase. She ran away from us. Returnd to our Anchorage. Lost our anchor and (30) Fathams chain. Got up another anchor and bend it in its place. Heard heavy fireing from the southard. Quite cool, wind from south.

> Cmdr. Parker conveyed to Adm. Lee what little he had been able to glean from the "colored refugees" WBG mentions: "Sir:—I have to report that this day three Contrabands were taken on board this vessel, having escaped from shore. I obtain but little information from them as they appear to be corn-field hands. Yet the same, is, perhaps, of sufficient importance to report. A large portion of the troops at Wilmington and from the Forts have been taken away and sent to Charleston. One of the 'rams' is finished (and has been seen at Fort 'Fisher' by the Blockading Steamers.) The intention is to run for the vessels here and destroy them. I would respectfully suggest that there is a probability that the Blockade may be broken unless 'iron clads' can be spared to re-enforce the vessels now here."[30]

TUES. FEB. 24TH

Off New Inlet. Got under way at 8 bells. Cruised all the Morning. Came to anchor about 2 bells. Heard that the "Montecella" had an engagement with Fort Caswell yesterday. She lost one Master Mate and A Boy. Still cold. Wind North West.

> The log for this date states: "The Mt Vernon having returned from the reef at 1-30 her Commander came aboard Reports that the firing yesterday (which WBG mentions in his Feb. 23 entry) was at a blockade runner. The rebel fort (Caswell) opened fire on the steamer Monticello killing and wounding some of her men."

WENS. FEB. 25TH

Off New Inlet. Got under way about 2 bells. Cruised all the Morning. Came to anchor about 2 bells. Weather quite fine.

THURS. FEB. 26TH

Off New Inlet. Got under way about 2 bells. Cruised until 3 bells. Came to Anchor. Quite foggy. About 5 bells the "State of Georgia" arrived. We are not to go north for the present. Return of Mr. Ordeorne who was takeen prisoner in December. Also return of Peter Trainer that was sent north in the Prize schooner Emma Tuttle. Quite rough with slight winds and thick fog all day.

FRI. FEB. 27TH

Off New Inlet. Got under way about 2 bells. Cruised all the Morning. Quite foggy. Came to Anchor about 2 bells. Light winds and warm.

SAT. FEB. 28TH

Off New Inlet. Got under way about 2 bells. Cruised as usual. About one bell A sail reported. Gave chase. Fog rise. Lost sight of the sail. Returnd to our Anchorage.

SUN. MARCH 1ST, 1863

Off New Inlet. Cruised as usual. Heard of an Iron Clad Ram inside.

MON. MARCH 2ND

Off New Inlet. Got up anchor about 2 bells. Cruised until 4 bells. Came to anchor. We received A mail. I received three letters. About 2 bells A steamer ran the Blockade. In the chase we broke our shaft. Anchord about 4 bells P.M.

TUES. MARCH 3RD

Off New Inlet. We got under way about 2 bells. Cruised until about 4 bells. Weather fine. Little cold.

WENS. MARCH 4TH

Off New Inlet. Got under way about 2 bells. Weather fine. Anchord about 2 bells.

THURS. MARCH 5TH

Off New Inlet fine day. Time verry dull. We got off New Inlet.

FRI. MARCH 6TH

Under way about 8 bells. Cruised until about 3 bells. Came to Anchor. We then put out Boats to sweep for our lost Anchor: we were furtunate enough to find it and after A great deal of pulling and hauling. We had it safely stowd (together with 4 fathams of chain) in the hold.

SAT. MARCH 7TH

Off New Inlet. We got under way about 8 bells. Cruised all day. Anchord about 6 bells for the Night.

SUN. MARCH 8TH

Off New Inlet. We got under way about 2 bell. Cruised until 1 Oclock. Came to anchor at 4 bells. Quarters and Serveace. Read the Articles of War. Also the Proclamation of Emancipation. Verry good.

> WBG was late hearing about the proclamation, which had been issued on Jan. 1, 1863. It was reproduced in the March 8 log.

MON. MARCH 9TH

Off New Inlet. About 3 bells saw two sails but could not give chase. Quite pleasant.

TUES. MARCH 10TH

Off New Inlet. At anchor all day.

WENS. MARCH 11TH

Off New Inlet. We got under way about 2 bells. Cruised until 8. Came to anchor. Sent 8 of our Men on board of the "Iroquois." Received four disable seamen from her to take North.

THURS. MARCH 12TH

Off New Inlet. Got under way about 4 bells. Ran to the shoals. Anchord about 2 bells. Sent 9 men to the "Dacotah." Heard that the small pox was at Smithville. In returning from the shoals we pass'd the Transports "—White", "Golden Gate" and "Nantucket" bound south. Sent our surgeon to the "State of Georgia." We received two sick and one discharged seaman and the surgeon from her to convey them North. We received the Mail and our Orders from the "Iroquois" and about 4 bells P.M. we set sail for Beaufort. Quite cold. Wind North East.

FRI. MARCH 13TH

This Morning we pass'd the Transport Island Home out from Beaufort, bound for Port Royal. We took A Pilot at 8 bells. Stood in and came to anchor in the Harbor of Beaufort about 2 bells the followings vessels were in port. "Maratanza" and "Daylight" sent the Colard Men to Morehead Citty. Quite cold. Strong winds from N.E.

SAT. MARCH 14TH

At Beaufort. Quite moderate. About 8 bells the Transport "Ocean Wave" arrived from Port Royal bringing the new of the destruction of the "Nashville" by the "Montauk." About 4 bells the "Ocean Wave" saild for Newberne. About 1 Oclock A.M. we heard heavey cannonadeing in land. We suppose that the Rebel Gen'l D.H. Hill have attack'd Gen'l Foster as it was known that he was at Kingston with A large boddy of troops for that purpose. The work on our shaft was repaird to day we sat up and tared down Rigging and about 2 bells we up Anchor for Hampton Roads. We rounded Cape Lookout about 4 bells P.M.

> John G. Barrett writes: "In arranging his forces to protect the supply trains in the eastern counties of North Carolina, Longstreet planned for Hill to 'make a diversion upon New Bern and surprise the garrison at Washington.' . . . The attack was to be launched from Kinston. . . . The opening round in the Confederate attack on New Bern occurred on Friday, March 13."[31]

SUN. MARCH 15TH

We pass'd Cape Hatteras about 4 bells. Weather verry fine with light winds from the N.W. about 4 bells we had Inspection and Devine Serveace. We made Cape Henry's light about 4 bells P.M. and came to Anchor in Chespeak Bay about 8 bells M.

> Lincoln's General Order of Feb. 10, 1863, requiring the observance of the Sabbath day in the army and navy, was copied into the log entry for this date.

MON. MARCH 16TH

Chespeak Bay. We got under [w]ay about 6 bells A.M. Stood up the Bay. Pass'd the Gaurd Ship "Mystic" at 8 bells. Arrived off the Flag Ship "Minesota" At New Port News about 4 bells Capt. Parker went on board the Flag Ship and reported to the Admiral (Lee). Our Captain returnd about 12 Oclock. About

2 Oclock there were sixty three of our Crew drafted for the Squadron. Then there was A great commotion geting ready for leaveing. Some of the Men done some pretty tall swearing by being disapointed in thair expectatin of goin home. I however escaped the Draft. This Evening we had A Ball on board. They sighn'd thair accounts and all are prepared to leave in the Evening.

TUES. MARCH 17TH

At New Port News. This Morning the first thing I was call'd into A Boat. Went along side of the "Minesota." On my return the Transport "Philadelphia" were along side with the Drafted Men on board. We bade them good Bye and they gave us three Cheers. We returnd them and they went on thair way but not rejoiceing. The Iron Clad Batery "Keokuk" saild about the same time for Charleston. Our ship looks desolate now. Our crew numbers includeing Marienes, Firemen, and Idlers, 48 Men. After clearing up Ship Offercers came on board to inspect the ship. After thair departure A Summary Court Martial conviend to try Perkins and Powers for descrting to the Enemy. We received orders to go to Baltimore for Repairs and A Pilot came on board for that place. About 5 Oclock the "Keokuk" returnd, haveing run into A Bouy and got the Chain entangle around her Propeller. The Pilot of her was put in confinement. I went on board took A good look at her. Saw her commander Lieut. Com. Rine. Perkins and Powers were releasd from confinement, haveing been confined in double Irons for six weeks.

WENS. MARCH 18TH

Off New Port News. Quite A gale this morning very thick fog. About 9 Oclock we had Quaters and Muster. Read the sentance of Perkins and Powers to the loss of three Months Pay to be disrated from Landsmen to first class Boys and to be transported to the "Brig Perry." I am now act. steward belongs to A Boat before the Mast and what ever therre is to be done.

THURS. MARCH 19TH

Off New Port News. Went asshore. Saw Mrs. Hall. Quite well. Quite cold wind from the North west. About 9 Oclock it began to sleet and about 11 Oclock it began to snow. We went along side of the Flagship. Not verry pleasant in A Boat at this time.

Mrs. Hall is probably Lucilla Moseley, whom WBG encounters aboard the
Mystic in November 1862. By now she has married WBG's fellow contraband
Joseph Hall. WBG tells the story of her escape and "interesting romance" in
an article published in *The Anglo-African*.

FRI. MARCH 20TH

Off New Port News. Went to the Flag ship, then asshore and again to Flag
ship and again asshore. This Evening we were near four hours pulling from
the Flag Ship to the "Cambridge." Verry cold. Snowing verry hard all day.
Wind from N.W.

SAT. MARCH 21ST

Off New Port News. I[t] have Moderated somewhat. Ceased snowing about
2 bells. Went to the Flag Ship. Braught on board the Prisone[r]s Perkins and
Powers. Thare chargees are incorrect. We returnd to the Flag Ship with
Prisoners, then asshore, took A look at the (Devel or What do you call it)
submariene Batry cigar shape that is propell'd by A screw and fires A gun
under watter after being submerged. Went asshore. I received some Delecacies
from Mrs. H for which that Lady have my thanks. We saw the
sun for the first time in A week. Raining lightly wind from N.W.

The submarine WBG refers to is the *Alligator*. It sank soon after, without ever
seeing any action, while being towed to Charlestown.[32]

SUN. MARCH 22ND

Off New Port News. Raind all Night and until about 4 bells this Morning
when it ceased. Went asshore then to the Flag Ship. While there Genl. Burnside went on board. He was saluted on his departure. Coaling ship. We went
again to the Flag Ship. In comeing down the Roads we were envelopeed in
A thick Fog and when it broke away we found ourselves among [a] fleet of
schooners and after many stopagees and starting we pass'd safely through and
arrived of[f] Old Point. About 6 Oclock we went asshore to carry the Pilot
and on our return we found the ship at Anchor and A Tug alongside geting
one of our Anchors. As soon as we had given them the Anchor we up Anchor
and stood down the Bay, bound for Boston. We got up another anchor from
the Hold and Bend it. Cleard up decks and turnd in about 2 bells. Wind
from the N.E.

By this time, Gen. Burnside, who had replaced McClellan in November 1862, had himself been replaced. Gen. Joe Hooker had been given his command on Jan. 25, 1863. Three days after this visit to the *Cambridge*, Burnside was given a new command.[33]

MON. MARCH 23RD

A verry fine day. Light winds and verry heavey swells. Feel in the Brig Elizabeth of Salem. 101 days from Malta for New York, eight days out of Provissions, supplied her with Wood, Coal, Bread, Pork, Beef, Rice, Coffee, Tea, Cheese and started on our way about 12½ Oclock. Slung clean Hammocks. All hands went through the opperation of scrubbing two apeice. We hove the lead about 7 bells found nineteen Fathoms. Wind light from the N.E.

TUES. MARCH 24TH

We are able to carry Fore and aft sails. Breeze quite Fresh from N.E. ship Rooling hea[v]y. this Evening quite foggy. Made A light (Fire Island) which we took for Montauk, ran along slowly, the wind increases. We are obliged to take in sail.

WENSDAY MARCH 25TH

This Morning quite rough and found us rather too close to Long Island for safety, as we were mistakeen in the light we passd Montauk Point about 1 bell n. A thick fog comeing on we came to anchor in 7 fathams of watter with 45 fathoms of chain out the ship quite steady. Wrote to C.W.R. and to J.L.H. The fog broke away about 8 bells and we found ourselves about three ships lengths from Gay Head Beach. We up anchor and ran into the Vinyard sound and came to anchor of Holm's Hole about 12 Oclock.

THURS. MARCH 26TH

Off Holmes Hole. We hoisted on Jack for A Pilot one came on board and we started about 7 bells for Boston. We sat sail. We did not proceed far when A thick fog came on and we were obliged to come to anchor. We again got under way about 12 Oclock. Took on board A Boston Pilot about 6 bells from the Boat Boquet, under full sail, about 2 bells we signalized at Chatam. Split topsails were obliged to take it in stood up the Bay.

FRI. MARCH 27TH

At Boston. We arrived and came to anchor off the Navy Yard about 2 Oclock.
I went asshore with the stewards to market. Set foot on the old Bey state.
About 8 bells I was orderd to prepare to go in the Gig as I belongs to all the
Boats of the ship. About 2 bells we carried the Captain to the Yard. Returnd
about 12 Oclock. The afternoon was spent in goin to and from the Citty. Saw
Thomas Taylor. Fred Myrick.

SAT. MARCH 28TH

At Boston. Went asshore. Took out our Powder. About 2 bells A Tug came
alongside. We up anchor and was tow'd along side of the docks. All hands
were mustered with Bags and Hammocks and march'd aboard of the "Ohio"
where we arrived about 12 Oclock. This Saturday March 28th 1863. So end
my first trip at sea.

SUN. MARCH 29TH

On board the "Ohio." My first time on board of A Receiving ship or Gaurdo
as they are calld by the Men. Here we meet with all Kinds and all clasees of
men. We had devine serveace on board our Lieut Strong came on board and
requested the commander to treat us well. Several of us went on board of our
ship and returnd in the evening.

MONDAY MARCH 30TH

On board the "Ohio." Wrote to my Aunt [Mary Moore (Mrs. Thomas Jones)].
All well.

TUES. MARCH 31ST

Heard from my Aunt in the afternoon she with her Daughter. Mary came on
board.

WENS. APRIL 1ST

On board the Garduo. Our Lieut came on board to day and got Liberty for us
for fourteen days (14). Rejoicing among us. We were soon ready for the shore
so the word is now off to Boston.

MON. APRIL 13TH

All Hands of us reported on board of the Garduo. All well now again for

Prison life. I remaind on board of the "Ohio" until the 22nd when all hands went on Liberty for 24 hours.

FRI. APRIL 24TH

We returnd on board this Morning. All night we remaind on board until Thurs. 30th when we all Hands. Got Liberty for four days.

TUES. MAY 3RD

We returnd on board this Morning where we remaind until the 15th inst. when we again got ten days Liberty. All hands went asshore. We returnd on board.

MON. MAY 25TH

I returnd with A severe cold and Headache. Went on the sick list. While on liberty I visited Nantucket. Meet Miss C.W.R. also had quite A good time in Boston and vicinety. Saw many of my aquaintances. I remaind on board of the Garduo until the 29th when the Measels broke out apon me and I was sent to the Hospital (Chelsea). I arrived at the Hospital on the 29th where I reamind until the 13th of Oct. While there sick, I was takeen good care of by the Surgeons Fox and Gilbert. Also the steward and Nurses were very Kind to me and when I goin to leave they insisted on my remaining but I have spent A verry long time on shore and now desires to be afloat one more. There is nothing like the whistling wind and the danceing Bark on the Bounding Billow bearing its precious treasure to the shores of some distant clime. While at the Hospital I acted as A nurse. There were two of my Patients Died there names are respectfully Henry Burrow of Hamilton Canada west and Louis B. Hoagland Brooklyn N.Y. Both were Burried in the Grave Yard attatchd to the Hospital. I had the priveledge of goin out whenever I had A mind to and frequently spent the Evenings at Boston. A friend woul[d] ocasionaly drop over to see me one instant while sick one of Cousins John J—s [Jones] came to the Hospital on buisiness. He came as near as the door of the ward that I was in and askd me how I was and amediately left. I did not know what to think of this treatment but on recovery I learnt that it had been reported that I had the Small Pox. That was the reason why they did not visit me at first. I remaind at the Hospital until the 13th day of October when haveing made an engagement with Dr. Fox who is orderd to the "Niagara" she being goin on A cruise to Europe. Dr. Beale, Dr. Fox successer insisted on my remaining but as this will be A good opportunity of visiting Europe I will avail myself of this opportunity and goin I will. So good Bye until you hear from me again.

Etc., Wm.B.G.

Aboard the U.S.S. *Niagara*

$\mathcal{T}$he U.S.S. *Niagara*, the ship that William B. Gould joined in October 1863, was one of six frigates the government had authorized in 1854, the first screw-propelled class in the U.S. navy. According to Donald Canney,

> *Niagara* was contracted by George Steers, famous for his yacht *America* and other fast vessels. He attempted to combine sharp clipper hull lines with a frigate's weaponry, apparently intending to have *Niagara* carry a battery comparable to her navy-built sisters (*Merrimack* and class). This was only possible by making her significantly larger than the other five—328 feet between perpendiculars and 5540 tons. When launched, she was the largest vessel built in the US to that time.
>
> Despite her commodious gundeck, she was only given spar deck weapons: twelve 11-inch Dahlgrens, all on pivot rails. She proved to be fast—10 to 11 knots under steam—and was known to exceed 16 knots under sail. Before the war, she laid the first Atlantic Cable (with HMS *Agamemnon*). During a mid-war refit she was given a complement of twenty 11-inchers on the gundeck, along with the dozen spar deck guns. This enormous battery brought her ports dangerously low and she reverted to her dozen guns shortly thereafter.[34]

This change was apparently at the instigation of the *Niagara*'s commander, Thomas Craven, who informed Secretary of the Navy Gideon Welles that "the batteries [were] entirely too heavy for the ship. . . . Her midships port was 5 feet 6 inches above the water line. . . . On our passage here, although there was little swell and the ports were lashed in—the gundeck was awash with water—demonstrating that in a gale of wind she would be exceedingly uncomfortable if not a dangerous ship and that under the most favorable circumstances, only two or three of her XI inch guns could be used. . . . I would suggest that her main deck battery be taken out."[35]

⌇

TUESDAY OCTOBER THE 13TH 1863

I was to day transferd from the Hospital at Chelsea (Where I have been since the 29th of May 1863) to the Receiveing Ship "Ohio" and again transferd to the Steam Frigate "Niagara" and went on board and reported then went ashore and spent the Night.

WENSDAY OCT. 14TH

I reported on board of the "Niagara" at 8 Oclock then went on board of the "Ohio" and sign'd accounts. The crew were then sent on board of the "Niagara." At ten Oclock the Niagara went in commission under the command of Comodore Thomas T. Craven. We then hauld out in the Stream and anchord off South Boston. A part of the crew of the Sabiene came on board.

THURSDAY OCT. 15TH

Off south Boston. Received on board our Amunition. All hands were musterd this evening and were devided into watches and Numberd and Stationd. Maild A letter to C.W.R. Also one to Aunt and one to F.C.

FRIDAY OCT. 16TH

Off South Boston. Morning verry foggy. Commenced raining at four bells P.M. All of the crew of the Sabeine came on board.

SATURDAY OCT. 17TH

Off South Boston. Raining verry hard this Morning commenced preperation for sea. Got under way at four bells and steam'd down the bay makeing ten and A half Knots. Off Gloucester we collaed [collided] with A schooner and carried away our Studing Sail Boom. The Ship roold verry heavey. Came to anchor of Gloucester. There was A great upheaveing among the crew.

> Canney writes of the difficulties the navy had recruiting sailors, and singles out the *Niagara* as an example: "The meeting of minimal, physical, and mental criteria certainly had its obvious down side. This, in addition to the competition

with the army . . . served to make the shortage of personnel a continuing problem throughout the conflict, often resulting in vessels with incomplete complements. More seriously, otherwise combat-ready ships sometimes remained at their berths for lack of manpower. In one instance, the frigate *Niagara* lay off Gloucester for several weeks in late 1863 attempting to complete her crew. In the end, she sailed with a significant shortage."[36] WBG makes several references to the calling up and discharging of men during the time the *Niagara* was in Gloucester. As *The Gloucester Telegraph* indicates, the *Sabine*, the receiving ship to which WBG went prior to his transfer to the *Niagara*, experienced the same difficulties. The *Telegraph* states that Gloucester had "already sent a great number of men to the War. Many, in fact, better suited to the naval than the military service, are in the army at this moment." Nonetheless, the paper advocated the wise engagement of "some public effort" to procure seamen for the Sabine "or such other government ships as may be waiting for a crew."[37]

SUNDAY OCT. 18TH

At anchor of Gloucester. Holy Stone decks for the first time. We Musterd at four bells. I was rateed asistant stweard Ward Room. We have verry fine weather for this season of the year.

MONDAY OCT. 19TH

At anchor off Gloucester all day. At 4 bells all hands were call'd to quaters and given thair stations at the guns. A heavy fog all day. Maild A letter for Mr. C.

TUESDAY OCT. 20TH

At anchor off Gloucester. About 2 bells heard fireing to the seaward. At 3 bells A.M. all hands call'd to quaters and giveen thair stations by devissions. About 2 bells A strang[e] steamer came in sight showing the American ensign with strange signals. We showd our numbers when she put to sea. We amediately got up steam and commence to get up ancher but did not go to sea. We loaded and trail our guns all ready for action. Last night it raind verry hard. A verry fine day. Late this evening again heard heavy fireing seaward.

WENSDAY OCT. 21ST

At anchor off Gloucester all day. Morning verry foggy. A number of visiters came aboard this Evening the Commodore and severl Jentlemens went on A fishing excursion. We take aboard wood for sea to day. About 7 P.M. two boys were brought up to the mast for fighting. They both were put on extra duty for punishment.

THURSDAY OCT. 22ND

At anchor off Gloucester. A verry fine day. At two bells we loosed sails. I
received A letter from C.W.R. At 4 bells we furled sails. A number of visiters
came aboard to day. This morning A man that deserted the day that the
Ship went into commission returnd. A man that deserted from the Army and
ship'd in the Navy was reclaimd by the Provost Marshall. Yesterday the
steerage stwerd went ashore but failing to return he was reported as A
deserter. At three bells P.M. all hands were call'd to quaters. Write A letter
to C.W.R.

FRIDAY OCT. 23RD

At anchor off Gloucester. Day verry fine. At four bells calld to quaters.
Stationd at the foot of shoot to pass emty powder boxes to day A man that was
caught stealing was lash'd up in his Hammock for three nights. Then he was
made to walk up and down the deck with A bag tied around him with a play
card attached with the word theif apon it. All hands put down for clothing at
three bells all hands calld to quaters. Maild my letter to C.W.R. A great maney
visiters came on board to day. We ship'd two recruits. The comodore went
fishing. Tattoo is beaten every night at eight Oclock.

> The *Oxford English Dictionary* states that in the military context the tattoo is
> "a signal made, by beat of drum or bugle call, in the evening, for soldiers to re-
> pair to their quarters in garrison or tents in camp." As defined by the *Ameri-*
> *can Heritage Dictionary*, it is "a signal sounded on a drum or bugle to sum-
> mon soldiers or sailors to their quarters at night . . . a continuous, even
> drumming or rapping."

SATURDAY OCT. 24TH

At anchor off Gloucester. Morning cloudy. Calld to quaters at four bells. It
commenced raining at 7 bells A.M. and continued all day. I commenced to
study French in company with C. Ross of N.Y.

SUNDAY OCT. 25TH

At anchor off Gloucester. It raind all night and cleard off this morning quite
cold. All hands calld to Muster at 4 bells A.M. Quaters at 3 bells P.M. Colder
this evening. Received A letter from Boston. This evening we had music for
the benefit of the men.

MONDAY OCT. 26TH

At anchor off Gloucester. Morning verry cold. Themometer down to (38) degrees. Quaters at 3 bells A.M. Several visiters came on board to day. Quaters at 3 bells. Received A letter from A.M. Jose. Also one from C.L.S. containing the good news that I drew A Pitcher at Chelsea which I took A chance for before I left the Hospital. Verry cold all day. Write A letter to Jose and one to Smith.

TUESDAY OCT. 27TH

At anchor off Gloucester. Verry cold all day. Our Paymaster and first Ass't Surgeon left to day for Boston. They served out clothing to the men. Quaters at 3 bells A.M. and 3 bells P.M. Our first Leiutenant's wife came on board this Evening.

WENSDAY OCT. 28TH

At anchor off Gloucester. Still verry cold. Quaters at 3 bells A.M. Two of our Ensigns went away on liberty this Evening A new Ensign joind the ship. We heard that we are to return to Boston to remove some of our guns. Quaters at 3 bells P.M.

THURSDAY OCT. 29TH

At anchor of Gloucester. This Morning more moderate. Quaters at three bells. Exercise in extinguishing fire. Shipd one recruite to day. Received A letter from C.L.S. The Comodore and surgeon went ashore to dine. A number of ladies came on board. Our Paymaster and ass't Surgeon returnd to day. Sent A Picture to C.W.R. Quaters at 3 bells P.M.

FRIDAY OCT. 30TH

At ancher off Gloucester. Quite moderate. Little cloudy. Quaters at 3 bells A.M. A schooner arrived to day from Boston with stores. Quaters at 3 bells P.M.

SATURDAY OCT. 31ST

At anchor off Gloucester. Morning verry foggy. Quaters at 3 bells A.M. A general overhauling of bags and marking clothing. Put down for small stores to day our Hospital stwerd were discharged for incompetancy. Another was

appointed in his place. Three men were sent to the Hospital. Dr. Fox left for
Boston. Quaters at 3 bells P.M. Our Master arrived to day this evening about
9½ Oclock. The schooner Annie ran into us. She struck us on our starboard
quater and lost her Jibboom. No damage to us.

> On Oct. 31, *The Gloucester Telegraph* noted that the "question of raising the
> men for the navy" was before the community and that public sentiment should
> be "fully alive to the importance of the work at hand." Said the *Telegraph*, "We
> trust that all hands will proceed to hurry forward the business of recruiting,
> and in thirty days, or less we trust the Niagara will have her full complement of
> men on board, ready to meet the highest expectations which the historic gal-
> lantry of our fishermen in the last war, has aroused throughout the country."[38]

SUNDAY NOV. 1ST 63

At anchor off Gloucester. This Morning clear and cold. To day there was A
fleet of about A hundred and fifty sails in the bay. Inspection at four bells.
Quaters at 3 bells P.M. This morning our steam conducters to the Ward
Room Registers burst.

MONDAY NOV. 2ND

At anchor off Gloucester. Quite cool. Quaters at four bells. We shipd two men
to day. Return of our Surgeon and cheif Engineer quaters at three bells. Our
chaplain sent aboard his baggage this evening received A letter from C.W.R.
Maild A letter to J. Fucher to Boston. Little cloudy.

TUESDAY NOV. 3RD

At anchor off Gloucester. Raining verry hard this morning, cleard off about
8 bells A.M. Quaters at 4 bells A.M. Received A letter from C.L.S. We shipd
one Landsman. We received orders to return to Boston. Arriveal of the Pilot
to take us up quaters at 3 bells P.M.

WENSDAY NOV. 4TH

At anchor off Gloucester. Day verry fine. Received A letter from New
Orleanes. Quaters at 3 bells. A number of visiters came on bord to day.
Quaters at 3 bells P.M.

THURSDAY NOV. 5TH

At anchor off Gloucester. Morning verry fine. Fire quaters at three bells.

Workmens on board repairing the heating apperratus. About 8 bells it commenced to blow verry heavely from the S.E. which lasted about four hours when it moderateed. Quaters at 2 bells P.M. This evening warm and cloudy.

FRIDAY NOV. 6TH

At anchor off Gloucester. Day verry fine. Qua[rters] at 3 bells Served our small stores. A number of visitores come on board to day. Quaters at 2 bells P.M.

SATURDAY NOV. 7TH

At anchor off Gloucester. Day verry fine. Quaters at 3 bells. Examination of bags. Discharges four men unfit for duty. We Shipd two men. Quaters at 2 bells. Write A letter to C.L. Smith. Men went ashore on Liberty. The Engineer stwerd was detected in bringing Liquor on board and was placed in confinement.

> The end of the liquor ration, or the "last call," was instituted by Asst. Secretary of the Navy Gustavus V. Fox on Aug. 31, 1862. "To quiet complaints about the action, the Navy compensated its sailors with an additional five cents a day in pay. Although based upon virtuous intent, ending the liquor ration . . . did not lead to better discipline."[39]

SUNDAY NOV. 8TH

At ancher off Gloucester. Day verry fine. Quaters at 4 bells. General inspections quaters at 2 bells P.M.

MONDAY NOV. 9TH

Off Gloucester. Quite cold. Quaters at 3 bells. Hears of A victory on the Rappehannoch. Sent A letter to C.W.R. Quaters at 2 bells. This Evening about 1 bell first watch it commenced snowing.

TUESDAY NOV. 10TH

Off Gloucester. It snow'd all night and until about four Oclock this evening still verry cloudy and freezeing. Ship'd two Men.

WENSDAY NOV. 11TH

Off Gloucester. Verry cold and blowing verry hard from S.W. Quaters at 3 bells A.M. and 2 bells P.M. arrival of our chaplain.

THURSDAY NOV. 12TH

Off Gloucester. More moderate. Quaters at 3 bells A.M. Ship'd one Man.
Quaters at 2 bells P.M.

FRIDAY NOV. 13TH

Off Gloucester. Day verry fine. Quaters at 3 bells. Ship'd one man. A summary
courts Martial convend at 6 bells to try Schreever for bringing Liquor on
board. A great maney visiters came on board. Quaters at 1 bell P.M.

SATURDAY NOV. 14TH

Off Gloucester. Quaters at 3 bells. Mark'd clothes with watch mark. Ship'd
four men. One of the Boat crew dezerted. Maild A letter to my Aunt. Quaters
at 1 bell P.M.

SUNDAY NOV. 15TH

Off Gloucester. Raining all day. We had serveace at four bells to day for the
first time.

> Donald Canney has written: "Prior to the war, culminating in the mid 1850s,
> there had been an extraordinary spiritual movement among the American
> sailors. Revival meetings and daily 'divine service' became staples on many
> vessels. One, the huge *Niagara*, had such a religious contingent that pews for
> hundreds were set up on her commodious decks and she came to be called
> 'The Gospel Ship.'"[40]

MONDAY NOV. 16TH

Off Gloucester. Morning verry fine. Quaters 3 bells A.M. Stations and
exercised in Looseing and Furling Sails. Ship'd two Men. Received A letter
from C.W.R. Maild one to the same. Quaters 1 bell P.M. Commence raining
at five bells.

TUESDAY NOV. 17TH

Off Gloucester. Raining all day and blowing verry hard from S.W. Ship'd
one man.

WENSDAY NOV. 18TH

Off Gloucester. Morning verry fine. Quaters at 4 bells. All hands to Muster.
Read the sentance of the court Martial. Three men for stealing were sentanced

to thirty days in Double Irons on bread and water and the loss of three months pay. Also the Engineers Stwerd for smugeling Liquor on board were sentanced to thirty days in Double Irons in bread and water and the loss of three months pay. About 12 Oclock it commenced to blow verry hard from S.W. Received A letter from C. Giles, W.H. Schenck, C. Brooks, T. Cowan. Answerd two. Put down for clothing quaters at 2 bells. My birthday.

THURSDAY NOV. 19TH

Off Gloucester. Verry fine day. Exercise at fire quaters. Also Exercise at looseing and furling Sails. Ship'd two men. Quaters at 1 bell.

FRIDAY NOV. 20TH

Off Gloucester. Day verry fine. Quaters at 3 bells. Shipd one Man. Quaters at 1 bell P.M. Shipd one Dog also one Cat.

SATURDAY NOV. 21ST

Off Gloucester. Raining all day. Quaters at four bells. Examination of bags. Received A letter from G.L.M. Our Lieut. ordered to the Minesota.

SUNDAY NOV. 22ND

Off Gloucester. Day verry fine. Quaters at four bells then Serveace. A verry good Sermon. Our Chaplain went ashore to hold serveace in Gloucester. Quaters at 1 bell P.M.

MONDAY NOV. 23RD

Off Gloucester. Day verry fine. Exercise in looseing and furling Sail. Quaters at 3 bells A.M. This Evening while furling Sails Henry Baxter Landsman fell from the top of the main Trysail to the deck and discolateed his shoulder. Ship'd one man. Quaters at 1 bell P.M.

TUESDAY NOV. 24TH

Off Gloucester. Raining all day. Quaters at 3 bells a.m. Ship'd one man.

WENSDAY NOV. 25TH

Off Gloucester. Fine day. Exercise in looseing and furling Sails. Quaters at 3 bell A.M. Shipd Six Men. Quaters at 1 bell P.M.

THURSDAY NOV. 26TH

Off Gloucester. Verry clear and cold. Quaters at 4 bells then Serveace, it being thanksgiveing day. A good many visiters come on board. Quaters at 1 bell P.M. Hears of A great victory by Grant over Bragg in Tenn.

FRIDAY NOV. 27TH

Off Gloucester. Verry cold. Quaters at 3 bells. Arriveal of Lieut. Commander Erbin and departure of Lieut Comman. Barnes. Quaters at 1 bell.

SATURDAY NOV. 28TH

Off Gloucester. Raining all day. Quaters at 3 bells. Put down for clothing. Shipd two men. Quaters at 1 bell P.M.

SUNDAY NOV. 29TH

Off Gloucester. Quite cold. Quaters at 4 bells. Serveace at 5 bells. Prayer at 1 bell P.M.

MONDAY NOV. 29TH [30TH]

Off Gloucester. Quaters at 3 bells. Exercise in looseing and furling sails. Shipd one man. Quaters at 1 bell P.M.

TUESDAY DEC. 1ST/63

Off Gloucester. Quater at 3 bells. Served out clothing. Went ashore and spend the evening. Verry cold. Received two papers from Boston.

WENSDAY DEC. 2ND

Off Gloucester. A heavey Gale. Blowing nearly all day. Quaters at 3 bells A.M. and 1 bell P.M.

On Dec. 2, *The Gloucester Telegraph* said of the ongoing difficulties confronted by the *Niagara* in the recruiting arena: "The trouble which the Navy Department is experiencing for want of seamen may be accounted for in this way. The landlords instead of endeavoring to ship men for the Navy, enlist them for the Army for the sake of getting the large bounties that are offered in that department of the service. The *Niagara*, now in our harbor, has succeeded in obtaining a considerable number of men but not as many as we had hoped she would obtain. It is, however, not altogether the fault of our citizens that she has not been more successful. As a general thing we have appreciated our duties to the government in this exigency but we lost time in providing ways and means for the accomplishment of our wishes and intentions. It would have been a proud day for this town if we had fully manned the ship for a cruise, with seamen enlisted at this port. A proper state of public feeling at the start would have turned the tide of men towards the ship rather than towards the railway trains, which have taken off at least one thousand able bodied and excellent sailors. We may yet learn that it is always best to launch an enterprise on the flood tide. There are other reasons which have operated to obstruct the course of enlistments here, which it will do no good to refer to in detail. The ship remains at anchor in our harbor and we hope to add still more to her company. But at any rate the Government will appreciate the honest effort which some of our fishing owners have made to meet public expectation."[41]

THURSDAY DEC. 3RD

Off Gloucester. Quaters at 3 bell A.M. Shipd two Men and two deserted.

FRIDAY DEC. 4TH

Off Gloucester. Fine day. Arrest the two Men who deserted yesterday. Received A letter from A.A. Jones.

SATURDAY DEC. 5TH

Off Gloucester. Shipd one man. Write home.

SUNDAY DEC. 6TH

Off Gloucester. Verry cold. Serveace at 5 bells. Prayer at 1 bell. Our Lieut's wife dined on board.

MONDAY DEC. 7TH

Off Gloucester. Verry cold. Received A letter from C.W.R. Maild A letter for home.

TUESDAY DEC. 8TH

Off Gloucester. One man deserted last night with bag and Hammock. Ship'd one man. Spent the Evening ashore.

WENSDAY DEC. 9TH

Off Gloucester. Verry windy and cold. Received A letter from Boston. Ship'd one man.

THURSDAY DEC. 10TH

Off Gloucester. Verry cold. The Themometer fell to 6 Degrees above Zero. Went on shore. Heard of the capture of the steamer Chesapeak by rebel Jrassingers of cape cod on the night of the 6th inst.

On this date, Dec. 10, Secretary of the Navy Welles instructs Comm. Craven to "proceed (to Pubnico Harbor) with the utmost dispatch and search the whole coast, and if (the captured U.S. steamer *Chesapeake* is) found in port call upon the British authorities to seize her."[42] Canney amplifies: "She [the *Niagara*] then was dispatched to Nova Scotia in search of the Confederate-held vessel *Chesapeake*," arriving Dec. 19 (as WBG noted in his entry of that date—though WBG states that the *Chesapeake* was captured by the *Ella & Anna*), "only after the vessel had been taken by the *Dacotah*."[43] According to *Civil War Day by Day*, "John C. Braine, leading (a) group of Confederate sympathizers, seized the Northern merchant steamer Chesapeake off Cape Cod" on Dec. 8.[44] WBG's version is confirmed by Cmdr. A. G. Clary of the *Dacotah*.[45]

FRIDAY DEC. 11TH

Off Gloucester. Verry cold. Went ashore. Receive sailing orders to cruise after the Chesapeak. Weigh'd anchor at 2 bells and started for Halifax N.S. About 4 bells exchange signals with the Ticonderoga.

Craven reported that 1:00 P.M., not two bells, was the actual time "when we sailed in search of the Chesapeake."[46] In reporting the sailing of the *Niagara*, *The Gloucester Telegraph* took on a somewhat apologetic tone in describing the difficulties she had experienced in recruiting men during her stay in Gloucester: "The 'Niagara' which has been lying in this harbor for nearly two months, sailed yesterday. She came here to add to her crew. Our citizens have exerted themselves to aid in the undertaking. About sixty men have been accepted and at least one hundred more would have gladly enlisted if the officers had chosen to receive ordinary seamen on board. Our recruiting officers were informed by the executive officer of the ship that able seamen only were needed, or at any rate, that boys were not wanted. It was therefore impossible to do more than has been done towards making up a crew for the frigate. . . . The officers of the Niagara, who had charge of the enlistment business, did not choose to wait for the development of the qualities needed, and therefore it was useless to send the men on board. As a community we have done our whole duty. We have paid money and have a fund in reserve devoted to naval enlistment. We appreciate our obligation to the country and before the Niagara came here we had sent 600 good men into the naval service, besides largely exceeding our full quota of soldiers for the army. The truth is, men for the navy are not easily obtained. The bounties paid for army recruits will attract seamen as well as landsmen, and it is not to be expected that individuals will hesitate in choosing between the army and navy while the advantage of enlisting in the army is so apparent, so far as money is concerned. The navy department has not had half a chance in conducting this war. But enough has been done already, with the resources at hand, to satisfy fair-minded that our naval affairs have been well and ably managed from the first moment of the opening of the rebellion.

"There is one other difficulty that we encountered in procuring seamen which we will mention. It is understood, and we believe rightly, that in Boston and New York men are enlisted in the navy for one year's service. This rule has not applied to the Niagara's crew, and enlistments for less than two or three years could not be effected. As to the matter of prize money the opinion prevails that the Niagara being destined for foreign service, will not be likely to afford much opportunity for captures. We give these statements by way of explanation for an apparent lack of enthusiasm among our fishermen to enter the government service. All considerate men will see the point."[47]

SATURDAY DEC. 12TH

Steering to the Eastward. Verry windy. Snowing all night and day. Set our fore and aft sails at 4 bells verry thick, At 9 bells set fore and main Topsails at five bells land reported on our port bow. We made it out to be Seal Island. Under close reef'd Topsails stood off to the so west.

SUNDAY DEC. 13TH

Change'd our course again to the Eastward with sail set makeing nine Knots. All hands call'd to shorten sail at five bells. Land reported at Six bells, ran in under steam and came to anchor of[f] Pubnico. Pilots came on board. Reported A steamer left thare three days before we arrive. Sent A boat ashore wich returnd without any tidings of the Pirats. Verry cloudy and windy.

MONDAY DEC. 14TH

Off Pubnico, blowing verry hard from the south west. Several visiters come on board. Quite foggy, fog cleard away about 3 bells P.M.

TUESDAY DEC. 15TH

Off Pubnico. Blowing A heavey gale from S.W. Two anchors down yesterday A Court Martial convened to try two men for desertion. The Court adjourned sine die at 1 Oclock. I was put on watch for two hours from 8 to 10 P.M. for punishment for sewing in the Pantry.

WENSDAY DEC. 16TH

Off Pubnico. Blowing verry hard from N.W. freezing all day. This evening A schooner came in from sea under close reef'd sails.

THURSDAY DEC. 17TH

Off Pubnico. Verry cold. The sea is less Boisterous. Sent A boat ashore at 6 bells. Returnd at 8 bells. Reported that the Cheasepeak is being blockaded

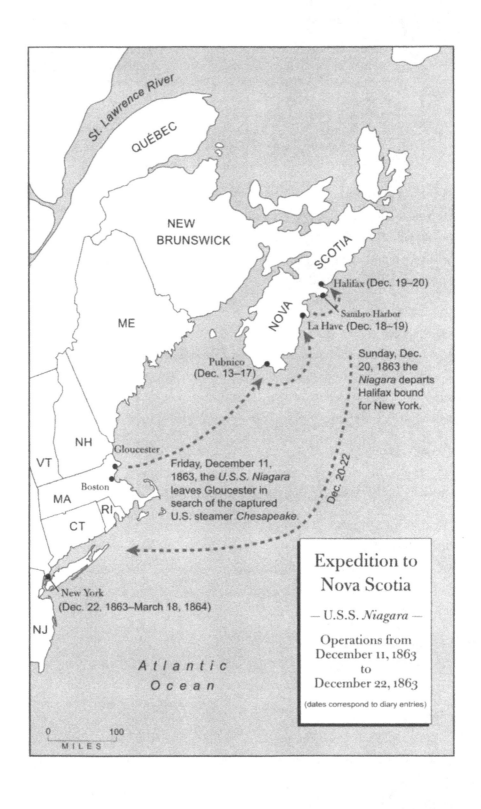

St. Lawrence River

QUÉBEC

NEW
BRUNSWICK

SCOTIA

Halifax (Dec. 19–20)

NOVA

Sambro Harbor
La Have (Dec. 18–19)

ME

Pubnico
(Dec. 13–17)

Sunday, Dec.
20, 1863 the
Niagara departs
Halifax bound
for New York.

NH

Gloucester

VT

Boston

Friday, December 11,
1863, the *U.S.S. Niagara*
leaves Gloucester in
search of the captured
U.S. steamer *Chesapeake*.

Dec. 20-22

MA

RI

CT

New York
(Dec. 22, 1863–March 18, 1864)

NJ

**Expedition to
Nova Scotia**

— U.S.S. *Niagara* —

Operations from
December 11, 1863
to
December 22, 1863

(dates correspond to diary entries)

*Atlantic
Ocean*

0   100
MILES

up the Lehave River by one of our Gun Boats. We got up anchor at 1 bell and started for the Lehave River makeing 9 knots after Night we reduced our speed to five Knots.

> Craven stated: "We were detained riding out a gale on a lee shore until the morning of the 17th instant. On that morning the gale abated, and communicating again with the shore learned that a steamer answering the description of the *Chesapeake* had passed by Yarmouth on the 12th instant, steering to the southward, and that on the same day she had entered the harbor of Shelburne, shipped four men, got on board 4 chaldrons of coals, and sailed the same day, steaming to the eastward. We also learned by a telegraphic dispatch that she (*Chesapeake*) was on the 17th instant at Le Have, blockaded by one of the gunboats. I immediately got underway."[48]

FRIDAY DEC. 18TH

We anchord off the Lehave River at 2 bells morning watch, snowing verry hard until Nine Oclock. Sent A boat ashore to make enquiries. The boat returnd with the tidings that the Chesapeak came in here on Tuesday night and left Wensday Morning. Also that A Gun Boat came in on Thursday Morning and saild Thursday Night. Blowing verry hard all day. We have two anchors down. They reported that Cheasepeak took in wood and ship'd some Men at 9 Oclock. More moderate.

> "At 5:15 a.m. of the 18th instant, in a blinding snowstorm, found my way in and anchored at the mouth of Le Have River. Sent Acting Master F.M. Green to the light-house on Ironbound Island, where he was informed by the light keeper that the *Chesapeake* had left the river on the morning of the 16th instant, following the next day by a gunboat, both steering to the eastward. Not feeling satisfied as to the truthfulness of this information, I delayed moving, intending to send boats in search of her up the river, but a gale coming on from the southeast I was compelled to let go a second anchor and start the engines to prevent being blown ashore."[49]

SATURDAY DEC. 19TH

Off Lehave. Call'd all hands at 8 bells a.m. got up anchors and started at 7 bells for Halifax. Ship rooling verry badly. About four bells pass'd A schooner with fore topmast carried away. Took A Pilot at 7 bells. Came to anchor in the Harbor off the citty at 3 bells. We found in the Harbor the Decotah, Ella & Anna, Cherokee, Ceres, also the Chesapeak. She was capturd by the Ella & Anna Friday Morning in the Harbor of Mud Hole and braught into Halifax.

Twelve of the Pirates were capturd on board. The others escaped. They ware takeen on shore and deliverd to the Athorities and the cheif one escaped from the Citty Athorities. She was demanded of the Athorities but they could not settle the affair until directed by thair Home Goverment. The Cheasepeak was coaling when she was capturd. After comeing to Ancher we sent A boat ashore to communicate with our Counsel. After the boat returnd we fired A salute of twenty-one Guns. This Evening all the other boats went to sea except the Ceres. After Night A boat with five Men pass'd around the Ship abuseing us for everry thing they could utter. The Commodore went on shore and returnd highly pleased with his visit to the Govinor in regard to the Cheasepeak. The statement of the arrest of twelve of the Pirates was eronious. Only three were arrested on bord of the steamer. There were twelve on shore at Sambro. The Athorities issued A warrent for thair arrest and three Poleicemen were sent down to arrest them but they being armed frighten'd off the Poleice the Goviner has promised to have them arrested at all Hazard.

> Canney erroneously states that it was the *Dacotah* that captured the Chesa-
> peake. WBG's account is confirmed by the commander of the *Dacotah* him-
> self, who reported on Dec. 18 that he had "made out two steamers in the har-
> bor of Sambro [Nova Scotia], steamed in to find the Chesapeake in possession
> of the U.S.S. Ella and Annie."[50]

SUNDAY DEC. 20TH

All hands were call'd this Morning at 8 bells. Weigh'd anchor and started from Halifax at 7½ Oclock for New York. We discharged the Pilot at 8½ Oclock. Snowing at the time quite hard. At 6 bells afternoon all hands were calld to Make sail, the wind being in our favor. Snow'd all day and night. Makeing 9½ Knots. Verry cold.

> On this day, Welles ordered Craven to "send all the vessels home and proceed
> in the Niagara to New York."[51] On Dec. 23, Craven reported: "After an ex-
> change of salutes and a night's rest in the quiet harbor of Halifax, at sunrise of
> the 20th instant we sailed for this [New York] harbor."[52]

MONDAY DEC. 21ST

While on the Eastern end of St. George Shoals we fell in with A schooner. Water Logg'd and abandond her Mainmast was carried away close by the deck. Foremast standing with shreeds of the jib hanging to the stays. She appeard to have had A deck Load of Lumber. About 1 hour after passing the wreck we saw A Brig to the Leward, it being about 6 bells A.M. Snowing alternately all day.

TUESDAY DEC. 22ND
On our way to New York. Verry fine day.

WENSDAY DEC. 23RD
About 5 Oclock A.M. we made Highland Lights and crossed the Bar at 7 bells. Came to anchor off the Citty at 4 bells A.M. There was in Port two Italian ships, one Rushan, one French. Our Comodore went ashore for orders. Moor'd Ship. One Masters Mate orderd to the Decotah. Received A mail, the first in thirteen days. Received A letter from Boston. Maild A letter to C.W.R. We saluteed the Admiral of the Yard with Fiften Guns. Verry cold. Freezeing all day.

THURSDAY DEC. 24TH
New York. Verry cold. Large Masses of Ice floating down the River. Received A letter from Giles. Maild A letter for Boston. Our Lieuts Wife dined abord. Departure of the Rushan Frigate.

FRIDAY DEC. 25TH
New York. More mild. Christmas day but no enjoyment. We received orders to proceed to Hampton Roads.

SATURDAY DEC. 26TH
New York. Preparc to coal ship. Went on shore. Went around in New York and Brooklyn. A great deal of Ice in the River.

NEW YORK MONDAY DEC. 28TH
Raining all day. Received A paper from A.A. Jones. Maild A letter to C.W.R. Still at anchor of the Batry.

TUESDAY DEC. 29TH
New York. A verry fine day. Loose'd sails this morning. One of our men by the name of Rollins died of consumption. His boddy was sent ashore for Interment. Two coal Bargees came alongside. We commence coaling ship at

1 bell P.M. I received A letter from A.A. Jones. We heard of an accident which happend to the Italian Iron Clad Frigate Re De Italia. She ran ashore near the Highlands. We received orders to go to her assistance.

WENSDAY DEC. 30TH

We coald ship all night and got under way about 4 bells and started for the scene of the disaster. Before we left we sent all of our sick to the Hospital Some thirty in number. When we got as far out as the Narrows we met the Re D. Italia comeing in in tow of three steam Tugs. We returnd to the Citty and anchord off the Batry. We being two close in we ware oblige'd to anchor farther off.

THURSDAY DEC. 31ST

This Morning two coal Bargees came alongside and we again commenced coaling. About 8 bells it commenced snowing quite hard. It snowd and raind alternately all day and night. We coald until 10 Oclock P.M. when we were obliged to Knock off and the account of the Storm. It blew verry hard from S.E. the Old year of (1863) went out Furiously as if it was angry with all the world because it had finished the time alloted to it. Sooner or lateer we must follow.

FRIDAY JAN. THE 1ST 1864

To day the first day of the new year (1864). The Morning quite foggy. It cleard off about 10 Oclock. Growing colder. About Eleven Oclock orders came for us to transfer all of our crew to the "Har[tford]" and for this ship to proceed to the Navy Yard for some alteration in our Batry. I was musterd this Evening among the other crew but was orderd to remain with the Ship. One man received some severe injuries by one of the Capstan bars flying out and strikeing him. Another fell down A scrittle and broke some of his ribs and another deserted from one of the boats.

SATURDAY JAN. THE 2ND/64

This is decideedly the coldest day of the season. The Themometer fell to 8 Degreess above Zero. A part of the North River was frozen over Ice. Verry plentiful in the River. This Morning the Powder boat came along side and we proceed to discharge our Powder and at 5 bells we weigh'd anchor to proceed to the Navy Yard but the wind being so unfavorable and after several attempts to get the Ship Round faild we were obliged to come to ancher again in the same place. It is a shame to the country that we laying in the Harbor of New York and have been three days without A mail. Such is the regulation of uncle sam to his children. Oh for A mail, A mail. A Kingdom for A Mail.

SUNDAY JAN. 3RD

Last night we received orders to transfer A part of our crew to the Hartford. This Morning I was told to get ready to be transferd to day. Then after I got all ready then they said they would not send me. Two hundred and fifty (250) of our crew were transferd to the Hartford. Out of nine boys in the Ward Room six (6) were sent away. Two steamers came along side at 7 bells. The Men were Musterd then transferd to the Steamers and left for the "Hartford." After the departure of the men three Tugs came along side. We weighd anchor and once more attemp'd to get into the yard with more success than yesterday. We succeeded in geting up to the yard but got aground about fifty yards from the warf. The Italian Frigate "Re De Italia" also came up to the yard to go into the Dry Dock. Mail A letter to C.W.R.

MONDAY JAN. 4TH

This Morning all hands were calld at 2 Oclock it being high water and succeeded in geting alongside the ward. We discharge'd our shot and shells at 4 Oclock P.M. Workmen came on board and commenced work clearing away to take out the Eleven inch Guns. I went ashore in Brooklyn and calld on Mrs. Culbreth. On my return I found Eighty of our crew that was transferd were returnd among them five of the Ward Room Boys. Write A letter to J.M.

> In a statement taken down by a scribe of the Charles W. Carroll Post 144, GAR, after the Civil War, WBG said of this period in New York "Here important changes and repairs were made in the vessel, twenty eleven inch guns being removed to reduce top heaviness."[53]
>
> Matilda Culbreth, a former slave, was widely known for her activities on behalf of blacks.
>
> The *Niagara* was ordered to search for the raider *Tallahassee*, "but at this point her immense armament betrayed her. She attempted to stand out of the harbor under steam against force 6 winds. Her log states 'The wind being too strong to handle the ship [we] returned to anchorage.' At precisely this point, Secretary Welles' telegram ordering the removal of her gundeck battery arrived and the guns were unshipped immediately."[54]

TUESDAY JAN. 5TH

Snow'd all day. Commenced to take out our Guns. Write A letter home.
Departure of the "Hartford."

WENSDAY JAN. 6TH

Brooklyn Navy Yard. Verry cold. Giveen charge of the Wine Mess Ward Room.

THURSDAY JAN. 7TH

At Brooklyn Navy yard. Takeing out guns. While removeing one of our guns
this morning one of the straps gave way and the Gun fell and struck one of the
workmen belonging to the yard and injured him so severely that he died in two
hours after. Maild A letter to C.W.R. About two bells it commenced snowing.

FRIDAY JAN. 8TH

It snow'd all night. This Morning the Snow was three inches deep. Went
ashore. Call'd on Mrs. Culbreth and Mrs. Hoagland. Write home. Two Men
deserted.

SATURDAY JAN. 9TH

At the Navy Yard. Verry cold. Buisey takeing out Guns. One man deserted.

SUNDAY JAN. 10TH

At the Navy Yard. Write one letter to Boston and one to New Bedford.
Indulge all day in thoughts of those far away and sigh for A letter. I hope
some kind friend will send me one.

MONDAY JAN. 11TH

To day we finished takeing out our Guns and shot and shell. The Carpenters
are buisey prepareing us for sea. Received A letter from J.M. Answerd it also.
Wrote one to C.W.R. To day more moderate than it have been for several days.

TUESDAY JAN. 12TH

The workmen are buisey engaged on the ship. We sent A draft of twelve men
to the Gaurdo to day and received fifty repentant Rebels in return. They all
have takeen the oath of Aleigeance and now will fight for uncle sam. Had an
interview with Mr. Neff. Heard of the arrival of Mr. O.S. Baldwin. Write to
Mr. C. Mallett. They commenced corking the Decks.

WENSDAY JAN. 13TH

A verry fine day. They buisey at work geting us ready for sea.

THURSDAY JAN. 14TH

Still buisey at work. Hurrying us up for sea. I received A letter from C.W.R.
One from C.G. and one from Aunt. I went ashore. Write to C.W.R.

FRIDAY JAN. 15TH

Raining this morning. Received A letter from C.M. Went ashore. Visited Mrs.
A.E.H. Write to C.G.

SATURDAY JAN. 16TH

Verry fine day. Received A letter from C.W.R. Also one from J.M. Went ashore
in afternoon. Served out Grog Money. We received $400 all round.

SUNDAY JAN. 17TH

In afternoon went ashore to the Howard House. Saw Benjamin Grier and
William McLauren. Went to Flett St. M.E. Church in company with Mrs.
A.E.H. Saw in church M.E.W. much to my surprise. Arrival of the
Vanderbilt at the yard.

MONDAY JAN. 18TH

Verry wet. Went ashore to New York. Calld on Mrs. A.E.H. and went in
company with her to Mrs. W. Heard from home. Arriveal of Ensign
Harrington.

TUESDAY JAN. 19TH

Received A letter from Boston. Shipd A new Master at Arms. Wrote to G.W.P.

WENSDAY JAN. 20TH

To day all were stationd at thair Guns. Received A letter from C.W.R. Shipd
A new steward, also A Ward Room Boy. Wrote to C.W.R.

THURSDAY JAN. 21ST

Received A letter from H.L. Brissar. Went ashore to N.Y. Visited Mrs. L.
We commenced takeing in coal and stores. H.L.B. co. A. 5th Regmt. Mass
Cavalry.

FRIDAY JAN. 22ND

Takeing in stores all day. Wrote to H.L.B., also to J.M. Our new steward came on board and reported for duty.

SATURDAY JAN. 23RD

Takeing in stores all day. Went ashore in the afternoon. Saw Abram Davis of Wilmington, now of the U.S.S. Vanderbilt.

SUNDAY JAN. 24TH

Still at the yard. A verry fine day. Ok for A walk ashore.

MONDAY JAN. 25TH

Takeing in stores all day. Afternoon went ashore. Visited Mrs. L. Staid ashore all night. Read A letter from Aunt Elsie.

TUESDAY JAN. 26TH

Takeing in stores all day and replaceing shots in our lockers. Received A letter from H.L.B.

WENSDAY JAN. 27TH

Takeing in stores and shot. Went ashore. Heard from home through M.E.L. Heard that S.Spicer was on board of the Colorado.

THURSDAY 28TH

Commenced coaling. The workmens hard at work fiting us out for sea. 1st asst. Surgeon Wells detachd.

FRIDAY JAN. 29TH

Weather verry fine. Coaling. Received A letter from Cousin M.C.G. Maild A letter for C.W.R. and one to H.L.B.

SATURDAY JAN. 30TH

Raining all day. Went ashore in afternoon.

SUNDAY JAN. 31ST

This Morning Dr. Abott arrived releiveing Dr. Wells. Visited New York. Raining all day.

MONDAY FEBUARY 1ST

Received A letter from A.A.J[ones, his cousin]. Raining verry hard all day. Went on shore in afternoon. Remaind all night.

TUESDAY FEB. 2ND

This morning I arose by the sound of the morning gun and returnd on bord. Received A letter from A.A.J. A verry fine day.

WENSDAY FEB. 3RD

Received A letter from C.W.R. They buisey at work painting and coaling Ship.

THURSDAY FEB. 4TH

To day after finishing coaling we hauld out from the ward and let the sloop of War. Brooklyn hauld into the warf. Went ashore in the Afternoon. Shipd A new Hospital steward.

FRIDAY FEB. 5TH

To day we holy stoned decks and moved all the Mess things apon the Main deck from the Birth deck. Wrote A letter to C.W.R.

SATURDAY FEB. 6TH

Verry fine weather. Went ashore in afternoon. Had some Pictures takeen.

SUNDAY FEB. 7TH

To day verry fine. Went over to New York. Saw John Howe. Returnd on board about 3 bells.

MONDAY FEB. 8TH

A verry fine day. Went ashore in afternoon. Visited M.E.L. Returnd on board Tuesday morning.

TUESDAY FEB. 9TH

Day verry fine. A little colder. Received A letter from J. Hall on board of the Receiving Ship Alegahny at Baltimore. This evening about 7 bells Richard Tilghman (signal Quater Master) fell over board from the gangway plank betwen us and the Brooklyn and was Drownd before he could be rescued. The diseease was A native of New Bedford Mass.

WENSDAY FEB. 10TH / 64

This Morning was verry cold and they was plenty of Ice. We drag'd for the boddy of Tilghman but without success. Wrote A letter to C.W.R. and one to J.H. Received one from my cousin M.G.

THURSDAY FEB. 11TH

A verry fine day. Went ashore in afternoon. Visited M.E.L.

FRIDAY FEB. 12TH

This morning we hauld ahead then along side of the Brooklyn one man was caught attempting to desert.

SATURDAY FEB. 13TH

A verry fine day. Went ashore. Visited A.E.H. Received A letter from G.W.P. Also one from C.G. Wrote one to C.W.R.

SUNDAY FEB. 14TH

St. Valentine's day. Quite windy. Went ashore in the Evening.

MONDAY FEB. 15TH

To day quite warm. I returnd on board at 3 bells. Went ashore to New York. Met M.E.L. on Broadway. Draw'd ($10.00) one of the W.R.B. was punishd for breaching his liberty. Our Mariens went ashore in full dress to attend the Funeral of Comodore McChinsy.

TUESDAY FEB. 16TH

The weather growing colder graduly. After supper I went ashore and had A gay time. It snowd several times during the day.

WENSDAY FEB. 17TH

This Morning is verry cold. The Themometer fell to 8 degrees above Zero. Cold. Verry cold.

THURSDAY FEB. 18TH

To day colder still. The Themometer stood at daylight four Degrees below Zero. Received A letter from C.W.R. and one from A.A.Jo. Went over to York in afternoon. Heard that George L.M. has joined the 5th Mass Cav.

FRIDAY FEB. 19TH

Still verry cold. Maild A letter to C.W.R. and one to my Nephew. Heard that war has brokeen out in Europe on the Holsteine question. The Prushen and Austrien nine thousand strong defeated by the Danes two thousand strong.

SATURDAY FEB. 20TH

To day quite cold. Received A letter from Mrs. H. went on shore in Afternoon. Visited Mrs. Culbreth. Two of our Ensign's Messers Bridgeman and Barker were detach'd from this ship and orderd to the Paciffice squadron.

SUNDAY FEB. 21ST

A verry fine day. We are still along side the warf under the shears. All the work is completeed and we only wants A crew to be ready for sea.

MONDAY FEB. 22ND

To day is like spring. Maild A letter To C.W.R. and one to Mrs. H. Went ashore in afternoon. There was A grand Parade in Brooklyn in honor of Washington's Birth day. Visited Mrs. L. Mr. Dana detachd

TUESDAY FEB. 23RD

Verry warm. Still at the yard. Hears that we are to haul out tomorrow. Received A letter from A.H.G. Last night two Men deserted and to night tow ware captured while attempting to desert.

WENSDAY 24TH

This morning we hauld off from the Brooklyn and again commenced the use of boats to get ashore. Also two more of our Ensigns have been detach'd and A draft of fifty men orderd to the Gun boat "Wattree" at the Washington Navy yard.

THURSDAY FEB. 25TH

This Morning all hands ware cald at 3 bells. After breakfast was over we hauld A little farther of then the draft for the "Glauceus" was musterd and after signing thair accounts they left for thair ship. Then the draft for the "Watree" ware musterd and sign'd thair accounts. They left the ship about 5 bells for Washington whare they will join thair vessel. It commenced raining about 8 bells.

FRIDAY FEB. 26TH

This morning Driziling all the morning until about 11 Oclock when it commenced snowing. Maild A letter to C.W.R. It snowd until about 4 Oclock when it cleard off. Quite cold.

SATURDAY FEB. 27TH

To day verry fine. One Lieut (Phoenix) and one Master (Kimball) reported to day for duty. Received A letter from C.W.R. Also read A letter from G.W.T. from Wilmington. Went ashore in the afternoon. Staid all night.

SUND[A]Y FEB. 28TH

I returnd on board this Morning. A verry fine day. Wrote five letters. One to C.W.R., W.H.S., A.A.J., H.L.B., J.M.

MONDAY FEB. 29TH

This Morning raining. Maild my letters. Went on shore in the afternoon. Visited Benjamin Grair and Wm McLauren. Remaind ashore in afternoon.

TUESDAY MARCH THE 1ST/64

I returnd on bord this Morning at 6 bells. All right. Dr. Fox returnd from Boston. He is Detach'd from the "Niagara" and orderd to the "Minesota" as fleet surgeon of the North Atlantic Squadron. It Began to snow about 7½ Oclock and continued to snow all day. Our Galley chimney took fire this morning and there was considerable commotion among the Men extinguishing it.

WENSDAY MARCH 2ND

This morning clear and cold. Received A letter from G.L.M. containing one from home bearing date Jan. 16th. All well. They received one from me. This is the second one that I have received.

THURSDAY MARCH 3RD

A verry fine day. We are still lying off the Yard uncertain what is to be done with us. Unbend sails.

FRIDAY MARCH 4TH

A fine clear day. Went ashore. Received A letter from C.W.R. Heard of the arrival at Cambridge of Edger Miller. Visited Mrs. A.E.H. Wrote to G.P.R.

SATURDAY MARCH 5TH

A verry fine day. To day I finish'd packing up Dr. Fox then took some of his
things to the steamer Newbern. In the Afternoon I took the remainder of his
things to the Astor house. I then took A stroll up Broadway. Departure of the
20th Regmt of U.S. (colard) Volunteers, the first colard Regement raised in
New York pronounce by all to be A splendid Regement. Recvd A letter from
H.L.B. one one from A.A.J. and one from A.E.H. Remain ashore all night.

"The 20th U.S. Colored Infantry, raised throughout the state of New York, pa-
raded through the streets of New York City, . . . thousands of people, both
white and black, lined the avenues to cheer these blacks in Union blue. In part
the draft had made the enlistment of black soldiers more acceptable to whites,
because blacks filled manpower quotas as did whites. But there was more to it
than that. Whites had come to realize that these one thousand black soldiers
were fighting for the same government and causes as were white troops, trying
in some small way to help win the war."[55]

On March 12, *The Anglo-African* described the events of March 5 by noting
that 200,000 were honoring the black regiment. The subheadline read: "A Partial Atonement for the Outrages of July" [the New York draft riots]: "March,
5th, 1864, was a great day to the colored citizens of New York—one long to be
remembered—a joyous day also to thousands of those of our white fellow-
citizens who delight in doing honor to the brave, regardless of color or clime. It
was the occasion of the reception and departure of the Twentieth Regiment
U.S. Colored Troops. Never before had we, or even 'the oldest inhabitant,' witnessed such a glorious demonstration. It seemed that New York, for once, was
anxious to acknowledge the manhood of her black sons, and to give them such
an ovation as their loyalty and bravery entitled them to. The wealthy merchant
vied with the humble employee in doing honors—the magnificently attired and
accomplished wife of the millionaire shared alike the joyous feelings of the most
tattered pauper. The aristocrat and plebeian were one that day."[56]

SUNDAY MARCH 6TH

To day verry fine (yesterday it raind). To day the Dr. took final leave of the
ship. I Know that I have lost A good Friend. Wrote A letter to C.W.R.
Yesterday two steamers ran into us but did no damage of any magnetude.

MONDAY MARCH 7TH

A verry fine day. This Morning the steamer "Agusta" ran into us and carried
away our spanker boom. Hauld A little farther off from the shears.

TUESDAY MARCH 8TH

To day A verry fine day. Went ashore in the Afternoon. Remain all night.

WENSDAY MARCH 9TH

This Morning I returnd on board at five bells. Found that a draft of one
hundred men (Rebs) came on board last evening. Also that they had up steam
ready to move the ship out from the yard after all things were ready. At ten
Oclock two Tugs came along side and we moved out from the yard after
hauling in almost every direction. We came to anchor of Wall street Ferry
about two Oclock we then Moor'd ship. We are again settled until the next
ordr comes from Washington.

THURSDAY MARCH 10TH

To day A verry fine day. There is A Rushan Frigate at the warf A short
distance from us with an unpronounceable name. We can now see A great deal
that is transpireing in the Harbor. Received A letter from G.P.R.

FRIDAY MARCH 11TH

To day verry fine. We took in our store of shots and shells and sharpnell. In
the Evening I went ashore and pass'd throug[h] some of the wealthey streets
of Brooklyn. I calld apon Mrs. C then I went to Plymouth Church (Rev. H.W.
Beecher). Listend to A verry good Lecture by George Thompson of England.
I remaind ashore all the night.

> *The Anglo-African* printed a letter from Rollin Brown, of Manchester, Eng., dated
> Jan. 22, 1864, urging black Americans to give Thompson, "the uncompromising
> champion of the negro in England, and the warm friend and earnest advocate of
> every movement which tends to our elevation," an enthusiastic reception. Brown
> was sure that Thompson would "receive a very different reception from what
> greeted him on his two previous visits. He is acknowledged as one of the most elo-
> quent champions of freedom in this country, and as such deserves to be especially
> received by the negroes in every town and city which he may happen to visit."[57]

SATURDAY MARCH 12TH

I returnd on board at 7½ Oclock. A verry fine day. We Holy stoned both
decks and otherwise regulate the ship. All hands ware station to thair
respective Devissions. In the Evening we ware call'd to Quaters for the first
time in two Months.

SUNDAY MARCH 13TH

To day A splendid day. Quaters at 2 bells. About 8 bells it commenced to
Rain and blow'd verry hard. It lasted about an hour, when it cleard of[f] as

clear as it was before. 8 bells this evening we had quite an excitement in consequence of the Masters Mates Store Room takeing fire from A light left burning in it by one of the boys. As we are to have A party tomorrow we are buisey prepareing for it. The Offercers will enjoy themselves but the men cannot even get ashore.

MONDAY MARCH 14TH

To day was A lovely day. The Powder boat came along side about 9 Oclock and we commenced to take in Powder. As we intended to have company to day I was obliged to go to New York after some of the Indespenciables. As I was leaveing the Ship the Band from the "North Carolina" came on board. I returnd about 12 Oclock to find quite A number of Ladies assembled and Danceing goin on. We now made preperation for the Luncheon wich pass'd off finely, when Danceing was again resumed wich lasted til four when the Band left. The Company remaind later and the last did not get away until about five. So end our trouble of to day. I received A letter from Mr. & Mrs. Hall. Quite well. The Water boat came alongside and we took aboard A supply of the chrystal licquoir.

TUESDAY MARCH 15TH

This Morning was clouded and quite cold. About Eleven Oclock it commenced to rain then it changed to snow, it snow'd about 2 hours when it finealy cleard off I went ashore and went to A concert (at fleet st. church) by Maddam Greenfeild (the Black Swan). I visited Mrs. C. and Mrs. L. I accompany'd Mrs. H from the Concert. Quite cold. I remaind ashore all night.

> "The Black Swan" was Elizabeth Taylor-Greenfield, born in Natchez, Miss., who was brought to Philadelphia as a child and who had been singing in public since 1851. In 1853 and 1854, she sang in England and was heard there by Harriet Beecher Stowe. After her English tour, she returned to Philadelphia, to "concertize" and teach until her death in 1867.[58]

WENSDAY MARCH 16TH

This Morning I went to the supply store and got our stores then came down to the warf to return on board here. I took an unintentional bath. The Ladder that we had placed alongside of the warf for our conveineance of geting in and out of our boats, the Ladder had become coated with Ice, and as I descended

the Ladder to the boat, I slip'd from the Ladder into the River. I was rescued
by the boats crew. It was verry cold and my face and clothes becamed coated
with Ice. I soon got on board and changed my clothes, in the Evening I felt
quite unwell from the effect of my bath. I received A letter from C.W.R.

THURSDAY MARCH 17TH

To day being St. Patricks day thare is lively times among the Irish portion of
our crew. Orders came on board for the ship to be readay to proceed to sea in
search of the Italian ship of the Seine "Re Galantuhomo" [*Re Galantuomo*]
reported to have been passd in A sinking condition on the 7th inst. We
commenced preperations accordingly we began to bend on sail and unmoor
ship, also took aboard A supply of wood, also got up steam and otherwise
prepared for sea. Wrote to C.W.R.

> According to the *New York Times*, the *Niagara* departed with only one-fourth
> of her full complement, and a large number of the crew were "inexperienced
> landsmen and boys." When she returned from this journey about 100 of the
> crew were on the sick list.[59]

FRIDAY MARCH 18TH

All hands ware calld at 3 bells, after takeing breakfast, they commenced to
bend on sails and got up the Port Anchor. Took abord our stores. The Pilot
came on board about 11 Oclock. At 1½ Oclock we commenced to take up the
starbord anchor. James Thompson was discharged, his time haveing expired.
We secured ancher and started for sea about 2½ Oclock. After passing Sandy
Hook we passd several vessels inward bound. About five P.M. we discharge'd
the Pilot. We now are one more on the boundless deep, blowing quite fresh
the ship rools heavaly. The greater portion of our Crew being Landsmen's
on thair first cruise thare is A large number of them sea sick. You can see
them trying to get forward by crawling and helping each other. They do not
like thair first feelings of A seafareing. After Night we set our foretopmast
staysail fore and mainsail and Foretopsail. Makeing ten knots our cours lay
to the Eastward.

SATURDAY MARCH 19TH

Not blowing as strong as yesterday. Steering E.N.E about ten Oclock A.M.
pass'd A sail in our starboard beam. We now set our Fore and Main

Degalantsails and all our Fore and Aft sails except the Spanker. 20 minutes
to 1 Oclock spoke the Ship Flora, Southard of and from Boston for New
Orleans. At 1 Oclock A sail reported on our Port bow. Pass'd the Sail (A Brig)
at 6 Oclock. Took in sail. Steering at night E.N.E.

SUNDAY MARCH 20TH

Quite moderate. Wind ahead until after 12 Oclock when it hauld on our Port
Quater. Set all our squaresails makeing about 5 knots pass'd a Barque to the
Leeward at sunset another sail on our Port Bow. About 8 bells took in sail
about 11 Oclock pass'd some heavy Spars.

MONDAY MARCH 21ST

The sea quite calm. The ship clouded and pleasant. Our course lay E.S.E.
About 9 Oclock made out A steamer on our starboard bow. We gave chase but
she ran away from us. Ship rooling heavaly.

TUESDAY MARCH 22ND

Verry cloudy. Our Course lay to the S.E. It tried to rain several times during
the day. We only carried our Fore Trysail and Foretopmast stay Sail. Ship
rooling verry heavaly.

WENSDAY MARCH 23RD

Verry cloudy with strong winds from South west. About 4 bells A.M. it
commenced to rain verry hard. We could not stow our Hammocks in the
Nettings. Sea runing verry high, the blow increasees to A gale, under double
reef Main Top Sail, ship'd several sea's over our bow. I[t] was realy amuseing
to see the Landsmans trying to keep thair feet. Manay A one sigh for thair
home they have left to become A sailor. The Gale increasees.

> In describing this journey—it was characterized as a "Perilous Voyage" in the
> headlines—the *New York Times* noted that "very severe weather [was experi-
> enced] the whole time." In respect to March 23, specifically, the paper de-
> scribed the *Niagara*'s situation as "appalling": "The whole of the day was ex-
> ceedingly rough; a severe rainstorm and a heavy gale."

THURSDAY MARCH 24TH

Blowing furiously from S.W. last night about 11 Oclock shipd A tremendious
sea wich carried away two of our Port waist boats. (3rd and 6th Cutters) filled

the Steerage and Engine room with watter. Set the Fore Topmast Staysail and
Fore sail (close Reef'd) the Comodore at the wheel. About 1 Oclock ship'd
another heavey sea, we ship'd several until after daylight when it moderateed A
little but still blowing A gale. One of our Coal heaveers was severely injurd last
night by the coal falling apon him. At ten Oclock steering E.S.E. We securd the
remaining boats by putting top liffts to the Davidts. To day we sent down our
main Degallant Yard and Mast, in Lowering the mast it was accidentally
brokeen. In the afternoon we shook the reef out of our Foresail and set the
Foretopsail. We took the Sun at noon and found that we was A great distance
out of our course. This Evening about 6 bells our Main Trysail stay parted.
The wind is more moderate but A verry heavey choping sea is running. Our
course lay S.S.E. We lost one of our 12 lb boat Howitzer and had A general
smash up of carragees Halyard racks our Main Deck wet Fore and Aft and all
our Main Deck hatches batten'd down steering at night East by North.

> The *New York Times* report continues: "About 11 P.M., the storm increased,
> and the gale assumed still greater violence; the waves were mountains high, the
> ship rolled franticly and labored heavily. In the middle watch the scene on this
> vessel beggars description; cutlasses, mess-chests, muskets, and, in fact, every
> movable thing were tossing about the decks promiscuously, and it required
> much courage to pass from one part of the ship to the other. At 1½ A.M., her sit-
> uation was so critical that the officers deemed it necessary to call all hands. At
> this time, the vessel was shipping heavy seas, and the main deck had some four
> feet of water upon it. This immense body of water would roll from side to side,
> carrying all with it; it had washed the ashes in the bilges, which rendered the
> pumps useless, and all momentarily expected it would extinguish the fires;
> two of her boats, the third and sixth cutters, were torn from their davits and
> carried away by the angry sea; for a while, her situation seemed utterly hope-
> less; at each roll of the ship her lower yard-arms dipped the water. But even
> more was to be endured, as two of the guns were broken adrift by the great vi-
> olence of the winds and water, were rolling about the deck, and all were fear-
> ful of being crushed; great apprehensions were felt lest they would break
> down the engine hatch, and be precipitated upon the engine. At the risk of
> their lives, some noble fellows succeeded in lashing the guns fast; the gun-car-
> riages were mashed to pieces. After hours of danger and suffering, and by the
> energetic and untiring exertions of both officers and crew, the hatches were
> battened down, the ship rid of much water, all hands made sail, and the *Niag-
> ara* safely rode the storm, but with a great amount of damage to the vessel.
> About daylight the morning of the 24th, one watch was relieved, and the fury
> of the storm was somewhat abated."

FRIDAY MARCH 25TH

A verry fine day light wind with A heavy sea running we send down Fore
Degallant yard and mast. Still steering E. by N. We took soundings to day at
11 Oclock and obtaind 45 Fathoms and again at 1 Oclock and we also got 45
Fathoms. We have been on the Banks of Newfoundland for the last three days
steering at night E.S.E. we also sent down to day our Mizzen Degallant Yard
and Mast, heavey clouds riseing all as around the horrizon wich betokeens
another storm.

SATURDAY MARCH 26TH

Cloudy with A slight Drizzle of rain, verry light wind and A heavey sea
running steering E.S.E. about ten Oclock we changed our course N.W.
steering homeward. It was reported that we pass'd an Iceberg last night but
I did not have an opportunity of seeing it being asleep at the time raining
verry hard all day carrying to night our Foresail, Foretopsail, Foretopmast
Staysail, Foretrysail and Main Topsail.

SUNDAY MARCH 27TH

The Morning was verry fine until about 10 Oclock when commenced to rain
quite hard we steering to the N.W. with all sail set until about 7 bells P.M.
when A sail was reported on our Port beam, the wind blowing from that
direction we ware obliged to furl sail in order to give chase, but night comeing
on we lost sight of the stranger. We again changed our course so as to get out
Fore and Aft sails to bear and stood on our course Homeward. Some of the
Boy's reported A Whale this afternoon but I did not get A sight.

MONDAY MARCH 28TH

This Morning cloudy and raining with A fresh breeze from the Eastward. We
avarage'd last night Eleven Knots, the wind increaseing and at 12 Oclock we
ware makeing 14 Knots. We carried all sail up to 1 Oclock when became
necessary to take in our Foretopmast staysails and to take A double reef in our
Main and Foretopsails, the wind at this time increaseing to A Gale and the Sea
running verry high at 3 Oclock P.M. our Forestaysail was carried away, when it
became necessary to take in all sail except the Fore and Maintopsails. We ware
making at this time 15 knots with her Engine stop'd, about two bells we made

A schooner on our Lee bow. We pass'd close by him but could not speak him on account of the Gale the "Niagara" pass'd him as if he was standing still. We now began to ship seas, as night comes on the Waves began to Mount higher about 5 bells our Main Topsail gave away. All the evening we stood on our course before the wind, under sail alone, sailing faster by five knots than we could steam, but the Gale has help'd us on. We tried to furl our Foresail but we only could get it clewd up and let it remain.

All last night we went before the gale under double reefd Foretopsail and fore storm Staysail. Our Main Topsail has blown to ribbons, also our Foresail. The Gale still blows fresh and the seas running verry high. We Ship'd several through the night and one sea fill'd the Ward Room with Water. I have got duck'd awfully last night. It was worth something to be apon the Deck, although thare is so much danger in A storm, thare is something verry sublime in one, to hear the roar of the storm, the hissing of the Waves, the whistling of the Rigging and the Cannon like report of the torn sail and above all this the stern word of Command and the shrill sound of the Boatswain's Pipe all adds to the granduer of the scene, for thare is something grand in A storm. All night with eager eyes both Offercers and Men pace'd the Deck watching our Foretopsail feeling in A measure of secure as long as we could carry Sail at all, it has stood through the night. Thare is no sign of the storm abateing, all the Galley fire is out, and nothing to Eat is the cry, and almost nothing to wear on account of the Water. Shine out fair sun and smote the Waves that we may proceed on our course and all be saved. It continued to blow until about 3 Oclock in the Afternoon when it moderated enough to enable us to send Men aloft to remove the remainder of our Main Topsail and to set A new one in its Place. Our course lay at night S.W. by W. After the sail was secured and spred to the breeze Grog was served out to all the Seamen's wich was takeen with A relish.

> Here is how the *New York Times* described this second storm: "On the night of the 28th, in lat. 42°, Ion. 53°, the *Niagara* again experienced a severe storm of hail, rain and sleet, and an intensely violent gale, and but for having a fair wind it would have been more terrible than the one above described; the vessel shipped heavy seas over her gangways, and the violence of the waves were such that some of her ports were stove in; nearly all her sails were literally torn

in shreds, and flying at the mercy of the winds; at this time the vessel had all canvas spread, was running before the wind, which as it sent the info to New York made all hands feel cheerful."[60]

WENSDAY MARCH 30TH

The sun rose clear this Morning but it was not long before it hid itself behind the murky clouds that obscured the horrizon at this time and we had alternately shunshine and rain during the day. We removed the remains of our Foresail and made everrything snug to day Grog Money was served out to all hands. I took up A subscription to assist in sending A News Paper (The Anglo Affrican) to the colard soldiers of the Army of the United States. [This subscription is acknowledged in "Three Cheers for the Boys of the Niagara!" *The Anglo-African*, April 9, 1864.] Verry little sea runing but it seems as it the ship has learnt to Rool so well that she cannot stop Rooling and tis with some difficulty that you can keep things in thair placees. We had Fair wind until late in the Evening when the wind showd A disposition to change and for some time it did not blow from any perticular direction until 8 Oclock when it settled dead ahead when we ware obliged to take in all sail.

> "On the morning of the 20th [sic] the *Niagara* presented a sorry picture on deck. On the 30th every one on board was pleased to see the sunshine, the first since the ship left port. On the days succeeding the trying scenes described the Chaplain summoned all hands to render thanks for their safe delivery from the very jaws of death; this was indeed a solemn time; the officers, the hardy sons of Neptune, young and old, all devoutly united in gratitude to the Almighty for His merciful protection while the storm-king reigned with such fearfulness. Indeed it seems almost a miracle that this ship has returned, or that one lives to tell the tale. The terrible scenes through which she and her noble crew have passed cannot be adequately described. All honor to the noble fellows who, while upon an errand of mercy, have so bravely encountered perils, and so miraculously escaped."[61]

THURSDAY MARCH 31ST

We still have the wind ahead and as it blows from the southard it might be fine if we did not Rool so verry bad. To day was the counterpart of yesterday in regard to the changees of the weather. We had head wind until about four Oclock when the wind hauld on our beam and we got our Fore and Aft sails set. About this time A sail was reported on our Port Bow. She was A schooner but night comeing on we did not speak her.

FRIDAY APRIL 1ST / 64

This morning cloudy and cool we took the wind on our beam carrying our
Fore and Aft sails until about 8 Oclock when the wind hauld ahead and we
ware obliged to take in sail, at daylight there was two sails in sight but by 12
Oclock we counted 22, land was reported earley this Morning. After dinner
they holy-stoned decks and scraped spars and otherwise put things in order.
At 6 Oclock we made the Highland light. We stop'd several times to take
sounds, late this evening sat all our Fore and Aft sails, which helpd us along
A great deal. We took abord A Pilot at 7 Oclock and bore down for the Bar.

SATURDAY APRIL 2ND

We Anchord of the Bar about 1 Oclock last night, but got under way by
5 Oclock. We took abord another Pilot this Morning and crossd the Bay by
6 Oclock, by 7 Oclock we passd through the Narrow and Anchord of Wall
street Ferry at half past Eight. To day while trying to Moore ship we lost one
of our Anchord and sixty Fathoms of chain. Two of our Ensigns Messers Hoff
and Harington is orderd to return to the Naval Academy and two other Mess
Chew [crew] orderd to the South Atlantic Squadron and Blake to the North
Atlantic Squadron. Maild A letter to C.W.R. I received A letter from C.W.R.,
W.H.S., C.H.B., J.H. With mutch regret I heard of the death of H.L. Brisar.
He died on the 26th of March of Consumption at Camp Meigs, Readville
Mass., he being A priveate Co. A. 5th Regmt Mass. Cavalry.

SUNDY APRIL THE 3RD

It being so stormy yesterday we could not moor ship we went to work at it
again to day, in the Afternoon I went ashore and visited Wm. McL at New
York, also M.E.L. at Brooklyn.

MONDAY APRIL 4TH

To day quite cold and rainy. In the Afternoon I went ashore, went to New
York, departure of Mr. Harrington.

TUESDAY APRIL 5TH

Quite cold. Went ashore in Afternoon. Took A walk though Fifth Avenue and
others of the Aristocratic streets, passd through 14th street whare they
holding the great Sanitary Fair for the benefit of disable soldiers. I visited the

Office of the Anglo Affrican. I remaind ashore all night as I was not in time for the Sun Down Boat.

WENSDAY APRIL 6TH

This Morning all hands were calld at three bells. I forgot to mention above that Dr. Maxwell came on board on Tuesday and commenced duties, also that two Ensigns reported for duty on yesterday.

THURSDAY APRIL 7TH

A verry fine day. We unbend all of our sails and housed them. The Rushan Admiral and his Fleet Captain and Flag Lieutenant came on board to take A look at the ship. We ware prepared to give them A salute but did not on account of the Absence of Comodore Craven. In the Afternoon some of our Offercers went on board of the Rushan Flag Ship to A party.

FRIDAY APRIL 8TH

A verry fine day. We took in Water from the supply boat. Reccived A letter from C.W.R. Went ashore in the Evening.

SATURDAY APRIL 9TH

I returnd on board to day we holystoned and had A general cleaning. The Men's time is fast expireing and every day thare is some leaveing with A general exclamation that they will never enter the Navy again. Would that I was in thair stead. In the evening it changed quite cool with verry strong winds, quite A Gale.

SUNDAY APRIL 10TH

Quite cool, windy and Rainy, in all A verry disagreeable day. We had serveace at 11 Oclock. Write A letter to C.W.R., To Mother and one to J.M.

MONDAY APRIL 11TH

Cold and Rainy. Today workmen came on board and commenced to make such repairs as are needed. In the afternoon I went on shore and went up to Union Square. Visited the Office of the Anglo.

TUESDAY APRIL 12TH

I returnd on board this Morning. Received A letter from A.E.H. Quite unwell. We commenced to transport Guns from forward to Aft.

WENSDAY APRIL 13TH

This Morning cold and wet sleeting. Late in the evening it changed to snow
then to Rain verry disagreeable. Received A letter from C.W.R. and one from
G.L.M.

THURSDAY APRIL 14TH

A verry fine day. Wrote W.H.S., C.B. and J.R. and C.W.R. Went ashore in the
afternoon. Visited A.E.H. Returnd on board at sun set.

FRIDAY APRIL 15TH

A beautiful day. Spring commencees to put forth in her beautiful dress of
green. A coal Barge came along side and we commence to coal ship. In the
afternoon another Barge came along side and we coald from both sides. In the
evening I went ashore and visited Mrs. H.

SATURDAY APRIL 16TH

I returnd aboard this Morning. Coaling ship. This Morning we heard of A
dredful accident that occurd in the lower Bay yesterday evening the the new
Double Ender "Chenango," while proceeding down the Bay explodeed her
Boiler, Injuring the Ship Badly and Scalding all of her Engineers and
Fireman's, about thirty six in all. They ware braught to Hospital whare about
twenty died. To day we also heard of the capture of Fort Pillow by the Rebels
and the Mascare of all the troops, both White and Colard. Still the
Goverme[n]t do not Retaileate.

> "The testimony of some of the officers and men who survived (Fort Pillow)
> shows that there was 'indiscriminate slaughter' of the Union troops, particu-
> larly of Negroes, after the Fort had fallen." The Confederate troops were led by
> Nathan Bedford Forrest. Though it is not clear whether Forrest ordered the
> massacre, the author of this quote, Dudley T. Cornish, feels that he obviously
> exulted in the bloodshed, and that no explicit order was necessary. It appears
> that the impending Overland Campaign dissuaded President Lincoln's Cabi-
> net from supporting retaliation against the Confederates. Black soldiers were
> to be left to "their own devices."[62]

SUNDAY APRIL 17TH

Quite A fine day but we cannot enjoy the day. We had serveace at ten Oclock.
Wrote A letter to C.W.R. and one to A.E.H. felt verry unwell to day obliged to
take Mediciene.

MONDAY APRIL 18TH

To day Rigers came on board and commenced to work on our Riging.
Takeing in Coal, fine day. Went ashore in afternoon.

TUESDAY APRIL 19TH

Returnd on board this Morning. Still coaling. This evening the Double
Turretted Monitor "Onondaga" went to sea under the convoy of the Tug
Boat Boose and Gun Boat Mattabessett.

WENSDAY APRIL 20TH

Still coaling. Heard of they intend makeing us A receiveing Ship.

THURSDAY APRIL 21ST

Coaling still. Received A letter from George Price. Quite well. Finishd coaling
late in the evening.

FRIDAY APRIL 22ND

We got Degallant Mast and Yards ready to send up. Holy stoned decks. The
Italian Minister came on board. One his Departure he was saluteed with
Eleven Guns.

SATURDAY APRIL 23RD

Verry fine day. Went ashore in afternoon. Visited the Office of the Anglo.
Also hears of the Rebel Ram descended the Roanoak and destroyed the
Union Gun Boats "Bombshell" and Southfield and disabled the "Miamma."
I returnd on board at Night. Departure of the "Mattacomet" and "Kerns"
for sea.

SUNDAY APRIL 24TH

To day A verry fine day. We had serveace at ten Oclock. Yesterday A summary
Court Martial convened to try Michal Simmons for Desertion and and
another Man for theft. Wrote A letter to G.L.M. and one to G.W.P.

MONDAY APRIL 25TH

To day Raining but warm. In the Afternoon we received 26 Seamen's and
6 Ordenary Seamens and 5 Landsmen wich is quite an addition to our
crew.

TUESDAY APRIL 26TH

Still raining. Heard of the capture of Plymouth N.C. by the Rebels and a
report of the Mascare of both White and colard soldiers belonging to North
Carolina. Commenced to send up Degallant Riging. Went ashore in afternoon, remaind all Night.

> Confederate troops under Brig.-Gen. R. F. Hoke attacked Plymouth, N.C., on
> April 17 and captured it on April 20. The Union army "lost about 2800 men
> plus a large quantity of supplies. The capture marked the first major Confed-
> erate victory in the area for a long time and brought hope to the defenders of
> the Atlantic coast."[63] The evacuation of "little Washington" followed on April
> 26 and was completed by April 30.[64]
>
> Regarding WBG's reference to the massacring of both white and colored
> soldiers at Plymouth, J. G. Barrett says in a footnote without comment that "it
> was rumored in Federal circles that during the afternoon of the surrender the
> sharp crack of 'Rebel rifles' could be heard 'presumably shooting Buffaloes
> and Negroes.'"[65]
>
> The account provided in *The Anglo-African* was much less muted: "It is
> positively affirmed that the rebels, on taking possession of Plymouth, ordered
> out the North Carolina troops who formed part of the garrison and shot them,
> and that all negroes found in uniform were murdered. We presume that the ac-
> count is correct, and it only proves that what was supposed to be an excep-
> tional barbarity at Fort Pillow has been adopted as the deliberate policy of the
> rebels. As the issue is made, it must be met."[66]

WENSDAY APRIL 27TH

I returnd on board this Morning. Rigers from the Yard came on bord and sent
up Degallant Mast and tar'd down Riging.

THURSDAY APRIL 28TH

We tar'd down Riging and also seized on Battins. paint ship. All hand were
musterd to hear the sentance of the Court Martial in the case of Michal
Simmons for desertion. Loss of three Months pay (30) day close confinement
on bread and water, for stealing a shirt (30) day close confinement, loss of one
Month pay.

FRIDAY APRIL 29TH

We finish'd taring down Riging. Prepare to put the ship in order. Heard of the
arrival of the Italian ship of the line "Re Galantuomo" at Cesara. Received A
letter from G.L.M. and Picture. Went ashore in the afternoon. Visited Mrs. C
and Mrs. W and Mrs. H.

SATURDAY APRIL 30TH

I returnd on board this Morning. Heard from J.M. Received A letter from
G.W.P. Heard of the destruction of the Rebel Salt Works by the Blockadeing
Fleet near Wilmington on Masonboro Sound. (Sunday May 1st went ashore in
the Evening. Went to Fleet street church. Heard Rev. Mr. Garnet.

> The Reverend Garnet was the man who alerted James Crawford, his brother-
> in-law, to the imminent sale of Cornelia and her mother.

SUNDAY, MAY 1ST

A verry fine day. Quarters and Inspection at 10 Oclock. Serveace at 10½
Oclock. See above.

MONDAY, MAY 2ND

I return on board this morning. A verry fine day. This being the Birth day of
the Rushan Emperor we hoisted the Rushan Flag at our Fore and at noon
fired a salute of thirty one (31) Guns in honor of the occasion. All the Rushan
Ships were gaily deck'd out with Flags and wasted a great quantity of Powder.

TUESDAY, MAY 3RD

This Morning raining and quite cold for this season. Heard of the Avacuation
of Washington N.C. by the Federals. Also of A verry destructive fire at
Wilmington N.C. wich destroyed the ware house and Berry's Railway the
Wilmington and Manchester Depot. The entire western side of the River. So
much for the Rebs.

WENSDAY, MAY 4TH

Quite cool. Received A letter from W.H.S. and one from C.W.R. and a
Photograph of Mr. C. We hears of A number of outrages commited by the
Rebs in the Avacuated district of North Carolina. Death of Comodore Porter.
Sent and escort of Mariens to the Furnal. Lieutenant French of Mariens left
the Ship to day, he being orderd to the Baracks.

THURSDAY, MAY 5TH

A verry fine day. Our Executive Officer Lieut. Commander H. Erben was to
day Detach'd and order'd to one of the Light Draft Iron Clads building at
Boston. Also Paymaster Watmough has been Detach'd. 2nd Lieut. Mariens
Beet, the successer of Mr. French, reported to day for duty. Mr Erben's

mother and his wife and others dined on board. Received A letter from
A.E.H. I went ashore visited Mrs White. Learnt of the whereabouts of Mr.
Benjamin Brown. Also heard that A.H. Galloway is in the Citty. Heard of the
advance of the Army of the Potomac and the passage of the Rapidan without
any opposition. Also the occupation of West Point on the York River by the
forces under Butler. Visited A.E.H. I have been suffering with A severe pain in
my face all day.

FRIDAY, MAY 6TH

I returnd on board this morning and found that they had Scrub'd Hammocks.
Received A letter from C.W.R. Heard of the departure of one Batalian of the
5th Regmt. Mass. Cavalry from Camp Meigs for Washington D.C. May God
protect them while defending the holiest of all causes Liberty and Union.
My face still verry painfull. Heard of the advance of Butlers Army up the
James River.

> On the back of a xerox copy of the page containing this entry, William B.
> Gould III wrote: "Camp Meigs was in Readville, Massachusetts. This was
> about 2 miles east of where William B. Gould made his home at 303 Milton
> Street, East Dedham, Mass."
> WBG's May 5 and 6 entries describe well the crossing of the Rapidan,
> which was "the beginning of the big Federal push in Virginia that culminated
> in the siege of Petersburg and finally Appomattox. From now on the pressure
> would not be relaxed. . . . Following Grant's many-pronged strategy to
> weaken the thin Confederate defense, Ben Butler's Army of the James assem-
> bled in transports in Hampton Roads."[67] The following day—May 5—Butler
> landed 30,000 troops at City Point and Bermuda Hundred aiming towards
> Richmond via Petersburg.[68]

SATURDAY, MAY 7TH

To day verry fine and hot. We spread Awnings. Went ashore in afternoon.
Went up to West Eighteen street. Visited Mr. Brown. Also went ot the
Office of the Anglo. Heard of three days hard fighting in Virginia resulting
in the defeat of Lee by Grant and the occupation of Citty Point by Genl.
Butler and marching forward on Petersburg. Visited A.E.H. returned
on board.

> This was the Battle of the Wilderness, which resulted in enormous casualties
> for both sides.

SUNDAY, MAY 8TH

A verry fine day. The Chaplain came on board and we had serveace at ten Oclock. Several visitors came on board. Heard of the Destruction of the Rail Road between Petersburg & Richmond by Genl. Butler. Also the retreat of Lee from before Grant.

MONDAY, MAY 9TH

Verry hot last night about 10 Oclock we had quite A lively time on the report that a man had deserted. There was a number of shots fired at the object supposed to be A man. A boat was lowrd and gave chase. When lo it proved to be a dead Horse. Maild a letter to C.W.R.

TUESDAY, MAY 10TH

A verry fine day. Quaters Regular at 3 bells A.M. Received A letter from C.B. last night A man attemptd to Desert after gaining the outside of the Ship, he remaind in the water for two hours hanging by a Rope and when he calld for assistance and was later on board and confined in double Irons another man that went on Liberty fell over board from the Pier and was drownd said to have been intoxicated at the time. About 5 Oclock we received 24 men from the Guardo. Looks like we will get A crew now as the draft commences to morrow. We are looking out for a muss.

WENSDAY, MAY 11TH

A verry fine day. We now have quarters regular every day. I went ashore at 1 Oclock. Up to 23rd Street. Visited the Office of the Anglo. Meet A.H. Galloway. Went to Sulivan street Church where there was A meeting to receive the Delegates from North Carolina. The meeting was verry poorly attended. Speeches were deliverd by Messers Hill on behalf of the Church and by Miss Pierson & Galoway in behalf of the Delegation. The object of the Delegation was to petition th Government for the rights of sufferage for the people of North Carolina.[69] Received A letter from G.W.P. We Received A draft of 24 men.

THURSDAY, MAY 12TH

I returnd on board this morning. Received a letter from J.M. We received a draft of 100 men to day from the North and furnish them with provisions and sent them off under Guard to Portsmouth N.H.

FRIDAY, MAY 13TH

To day Cloudy and cool. Still hear of victories of Grant and the retreat of Lee. All hands were musterd at 5 bells P.M. and given our watch numbers. Still discharging men every day. Maild A letter to C.W.R. Went ashore for A short time to day.

SATURDAY, MAY 14TH

To day quite Rainy. Went on shore. Calld at the Office of the Anglo. Learnt of the departure of Gary. Returned on board at 3 Oclock.

SUNDAY MAY 15TH

Raining all day. Still reports come of heavy fighting in Virginia. Went ashore in the Evening.

MONDAY, MAY 16TH

I returnd on board this morning. Cloudy all day. The Report confirmd of the capture of Dalton Ga. by Shearman. Wrote A letter to C.W.R. and one to G.W.P.

TUESDAY MAY 17TH

Morning Cloudy. Cleard off about noon. Verry warm. Packd up Dr. Maxwell and Paymaster Watmough. Went ashore to the Dr's also up to 14th street, remaind over all night. Maild my letters. Visited Mrs. Culbreth

WENSDAY MAY 18TH

I returnd on board this morning. Quite warm. Yesterday about 300 men of the Maryland (colard) Regiment came on board (they being transfer to the Navy) and took dinner then departed for Portsmouth N.H. They were treated verry rough by the crew. They refused to let them eat of[f] the mess pans and calld them all kinds of names, one man his watch stolen from him by these scoundrels in all they was treated shamefully. About 5 bells A draft of men came on board for us from the "North Carolina."[70]

THURSDAY MAY 19TH

To day quite warm. A great deal of excitement in New York on the suppression of the Papers. (World and Journal of Commerce) for publishing A Forged call for 400,000 volunteers. We took in A supply of Water. Also some stores.

Act. Lieut. Green was detached and orderd to the "Louisianna." We to day
had several visitors on board and two Ladies Diend [dined] with the Ward
Room Officers. One of the Rushan Officers Died on board of the Alexander
Nevski, lying abrest of us. No news of fighting on any magnitude.

FRIDAY MAY 20TH

Quite warm. Departure of Lieut Green, Paymaster Watmough and Sarg.
Maxwell. Also of the arrival of Paymaster Williams. Went on shore in the
afternoon. Remaind all night. Received a letter from C.W.R. Orders to
prepare for sea.

> The order was indeed given that date. Secretary Welles wired Rear-Adm. Hi-
> ram Paulding, the commandant of the Navy Yard in New York: "Get the *Ni-
> agara* ready for sea as early as convenient and report. Not longer than ten
> days."[71]

SATURDAY MAY 21ST

Arived on board early this morning. Verry warm. Went ashore in the afternoon. Remaine all night. Visited Washington Morllet Also went to 24 St.
Commence to remove the Ward Room on the Main deck.

SUNDAY MAY 22ND

I returnd on board this morning. A number of visitors come on board. This
morning the Iroquois came in and anchord it short distance from us. Wrote A
letter to C.W.R. and one to E.A.M. See by the papers that the Italian
Government conferd An honery title apon Comodore Craveen for his search
for the Italian Ship of the Line Re Galantuomo. Rain in the evening.

> As he did on March 14, WBG may be understating things here when he says
> that "a number of visitors came on board." In reference to this occasion, one
> of his shipmates, Fred White, wrote to a friend that there were "quite a num-
> ber of Ladies on board to day some of them of rather doubtful character but it
> don't make any difference to the men you know if they only get a bit of whiskey
> they are all right but I don't drink now."[72]

MONDAY MAY 23RD

A verry fine day went ashore in the Afternoon, returnd on board at sun set,
arrival yesterday of the Sloop "Iroquois." She belongs to the squadron that
this ship do.

On this day, Secretary Welles instructed Rear-Adm. Paulding: "Have the *Niagara* ready to go to sea on Wednesday, June 1."[73]

TUESDAY MAY 24TH

Verry warm went ashore in afternoon visited A.E.H. Maild A letter to C.W.R. one to E.A.M. returnd on board at sun-set. Saw the procession of the School Children celebrateing thair school Aniverseery, evening verry misty.

WENSDAY MAY 25TH

To day verry misty with rain at intervals. A coal barge came along side and we took in all the coal that we could carry. Some of our men returnd from the Hospital. At night there was A malee on Deck between the white and colard men.

THURSDAY, MAY 26TH

Weather still verry thick and misty. I spent the night ashore. They had A verry large turn out to receive the 14th Regement on thair return from the seat of war. This morning Henry Smith (steerage steward) was detected bringing liquor on board and was confined in double Irons. Received a paper from C.W.R.

FRIDAY MAY 27TH

It cleard of[f] to day fine. At Eleven Oclock to day A Summary Court Martial convend to try Henry Smith on A charge of bringing on board Liquor to sell to the men. The water boat came along side and we took in A fresh supply of Water. We also took in five months stores of provissions and Clotheing in order to get us off to sea. The Carpenters are at work apon us night and day verry warm. Went ashore in the Evening.

SATURDAY MAY 28TH

I returnd on board this morning in order to have us go away at the appointed time the work men were buisey at work last night. This evening I went on shore at 3 Oclock and went up to 23rd St. remaind all night ashore.

SUNDAY, MAY 29TH

I returned on board this morning A fine day. We had Inspection at ten. Then Serveace. The Carpenters at work all day. All hands were calld to Muster to hear Read the dismissial of surgeon and Act Master by General Court Martial for Maltreatment of A Seaman. One for striking the man producing sickness and the Surg. For sheilding said Act. Master by alleiging Ignorance to the Man's disease.

MONDAY MAY 30TH

We are making great preparation for Sea. Went ashore to day. Returnd on board in the Evening. The Sentence of Henry Smith for the offence above stated were thirty days confinement in single Irons with the loss of two months pay. Maild A letter to C.W.R.

> The "great preparation" WBG noted was in response to an order Craven had just received from Welles, telling him to "proceed to sea . . . on Wednesday, 1st June next, and after getting to sea you will break the seal of the enclosed instructions and carry them into execution."[74]

TUESDAY MAY 31ST

Still verry buisey at work apon us and A general bustle among the Officers getting ready for Sea. Last night in the Mid Watch. A Man by the name of George Williams attempted to desert by swimming to A Brig lying close to us but he was discovered and brought back. I went ashore in the afternoon. Went up to the Chaplains House. Got his things. Sent them on board. I remaind on shore all night. Visited A.E.H. Also M.E.L.

WENSDAY JUNE 1ST

After goin to our Provission dealer and getting all our Fresh stores I returnd on board and found them verry buisey some bending sails and some unmooreing ship. Also the carpenters had completed thair Job on yesterday now begins A great confusion Officers comeing on board with A great deal of Baggage some moveing up into thair new Rooms not waiting for the Up Holsters and Painters to finish thair work. About Eleven we found that A part of our stores were not on board. Here was troubble however it was soon overcome. Then A draft of men came for us all all the men haveing less than three months to serve were transfered to the North Carolina. Among them was Charles E. Profs and Charles H. Scott, Ward Room Serveants and Hutcheson Allen Ward Room Cook. Here we was left without A Cook but I attempted to get the dinner ready amid the greatest confusion immaginable. By three Oclock all our stores arrived and the Pilot being already on board, the shrill notes of the Fife, and the regular tramp of the Men together with the clank of the Capstan, all told that we were soon to feel the motion of the swelling sea. Our anchor being weighd and cated we steamd out. Discharge our Pilot and before dark we were outside of Sandy Hook. To night feeling very tired from my new occupation that I must leave off. Hopeing that on the morrow will bring some one to fill the place made vacant by the transfer of H. Allen. Maild A letter to C.W.R. and one to A.E.H.

> Craven opened the sealed instructions he had received after he discharged his pilot on this day or soon thereafter. His main objective, he was told, was to be on the lookout for the *Florida*, which was thought to have left Bermuda on May 14 and headed north. "It is possible that under sail she may follow the track of our vessels bound to Europe. You will therefore, under sail when possible, or easy steam when otherwise, work along to the eastward in said track, overhauling vessels for information concerning any pirates, and, receiving such, you will act according to your best judgment relative to pursuing and destroying such craft. If no information is obtained in the route, you will cross the Atlantic in from twenty-five to thirty-five days, and go into Antwerp for repairs." But though the search for the *Florida* was the chief object, he was instructed "not [to] omit due diligence in all cases during your cruise, and [you] will seize and send into port any vessel of the enemy engaged in depredating on our commerce, or in the transportation of arms, munitions, or contraband of war to the insurgents." He was to advise the department frequently of his movements and get in touch with the U.S. minister or chargé in any country he visited. The document cautioned him to be "careful that you do not permit any information in regard to the movements of your vessel to be promulgated."[75] The *Florida* was commanded by John Newland Maffitt, who had owned Cornelia Read and sold her to her uncle, James Crawford, in 1858.
>
> Reflecting on this situation after the war, WBG says: "After the fight of the Iron Clads at Hampton Roads, Va. March 8 and 9, 1862, the Confederates contracted with the Lairds ship building Co. of Liverpool, England, for two Iron Clad rams. News of the progress of the work on them reached the United States from time to time until finally it was known that they were launched. It was also reported that the Confederates were trying to get a fleet together of which these rams were to be the nucleus and that the Privateers 'Georgia' and 'Alabama' were on the way to Liverpool to be refitted. The American minister, Charles Francis Adams had notified the English Government that if these vessels were allowed to go to sea, it would be construed by the United States as a declaration of war. That was the situation June 1, 1864, when the 'Niagara' sailed for the European station having been assigned to the Irish Sea and ordered to keep a sharp lookout for these rams. The U.S. ship 'Kearsarge' was already cruising in the English Channel intending to head off any vessel trying to make port. The 'Wachusett' and the 'Sacramento' were to follow the course of the Rebel ships."[76]

THURSDAY JUNE 2ND

A verry fine day. Ship verry steady, steering E.S.E. sent up Degallant and Royal yards, set Degallant sails, passd several sails.

FRIDAY JUNE 3RD

Still verry fine. Set Royals, pass'd several sails find it quite hot cooking, to day A Summary Court Martial convend to try George Williams for Desertion.

SATURDAY JUNE 4TH

Holy-stoned Decks. Also had A regular drill at the Guns. Pass'd several sails but did not speak them.

> After the war, WBG said: "The 'Niagara' crossed the Atlantic leisurely head-
> ing for the Bay of Biscay. The men were drilled daily in gunnery as the only
> hope of being able to affect a capture lay in the amount and accuracy of fire,
> the 'Niagara' being an old wooden ship, while those of the enemy were mod-
> ern iron clads. The 'Niagara' was armed with twelve two hundred pound Par-
> rott rifles, four twelve pound Napoleon rifles, and twenty-four pound How-
> itzers for close work."[77]

SUNDAY JUNE 5TH

At Daylight A sail was in sight. We gave chase. She did not notice us but kept steady on her course when about three miles from here we fired A blank catridge when she show'd her collars and we stood off. She was one of the English Mail steamers. We also spoke and boarded the English schooner "Empire" of and from Burmuda for New York. Two weeks out reported the Rebel steamer "Florida" at Burmuda. When the Empire left we had quarters at ten. Then mustered to hear the sentance of George Williams for desertion which was thirty days double Irons solitary confinement on bread and water except on every seventh day. Then he was to have full rations with the loss of three months pay. We have prayers every Evening at sun set.

MONDAY JUNE 6TH

Verry foggy. Last night sent down Royal yards. Ship Rooling cruiseing on the grand Banks. Quite cool. All the Devissions puting down for clothing.

TUESDAY JUNE 7TH

Still quite cool. Cruiseing to the Eastward. Saw two sails but did not speak neither of them. Henry Belt was put into the Brig for refuseing to do duty.

WENSDAY JUNE 8TH

Still cruiseing to the Eastward. Quite cool all night. At daylight saw A sail ran
for it spoke and boarded her. A Fishing Schooner three day out from Boston.
Made A Brig ran down and spoke her. A fisherman of Halifax. At 7 bells all
hands calld to Reeve Topsails, chaseing A schooner. A fisherman served out
fishing lines to the men which looks verry much like haveing some fresh fish.

THURSDAY JUNE 9TH

At daylight A sail in sight. Ran down and spoke her, A fisherman, made
another sail, ran for it, A fisherman at anchor boarded him and procurd A
large lot of Fish, enough for all hands. We are now on the Grand Banks of
Newfoundland among A fleet of Fisherman's. We can see from six to Eight at
any time. At 5 bells P.M. all hands were call'd to Reef Topsails, steering N.W.
by N. blowing quite fresh and quite cool for June. We have not been able to
find out where we are goin.

FRIDAY JUNE 10TH

Cruiseing on the banks blowing A Gale and verry foggy quite rough the ship
rooling verry much courseing under Forestaysail, Foresail, Fore and Main
Trysails Fore and Main Topsails double Reef'd steering W.N.W. I find it
quite hard cooking when the ship is Rooling. We had to day fish chowder for
all hands.

SATURDAY JUNE 11TH

Still blowing quite fresh ship Rooling heavealy carrying sail as yesterday
except our Topsails are close reef'd. Last night A seaman by the Name of
Antonia Arletta fell out of his Hammock and died soon after. He had been
sick for A day or two. He was burried to day at 11 Oclock in the useual mode
of Burrial at sea. I feel quite unwell this Evening.

SUNDAY JUNE 12TH

This Morning I am sick so as to be obliged to leave off Cooking, voilent pains
in my head and A severe Caugh also A Riseing in my left thumb which pains
me verry severe. We crossd the Banks this morning and find the ship A great
deal steadyer than she have been for the last three days. We had quarters to
day, then serveace in the Evening changed our course again for the Banks. It

seems that we are to cruise around here for some purpose or other that we know not of.

MONDAY JUNE 13TH

Still verry unwell. Went on the sick list. They served out cloathing. Ship Rooling very heavaly. Shiping seas quite freely. Have not eaten anything for two days.

TUESDAY JUNE 14TH

Still on the sick list, feel A little better. Ship Rooling heavaly, shiping seas all day under sail alone. Making from twelve to fifteen knots. Feels A little better.

WENSDAY JUNE 15TH

Still blowing verry fresh. Under sail alone. Spoke A schooner bound for Liverpool. Also spoke at 1 Oclock the ship Empire State of and from New York for Liverpool twelve days out. All well. Reports our Army nearer Richmond than when we saild. I feels much better expects to go to work to morrow.

THURSDAY JUNE 16TH

Quite cool for June, still steering to the Eastward. Saw A Barque. Kept her company all day but did not speak her. I went to work to day in the Ward Room. The Offercers verry glad at my return. They overhaul all the Boats and the two Launches got up awnings and all other things Requisite for them. We all believe that we are on A cruise to some Foreign Port.

FRIDAY JUNE 17TH

Weather quite fine. We shook out the Reefs from our Topsails and set Degallant sails. During the day several Vessels were in sight but we did not speak any except A four Masted Steamer passd close to us on our port beam and exchanged signals. Steering E.S.E.

SATURDAY JUNE 18TH

Blowing A little fresher this morning. Furld Degallant sails. About four bells a.m. A sail in sight, gave chase spoke at 4 bells P.M. the Ship Lady Russell of Liverpool, fourteen days from Quebec for Liverpool, all well. In the Evening it began to Rain and A Fog set in still steering to the S.E. to day A court martial convend to try several persons charged with different offencees.

SUNDAY JUNE 19TH

The sun rose clear but by 9 Oclock it had clouded up and began to Rain. We had Quarters at ten then serveace. Ship rooling very heavaly. Signalized the Ship Minnie from Nova Scotia for Liverpool. The water has changed from Blue to green.

MONDAY JUNE 20TH

A great deal colder in this part of the world that I have been acustomed to, we find Overcoats to be quite comfortable all day and Blankets at night. We are now off the coast of Ireland or at least steering in that direction. Served out small stores and commence making Hats.

TUESDAY JUNE 21ST

We have changed our coast more to the southard. Still quite cool. Carrying Degallant sails.

WENSDAY JUNE 22

Bay of Biscay. More moderate. At daylight made A sail. Ran down to her but did not speak her. On yesterday we Furld Degallant sails and took down our Fore Degallant Yard to repair damages. After compleeting all the necessary repairs we sent up the yard again and spread our Degallantsails to the Breeze. Saw several sails but did not speak any of them. Bearing up for the English Channel. I have been takeing lessons in Hat Makeing. The ship at present looks like A Hat Manufactory. All hands Mark thair clothing with thair Name and Number. My Number is 44. Ships Number.

THURSDAY JUNE 23RD

The weather is much milder. We are standing in for the English Chanel and leaveing the Bay of Biscay. Made A sail about 7½ Oclock. Ran down to her. She showd the Flag of Holland. Also saw A steamer on our Port Beam skid carrying full sail gave chase but haul'd off.

FRIDAY JUNE 24TH

Runing up the English Chanel under sail alone. Verry light winds. Carrying Degallant Sails. The crew drills regular each day in the Morning at the Guns and Afternoon with small Arms. They can handle the Guns quite fast. Began

Drilling the Mariens in the Bayonet Exercise. Made Land about 8 bells P.M. on the coast of England. Shorten sails. Pass'd two Flash lights in the mid watch. About 2 bells Morning watch pass'd Pilot Boat showing French Collars. Quite Foggy with light Rain. Cleard up about 6 bells. Passd A great maney Sails. About 3 bells took on board an English Pilot who braught us the thrice Glorious news of the sinking of the "Alabama" by the sloop "Kerasage" off Cherbourg. Framed on Sunday June the 19th after a fight of 2 Hours. All honor to Capt. Winslow and his brave crew. The "Kearsage" Rescued 72 of the crew of the "Alabama" and an English yacht (the Deerhound about 40 including Semms the commander of the "Alabama." The Deerhound landed the men she rescued at cours. The "Kerasage" took hers to Cherbourg. We also heard that that Sheerman had captured Marietta and advancing in Atlanta, Geo. We had news up to the 7th of June from home, the first since we saild. Grant was still striking for Richmond. Although we have been disappointment to us in not getting A shot at the "Alabama" we are satisfied that she is out of the way. We made cape. About 6 Oclock pass'd quite A fleet of sails.

> Years later, WBG said that when the crew got the news of the sinking of the *Alabama*, they "were as delighted and as proud of the deed as if they had done it themselves."[78] Says William Marvel about the feelings of the sailors on the *Kearsarge*: "Before, some had greeted word of a nearby Confederate glumly predicting the monotony and misery of the long vigil that would follow, and the presence of the *Alabama* guaranteed no opportunity for excitement. But this was the cruiser that Federal sailors coveted above all others and no Union officer had yet put a spyglass on her, let alone come within broadside range. For the chance to see this ship, and perhaps have a crack at her, the bored and homesick crew might have given a great deal."[79]
>
> WBG's shipmate Henry Smith sent a letter to *The Anglo-African* from Antwerp several days later implying that it was there that the crew got word of the sinking of the *Alabama*. At any rate, he was excited to read in the morning papers that Semmes, the *Alabama*'s commander, "is to have another vessel and to fight the Kearsarge again. I only wish we could have the chance to try the guns of the old Niagara."[80] Ironically, it has been persuasively argued that the *Niagara* would have been a more formidable foe for the *Alabama* than the *Kearsarge* was: "The significance of the *Kearsarge-Alabama* struggle lies less in the battle itself than it does in the location of the battle. The course of the war was affected not one whit by the battle. Had Semmes won, he would have had to face the U.S.S. *Niagara*, which was then en route to Europe and more powerful still than the *Kearsarge*." The footnote here goes on to state: "The *Niagara* was a ship of 4,582 tons, compared to the *Kearsarge*'s 1,031 tons."[81]

SUNDAY, JUNE 26TH

Pass'd through the straits of Dover early this morning into the North Sea. The
Sea verry smooth ship verry steady. Cast off our Gun lashings. I have a very
severe Boil under my Arm. Had it Lanced. About 8 bells A.M. Pass'd the
Light ship West Hinder. A thick fog. Serveace about 5 bells A.M. We took on
board A Belgian Pilot. We enter the River Scheldt 20 minutes past 12 Oclock
passd Ostend. We arrive off Flushing about 3 Oclock. Took another Pilot and
discharge the one that brought us to Flushing [now Vlissingen]. Stood on our
course up the River. The Country presents beautiful scenery as we pass up
the River beautiful Cottages, and Farms looking verry Beautiful. A plenty of
Shiping among them several American Ships. We came to Anchor of of the
town of Uderskeric about 6½ Oclock. A light Drizzell of Rain.

> His shipmate Henry Smith wrote: "After cruising around and overhauling every-
> thing we sighted, we made the coast of England on June 24, passed Dover, Eng.,
> the 26th, and arrived at this place June 26th. Left here June 28th, proceeded
> some sixty miles up the river to the city of Antwerp, in Belgium, which lies on
> the left hand side of the River Scheldt, which empties into the North Sea."[82]

MONDAY, JUNE 27TH

Last night we sent A boat out to look for sand but return'd uncuccessful. We
got under way about 6 bells and started up the River passing Villages and
quite a number of Vessels. We arrive at Antwerp at 20 minutes to Eleven and
anchord of[f] the Hotel De la Crux Blanch. The Counsel Mr Crawford came
on board. The Comodore and several of the Officers went on shore. On our
way up we ran against a schooner an knock'd of[f] A part of her Stern. We
commence seeing Gold and Silver wich is good for our Eyes. Wrote to C.W.R.

ANTWERP, TUESDAY JUNE 28TH

A little Cloudy. Several persons came on board yesterday. We fired a salute of
21 Guns. Here every one is A Military. 1 Coal Barge came along side.

ANTWERP, WENSDAY JUNE 29TH

Coaling Ship. Another Barge came along side. To day we have two whips
goin. They answerd our salute to day. The Comodore and Staff went to
Brussells to day. To be real Belgium wether we must have rain every day. A
great many visiters to day of both sexes.

ANTWERP, BELGIUM, THURSDAY JUNE 30TH

We Cleand Ship this Morning then All hands Dress themselves. We were visited by the Govener and the Minister of War several Brigedares and any quanities of other Dignataries. A great many Ladies and Gentlemens. We was throng'd all day. We fired a salute of 17 Guns and one of Nine. We Drilld one of our Guns Crew to show them how we handled our Parrott Carragees. We fire off one of our 150 lbs. Rifles twice to see how they liked the noise. After the Visiters left we went to coaling ship on both sides.

ANTWERP FRIDAY JULY 1ST

All Hands were calld at 8 bells. Coald ship all day. We saluteed the American minister. Some of the Crew went on liberty. Gold up higher. We are orderd to sea on tomorrow. A great many visiters came on board.

ANTWERP SATURDAY JULY 2ND

All hands call'd at 8 bells. Coald ship untill 10 Oclock. We then unmoor'd ship and got ready for sailing. All the men came off Liberty. We got under way about 11 Oclock and started down the River. When passing the first Fort from the Citty they gave us A salute of 21 Guns which we returnd. We were obliged to come to anchor off Uderscaric to prevent us from runing into A ship. We got under way again and anchord (at the same place where we anchord on our way up) for the Night.

> Wrote Commodore Craven to Secretary of the Navy Welles: "Sir: For the information of the Department, I take leave to enclose herewith a copy of a letter addressed to our minister at Brussels, and which Mr. Sanford sent to me by express yesterday afternoon. As I am yet without instructions from the Department, and as it is possible that the *Florida* may be fallen in with somewhere upon the French coast, I shall get underway immediately and proceed in search of her, and if possible communicate with Commander Winslow. The opinions expressed by Mr. Beckwith are in accordance, I believe, with those entertained by our three ministers at Paris, The Hague, and Brussels. After making a thorough search for the *Florida* I purpose in the course of two weeks to return to this port, where I hope to receive further and full instructions for my future guidance."[83]

SUNDAY JULY 3RD

We were calld at 8 bells and after performing our regular duties we got under way at 6 bells and started again for Flushing where we arrived at 3½ Oclock and came to Anchor. Flushing is A town of 9000 Inhabitants. It belongs to Holland. There is A Navy Yard here. The Town is Wall'd in.

FLUSHING MONDAY JULY THE 4TH

At 8 Oclock we saluteed the Flag of Holland with 21 Guns. They returnd it from shore at 9 Oclock all hands were calld to up anchor out Pilots being on board. We soon had our Anchor cated and Fish'd. We steamd out and discharged the Pilots at 11 Oclock we pass'd Ostend about 5 bells. We are again in the North Sea A plenty of sails in sight. We made the lights of Dover about 3 bells P.M.

TUESDAY JULY 5TH

Runing along the coast of England with land in full view, day verry fine perfectly lovely in the Chanel. About 1 Oclock we chased A steamer but after Running down to her we pass'd her by. Ten minutes before 5 bells P.M. we Gave chase to A steamer. She attempted to run away from us. We beat to Quarters, first fired A Blank Catridge, then A shot and another Blank, when she hove to, show'd English collors, then we haul'd off. We can see A large Citty in the Distance suppose to be Portsmouth.

WENSDAY JULY 6TH

We made land on the French coast at sun Rise made several sails. We arrived off Cherbourg about 12½ Oclock, sent A boat asshore, first A Pilot came on board of us. A Beautiful day. We sent A Lieut ashore who returnd about 6 bells accompany'd by the American Counsel and the Capt of the "Saccremento." The Counsel and Capt left about 3 bells. We Fired A salute of 7 Guns then stood out to sea. This Place Cherbourg, is verry strongly Fortyfied Place. The "Saccremento" is in the Port. Also the "Kersage." There is A great Breakwater in front of the Harbor and answers the double purpose of Breakwater and Fort.

THURSDAY JULY 7TH

Cruiseing in the Chanel. Verry fine day. All hands Mustered in Straw Hats. Read the Articles of war. This Morning we sent up Royal Yards and set Royal sails. Procurd some Fish from A Fisherman. To day I was returnd to the Galley as Ward Room Cook. To day A Court Martial conveind.

FRIDAY JULY 8TH

Cruiseing in the Chanel. Verry fine day. Pass'd several sails. Had A distant View of A Castle. All hands calld to Muster to hear the sentance of the Court Martial. Verry fine day.

SATURDAY JULY 9TH

Cruiseing off the English Coast with A verry fine breeze all day we are goin along quite lively. All hands orderd to wear thair Watch Mark. The weather somewhat Misty. Burst one of our Cilender heads.

SUNDAY JULY 10TH

We are goin along quite briskly with A favorable breeze. Rooling A little. Pass'd A large steamer this Morning and any number of sails. Quaters at 4 bells then Serveace.

MONDAY JULY 11TH

Cruiseing up the Chanel. Pass'd several sails day verry fine.

TUESDAY JULY 12TH

Running up the Chanel. Pass'd Dover about 7 Oclock P.M. quite cold.

WENSDAY JULY 13TH

Runing up the North Sea. Pass'd Ostend about 10 Oclock. Took on board A Pilot. Came to Anchor off Flushing. About 2 Oclock the Dutch Commander came on board also the American Counsel. We saluted the Commander, also the Counsel. The Fort returnd our salute severl visiters came on board. We repaird the Cilender by puting on A new head. Verry fine weather little cool.

THURSDAY JULY 14TH

Holy stoned Decks. Two Dutch Offercers came on board. Sign'd accounts $125.57.

FRIDAY JULY 15TH

A coal schooner came along side and we commence coaling. Gave some of the Men Liberty yesterday had five teeth drawn. One man Deserted.

SATURDAY JULY 16TH

We coald ship all night got under way at 6 Oclock and started up the River
(Scheldt) for Antwerp. In goin up the River we pass'd the Quarenteen station
without stopping. We ware oblige to return again to the station. After the visit
by the Quarenteen Offercers we were allowd to proceed on our way to
Antwerp where we arrived at 9 Oclock, all safe. We were soon safely Moor'd
and throng'd with visiters. My face A little better but still quite sore. The
Counsel came on board. We saluteed him on his departure. Then we saluteed
the Citty. They returnd our salute.

SUNDAY JULY 17TH

Verry fine day. We had Quaters at 4 bells then serveace. Several strangers was
on board to serveace. We were throng'd all day with visiters. All hands wore
white Frocks and straw Hats.

MONDAY JULY 18TH

Antwerp harbor, dress as yesterday. A great many visiters came on board. The
"Sacramento" arrived to day all well. The Men had liberty. Every day full of
visiters. Fird A salute.

TUESDAY JULY 19TH

Morning cloudy. Cleard off after Breakfast. Made preperation to receive the
King as it is Reported that he intends to pay us A Visit, but he appeard not.
Three men Deserted last night give liberty every day.

WENSDAY JULY 20TH

At Antwerp. Morning Rainey. Many visiters on board. Among them some
offercers of destinctions. Two Men Deserted to day.

THURSDAY JULY 21ST

At Antwerp. Morning Rainy. Lost my Port Monnie. Went on shore. Had a
fine time generaly. Went up to the top of the Tower of the Cathedral by
ascending six hundred and sixteen steps (616). F[o]und every boddy
verry kind.

> Henry Smith wrote, of this cathedral: "In Antwerp there is a very large church,
> built in the year 1429, which is very high and magnificent. Inside of the Church

are some paintings, done by Quintin Mastly, the Blacksmith of Antwerp. There is a chime of five hundred bells, which is played every fifteen minutes by machinery; and for the small sum of ten cents, we are guided through the church by a young lady, and a book to endorse our names in. The Niagara's crew have climbed to the top, and cut out their names and wrote them on the bells."[84] WBG does not mention either the book or cutting out names on the bells.

FRIDAY JULY 22ND

At Antwerp. I returnd on board this Morning I found that in swinging around the ship got aground. All hands were hard at work trying to get her off. We got up steam and with the assistance of two Tugs and high Water we got Afloat again, sustaining no damage. We moord ship again and will try in future to keep off ground. Several of our Men were put into the Brig for being Drunk. Some of them deserts every day.

JULY 23RD SATURDAY

At Antwerp. Fine day. Four men deserted last night. This Evening about 6 bells while one of the Firemen were at work about the safety valve it flew open and he was badly scalded. The "Saceramento" saild this Morning. Saw A paper from home of July the 8th. saw that Grant was buisey around Richmond and Petersburg. Also saw that the Rebs have invaded Maryland for the third time. The Rebs are offering A Bounty of $300 in Gold for Men to Man thair ships in France. Our men are deserting verry fast we suppose to join them.

> At the beginning of July, Grant's army was bearing down on Petersburg. The "Reb" invasion WBG speaks of was Jubal Early's crossing of the Potomac on July 5. The advance continued to the outskirts of Washington itself. The Confederate forces did not recross the river until July 14. Like Lee before him, Early was allowed to retreat unhindered.

SUNDAY JULY 24TH

At Antwerp. Fine day. Sent our Mariens on shore to bring abord liberty men. They braught off thirteen. Many visiters on board. A small Mail from the states but nary [a] letter have I.

MONDAY JULY 25TH

Fine day all hands dress for Muster. Full of visiters all day.

TUESDAY JULY 26TH

At Antwerp. Morning Rainey. Cleard off after Breakfast. Full of visiters all day. One colard Jentleman from Brussels came on board, the first that I have seen belonging to the Country.

WENSDAY JULY 27TH

At Antwerp. Fine day full of visiters. Saw papers from home. Heard of the capture by Hinks. Devission of 7 Peicees of Cannon in one charge before Petersburg on the 15th ult.

THURSDAY JULY 28TH

At Antwerp, fine day. Many visitors on board. Last night two Men that was confined escaped and took A Boat that was towing astern. The Boat was recovered but the Men es non est. Another attempted to Desert by dressing in Citizens clothes and tried to pass the sentry but he was detected. The Prisoners in the Brig (about twenty five) had A free fight among themselves until the Marienes were call'd to them. Wrote to R.H.

FRIDAY JULY 29TH

At Antwerp. Morning cloudy with slight drizzle of rain at intervals. About four bells A.M. unmoor'd ship. Took Breakfast, at one bell all hands were call'd to up Anchor. We started at 3 bells. First fird A salute of fifteen guns then one of twenty one. We descend the River in safety and anchord of Uderskaric where we spent the night. We sent ashore and procurd some Poultry and Lambs, also vegetables. Visiters came on board. One Man deserted from our boat.

> Craven was struck by the warm welcome the *Niagara* received in Antwerp and noted that she was "the first American vessel of war and the largest ship which had ever visited the waters of Belgium."[85]

SATURDAY JULY 30TH

Off Uderskaric. We up anchor about 9 Oclock. Soon after starting one Man named Ellis Died of consumption. We arrived off Flushing where we anchord. The Counsel came on board. Sent the corps ashore for Burrial. Then up anchor and put to sea. Pass'd Ostend about 5 Oclock.

SUNDAY JULY 31ST

North Sea. Discharge the Pilot about 8 Oclock. Enterd the Chanel. Spoke severl Pilot Boats. Took no Pilot. A great many sails in sight.

MONDAY AUG. 1ST

English Chanel, fine day. Many sails in sight. Served out Hat Bands with Name of the ship.

TUESDAY AUG. 2ND

At 7 Oclock pass'd Lands End of England. Stood for the coast of Wales. About 4 bells P.M. made Cape Clear on the coast of Ireland. Enterd at Georges Chanel, stood up for Liverpool.

> Perhaps unknown to WBG, new problems for his ship were on the horizon at this time. American officials were becoming increasingly concerned about the movements of the C.S.S. *Georgia*, which, though she had passed into British hands, was assumed to still represent a threat to the Union fleet. "She is still rebel and is going out on her old trade," said a U.S. representative in Britain."[86]
>
> Only a week earlier, on July 27, Amb. Charles Francis Adams had written Comm. Craven, as well as Capt. John Winslow of the Kearsarge, about the *Georgia*: "I learn from the vice-consul of the United States at Liverpool that the steamer heretofore known as the *Japan*, or the *Georgia*, purporting to have been sold or transferred to British subjects, is about to sail from Liverpool for some destination unknown, but believed to be with unfriendly intentions to the United States. The validity of a sale of a belligerent vessel in a neutral port in time of war has ever been denied by Great Britain when a party to the war and is now denied by the United States. This vessel is therefore open to capture and condemnation as lawful prize of war wherever she may be found upon the high seas, no matter what may be the national character she assumes."[87]
>
> On the same day, the assistant secretary of the legation in London wrote to Capt. Winslow: "The *Georgia* or *Japan*, is still at (Liverpool), but evidently preparing for mischief. Her brass tracks, or rails, for the gun carriages have been taken up from the deck and stowed in her stokehole, but no other change has been made in her as a man-of-war, although it is pretended that she was lately sold for commercial purposes. . . . Semmes (previously of the *Alabama*) is at Liverpool with Bulloch concocting some roguery. It is reported that her nettings are to be fitted up for the hammocks. She has not made any preparation yet for sea, but she could be coaled and ready in twenty-four hours."[88]

WENSDAY AUG. 3RD

Standing up for Liverpool. Took A Pilot about 8 bells a.m. Made the Citty
about 1 Oclock. Passd two ships of the Line and and one Frigate pass'd near
the two Rams that was intended for the Rebs. Anchord near one of them.
They looks like they would give our Gun Boats some troubble. One of the
English Comodores came on board. Saluted the English Flag.

THURSDAY AUG. 4TH

At Liverpool. Morning Rainy. Saw papers from home of the 21st ult. Heard of
the invasion of Maryland and attack upon Washington and thair repulse and
Retreat, also the deppredations of the "Florida." Made preparations for coaling
ship, as we are to sail on the morrow, so as not to break the English *Newtrality*
Law. Our coal arrived about 10 Oclock P.M. We at once began to coal ship.[89]

FRIDAY AUG. 5TH

At Liverpool. We coald ship all night. Finish'd about 9 Oclock when we at
one proceed to up anchor. While geting up Anchor Charles Johnston (ord.
sea) died of consumption, native of Boston Mass. being in great haste we were
obliged to take his boddy to sea for Burial. We left Liverpool about 10 Oclock,
as soon as we were well down the Chanel we began to Disguise ship, sent
down Degallant Mast and yard, in sending down our Main Degallant Mast.
We brook it at the sheaf. At 6 bells all hands were musterd to bury the dead. I
acted as one of the bearers.

SATURDAY AUG. 6TH

This Morning we looks quite alterd. After working all night disguiseing ship
we would hardly know her at A distant. We have been cruiseing about in St.
George's Chanel. Pass'd many sails of all kinds. At 6 bells all Hands were
musterd to hear the sentance of the court Martial. There were several
disrateed for Drunkenness and Desertion. Very cool. We Holy Stones Decks
and clear of some of the coal dust. Tis very different from our coal, so much
more dust. Quite cool.

SUNDAY AUG. 7TH

Cruiseing in the Bay of Biscay. Quite cool. Steering to the southard. Quaters
at four bells then serveace at five five bells. Passd many sails in Evening. All

hands were musterd to hear the sentance of two Men by Court Martial for Drunkenness and Riotous conduct, each to loose six months pay and to be disrateed.

MONDAY AUG. 8TH

Cruiseing in the Bay of Biscay, quite cool to day we rous'd up our sheet cable and over haul them, then stowd them away again in the Evening we saw A steamer and gave chase. Carried no lights all our Fore and aft sails set.

> As the *Niagara* was cruising in the Bay of Biscay awaiting the *Georgia*, Craven received word from the vice-consul in Liverpool that the *Georgia* was still there. "Commodore: It was unfortunate that your boat came so late on Friday morning, for when I returned I found a message waiting that the *Georgia* had been detained at the request of the Portuguese minister, and it was then too late to let you know. The *Georgia* is here yet. She was just going through the gate on Friday when the order came by telegraph to stop her until further orders. To-day orders came to let her go, and at tide turn she left the dock and is now at anchor off the Rock Fort. I think she will go during the night, and when she has gone I will telegraph you, care of consul at Lisbon."[90]

TUESDAY AUG. 9TH

Cruiseing in the Bay of Biscay. A little warmer than we have felt it for several days we chase'd the steamer and overtook her about 4 Oclock A.M. one of the Meditterainian Mail steamers. We again hauld our cours to the southard. To day we set all our squinsails, goin along quite briskly.

WENSDAY AUG. 10TH

On the coast of Portagual. Quite warm. All hands were Musterd at three bells. Read the Articles of War. Made Land about 8 bells. Noon, passd An English mail steamer. We took A Pilot at 8 bells P.M. got out Boats. We expects to see Lisbon on the Morrow. The country is verry High and Hilly.

THURSDAY AUG. 11TH

Off the Port of Lisbon. Last night A steamer (Brig. Rig.) pass'd close to us. When we attempt'd to speak her, she douse'd her lights and attempted to pass her we also douse'd lights also and gave chase. We overtook her and spoke her thair reply was the Schottish steamer Julia. We askd where from and where bound but we got no answer. We stood of[f] and on all night. This Morning we saw A steamer (Brig. Rig.) suppose to be the same steamer that we spoke

last night. Also another steamer (Barque Rig). We kept about A mile from
them all day towards Evening we stood in for land and ascended the River
and came to anchor below the Citty about 7 bells. The country is very hilly.
As soon as we cast Anchor Boats were along side with Washerwomen and
all kinds of Fruits. Verry warm. Write to Aunt Jones (No. 2 Sears Place
Boston Mass).

FRIDAY AUG. 12TH

At anchor in the harbor of Lisbon. Verry hot. At Eight Bells we fired A salute
to the Counsel and one to the Admiral and one Nanational to the Government. Spread awnings verry hot. A plenty of Fruit. The Country aboat here
is verry hilly and Rocky. After Quaters all hands had A general swim. We
made preperation for coaling ship. Spread Awnings. The most of the crew
slept apon the spar Deck under the awning. It was much more pleasanter
thare than below.

SATURDAY AUG. 13TH

Last night verry warm but pleasanter this Morning. Coal came along side by
7 Oclock we made preperations for coaling ship. Commenced to coal about
10 Oclock we coald ship all day verry hot this Evening unmoord ship got up
one anchor and stowd away awnings and awning stancions.

SUNDAY AUG. 14TH

At Anchor in the Port of Lisbon. It was not so warm last night. This Morning we Fird A salute to the Counsel then we got up anchor and by 11 Oclock
we had gaind the sea, when we discharged the Pilot and stood to the Eastward quite warm we was hard at work all day puting coal below then
scrubbing decks. After all the work was over we had serveace. Still goin
to the Eastward.

MONDAY AUG. 15TH

Cruiseing of[f] the coast of Portugaul. We saw many sails. About 7 Oclock we
made A steamer and stood for her. She kept on her cours until we got within
five miles of her when she sudenly changed her cours. We Beat to Quaters and
Fird A shot. She show'd the English Collors we Fird another when she came
to we boarded her and found her to be the Rebel Privateer "Georgia" from

Liverpool on her way to refit as A cruiseer, but the next cruise that she makes will be for Uncle Samuel. She is A verry pretty vessel. Brig Rig. A propeller and tis said that she steams verry fast. She have two New Engines and Boilers. What her cargo is we do not know. This capture makes our Crew feel verry proud. We gave her Provissions, Coal and Water, also some chain. Put A Prize Crew on board in charge of Act. Master Jacob Kimball. We then transferd her Crew to our ship. Some in number. All Englishmen. They said that they ship'd in her to go to the Coast of Affricca but they made A short voyage. The "Georgia" takes A Mail to the states so I avail'd myself of the opportunity of sending A letter to C.W.R., A.C.H. and one to my Aunt. We also sent home some invallids. That is one good deed for the "Niagara" and we hope that she will do many more before the cruise is up.

TUESDAY AUG. 16TH

Off the coast of Portugal. It took us the greater part of the Night to put the necessary articles on board of the "Georgia." We sent on board some water to day and stood on the Coast for the States with her. About noon or A little later she (the "Georgia") Squaird away for the states with many A good wish from the Boys of the "Niagara." We will now take A look for some of the other cruiseers of would be King Jeff. We have verry fine weather.

> Craven advised Welles of the great events of the preceding days: "Sir: I have the honor to inform you that in compliance with the instructions contained in a letter from Mr. Adams, our minister at London[,] I sailed with the 'Niagara' from Antwerp on the 29th of July for Liverpool, where I arrived on the 3d of August, and ascertained that the *Georgia* would sail for Lisbon in a day or two. Supposing my best chances for falling in with her would be on this coast, I left Liverpool on the 5th instant, arrived at Lisbon on the 11th, coaled ship, and sailed again yesterday morning; and this morning at about 9:30 o'clock discovered the *Georgia* on our port bow, standing to the southward. At 9:45 brought her to, and at noon put a prize crew on board under charge of Acting Master Kimball, with orders to proceed to Boston, Mass."[91]
>
> Craven sent instructions about the disposition of the *Georgia*, described in some measure by WBG on Aug. 16, to the *Georgia*'s acting master, Jacob Kimball, on the very same day: "Proceed with the steamer *Georgia* under your charge to the port of Boston, Mass., and there deliver her, together with the accompanying papers (which are all that were found on board) and the persons retained as witnesses, to the judge of the U.S. district court, or to the U.S. prize commissioners at that place, taking his or their receipt for the same. You

will not deliver either her, the papers, or the witnesses to the order of any other person or parties unless directed to act otherwise by the Navy Department or flag-officer commanding the station. The *Georgia* was seized by this vessel, under my command, on the 15th day of August, 1864, off this coast as a pirate, formerly cruising under the rebel flag, and after committing numerous acts of piracy upon our commerce, being illegally sold in a neutral port; and of the circumstances attending the case you are sufficiently aware, and will communicate them when required to do so by competent authority. On your arrival at Boston, Mass., and immediately after you have visited the judge or prize commissioners, you will call upon the U. S. district attorney thereat, show him these instructions, and give him any information concerning the seizure he may solicit. Then you will next report yourself in person to the commanding officer of the navy yard thereat, show him also these instructions, and ask his directions, when needed, as to the disposition of yourself and the rest constituting the prize crew. Finally, when duly notified by the judge, prize commissioners, or district attorney that your services are no longer wanted by the court, you will at once return to your vessel, taking with you the men under your command and the receipt above alluded to, unless otherwise ordered by superior authority. You will receive herewith a communication for the Secretary of the Navy, giving him a detailed account of the seizure. This you will mail immediately on your arrival at Boston."[92]

WBG's shipmate Henry Smith expresses outrage at the British involvement with the *Georgia*: "I wish this to be the fate of all cruisers that are in rebel hands, fitted out and manned by English subjects. This is their neutrality—sheltering pirates from the laws. But there is a reckoning day coming. English gunners and seamen could not fight with the gallant Kearsarge. Glory be the little ship which wiped out the greatest piratical craft that ever floated!"[93]

But there was considerable controversy about the *Georgia* because she was flying under the British flag, as WBG had noted, and was purchased by Mr. E. Bates, a Liverpool shipowner, and registered as a British vessel. Craven seems to have anticipated the controversy in an Aug. 24 report that he sent to Secretary Welles from Dover: "On the 15th instant, in lattitude 39° 16' N., longitude 9° 38' W., I fell in with the steamer *Georgia*, formerly the priate *Japan*, and sent her as a good and lawful prize to the United States, under charge of Acting Master Jacob Kimball. . . . As the *Georgia* was sailing under the English flag, and was chartered by the Portuguese Government, and as her officers and crew were evidently engaged in good faith to sail on a lawful voyage, and could neither be treated as blockade runners nor as belligerents, it seemed to me to be improper to send them to the United States, excepting the chief mate and engineer. I have brought the master (Captain Withacomb), his officers and crew, here. There appears to be no doubt as to the *Georgia*'s being a good and lawful prize, but it seems that some more positive evidence than we now have to identify her as the 'Japan' is necessary, and I have written to Mr. Adams for information as to how that evidence is to be obtained."[94]

On Sept. 3, *The Law Times* of London noted that the *Georgia* had been refitted as a "passenger ship" and was twenty miles off Lisbon where the *Niagara* was "seen apparently waiting for." The *Times* noted that in both the United States and Great Britain, the transfer of merchant ships by a belligerent to a neutral was considered valid in time of war so long as the purchase was bona fide. The assumption was made that communication relating to the sale should be made, given the possibility that a vessel might find her way back into the hands of the seller. Suggesting that the U.S. government might have to back down as it had in the famed *Trent* incident when the Confederate envoys were taken off of a British ship, the *Times* said: "If ever the sale of a ship used for war could be free from suspicion that, by a colourable transaction, she was being reserved for the future use of the selling belligerent when the belligerent might find itself in a favourable position for repurchase, that sale would, to all appearance, be the sale of the *Georgia*."[95]

The following week, Sept. 10, the *Times* noted the promulgation of an Order in Council subsequent to the transfer of the *Georgia* that prohibited all such sales. The article stated that the legislation had taken account of British interests and did not "require the sacrifice of the *Georgia* on the altar of precedent."[96] On Sept. 17, the *Times* noted that Lord Russell had refused any kind of diplomatic response to the seizure of the *Georgia* and had stated to Mr. Bates that a prize court in the United States would have to resolve the matter. The *Times* now considered this case "entirely different" from the *Trent* dispute: "There no ship or anything was captured which could legitimately become matter for judicial determination. Passengers were seized in a British mail ship, and forcibly taken away. The present is no occasion for angry feeling. The British flag has received no insult."[97] The British were now ready to accept American judicial resolution. That was to come at the end of the war in the District Court of Massachusetts, which found for the United States, essentially charging that the British had used a ploy to protect a ship of war in imminent danger of capture. The court concluded that the sale was genuine and bona fide. It cited the authority of the proposition that the doctrine of a sale of ship of war is illegal. Said the court: "The duty of a neutral is to give no aid to either belligerent. This duty is evaded if ships of war in great danger of capture, as was notoriously the case here, can be turned into money in a neutral port in which they have taken refuge. The standing order which the British government had adopted, limiting the time that such vessels should stay in the ports of the empire, was in fact evaded by the sale of the *Georgia*, against the protest of our representative."[98]

The matter was appealed to the U.S. Supreme Court, which also assumed the bona fide nature of the sale and that the intent of the purchaser was not to equip the *Georgia* as an armed vessel. The Court, speaking through Justice Samuel Nelson, adhered to the principle against the purchases of vessels of war from a belligerent. "The removed armament of a vessel, built for war, can be readily replaced, and so can every other change be made, or equipment furnished for effective and immediate service. The *Georgia* may be instanced in part illustration of this proof. Her deck remained to the same, from which the pivot guns and others had been taken; it had been built originally strong, in order to sustain the war armament, and further strengthened by upright and stanchions beneath. The claimant states that the alterations, repairs and outfit of the vessel for merchant service, cost some £3000. Probably an equal sum would have again fitted her for the replacement of her original armament as a man of war. . . . That *The Georgia* in the present case, entered the Port of Liverpool to escape from the vessels of the United States in pursuit, is manifest. The steam frigates *Kearsarge*, *Niagara* and *Sacramento* were cruising off the coast of France and in the British Channel, in search of this vessel and others that had become notorious for their depredations on American commerce. It was but a few days after the purchase of the Georgia by the claimant, *The Alabama*, was captured in the Channel, after a short and brilliant action, by *The Kearsarge*. *The Georgia* was watched from the time she entered the Port of Liverpool, and was seized as soon as she left it."[99]

The Court noted that under French and Russian law, in contrast to that of England and America, the question posed could not even arise because their law prohibited even sales of merchant ships in addition to warships. In conclusion, it said: "It may not be inappropriate to remark that Lord Russell advised Mr. Adams, on the day after *The Georgia* left Liverpool under the charter-party to the Portuguese Government, August 8th, 1864, Her Majesty's Government had given directions that, 'In future no ship of war, of either belligerent, shall be allowed to be brought into any of Her Majesty's ports for the purpose of being dismantled or sold.'"

WENSDAY AUG. 17TH

We changed our cours to the Northard. Verry fine weather. Saw several sails but spoke none. One Italian Brig pass'd close to us. We carried full sail all night and day. Cleand ship. etc.

THURSDAY AUG. 18TH

Still cruiseing to the Northard. General Quaters at 3 bells. No. one Gun came in by the run and and injured her carrage. A little after Quaters we got up and bend studinsails. Carried them all day. Fine weather. A little cooler than we have had it for several days.

FRIDAY AUG. 19TH

Cruiseing to the Northard. Cloudy and cool. Nothing of interest transpireing except that we have A Band of four Peicees and they have begun to Practice. Also that they have begun to drill the Men with single sticks. This Evening all hands were Musterd. There were several of the crew Rateed. Also severel that was disrateed was restored to thair former rateing.

SATURDAY AUG. 20TH

Still cruiseing to the Northward. Quite cool. We had A general cleaning. Pass'd several sails.

SUNDAY AUG. 21ST

We Made Land from the Mast Head about 1 bell A.M. we stood up the Chanel. Quaters and Inspection at 4 bells. Quite A number of the crew were punish'd by being kept apon deck six hours for haveing on dirty shirts and for not haveing on thair watch Mark after Inspection. Serveace pass'd A number of sails. Geting quite cool. All hands were orderd to appear at evening Quaters with thair Pea Jackets as they are A verry necessary article at this time.

MONDAY AUG. 22ND

Cruiseing up the Chanel. Quite cool. During the Night we carried our Fore and aft sails but the wind changeing to the Northard and Eastward. We were oblige'd to take them in. It clouded up and the wind increasd so much that by ten Oclock we had quite A storm. Saw many sails. About 8 Oclock we made the Ile of Wight. We stop'd once about 9¾ Oclock to take soundings. Still blowing verry hard and Raining.

TUESDAY AUG. 23RD

Cruiseing up Chanel, blowing verry hard and Raining. About Noon we set our Fore and Aft sails after the Wind changed to the westward it became more moderated. The sun shone out as it was goin to red so we shall look for A Fair day on the Morrow.

WENSDAY AUG. 24TH

At Daylight the Highlands of Dover is in sight. After takeen on board A pilot we ran in and (to Dover) and anchord about 9 Oclock A.M. we then put the Prisoners (the crew of the "Georgia") on board of A Pilot Boat and sent them in Charge of Lieut Phoenix on shore to deliver them up to the Athorities. While the Negociations were pending one Man Deserted from the Boat. We got up anchor about 11 Oclock and set sail for Flushing where we arrived about 7 Oclock. We made A verry quick run averadgeing fourteen and A half knots all day (14½). That is quick time. At Flushing we met the "Saccramento." We heard that she colied with A Brig in the Chanel and sunk her.

(the Brig. We heard at Dover of the capture of Mobile by the Federals. We had
A small Mail to night.

THURSDAY AUG. 25TH

At Anchor at Flushing. We ha[d] Rain to day. Quite cool. The Kings Birth
day. We Fird A salute. We heard that we are to go to sea amediately and
commenced preperation for coaling. We received another Mail. I received
three letters. One from C.W.R. Heard of the Death of Mrs. White. Also of
the Wounding of J. Kellogg and that Virgil Richardson is engaged to
Miss R.K.

FRIDAY AUG. 26TH

At anchor at Flushing. Quite cool and cloudy. This Morning we got A Brig
along side with Coal and began to coal ship amediately after Breakfast
another Vessel loaded with coal came Along side and we coald ship from
Both sides at work on the Engine and Riging. Arrival of tender to Royal
Yach[t] of England.

SATURDAY AUG. 27TH

At Anchor. At Flushing. Still coaling ship. We had A shower this Morning. We
cleard up the ship and Made preperation for the sabath. Two men deserted.

SUNDAY AUG. 28TH

At Anchor at Flushing. Raining in Morning. Last evening the American
Minister and Lady from Hauge came on board. We saluted him. We Fired A
salute this Morning on the arrival of the Queen of England's Yacht. We had
Quaters at four bells. Serveace at 5. The Minister and Lady on board to
serveace. Smiths time Expired.

MONDAY AUG. 29TH

At Flushing. Fine day. Cleaning ship and seting up rigging scrubbing ship
outside. A few visitors on board. Arrival of the Counsel from Antwerp.
Coaling ship. Arrest of the men who deserted on Saturday. Servd out Grog
Money to some of the crew.

TUESDAY AUG. 30TH

At Flushing. Fine day. Coaling ship. Battle down Rigging. Write to C.W.R.

WENSDAY AUG. 31ST

Arriveal of A Mail. Heard the Details of the Capture of Mobiele and the loss of
the Monitor "Tecumsa" with all on board including Captain Craveen, brother
to Comodore Craven. It was call'd the Greatest Naval Battle of the War.
Admiral Buchanen of the Rebel Navy was taken Prisoner. The Royal Yacht of
the King of Belgum came down the River and pass'd around the ship. I had A
look at his Highness the King from the Deck. He is a Man about fifty medium
hight, quite Robust. We saluteed him with a Nanational salute.

> News of the U.S victory at Mobile Bay had begun to spread on Aug. 11. The
> U.S.S. *Tecumseh* was sunk after proceeding toward the C.S.S. *Tennessee* on
> Aug. 5.[100]

THURSDAY SEPT. 1ST

Last Evening we had quite A blow for A few Minutes, then Rain all night. To
day we sent down our Degallant Mast and Yards and sent up our Degallant
and Royal Mast. Some of our Men had A fight and was giveen Quaters in the
Brig. Served out Grog Money. Some one of the Crew wrote A letter to the
Comodore dielateing [dilating] him on the treatment of the Crew in not
giveing them liberty. The Comodore apon this stop'd the Paymaster from
serveing out Grog Money and stop'd the *Sehouse* until the party who wrote
the letter was found out. The ship was all excitement for about two Hours
when the Man that wrote the letter came forward and acknowledge'd to the
letter. He was placed in double Irons to await his trial by Court Martial and
every thing soon return to thair usual way.

FRIDAY SEPT. 2ND

At Flushing. Morning quite pleasant for the season. Strike the coal below that
we had apon Decks and had A general cleaning spell every day more or less.
Some one of the crew is put into Durance vile for some petty offence among
so many it is almost impossible to keep the Run of so many. About 7 bells it
commenced to Rain slightly.

SATURDAY SEPT. 3RD

At Flushing. Raining alternately all day. We got up steam which looks like leaveing for some other part of this Hemisphere. To day A court Martial convend to
try several Men for different offences. We received our Grog Money for August.

SUNDAY SEPT. 4TH

At Flushing. Raining all day. We display'd the Dutch Flag at our Main and American Flag at our Fore Mizzen and Peak, the "Saccramento" the same. We had serveace at 5 bells. We received A Mail from the states in the afternoon. Some of our Men went on board of the "Saccramento" and some of her crew came on board here. Lieut Pheonix returnd this Evening.

MONDAY SEPT. 5TH

At Flushing. Raining all the Morning. In the Afternoon I went ashore, had A good time and returnd on board at sun set. All hands were musterd to hear the sentance of the Court Martial. The streets of Flushing are verry narrow but clean. The Buildings are on the Ancient style. End of book No. 3

⌐

From September 6, 1864, through early February 1865 there are no diary entries. WBG clearly kept up his diary in these months because it picks up on an obviously incomplete entry. It is likely that this section was thrown out in 1958 by someone who went through Lawrence Gould's home before my father's arrival. Note that, in contrast to the previous parts of the diary, there is a host of illegible gaps owing to the deterioration of this swatch of pages, which are not bound between covers as the other sections are.

During the months of the lost entries, the *Niagara* fruitlessly pursued the screw-steamer *Laurel*.[101] And November 1864 was a major turning point—the presidential election between Lincoln and Gen. McClellan. In a Nov. 22 report to Welles, Craven said: "Telegrams yesterday announced the reelection of his Excellency President Lincoln. The *Niagara* was immediately dressed, with our national flag flying at her mastheads. Considering this to be the greatest and most important contest of the war, and most glorious in its results, I have again dressed ship to-day, and at noon fired a salute of twenty-one guns. It is, I believe, the first time since our national existence that such a demonstration was made by any of our ships of war, but the occasion seems so momentous and all-glorious to me that I could not resist the impulse to thus manifest my joy."[102]

⌐

[FEBRUARY 4, 1865, FLUSHING]

. . . make preparation for leaveing the land of sour krout About 6 bells. [all] Hands were called to up Anchor. An[d] soon the sharpe notes of the fife, a[nd] the steady tramp of the men told th[at] we were soon to be Afloat again apon the Deep Green Sea. We left Flushing and descended the Scheldt and came to Anchor of Ostend at about 1 bell P.M.

SUNDAY FEB. 5TH

This Morning all Hands were called about 2 bells. We amediately got underway and proceeded down the North Sea. We had Inspection at 10 Oclock and Quarters at 10½ Oclock, we anchord off Dover about 4 bells. Afternoon sent a Boat asshore. Made preparation for leaveing but on the return of the Boat, we secured everything. We heard that the Rebels have got hold of an Iron Clad Ram and that she have gone to sea. They obtained her throu[gh] the French and Danes. We sail [on] the morrow in search. We [also] heard that the A[rmy] have captured Fort Caswell and Johnston and of cours the town of Smithville. A report is that the Gun Boats had gone up the River. A verry thick fog all day.

[M]ON. FEB.6TH

This Morning all Hands were called at 2 bells. Got Breakfast, then up anchor. Stood down the Chanel. Verry fine weather. About 1 bell P.M. all hands were called to make sail.

TUES. FEB. 7TH

Running Morning. E.S.E. A[t] noon W.N.W. the wind hauld ahead in the mid watch last night when it became nessary to shorten sail. A[t] night we are running due W. Night verry fine. Moonlight but wind dead ahead.

WENS. FEB. 8TH

Running along quite Brisk. Light rai[n]. Wind in the quarter. Morning wa[rm]. Made sail. Cours lay S.W.S. We [are] evidently in the Bay of Biscay. [I] feel quite unwell.

THURS. FEB. 9TH

Bay of Biscay. Cours lay S.W. by _____. Light wind on the Quarter. Fur[ld] [Dega]llantsails. We are not ma[king] much speed to day. In the After[noon]

we had General Quarters make e[very]thing ready for A General Engage-
m[ent]. It realy looks as if we are to have [a] fight of some kind.

> The Confederates, frustrated by the British government's rigorous policy
> against the construction of Confederate ships in the country, moved toward
> France, which had pioneered in the development of ironclads for similar serv-
> ices. As Warren F. Spencer has said: "John Slidell and James Bulloch did not
> have to read the diplomatic correspondence during the first half of 1863 to
> know that conditions in Paris were favorable to the South. They could add the
> factors—unemployment, . . . the Mexican situation,[and others, including the
> domestic political popularity of President Lincoln's opponents]—and logi-
> cally conclude that Napoleon III, with or without Great Britain, would favor
> two republics in North America. They could hope and even scheme for offi-
> cial recognition and ultimate intervention in the Civil War. King Cotton had
> not yet been dethroned."[103]

FRI. FEB. 10TH

Bay of Biscay. Blowing verry stro[ng] from the N.W. Our course lay to the
southard and westward. During the night we shorten sail and close reef[d]
Topsails, lay to all night, in the morning we sat Foresail, Foretrysail and main
Trysail. About 7 bells. N. the Port Fore Tack gave away the sail began to shift
up, we clew'd it up and unbend it amediately but before we got the Foresail
secur'd the Fore Trysail sheet gave away when we were obliged to furl that
also. We made land about 12 Oclock and stoo[d] for it blowing verry strong
ship laboring verry heavaly all the time. We bend another Foresail after we got
under the lee of the land everything became quite control[able] _____ ran in
until about _____ we about ship and stood off again[st] several sails and one
steamer in sight. We being now off Cape Feniston, Portugal. This morning we
also carried away our Forestaysail and were obliged to Bend another. This
being the Roughest weather that we have had since we left York.

SAT. FEB. 11TH

Off the Island of Gallica. We stood off and on all night. This morning we
stood in hoisted the Jack. A Pilot came on board about 8 bells and we ran into
the Bey and anchor[ed] of the Citty of Corruña about 11 Oclock. We saluted
the Spanish Collars. They answered us from one of thair For[ts] when the
Pilot came on board h[e] braught the report that the Rebel Ram Stonewall
was in Port i[n] A disabled condition we were __ on to him. Now there looks

lik[e] A fight certain. The Crew were o[rdered] to sharpen their Cuttlasses
an[d] we took up A plenty of shots. _____ plugs and packing rea[dy]

The "fight," as WBG noted on Feb. 11, was to be with the C.S.S. *Stonewall*. As
the Prussian-Danish war drew to a conclusion in the fall of 1864, James Bulloch, the head of Confederate operations in Europe, saw an opportunity to purchase an ironclad for the Confederacy. The *Sphinx*, destined for Denmark from
Bordeaux, France, suddenly became available because Denmark had no more
use for her at the end of the war with Prussia. The stage had been set in July
1863, when Bulloch and Arnous de Riviere contracted for the *Sphinx* and another ironclad to be built for the Confederacy. But after the *Sphinx* was three-
fifths finished, in September or October 1863, the fortunes of the Confederate
naval construction program began to fade. The appearance of the C.S.S.
Florida, commanded by John Maffitt, created two developments: (1) a demand
for munitions and assistance that bordered on the "arrogant" and (2) an attraction provided for major northern vessels, including WBG's *Niagara*, to come
into European waters. Says Spencer: "From the autumn of 1863 until the spring
of 1864 major war vessels of both belligerents plied the seas from the Madeira
Islands, around Portugal and Spain, and on into the Bay of Biscayne and the
English Channel. These maritime hostilities in European waters climaxed dramatically in June 1864 with the decisive and classic *Kearsarge-Alabama* battle
(adverted to by WBG above) and continued with the United States vessels *Niagara*, *Sacramento* and *Iroquois* keeping watch over the Bordeaux ironclads
and in 1864 eventually confronting the only ironclad that fell into Confederate
hands, the C.S.S. *Stonewall*. But it all began that September day when the
Kearsarge dropped anchor not far from the docked *Florida*."[104]

These changes, which presaged conflict close to France, produced more reticence on the part of Napoleon III toward Confederate activities. The invitation
to build ships in France was withdrawn as the fortunes of the Civil War began to
change in late 1863 in the wake of Gettysburg and Vicksburg and as an upsurge
in cotton imports and a decline in unemployment persuaded the French that a
more conciliatory posture toward the United States was now compatible with
their designs upon Mexico. In May 1864, Napoleon III ordered Arnous not to
sell the ship to the Confederacy. As a result it appeared as though the Confederates' chances of getting anything from the French shipyards were remote.

But in December 1864, with Denmark no longer a willing purchaser, the
prospect of a deal with the Confederacy revived. In the hope that the ironclad
would spread fear throughout the North and scatter the U.S. Navy, which had
blocked off all ports except Wilmington, a new agreement was signed that
brought the *Sphinx* to the Confederate Navy. The ironclad was to proceed to
Copenhagen and then rendezvous with a Confederate crew and supplies. Sailing on Jan. 7, 1865, under the Danish flag and with a Danish crew, the ship was
temporarily named *Olinda* by the Danes and then transferred to the authority
of the Confederates. It was renamed the C.S.S. *Stonewall* by its commander,
Thomas Jefferson Page.

On Feb. 8, John Bigelow, U.S. chargé d'affaires in Paris, noted the arrival of the *Stonewall* in Ferrol and the possibility that a contest between the *Stonewall* and the *Niagara* might be "sufficiently uncertain to make it bad policy to risk one unnecessarily." Horatio J. Perry, U.S. chargé in Madrid, wrote to both Craven of the *Niagara* and Bigelow complaining of the unwillingness or inability of France or Spain to take action against the *Stonewall* while it was in Ferrol for repairs.[105] According to Craven, it was on this date—Feb. 11—that he had "learned that an ironclad ram under the Confederate flag, called the *Stonewall*, had put in here some ten days previously for repairs, but remained only three days and then went to Ferrol, and would be ready for sea in about three days."[106]

SUNDAY FEB. 12TH

Off the Citty of Corruña. Fine [day] we had Inspection at 10 Oclock. Devine serveace at 10½ Oclock. Full of visitors all day. Boat came along side with Fruit and other articles for sale. All of the talk is of the Ra[m]. We expects that she is an ugley customer to handle, but we will not be dismayed.

On this day, Thomas Jefferson Page writes James Bulloch in Liverpool: "The necessary repairs—that is, such as I suppose the authorities will allow to be made—would require not less than ten days. They may take less, for so anxious are these people to get rid of us they are doing everything in the most hurried manner, not securing the serious damage (the leak around the rudder-heads) as it should be; [and] they will doubtless not allow [Sundays and] feast days to stop them. The Yankee frigate, *Niagara*, having arrived yesterday in Coruña, about nine miles from here, has given them additional uneasiness and apprehension."[107]

MON. FEB. 13TH

At Corruña. A verry fine day. We have been verry buisey all day unbending and bending Sails geting up shots and geting sand on board for Batries and otherwise prepareing the Ship for the desperate engagement that is to come off. We have been crowded with visitors all day among them many Ladies. Nin[e] men from one of the Boats stop'd asshore. All was braught off except three. It is the opinion of the People here that the Ram will be too much for us but time will tell. Old T[om] not the Man to stand.

[TUES.] FEB. 14TH

At Corruña. A verry fine day. This morning it was reported that A Rebel Steamer had come in during the night and went up to the Navy Yard but it proved to be an English steamer with men and material of War for the Ram

but the athorities would not allow them to be deliver'd in Port. About 1 Oclock
we rig'd Capstan and ran in about thirty Fathoms of Chain. About the time
every thing was made snug it was reported that the Ram had run out and put
to sea. We were all confusion and excitement. There were several Men and
Women on board and such A bustle and tumbling up the gangways you would
have been much amused at thair fri[ght] it proved however to be the steam[er]
above mentioned. We up Boats and hoisted the Flag for the Pilot. Mad[e]
preparation for sea at 1 bell P.M. all Hands were call'd to up an[chor. All] the
evening we were surr[ound]ed with Boats, loaded with visiters [but] they was
no[t] allowed to come on boar[d]. It occasion'd much disapointment [to] them
but thair visit will be received [an]other time. By the time the Capstan was
man'd the order was belayed. We than let every thing remain until about four
Bells. It being somewhat dark we then up Anchor and proceed (with darken
Lanterns) for the River leadeing to the Navy Yard. As soon as we reach'd the
River we [un]cover'd lights and ascended the River. The pasage is A verry
narrow one bu[t] verry cold Watter. The whole passage for A mile in length is
one continued line of Fortifacations. The River opens into a beautiful Bay not
verry large but surrounded by lofty hills and great Mountains. (Pryernees) in
the distance on the Base of these hills stands the Citty of and the Navy Y[ard]
of wich the Rebel Ram St[onewall] was lying we came _____ close to A
Spanish *Sloop* of War a[bout] 8 bells P.M.

[WE]NS. FEB. 15TH
At Ferrol. As soon as day dawns the Crew was all eagerness to see [the] monster
that have vow'd vengeance for us. We are lying about one Thousand yards from
her (Ram). She looks like an ugly customer for anything that she can hit with
her Prow but we do not think she can come it over this ship. At Nine Oclock we
saluted the Port and the Band Play'd two nanational Airs then we saluted the
Admiral wich was returned amediately. The same time we show'd our B__ing,
the Ram show'd hers. She lo[ok] defiantly. Some of our men meet some of her
crew on shore and they Braught of[f] A Rebs cap as a trophy. It was of gray
stainnett, [the] Pants of the same, and shirts of Flanel trim'd with white. In the
Afternoon two of them pass _____ the ship exclaimein[g] that we will be A
Bully Prize to the[m] but I am inclined to believe that [they] are of the wrong

opinion. We were visited by several Offecers and some of the Spanish Offercers. The Bay is coverd all day with Fishermans. We had some large oysters to
day the first since we left the states. The Farms covering the sides of these
Hil[ls] looks verry Beautiful from the Basin like appearance of the Bay. It looks
verry strange that in this country where Nature have lavished her riches that
there should be so many Poor People.

> In a report of Feb. 28, Craven says: "On the evening of the 15th instant I pro-
> ceeded with the *Niagara* to Ferrol, and on the following morning called upon
> the military and civil governors of the place, who informed me that her com-
> mander, Thomas J. Page, had reported the *Stonewall* ready for sea, but had
> not as yet appointed a time for sailing."[108]

[TH]URS. FEB. 16TH

At Ferrol. Raining and blowing verry hard all day. About 11 Oclock the
Spanish Admiral came on board on his departure. we saluted him on his
return to this ship. He returned our salute. About 12 Oclock we were obliged
to pay out more chain in consequence of the Blow. In the Afternoon it haild
and continued to Rain all day. We [had] no news since leaveing ____

[FRI. F]EB. 17TH

At Ferroll. Morning fine. Loos'd s[ails] at two bells, we had several showers
during the day. It is reported that the Commander of the Rebel Ram have
gone to Parris. Also that the Athoritie[s] will not take her into the Dock and
she cannot get the necessary repairs without goin into Dock. I hope that she
will soon leave this Port so that we can try her spirit. We fired A salute for the
Counsel about 12 Oclock. We furld sails at 6 bells.

> The U.S. chargé d'affaires in Paris, John Bigelow, was advised that "the Con-
> federates were using the *Rappahannock*, still tied up at Calais, as a collecting
> point for a crew for the *Stonewall*. This was absolutely contrary to French
> neutrality laws. Bigelow protested in as strong language as diplomacy permit-
> ted."[109] Apparently this effort was successful in obtaining French governmen-
> tal action to stop the recruitment.

SAT. FEB. 18TH

At Ferroll fine day. To day we aird Beding, served out clean Hammocks. In the
Evening there was A repo[rt] that peace was declared in the state[s] but I do
not credit it.

> This report was undoubtedly triggered by the Hampton Roads Conference,
> where President Lincoln met with three Confederate representatives on Feb. 3.
> The President was quite firm in demanding an acceptance of the national au-
> thority of the United States before any discussion of other matters. This was the
> "last and only real effort at peace before surrender."[110]

SUN. FEB. 19TH

At Ferroll. Verry fine day. Inspection at 10 Oclock. Devine Serveace at 10½
Oclock. Several Visiters on board. We see that they are verry buisey at work
apon the Rigging of the Ram.

[MON.] FEB. 20TH

At Ferroll. Verry fine day. We lo[osd] sails at 9 Oclock. Several visiters c[ame]
on board among them many Lad[ies]. They enjoyed A pleasant hop on t[he]
light fantastic. Earley in the morning there was an altercation between some
of the Boardsmen and one of the Ships Corperals. We furld sails at 2 bells.
We see the Ram takeing in Coal to day. That look verry much like showing
fight. I hope that it will not be put off much longer. Several of our Officers
went ashore to A Ball at the Counsel's.

[TU]ES. FEB. 21ST

At Ferrol. Verry fine day. About 6 bells the "Saccramento" arrived from
Lisbon. She anchord close to us. We have no news from the states. We
received her with music by the Band.

[WEN]S. FEB. 22ND

At Ferrol. Last night about 10½ Oclock our lookout reported steam up on
the Ram. We sent the Lieut asshore and made everything read[y] to slip the
cable should she [a]tt[empt] to run out but when _____ was at her
anchorage with steam up every thing the same. A verry beautiful day. It being
Washington's birth day we dress'd ship and at noon fired A salute of 21 Guns.
The Spanish Frigate also saluted our Flag. At four bells we Rig'd Capstan
and prepared to get under way. About 6 bells we up anchor and saluteed
the Spanish Flag with 21 guns and stood out the Bay the "Sacramento"
following we anchord in the Harbor of Corruña about 1 bell P.M. the
Sacramento comeing in soon after. This Morning the Starboard Watch
scrub'd Hammocks.

THURS. FEB. 23RD

At Corruña. Verry fine day. Port Watch scrub'd Hammocks. Many Visiters
came on board. At 12½ Oclock we fired a Salute of 15 Gu[ns] and again at 2
Oclock. We were [vis]ited again by the Governer. On departure we saluteed
him. [The "Sacra]mento" is lying close to u[s].

A general fight tis certain the [Ram] is here and if she comes out we will
have A fight. The Ram carr[ies] one 300 lb. Armstrong Gun an[d] the
Forecastle and two 70 ib. Wh[it]worth Guns in two stationary Turrets (one in
each). She is plateed with 4½ in. of Iron and have al[so] a Prow extending
from her bow (below the watter) 22 feet. She have two separately acting
engines so that she can go ahead with one and back with the other and is
called fast. She have at present A crew of about 75 men and 14 Offercers. She
is Commanded by A Man named Page, A native of Norfolk VA. He formerly
was in our Navy. He says that h[e] is prepared for any single ship in the
United States Navy. She was built at Bordaux France for the Danish Government as it is said but the Danes makeing peace d[id] not want her when
the Rebs [came] in and baught her. _____ion that she was built
expressly for the Rebs and by Designs furnish'd by them. We are expecting
to fight but who will be the victors remains to be seen. Several visitors came
on board, Citizens and soldiers and several cadets from A Milatary school
that is situated here. Several of our Officers went asshore. The Citty is small
and looks verry Ancient. We can see several very ancient looking Churches
and two verry fine lighthouses. There are six Forts in sight commanding the
Citty and the entrance to the Bay wich is A verry fine one. The place is noted
for the many Battles faught in this vi[cin]ity during the Peninsular War and
also the death place of the [En]glish General Sir Thomas Moor[e] and also
the first place that We[lling]ton was distinguished. Well figh[t] is to be and
victory I pray wil[l be ours.] We are looking very anxiously [for] the
Rampages appearance bu[t it] comes not yet.

> WBG did not mention the length of the *Stonewall* here, 170 feet, which made
> her smaller than both the *Niagara* and her companion ship, the *Sacramento*.
> The *Stonewall*'s top speed was 13 knots, which meant that she could "outrun
> the *Sacramento*, whose top speed was 12.5 knots, but would be hard pressed
> to match the 14.5 knot maximum speed of the *Niagara*."[111]

[FR]I. FEB. 24TH

At Corruña. Raining all day. About __ Oclock two Coal Bargees came
alongside. We began to coal ship. Two Boys were conf[ined] for refuseing to
swab the Deck for the Offercer of the Deck and also for the Executive
Offercer.

[S]AT. FEB. 25TH

At Corruña. Raining alternately all day. Coaling ship. Maild A letter to C.W.[R.]

SUN. FEB. 26TH

At Corruña. Raining. Inspection at 10 Oclock. Devine serveace at 10½
Oclock. About 1 Oclock we were visited by the Govener General of the
Province and staff. On thair departure we saluteed him with 17 Guns. In the
afternoon some of our men went on board of the "Saccramento" and some of
her men came on board here. I have A verry severe Headache this evening.

[MON.] FEB. 27TH

At Corruña. I feel somewhat better this morning. Coaling ship and scrapeing
of Whitewash from [the fore]castle. We were visited [by] _____ dignataries
we Fired A salute of 13 Guns.

[TU]ES. FEB. 28TH

At Corruña. Fine day. Many visit[ors] on board. Last night several Men were
intoxicated and several fights occurd during the Evening and attempt was
made on the life of the Master At Arms as he allieged. They were oblig[ed] to
put extra sentries on the Main Deck. Five Men Deserted last nig[ht] among
them the Drummer of the Mariene Corp. One of the men that Deserted one
the men that Desertd on the 13th inst. was arrested asshore h[e] claims
English protection. He is in prison. What will be the decission of this case
we cannot conjecture.

> On this day, Craven expressed considerably more doubt than WBG had
> articulated on either Feb. 15 or Feb. 23. Said Craven in a letter to Horatio
> J. Perry in Madrid: "The leak (in the *Stonewall*) has been but imperfectly
> stopped, and might at any time break out and become as inconvenient as ever.
> Notwithstanding the pledges given you by the Spanish minister that strict or-
> ders had been issued to the commandant at Ferrol not to allow any repairs,

except such as were indispensable for the security of the crew of the *Stonewall* at sea, to be put upon her; notwithstanding the assurances of the naval commandent at Ferrol that those orders had been strictly obeyed, and notwithstanding I place implicit confidence in the honesty of purpose of these assurances, I cannot help feeling that in spite of their care and watchfulness to prevent it the pirates have had the opportunity and have clandestinely improved their time, and have done much more than they have proposed to do, not only toward the repairs but to the fitting out of their vessel in the bay of Ferrol. Besides other occupations, they were busily engaged for one or two days after my arrival at that port in filling up their shells and otherwise preparing their battery for work.

The *Stonewall* is a very formidable vessel. . . . If as fast as reputed to be in smooth water she ought to be more than a match for three such ships as the *Niagara*. Should we be so fortunate, however, as to catch her out in rough water, we might possibly be able to put an end to her career. Our main chance now depends upon the possibility of detaining her where she is until the Government sees fit to send out reenforcements. In the meantime . . . I shall strive to do my duty."[112]

WENS. MARCH 1ST

At Coruña. Fine day. We scrubd Pa__ work and got rid of some of the dirt of Coaldust and Limedust. One of the Men that deserted night before last [re]turnd on board this morning. He w[as] confined to await his trial by Court [Mar]tial. One the man who claim[s English] protection and one of the [men] that deserted night before last were br[ought] on board this Evening and we heard th[at] Morgan, another of the five is arrested ____ yesterday we ship'd A tenor Drumer for the Band. We had some visitors on board this Evening.

[THURS.] MARCH 2ND

At Corruña. Fine day. At 2 bells we loo[s'd] sails. At 9 bells we had General Quarter[s]. Many visiters on board. In the afterno[on] they braught Morgan on board. We heard that Charleston was evacuated by the Reb[s] and that the Federals occupied the Citty. About 6 bells we furld sails. The Peace Commissioners was not able to arrange the present difficulties so the War must go on.

[FRI.] MARCH 3RD

At Corruña. Verry fine day. Many visiters on board. We are almost tired waiting for the Ram to come out.

[SAT.] MARCH 4TH

At Corruña. Fine day. Many visiters on board. We had A Danceing Party on
A small scale. They are verry common thing here at this time.

[SUN.] MARCH 5TH

At Corruña. This morning we _____ then it cleard off. We had _____ at
10 Oclock and Devine serveace at 10½ Oclock. We received A Mail. I was
Joyful to receive 7 papers and a letter from Mr. W.H.H. We also heard of the
occupation of Charleston by ou[r] troops. Also the loss of the Monit[or]
"Patapsco" of Fort Sumptor. I saw an account of A light Batry wi[th] colored
Offercers also that Lieut Swails had his commission app[roved] by the
War Department.

MON. MARCH 6TH

At Corruña. A verry bad day. ____ing and Blowing all day. We received A mail
from the Sta[tes]. I received a letter from D.C.__

TUES. MARCH 7TH

At Corruña. Still blowing verry strong. Ship Rooling as heavaly is she was at
sea. We received dispatch this morning confirming the capture of Charleston
and Columbia. We together [with] the "Sacramento" dress'd ship an[d] Fired
at Noon A narrational [sa]lute of 21 Guns. We receive [mail] from the states.
I re[ceive] one letter from C.W.R. and five [pa]pers. We have an account of
the passage of the amendment to the Con[sti]tution prohibiting slavery
througho[ut] the United States. C is quite well. ____ have had A fair at N.
for the Benefit of the Freedmen. We now have plenty of news.

WENS. MARCH 8TH

At Corruña. Blowing quite fresh and cool. Several visiters on board in the
afternoon. Some Ladies came on board and they enjoyed A Fandango. At
3 bells A.M. all Hands were calld to Muster. Read the Articles of War. Feel
quite unwell.

> "The Spanish are said to have invented the Fandango (meaning Go and Dance)
> as a courtship dance. However, the primative Fandango may go all the way
> back to Phoenician soil. The Fandango was always danced by only two per-
> sons, who never touch each other with the body or the hand, but face each
> other.[It] is said to be a foundation to all the other Spanish Dances."[113]

[TH]URS. MARCH 9TH

At Corruña. Verry fine day. We had General Quarters at 9 ¼ Oclock. We received A Mail from the States. I received An Anglo. Several visiters on board.

[FRI.] MARCH 10TH

At Corruña. Fine day. Many visitors on board. In the Evening some Ladies came on board and they enjoyed A fandango.

SAT. [MAR]CH 11TH

At Coruña. Fine day. We had [In]spection at 10 and D[evine service] at [1]0½ Oclock. We received A Mail from the states. I received A letter from the 4th Auditor. No prize money ready. Arriveal of A corospondt Heral[d].

[S]UN. MARCH 12TH

At Corruña. The above was intended for this day. On Saturday nothing transpired of note.

[M]ON. MARCH 13TH

At Coruña. Fine day. "Saccramento" saild 7½. We have been verry buisey all day passing to and from shore. About 2 bells A.M. loose'd sails. Furld about 2 bells P.M. Securd everything for sea at 4 bells. Braught to the cable and Riggd capstan at 7 bells we up Anchor and stood out for S[ea]. As soon as we cleard the Harbor we saw the Sac—comeing in when she put about and follow'd us. About 4 bells all ha[nds] were call'd to make sail. Th[ere] is something in the Wind.

TUES. MARCH 14TH

All night we cruised off and on [wind] blowing verry strong and the s[ea runn]ing very high, durin[g] mid watch We were obliged to short[en] sail and double Reef the fore and main Topsails. The "Saccramento" [keep]ing near us all the time. There was A great many sick I being one of the number. We stood in and anchord of the mouth of the entera[nce] to the Port of Ferrol it being mor[e] moderate.

> Again, doubts are expressed about the prospects of the *Niagara* and the *Sacramento* against the *Stonewall*, this time by Vice-Consul Wilding in Liverpool in a March 14 letter to Perry in Madrid: "A person here who was formerly in one of the rebel privateers holds a commission and is waiting orders; has re-

ceived a letter from a man on board the *Stonewall*, in which the writer gives
some particulars of the vessel which it might be well to communicate to Commodore Craven. He says she is brig-rigged, topgallant forcastle; has a ram
(spur) projecting 40 feet; two turrets; forward turret has one rifled gun; shot,
11-inch shell, 50 pounds in cartridge, 10 pounds in shell; steel shell and shot
and segment shot; has four engines, two screws; speed, 12 knots; plates of turrets, 5, 7, and 8 inch. He says the *Niagara* and *Sacramento* are outside, but
give us little concern, as we shall run right into one of them and send her to the
bottom. The man to whom this is addressed has told my informant that he expects to go to the *Stonewall* as gunner, and that men are still being engaged for
her, and that a Dutch vessel is to take them to her."[114]

[WEN]S. MARCH 15TH

At Corruña. Fine day. This Morning w[e] up anchor at 6 bells ran into the
Harbor of Corruña and anchord at 8 bells. Scald my right hand.

[THU]RS. MARCH 16TH

At Corruña. Fine day. Nothing of interest transpireing.

[FRI.] MARCH 17TH

At Corruña. Fine day. A few visiters on board. Hand better.

[SAT.] MARCH 18TH

At Corruña. Nothing of note goin on excepting that we have A great deal of
Rain and storm during the mid watch. We were obliged to let go our starboard
Anchor.

[SUN.] MARCH 19TH

This morning we took up our starb[oard] Anchor. Raining. Serveace at ____.
Still blowing quite hard _____

[MON.] MARCH 20TH

At Corruña. Last night we were ob[liged] again drop our starbord anchor
a[nd] got up the sheet chain and after all became calm we struck it below
aga[in]. I received A letter from C.W.R. also 3 Papers. We hear of the occupation of Charleston S.C. by Gilmore and Columbia by Sheerman. Also t[he]
advance of Terry on Wilmington. I also received A speech of senitor Kassion
from Mr. J.E.C.

The reference here is to Alfred Howe Terry, who had led the second Ft.
Fisher–Wilmington expedition and captured the fort on Jan. 15.[115]

TUES. MARCH 21ST

At Corruña. Fine day. Coaling sh[ip]. About 11 Oclock we received A
repo[rt] that the Ram had sent down h[er] spars and would appear on the
M[or]row. And again at 1 Oclock that [the] Ram would be out at 2 Oclock
and about 2½ Oclock she did. We imediately beat to Quarters up anchor
and gave chase. B[ut] by the time that we were fairly under way the Ram
put ab[out] and Ran into Ferrol again _____ was followd by A
Spanish F[rigate] [c]ome I suppose to see a fight. We all were sadly
disapo[inted] for we know not when he will [come out] again. This
Morning four or fiv[e] white fellows beat Jerry Jones (co[lored]). He
was stabd in his left shoulder. Verry bad. I received A letter from G.L.M.
Quite well.

[WENS.] MARCH 22ND

At Corruña. Coaling ship all day. We received A Mail from the states. I
recei[ved] two papers from C.W.R. Heard of the capture of Wilmington.
Oh for A [mail].

> Wilmington had been liberated on Feb. 22. Federal troops entered the city
> without opposition that day.[116]

[THURS.] MARCH 23RD

At Corruña. Quite moderate but ch[illy] after breakfast we wash'd down
De[cks] and made everything ready. About 5 bells the Ram was reported. We
amediately up Anchor and stood out for her followd by the "Saccramento"
when the Ram put about and ran into Ferrol again she was accompanyd by
the Spanish Frigate. We was much disapointed b[ut] [w]as obliged to return
to Corruña ____ where we Anchord a_____ _____k_____ to the
Ra[m] _____ _____ much _____.

> According to the ship's log, "At ten the rebel ram *Stonewall* came out from
> Ferrol. Got under way and stood out to meet her, the men at quarters and ship
> cleared for action; At 10:45 the ram returned to Ferrol; this ship stood to the
> entrance of that harbor and then returned to Coruña."[117] Craven informed
> Welles: "On Tuesday, the 21st and on Thursday, the 23rd, having stripped ship
> to her lower masts, she (*Stonewall*) left her anchorage and stood out some 2
> miles from the entrance of the harbor; but the state of the sea was not favorable
> for her purposes, and as the *Niagara* and the *Sacramento* were steaming out
> of the bay of Coruña to meet her, she turned and ran back to her old berth. Af-

ter shoving ourselves off the mouth of Ferrol we returned to our former positions in the Bay of Coruña."[118]

[FRI.] MARCH 24TH

At Corruña. Fine day. We received A Mail. I received An Anglo. Here of the commission of A colard Man as Major U.S.A. 5 bells all hands were call'd to muster to hear the sentances of court Martials and Gene[ral] Orders. While at muster the Ram w[as] reported goin out. We were piped dow____ braught to on the Cable but did no[t] go out. A Spanish Offercer came on board for what purpose we know not. The Ram was manouvering [all] day accompanyd by the Spanish F[rigate.] We expect A fight to morrow. The Sea was perfectly calm all day. The Ram, after manouvering all day came to the mouth of the enterance [to] Ferrol hoisted three Flags and ste[ered] off. We layd quietly at Anchor al[l] th[e] time. Why we know not.

The log for this date says: "The rebel ram *Stonewall* went to Sea at 10:30 followed by the Spanish frigate *Conception*; made preparations for getting under way."[119] Here is what Craven reported to Welles: "On the morning of the 24th, at dead calm prevailing, with a smooth glassy sea, she again made her appearance outside and to the northward of Coruña, accompanied, as on the two former occasions by the Spanish steam frigate *Conception*. At this time the odds in her favor were too great and too certain, in my humble judgment, to admit at the slightest hope of being able to inflict upon her even the most trifling injury, whereas, if we had gone out, the *Niagara* would most undoubtedly have been easily and promptly destroyed. So thoroughly a one-sided combat I did not consider myself called upon to engage in. As she had left her boats behind her, my impression was that she would return again to Ferrol, but on Saturday morning she was reported as being still outside and lying under a point of land to the northward of Ferrol. In the afternoon, however, I learned that she was last seen early in the morning steaming rapidly to the westward, when, immediately after paying off bills on shore for coal, etc. we got under way and made the best of our way to this port, our progress being considerably retarded by the inability of the *Sacramento* to keep up with us."[120]

Meanwhile, on March 25, Thomas Jefferson Page of the *Stonewall* stated that it had been his expectation to "encounter the two Yankee men of war." He stated that he had taken out forty tons of coal so as to lighten the *Stonewall* somewhat and that, having left at 10:30 A.M., he remained off the harbors of Ferrol and Corruna until 8:30 P.M. "in full view" of the *Niagara* and *Sacramento*. Said Page: "This will doubtless seem as inexplicable to you as it is to myself and all of us. To suppose that these two heavily armed men of war were afraid of the *Stonewall* is to me incredible; yet the fact of their conduct was such as I state to you."[121]

SAT. MARCH 25TH

[At] Corruña. Verry fine day it i[s] _____ that the Ram have _____ _____ __
[kn]ow not. But sup_____ _____ [c]haseing her is _____ she is gone
_____ another. We remaind at Corruña until about 5 Oclock P.M. when
w[e] up Anchor followd by the "Saccramen[to"] and stood out for sea. Maild
let. to sister and _____

> The log for March 25 states: "At 5:45 called all hands and and shook out all
> reefs in fore and main topsails and furled them. . . . At 10:20 lost sight of
> Coruña. . . . The Sacramento about one mile astern of us at 12 midnight."[122]

[SU]N. MARCH 26TH

At sea. Verry fine day. Carrying Topsails, Trysails and Foresails. Makeing
good time. We suppose from the course that we are steering for Lisbon.
About 3 bells A steamer was Reported. We stood up for her followd by the
"Saccramento." Verry fine weather. We lost sight of her during the night.

> Here is what Craven had to say about March 26: "On our arrival in the Tagus,
> an officer from the Portuguese guard ship came on board and informed me that
> the *Stonewall* had arrived here on Sunday, the 26th instant, thirty hours from
> Ferrol; that she had just finished coaling, and, in conformity with the positive
> order given by his Government to leave the port, she was at that moment in the
> act of getting under way. At the same time this officer stated that it was the ur-
> gent desire of his King that I should anchor where I then was, about a mile to
> the eastward of the Tower of Belem, and not attempt go out of the harbor until
> twenty-four hours had elapsed after the departure of the *Stonewall*."[123]

[MON.] MARCH 27TH

This Morning it Began to Freshen up A little so that by 8 bells we were ab[le]
to take A Reef in our Topsails about the time all was made snug we were
orderd to take another Reef in the Topsails. We freequently were obliged to
wait for the "Saccramento" to come up with us. We pass'd several sails during
the Night and Morning about 8 bells. Noon land was reported off the
starboard Bow. We stood in and took A Pilot and started up the Ri[ver] and
anchord half way [up] _____. We heard that the Stonewall arrive[d] here on
Sunday Morning. We ran o[ff] some of our Guns as a precautionary measure.

> Again, Cmdr. Page of the *Stonewall* to Bulloch in Liverpool: "The *Niagara* and
> *Sacramento* are off the bar, and I suppose will come in. . . . These ships are
> dogging us to take an opportunity most favorable to them. The wind is strong

from the north—very much against us; but we must go out to-morrow as, we are ordered out. We must encounter them."[124]

[T]UES. MARCH 28TH

At Lisbon. At 8 bells we saluteed [the] City. The Salute was returnd about 9½ Oclock the Comodore went asshore and about 10½ Oclock the Stonewall went [to] sea. She passd closed to us and it was verry mortefying to see her go out so close to us flaunting the Rebel Rag in our verry face and we dare not follow. The day was Beautiful. About 2½ Oc[lock] we up anchor. In order to go higher u[p] the River we were obliged to go do[wn] the River in order to turn around. ____ Castle Bellam near the Fort they opend Fire on u[s] with shot and shell. We dipd our [flag] but they took no notice of it but [con]tinued to fire until we put about and stood up the River. One shot st[ruck] us forward of the Beam and an[other] struck our smokestack and sever[al] passd over us. An Officer cam[e] _____ to appologize but the ____ accept no apology. We anchord neare[r] to the Citty, the "Saccramento" close [by]. This evening the "Saccramento" Etheopeon Troupe are to have A performance and several of our crew have gone over to en[joy] the fun. We hear that Gold have fell to 170.

> Log: "*March 28.*—Lisbon, Portugal. At 8 a.m. saluted the Portugese Flag with twenty-one guns; the salute was returned from the fort. The rebel ram at anchor off the City. . . . At 11 a.m. the rebel ram *Stonewall* went to sea. . . . At 2 p.m. . . . got ready to get underway. At 3:15 got underway and stood down the river toward Belem Castle for the purpose of turning. The Fort opened on us and fired nine shots, and continued to fire on us after we had turned and dipped our colors several times."[125]
>
> Craven reported the incident to James E. Harvey, U.S. minister in Lisbon, stating that "at about 3:15 p.m. the *Niagara* was got underway and was about being turned head upstream when three shots were fired in rapid succession directly at her from Castle Belem. Supposing that the officer commanding the fort might have been under the impression that I was in the act of following the pirate *Stonewall* out to sea, and had fired those guns warning not to proceed, I immediately ordered our flag to be dipped or hauld part way down, as a signal that his warning was understood, and that I did not intend to pass the fort; but, to my astonishment, so soon as those guns could be reloaded they were again fired at my ship and this, too, when my flag was at half-mast and the ship's head was being rapidly turned upstream. The firing having then ceased for some three or four minutes, my flag was hoisted up to its place at the peak, when immediately a third volley of three shots was fired at us."[126]

Craven went on to say that no one but an "idiot" could have thought, for a moment, that he had any intention of violating his pledge to comply with the rule of holding off for 24 hours when another ship left port, and that the officer who "perpetrated this insult upon our flag can not invent the least possible excuse for his conduct."

The *New York Times* railed against Portugal's double standard in allowing the *Stonewall* to leave immediately and yet holding the *Niagara* to the 24-hour rule and firing on her when it appeared to someone at Belem that the rule was being violated. Said the *Times*: "The ram, it seems, was promptly required to leave Portuguese waters by a government order. But our fleet was, at the same time, required to remain twenty-four hours behind. The circumstances seemed to the United States Commander such, that he took upon himself to disobey this mandate, and prepared to sail before the time designated. There-upon our fleet was fired upon from the Belem Fort, and the *Niagara* was struck on the poop and one seaman killed. Our fleet then returned to its anchorage.

"These are the bare results thus far, materially regarded. Of course this new scourge is now on the high seas, and will doubtless prove to us still further the advantages of European neutrality at this particular crisis. In these acts the Spanish and Portuguese Governments do but copy, and scarcely improve upon, the neutrality of England and France. They have been guilty of an essentially unfriendly act; and their joint action—for such we must call it—of letting loose this pirate at this time, is particularly foolish and criminal."[127]

[WEN]S. MARCH 29TH

At Lisbon. Quite pleasant. Several of the Officials visited the ship to day. Also the Dutch Commander he being on the way to the States. We began to coal ship.

[THUR]S. MARCH 30TH

At Lisbon. Verry fine. We coald ship all night. Finish'd this morning. Cleand up. Wrote to G.L.M. There was great talk of his Highness the King of Portugal visiting the ship but he came not.

[FRI.] MARCH 31ST

At Lisbon. Quite pleasant. Several visiters on board. Arrived two verry large English ships, one of them useing her Mainmast as A smoke stack, they being of Iron. Something that I never ha[ve] seen before.

[SAT. APRI]L 1ST

At Lisbon. Fine day. This being all fools day many A joke was pass'd ap[on one an]other. One ap[on] the _____ Blockaderunner. She went to sea a[bout] 3 bells P.M. pass'd the ship with A Rebel Flag at the Fore and the

English at the Main and Peak. The Captain waved his Hat and da[red] us to follow. The Crew was awful indignant at this treatment.

SUN. APRIL 2ND

At Lisbon. Verry fine. We had Inspection at 10 Oclock then Devine serveace at 10½ Oclock.

MON. APRIL 3RD

At Lisbon. Verry fine. Several visite[rs] on board. We hears cheering news f[rom] home and only feels wrongd becaus[e] [we] cannot fight the Ram.

> As noted, Craven had contended that the *Stonewall* had returned on March 21 and 23 to Ferrol because the "state of the sea was not favorable for her purposes," and that on March 24, with a "smooth, glassy sea, . . . the odds in her favor were too great and too certain . . . to admit at the slightest hope of being able to inflict upon her even the most trifling injury, whereas, if we had gone out, the *Niagara* would most undoubtedly have been easily and most promptly destroyed. So thoroughly a one-sided combat I did not consider myself called upon to engage in."[128]
>
> Secretary of the Navy Gideon Welles was apparently of a different view. (As we have seen, so was his potential opponent, Thomas Jefferson Page.) A court martial was convened by the Navy Department in Washington on Nov. 7, 1865, and Craven was charged with "failing to do his utmost to overtake and capture or destroy a vessel which it was his duty to encounter."[129] The hearings continued through most of November and were completed on the fifteenth day of testimony, Nov. 23.
>
> The testimony was that on March 21 and 23 the *Niagara* was ready for "action." Lt. Cmdr. Henry D. Todd, attached to the *Sacramento*, testified that there was no chance of prevailing on March 24, and that both ships would have been "destroyed," noting that the *Niagara* could not steam as fast as the *Sacramento*, which had "a little more steaming power or speed than the ram." Todd, in response to the question of why matters were more "hazardous" vis-à-vis the *Stonewall* on the 24th as opposed to the 23rd, testified: "because of there being a smooth sea and no wind. The way I looked upon it was that the chance of one of the wooden vessels ramming the *Stonewall* was much better on a day when there was sea and wind; because, if there was much of a sea by getting up to the windward, and coming down at a greater speed, the *Stonewall* would hardly be able to fire her 300-pounder guns at the same time, just before striking. In a heavy sea the water would come into the port."[130] He stated that under such circumstances, the aim of the gun would have been more difficult. Capt. Henry Walke of the *Sacramento* testified in much the same manner. Thomas L. Wilson, gunner of the *Niagara*, and many others testified that there was no chance on March 24.

The court, which included Vice-Adm. David Farragut, Comm. Winslow of *Kearsarge* fame, and Rear-Adm. Dahlgren, censured Craven's "defective judgment" on March 24, which it saw as arising out of a "want of zeal and exertion in not making constant and personal observation of the rebel ram while at Ferrol, and thereby endeavoring to ascertain the truth or falsehood of the received reports of her character." The court also "reflected" on Craven's conduct in "remaining quietly at anchor in the Bay of Coruña while his enemy was parading about in neutral waters, flaunting his flag," when it was his "duty" to seek out the *Stonewall* and to make personal observations of her capabilities and vulnerabilities. The court also stated that Craven had not formed a plan of attack with the *Sacramento* and thus found him "guilty of the charge in a less degree than charged."[131] Accordingly, Craven was suspended from duty on leave pay for two years.

The Secretary of the Navy on Dec. 1 condemned the court martial proceeding and said that such findings and conclusions would render the applicable provisions of law a "dead letter." The court then revised its judgment and excluded its reference to Craven's "duty to have done" now that the charges were proven. The same suspension with pay was imposed. At this, Welles issued an order commenting upon the court's "manifest inconsistency in finding the charge proven" but removing the language relating to duty. Thus the proceedings of the court were set aside, and Craven relieved from arrest.

The ultimate question is whether the *Stonewall* would have made a difference in the war at that particular juncture. All of this took place in February and March on the eve of Appomattox when the war would begin to conclude. On the question of whether the *Stonewall* would have made a difference to the Confederacy, opinion is divided. Although Frank Merli is of the view that the result would have been a factor, Edward S. Miller has written that the court was reticent in establishing "the principle that it is always imperative that two wooden vessels should attack an ironclad," notwithstanding its "censure" of Craven.[132] For him, "Craven's case highlighted a commander's dilemma when adverse odds are high and the stakes are small. It is clear by the end of March 1865 that the war could end only one way and that it was going to end very soon. The Confederacy lay in ruins; its armed forces were facing defeat, and the *Stonewall* could have been, at worst, only a nuisance. It would surely have been difficult to explain to newly bereaved families why wooden warships had been unnecessarily pitted against an ironclad when the war had been so near a victorious conclusion. Possibly by returning the verdict a second time, the court was gently admonishing Welles for insisting on strict adherence to procedure in the face of so many mitigating circumstances."[133]

TUES. APRIL 4TH

At Lisbon. Verry fine. Several visi[ters] on board. Among them some Ladies. we had Danceing on board. We receive A Mail from the states. News Anticipat[ed] we shipd two Musicianers one sea[man].

WENS. APRIL 5TH

At Lisbon. Fine day. Maild A [letter] to G.L.M. This evening all hands made an attempt to go on board the "Saccramento" to an entertainment. Served out Grog Money.

[THURS.] APRIL 6TH

At Lisbon. Fine day. The boys [re]turnd from the "Saccramento" m[ost] delighted with the performance. _____ vows to have something of the kind on board here. To day we shipd Bat__urst an old ship mate of mine.

[FRI.] APRIL 7TH

At Lisbon. Verry fine. Shipd one man to day. We were visited by the English Minister. We received A Mail from the states. I received three Journals (Boston) and two Anglos. Nothing of great interest. Served out Clothing.

[SAT.] APRIL 8TH

At Lisbon. Verry fine in fact ve[rry] hot. Oh for the fresh Breeze of the Oceon. We cleand ship and made preparation to receive some of the dignataries but they came not. On Wensday the Govener of the Fortress that fired upon us were dismiss'd an Another instated. They saluted us and we returnd the Salute.

> On March 31, only two days after receiving U.S. minister James E. Harvey's letter of protest, Portugal's foreign minister, the Duke de Loulé, responded by saying that he deeply "deplored" the shots being fired, and that the governor of Belem Tower would be dismissed "without delay."[134]

[SUN.] APRIL 9TH

At Lisbon. Verry fine day. Inspection at 10 Oclock. Devine Serveace at 10½ Ocl[ock]. We were visited by two Jentlemen from the "Saccramento"_____

[MON.] APRIL 10TH

At Lisbon. Verry fine day. We began to Rattle and Tar down Riging [and] paint ship. We received a A mail from the states. Yo no receba nada.

[T]UES. APRIL 11TH

At Lisbon. Cloudy and Rainy. Fin[ished] the work on the Riging. This afternoon the Comodore had several Gu[ests] Destingue to Dine.

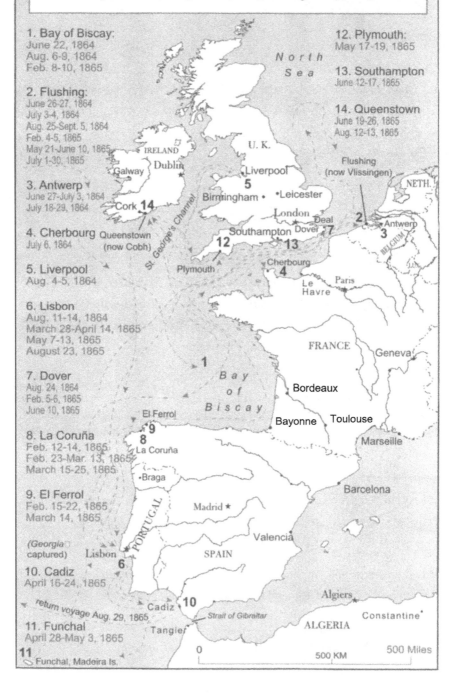

Principal European Ports of Call — U.S.S. *Niagara* —
Operations from June 21, 1864 to August 29, 1865

1. Bay of Biscay:
June 22, 1864
Aug. 6-9, 1864
Feb. 8-10, 1865

2. Flushing:
June 26-27, 1864
July 3-4, 1864
Aug. 25-Sept. 5, 1864
Feb. 4-5, 1865
May 21-June 10, 1865
July 1-30, 1865

3. Antwerp
June 27-July 3, 1864
July 18-29, 1864

4. Cherbourg
July 6, 1864

5. Liverpool
Aug. 4-5, 1864

6. Lisbon
Aug. 11-14, 1864
March 28-April 14, 1865
May 7-13, 1865
August 23, 1865

7. Dover
Aug. 24, 1864
Feb. 5-6, 1865
June 10, 1865

8. La Coruña
Feb. 12-14, 1865
Feb. 23-Mar. 13, 1865
March 15-25, 1865

9. El Ferrol
Feb. 15-22, 1865
March 14, 1865

(Georgia□
captured)

10. Cadiz
April 16-24, 1865

return voyage Aug. 29, 1865

11. Funchal
April 28-May 3, 1865

12. Plymouth:
May 17-19, 1865

13. Southampton
June 12-17, 1865

14. Queenstown
June 19-26, 1865
Aug. 12-13, 1865

Flushing
(now Vlissingen)

North
Sea

U.K.

IRELAND
Galway   Dublin
Liverpool   NETH.
Cork   **14**   Birmingham •   •Leicester   Antwerp
London   Deal   **2**
Queenstown   Southampton Dover   **7**   **3**   BELGIUM
(now Cobh)   **12**   **13**
Plymouth   Cherbourg
4
Le   Paris
Havre

FRANCE   Geneva

1   Bay
of   Bordeaux
Biscay
El Ferrol   Bayonne   Toulouse
9
8   Marseille
La Coruña
•Braga   Barcelona

Madrid ★

PORTUGAL   Valencia
SPAIN

Lisbon
6
Algiers
Cadiz   **10**   Constantine•
Strait of Gibraltar   ALGERIA
Tangier

11   0   500 KM   500 Miles
Funchal, Madeira Is.

WENS. APRIL 12TH

At Lisbon. Little cloudy and verry wa[rm]. We had quite an uproar this
mornin[g] by dischargeing the Ward Room Stew[ard] (A.F. Gomez) and
appoint me [in] his place. Shipd A Portugue cook. We were visited by the
Austrian, Sardienian and and Rushian [v]isters. We saluted them on thair
[de]parture. About 5 Oclock the ste[ward] left the ship for the states. We got
Deck Tacles and got everything rea[dy] for getting up Anchor but the Ord[er]
was beleyd and we securd every [thing] again.

THURS. APRIL 13TH

At Lisbon. Verry warm. I enter[ed] the duties as stewrd. I do not exp[ect]
_____ long. About four Bells w[e up] anchor and stood down the River.

[FRI.] APRIL 14TH

At sea. Fine weather. We are runni[ng] to the Westward. Verry fine indeed.

[SAT.] APRIL 15TH

At sea. Fine weather. Took A Pilot a[bout] 7 bells ran in the Harbor of Cadiz.
We anchord of Quarenteen. We were visited by the health surgeon. Our
papers were not properly signd. We were quarenteend until about 3 Oclock
when we were allowd to visit the Citty. I was among the luckey ones that went
on shore. I found Cadiz to be quite clean but the streets are verry narrow and
the Citty must be verry hot in consequence. On my return on board I heard
the Glad Tidings that the Stars and Stripe[s] had been planted over the
Capital of the D—nd Confedercy by the invincible Grant. While we honor
the living soldiers who have done so much we must not forget to whisper for
fear of desturbeing the Glorious sleep of the ma[ny] who have fallen. Mayrters
to the cau[se] of Right and Equality.

APRIL 16TH

At Cadiz. Quite warm. Went to [mar]ket. After all went well we disp[layed]
the nanational collors on the For[e] Main and Mizzen. Devine serveace at
10½ Oclock.

MON. APRIL 17TH

At Cadiz. Fine day. At 8 Oclock [we] fired A salute of 21 Guns with our

Big Guns another at 12 Oclock and at sunset. Also A salute of fi[ve] guns
for one of the Spanish Offi[cers]. We began liberty on Sunday. Give [lib]erty
to day.

TUES. APRIL 18TH

At Cadiz. Fine day. Gave Liberty. [No] news except by Telegraph. Oh for [a]
mail. Received two Men belonging to St. Louis.

WENS. APRIL 19TH

At Cadiz. Fine day. Gave Liberty. Hea[r] of the occupation of Richmond by
Army of the James. Ship'd A Cook.

THURS. APRIL. 20TH

At Cadiz. No Liberty today in [con]sequence of some of the Men not
returning. Shipd three men. Gave Li[berty]

FRI. APRIL 21ST

At Cadiz. Fine day. Yesterday we_____ to take in stores. Took in store[s] __
day. This Morning we put out _____ Launch and first _____ took them
in again. Gave Lib[erty]. Received A mail from the states. I received A letter
from C.W.R. hear[d] of the marrage of Miss R.K. to V.R. Heard of the
Surrender of Lee to Gran[t] of his entire force.

[SAT.] APRIL 22ND

At Cadiz. Very fine. Shipd three Men yesterday and to day took in stores and
Clothing continues to come from the states.

[SUN.] APRIL 23RD

At Cadiz. Fine day. Asshore three times. Paid all Bills. Returnd on board
at 9½ Oclock. Heard of the advance on Mobiele. We had Inspection at
10 Oclock and Devine Serveace at 10½. Also Prayers every Evening at
6 Oclock.

[MON.] APRIL 24TH

At Cadiz. Calld all Hands at 4½ Oclock. Secured Boats for sea. Up anchor
at 2 bells and stood out for sea bound for Madera. Discharged the Pilot about
7 Oclock and bid the land of the Castille adue. Verry fine indeed. Caryng full
sail abo[ut] _____ Royals and Studinsails.

[TUES.] APRIL 25TH

At Sea. Verry fine weather carrying full sail, no steam. Towards even[ing] it began to freshen up.

[WE]NS. APRIL 26TH

At Sea. Carried full sail all night. This morning we took in Stunsails and Furld Royals, carrying every th[ing] else. On the course to Madera.

THURS. APRIL 27TH

At Sea. This Morning we furld Degallant sails and double Reef'd Topsails. Quite fresh. About 9 Oclock we made Land right ahead. The Deserters Mountain in full sight. Keept on the course all night.

FRI. APRIL 28TH

This Morning we be close in the Island we ran in and Anc[hor] of[f] the Citty of Funchal. Close along[side] of A French Gun Boat. We we vi[sited] by the Health Offercer, the Com[man]der of the Gun Boat, Captian of ____ Port and completely surrounded [by] Boats and Divers who much [am]used the crew by Diveing for [some]thing that was thrown overboar[d] At 8 bells we saluted the Citty and our salute was amediately [re]turnd. After Breakfast we were _____ed by pedlers with all Kinds of trinkets for sale. Some verry fine fine fea[thers] flowers and work Boxes. We Rous'd up b____ sheet cables and bend them. Also scraped spars.

[SAT.] APRIL 29TH

At Funchal Madera. Verry fine day. Some visiters on board. Everything lovely. Gave Liberty.

[SUN.] APRIL 30TH

At Funchal Madera. Verry fine day. Inspection At 10 Oclock. Devine Serveace at 10½ Oclock. Many visitors on board. This is A second Antwerp for visiters.

[MON.] MAY 1ST

At Funchal Madera. Fine day. Wrote to C.W.R. Many visitors on board. Oh for the shores of America where I can clear my self from this awful situation. Gave Liberty.

[TUES.] MAY 2ND

At Madera. Verry fine. Many visiters on board. Several Ladies. Enjoyed A hop.
Arriveal of the Mail Steamer outward bound. Also arrived Her Magest[y's]
Frigate Naracisus bound out to [the] Indies.

> According to the commander of the U.S.S. *Kearsarge*, the *Stonewall* "was at
> Teneriffe (directly south of Madeira) when last heard from."[135]

[WENS.] MAY 3RD

At Madera. Fine day. About 8 Ocl[ock] we heard that we are to sail this [day].
There was any amount of confusion. Verry busey unbending sheet Chains
and stowing them below. About 3 Oclock we up Anchor and stood ou[t]
when in the Offing the Islands presented A Beautiful specttacle in the seting
sun, one that one w[ill] travel miles to behold. We are bound for Lisbon.
Richard Johnston left _____. Shipd A Cook.

THURSDAY MAY 4TH

At Sea. Bound northward. Sat studinsails. Makeing 11½ knots with steam
and sail we are doing fi[ne]ly. Carried full sail all night.

FRI. MAY 5TH

At Sea. Steering Fine wea[ther]. Changed our stunsail from starboard to
Port. Finely took th__ in and put on steam abo[ut] 11 Oclock. Makeing
good time.

SAT. MAY 6TH

Off Cape Vincent. We made light _____ about 12 Oclock M. We _____ this
morning until A Pilot [came] on board. When we ascended th____
[sal]uted the Port. We fo[und] here an English fleet of four [iron] clads and
one Line Ship. We saluted [the] Admiral of the Fleet. We went to the upper
part of the harbor and turnd round and came to Anchor of the same place
that we formerly laid. We also found the "Keresage" direct fro[m] the states.
She braught us the awful tidings of the assasination of President Lincoln at
the Theatre in Washington. He was shot through the head by an English
actor by the name of Booth. Also the assasanation of the Son of Sect. Seward
and attempt Murder of the Sectetary himself in his bed, he being sick at
the time. He was stabd seven times. The Murderer escaped. I received a

note from Wm Morriss who left this ship last December. He is now Ward
Room Cook. We received A Mail. I received an Anglo. We began to
coal ship.

[SUN. MA]Y 7TH

At Lisbon. Coaling Ship all day. Raining alternately all day. We had A short
serveace this Morning at 8 Oclock w[e] hoisted our colars at half M[ast] _____
President. Went on shore to market.

MAY 8TH

At Lisbon. Raining alternately a[ll] day. We comemorate the death of
President Lincoln by fireing A Nanational Salute of 21 minute guns at
Morning Noon and N[ight] accompanynd by the "Kerasage" at N__ the
English Frigate Defence fired at sun set the Portugues Friga[te] fired. Our
Flags were displeyd at half Mast. The Englishman also had his flag at half
mast an American flag at the Main. [We] had news from the States to
the __ ult. Mobiele captured. All the mo[ve]ments seems to be in North
Carolina. We were visited by the Rushan Minister.

> In another letter to *The Anglo African* signed by Oley, WBG wrote: "With
> deep sorrow we heard of the death of our beloved President, sad the news has
> cast a gloom over all. We being, when the doleful news arrived, in the port of
> Lisbon, Portugal, displayed our colors at half-mast and fired a national salute
> of minute guns, and the Portuguese and English ships in port joined in paying
> this last tribute of respect to a just and good man, of whom the American peo-
> ple will ever be proud."[136]
>
> The Portuguese King issued instructions on the protocol his ships in Lis-
> bon harbor were to follow on the 8th: "The Secretary of Affairs of the Por-
> tuguese Navy is to instruct the Major General of the Fleet to order the ships of
> the Navy, located actually in the Tejo, to follow the funeral rites for President
> Lincoln on the American Frigate Niagara by strictly observing the same pro-
> cedures that are made by the Navy's ships of her Britannic Majesty, now an-
> chored in this harbor."[137]

TUES. MAY 9TH

At Lisbon. Morning Rainy. [Noth]ing of importance. We hear that [the]
assassain of Mr. Lincoln have [been] arrested. His name is Wilks [Booth]
and that Sect. Seward and _____ are recovering. Also that Jhon[son] _____
[a]bout to surrender hi[s] [troops] to Sheerman.

[WENS.] MAY 10TH

At Lisbon. Fine day. We received [a] report that Jhonston had surrenderd.
The Rushan Fleet arrived this Morning of four ships [*Alexander*, *Newski*, and
Oleg as well as the yacht *Almaz*] with the Boddy of the late Czar on board.
They was much saluteing on every hand. We cockd Billd our Yards (and all
its naval ships in port).

> In fact, as WBG noted in "A Portion of the Cruise," the body was that of a
> Prince, not a Czar—Prince Nicholas Alexandrovich Romanov—who had died
> at the age of 22.
>
> On this day, President Andrew Johnson proclaimed that the insurrection
> and the armed resistance to the authority of the United States were virtually at
> an end, and that "the Navy should arrest the crews of commerce raiders still
> on the high seas and bring them in. He also warned against continued hospi-
> tality by foreign powers to Confederate cruisers."[138]

[THURS. MAY 11]TH

At Lisbon. Fine day. We had news to the effect that Booth the Assinnator of
President Lincoln was shot dead by some one who regonized him. We were
calld to muster to day to hear read General orders in regard to pay of Masters
Mates. Also in regard to the death of President stateing the length of time that
the nation shall mourn for him that we have lost. We were visited to day by the
Portuguese Admiral. Also by several of the Rushan Officers. We fired several
salutes during the day. Thats common.

> Craven wrote to Welles from Lisbon: "Sir: I have the honor to inform you of
> the return of the *Niagara* to the Tagus. I sailed hence on the 13th Ultimo for
> Cadiz, arrived there on the 15th, and, after filling up with such provisions and
> articles of clothing as were there in store for us, sailed thence for Madeira,
> where we arrived on the 28th ultimo. We could learn nothing at either of those
> places of the movements of any rebel vessels.
>
> "While at Cadiz the joyful news of the capture of Richmond, Petersburg,
> and Lynchburg, with the surrender of Lee's army, was made know to me by
> telegrams from our minister at Madrid. That glorious news was more than
> counterbalanced by the shocking accounts which were communicated to us
> on our arrival here on the 6th instant of the diabolical act which deprived us,
> on the 14th ultimo, of our most excellent and justly beloved President. The
> same flags which were hoisted at our mastheads on the first occasion, and sa-
> luted with three times twenty-one guns, were on Sunday and Monday, the 7th
> and 8th instant, displayed at half-mast, and minute guns were fired at morn-
> ing, noon, and sunset. The Portuguese promptly joined us in celebrating this

our terrible national calamity, by hoisting the American flag at half-mast at their main and firing minute guns from Belem Castle and their ships of war. The English ironclad frigate *Defense* simply displayed our flag at half-mast, without firing a salute. . . .

"So soon as I learned that it was the intention of the Russian admiral to touch here on his way to Cronstadt I called upon M. M. de Koudriaffsky, the Russian ambassador at this court, to express the sympathy which we all feel in their great national bereavement, and offered the services of the *Niagara* as a part of the escorting squadron from this port to the Baltic. My offer was gratefully and most courteously accepted and to-morrow we sail hence for Plymouth. On the arrival of the Russian squadron our flag was hauled down at half-mast, our yards were canted crosswise acockbill, the Russian flag hoisted half-mast high at the main, and a salute of twenty-one guns fired, and when they anchored I immediately called upon the admiral and renewed the expressions of our condolences and my offer to escort him on his homeward voyage. At 11 o'clock, two and a half hours after they had anchored, accompanied by several of my officers in full dress, I attended, on board of the admiral's ship, the celebration of their funeral services, a most imposing ceremony, at which were present the brother of the King of Portugal and several foreign ambassadors.

"The *Kearsarge*, Commander Harrell, which I found at anchor here on my arrival, will accompany the Russian squadron as far as Cape Finistère, and then return to this port."[139]

[FRI. MAY 1]2TH

At Lisbon. Fine day [We make] every preperation for sea but postpond our departure until the Morro[w] We were visited to day by several Officers Destingue and of cours there was A great quantity of powder _____ on thair account. To day one man _____ left one of the Boats.

SAT. MAY 13TH

At Lisbon. Raining after Breakfast. We unbend and stowd sheet Anchor. After all were in rediness the Flag Ship (Alexander Nevskie) under way followd by the Rus[han] Frigate then the English Ram (Defence), then this ship (Nia[gara]) "Kerasage," Rushan Corvette, [in] this order we went to sea. [the] Defence lost A Man Overboa[rd] when she was getting under way. Blowing quite strong. Our co[urse] lay to the northerd and Ea[st]

In a subsequent communication to Welles, Craven said: "On the 13th instant the Russian squadron accompanied by the English ironclad frigate *Defense*, a Portuguese steam corvette, the *Niagara*, and *Kearsarge*, left the port of Lisbon. Late in the evening the Portuguese corvette and the *Kearsarge* parted company and put back for Lisbon."[140]

SUN. MAY 14TH

At Sea. Blowing quite stro[ng]. Have been exerciseing all __ makeing and takeing in s____ have carried studinsails _____ the day and by night ____ oblige to reef Topsails. Some tim[es] were ahead and sometimes behin[d].

[MON.] MAY 15TH

At Sea. Fine day. Morning we ca[rried] full sail and at Noon the wind h____ ahead. We were obliged to furl sail. Cours to the Northd and Eastward. Nothing of note occurd excepting that all the other ships out steam us.

[TUES.] MAY 16TH

Bay of Biscay. This morning we were far behind the fleet. About 8 bells. We were able to make sail and we were soon crawling up on them. At sun set we were up with them. Fine weather.

[WENS. M]AY 17TH

Off the coast of England. Before day light we made the Light at Lands End and stood up the Chanel. We expect soon to be in the Port of Plymouth. We arrived in Port about 10 Oclock and after the acustomery salute we moor'd Ship. Here we had A view of A fine Harbor and the celebrated ships Achill[es] Black Prince. We received quite A lar[ge] Mail. I received A letter from C.[W.R.] 2 from W.H.H. and on[e] _____

[THUR]S. MAY 18TH

At Plymouth. Fine day. A little coo[ler] than we have been acustmd to[for] A time. Went ashore. Found the [British] verry friendly. All seem to feel happy at the conclusion of the War and [to] denounce the Assassination of the President. England have removed th[e] Restrictions of our Ships in thair ports. The[y] see that it is time. We coald ship_____ and day. The Rushans held Serveace on the Frigate ship to day at 11½ Oclock.

FRI. MAY 19TH

At Plymouth. To day we are to _____ Went on shore. Maild A letter to Anglo. About 12 Oclock began pr[ep]eration for sailing. Last night [we] lost twelve men. Four deserte[d] one of the Boats and the others the Ship. All were Englishmen. They [were] arrested but claimd English pro[tection] and they would not give them u[p]. We saild about 9 Oclock.

SAT. MAY 20TH

English Chanel. With the Fleet _____ far behind at daylight about 8 O[clock]
we sent down Degallant yard [and] mast. The Fleet done the sam[e] [at]
9 Oclock. We came up with the _____ arrived off Dover about [sun]down
the Fleet stopd. We made sail __ Stood away for the Scheldt.

SUN. MAY 21ST

About 7 bells this morning we ran into shoal watter and were obliged [to]
anchor, it being verry foggy at the t[ime]. The fog cleard off about 10 Oclock
when we found ourselves near the light ship West Hinder. We amediately
got under way and stood for Flushing where we arrived about 4½ Oclock.
At 11 Oclock we had serveace. On our arriveal we received A verry large
mail. I received A letter from W.H.H. one from M.C.G. and papers. A letter
from C.W.R.

[MON.] MAY 22ND

At Flushing. A little Rain. Nothing of much much importance excepting that
one watch of Marienes were put in double Irons for refuseing to obey the
Offercer of the Deck.

[MAY 23RD] TUES.

At Flushing. Fine day. We dreesd in white Frocks. The first time this season.
Nothing of great importance transpireing. Maild A letter to C.W.R., S.C.,
A.E.[H.]

[MAY 24TH] WENS.

At Flushing. Fine day. I re[ceived] A letter from J.M. _____ he had visited
Wilmington. Saw m[any] people all well. I felt verry much releived but my joy
was of short duration, for this evening I recei[ved] A letter from my Sister
bring[ing] me the sad news of the death of [my] Mother. She died March the
13th. ____ sad news for me. The first lett[er] that I receive from my Sister
s[hould] contain such news. Wrote to my Sister.

THURS. MAY 25TH

At Flushing. Fine day. This bei[ng] [a] Holyday asshore (Assencion day) [I]
took a stroll through the town. Arrival of A dutch ship. Her Offer[cers] visited
our ship.

FRI. MAY 26TH

At Flushing. Fine day. We ove[rhauled] and repaird Riging. We received [A
Mail] from the states. I received A pap[er]. We heard A report that Davis [had]
been Capturd. Also that our ____ are being disbanded and th[e] discharged
soldiers are goin i[n] ____ numbers to Mexico. Look ou__ _____.

MAY 27TH, 1865

At Flushing. Fine day. Takeing in wood all day. Last night I received an Anglo.
To day I received A letter from Miss S.S. from Antwerp. Our Band went
asshore to play. One Man Deserted. The first Colord Man that left on this
side of the watter.

> "Generally, contraband sailors proved enthusiastic, hard working, and most im-
> portantly, better disciplined than white sailors. [Rear-Adm.] Albert S. Barker
> opined, 'to their credit be it said they were as a rule, a very well-behaved set of
> men.' They deserted less frequently."[141]

MAY 28TH SUN

At Flushing. Fine day. We had Quarters and Inspection at 10. Devine
Serveace at 10½ Oclock. Last night A Boat came alongside to bring off some
Offercers, when she got caught and swampd, the Men were saved. To day the
Dingy was being carried out to the Boom when she got caught under the Bow
of another Boat and swampd all were saved. We recoverd the Boat this
Evening We received A Mail from the States. I received A letter from C.W.R.
Quite well. She spoke of the Death of my Mother. Also of Abram Price. We to
day received news confirming the Capture of Jeff Davis (he was in Female
Disguise) by Wilson Cavalry. We also heard of the arriveal of the Stonewall at
Havannah. She no doubt will try her hand on the Texan Coast. We hears that
the Conspiretors are being tried at Washington. I hope that they shall reap
thair reward. Cloudy all day. Moderately Cool.

MAY 29TH MONDAY

At Flushing. Fine day. Visited Mr. Myer. A relative of Maddam Flora at
Antwerp. Asshore this Afternoon at Flushing.

MAY 30TH

At Flushing. Quite windy. Blowing so hard that we were obliged to let go both
sheet Anchors. About 9 Oclock we went down Degallant yards. At 6½ we sent

down Degallant Mast. Our Minstrel Troup give one of thair entertainments this evening. I wish them success.

MAY 31ST

At Flushing. Verry fine. Last night the Minstrel Troup acquited themselves creditabley. We got up our sheet anchor and sent up Degallant Mast etc. This afternoon A steamer on an excursion pass'd around the Ship. They cheerd us, We man'd the Riging and returnd the cheer. Our band played the Nanational Air of Holland.

JUNE 1ST

At Flushing. Fine day. This Morning we up Anchor and returnd to where we drifted from on Tuesday.

FRI. JUNE 2ND

At Flushing. Fine day. We received A mail from the states. I received A paper.

SAT. JUNE 3RD

At Flushing. Fine day. Little rain in the Morning. Cleard off about noon. Nothing of importance. Our Band went asshore.

> On this day when "nothing of importance" happened, in fact Acting Secretary of the Navy G. V. Fox had determined that the *Niagara* would return to Boston on Sept. 1.[142]

SUN. JUNE 4TH

At Flushing. Fine day. Inspection at 4 bells. Devine serveace at 5 bells. The Paymasters wife came on board to serveace.

MON. JUNE 5TH

At Flushing. Fine day. We received A Mail from the states. Nary letter for me. Coaling ship.

TUES. JUNE 6TH

At Flushing. Fine day. Went out to the Farmers Fair. Seem'd to be the Rule for every boddy to drink as much Gin as they could stand under and many both Male and Female could not stand but A verry short time. Call'd on Miss Scott from Antwerp. Found her well.

WENS. JUNE 7TH

At Flushing. Fine day. We heard of the Surrender to the Spanish authorities of the Rebel Ram Stonewall at the Port of Havanah, Cuba. Wrote to Mr. A. How.

THURS. JUNE 8TH

At Flushing. Fine day. Gave liberty every day. To day A man was confined for abuseing the first Luff on the Quarter Deck.

FRIDAY JUNE 9TH

At Flushing. Fine day. Verry buisey takeing in stores as we are to sail on the morrow. When goin off to the ship I saw Miss S. Bade her good bye. We are to have A performance on board to night. Unbend sheet chains prepare for sea.

SAT. JUNE 10TH

This Morning about 9 Oclock we began to up Anchor. The performance last night was well attended from shore and all seemd to enjoy it verry much. We discharged the Pilot about 12 Oclock off Ostend and arrived at Dover about 5 bells P.M. Quite sick all day. Chills and Fever. The Paymaster have his better half on board with him.

SUN. JUNE 11TH

About 2 bells a.m. we up anchor and saild for Southampton without communicateing with the shore (Dover). At 4 bells call'd all Hands to Make sail. At 3 bells calld all hands to shorten and furl sail. We took A Portsmouth Pilot about 2 bells pass'd Portsmouth where there was quite A fleet of large ships one Iron Clad having four Turretts. We also saw the "Black Warrior." We came to anchor off Cowes about 8 bells. Quite cool for the season. I feels A little better though my throat is quite sore.

MON. JUNE 12TH

Off Cowes. Calld all Hands to up anchor about 2 bells stood up the Roads. Anchord of the Victorior Hospital Southampton about 9 Oclock. Fine day. Heard of the surrender of Smiths forcees in Texas. Also the new Amnesty proclamation to the Rebels. All of the leadeing Rebels are to be tried for Treason. I found Southhampton to be quite A Citty. The People verry obligeing. Still have A bad cold.

WBG has reference to the proclamation of President Andrew Johnson granting amnesty and pardons to all persons who "directly or indirectly participated in 'the existing rebellion' with a few exceptions. All property rights were restored except to slaves and in special cases. Of course an oath was required that such persons would 'henceforth' fully support, protect, and defend the Constitution and abide by the laws. This oath was opposed by the Radicals, who wanted an oath that could be taken only by those who had never directly or indirectly voluntarily supported the Confederacy. Johnson's proclamation followed the pattern laid down by Lincoln except that persons who participated in the rebellion and had had taxable property of over $20,000 were excluded from amnesty. Others excepted were those who held civil or diplomatic offices; those who left U.S. judicial posts; officers above the rank of colonel in the Army or lieutenant in the Navy; all who left Congress to join the South; all who resigned from the U.S. Army or Navy 'to evade duty in resisting the rebellion'; all those who mistreated prisoners of war; all who were educated in the U.S. military or naval academies; governors of states in insurrection; those who left homes in the North to go South; those engaged in commerce destroying; and those who had violated previous oaths. But any person belonging to these excepted classes could apply to the President where 'such clemency will be liberally extended as may be consistent with the facts of the case and the peace and dignity of the United States.'"[143]

As we see below on July 11, William B. Gould seems to express some concern about the extent to which the rebels are being pardoned, and comments sarcastically that "quiet" will reign throughout the United States.

The reference to the surrender of Smith's forces in Texas is to General E. Kirby Smith, Confederate commander of the Trans-Mississippi Department and the surrender of forces on May 26, later to be confirmed by him on June 2 at Galveston.[144]

TUES. JUNE 13TH

Off Southampton. Fine day. We were visited by some of the Officials to day we received A mail from the States. I received an (Anglo). We see the 25 Corps have gone to Texas. We hope soon to see the Rebellion finished in that section.

WENS. JUNE 14TH

Off Southampton. Fine day. We made preperation to Receive the English Admiral but he came not. We see by the papers that the President in A speech intimates Colinization for the colard people of the United States. This move of his must and shall be resisted. We were born under the Flag of the Union and we never will know no other. My sentement is the sentement of the people of the States. Arrival of the "Saccramento."

James McPherson has summed up the prevailing view among blacks during the war: "Colonization failed primarily because few Negroes wanted to be colonized. Lincoln and other proponents of colonization thought that colored men would prefer to emigrate rather than remain in America as second class citizens. But most Negroes were determined to stay in their native land and struggle their way upward to equality. The opportunities of the Civil War seemed to be opening a new and better future for the black man in America."[145] Ironically, Henry Highland Garnet, who figured so importantly in Cornelia Read's life, had long been a great proponent of emigration to countries such as Haiti, but he altered his view around this time.[146]

THURS. JUNE 15TH

Off Southampton. We are lying of the Victoria Hospital. A verry fine and large Building (¼ of A mile in length) and is for the Army and Navy. Fine day. Arriveal and departure of one of the American steam Packets. We received A Mail. Received two papers from C.W.R.

FRI. JUNE 16TH

Off Southampton. Fine day. Several visiters on board. We heard that Davis have been carried to Washington to be tried by Court-Martial on the on the indictment of Treason. We hope that the sour Apple Tree is all ready. Wrote to C.W.R.

The expression "sour apple tree" is apparently based upon the song "Good Bye, Jeff," by Philip Bliss, which concludes: "But the soul of famous Old John Brown has not stop'd marching, Jeff, / And the last of Southern Chivalry we'll see, / When the echo of the 'Hallelujah Chorus,' Jeff, / Finds you hanging on a 'sour apple tree.'"[147] Davis was captured by Federal troops on May 10 in Georgia and imprisoned in Fort Monroe, Va.[148] Even though he had taken up arms against the constituted U.S. government, Davis was not tried for treason.

SAT. JUNE 17TH

Off Southampton. Fine day. We were visited by the American Counsel. We saluted him on his departure. About 1 Oclock we unmoord Ship. The Pilot came on board quite earley. I went on shore in the Morning about half an hour. About 4 Oclock we began to heave up anchor. We started about 4½ Oclock. About 6 Oclock we pass'd the Needles, discharged the Pilot and stood on our way down the Chanel bound we believe for Queens town [now Cobh] Ireland. Fine weather.

SUN. JUNE 18TH

English Chanel. We had Quarters and Inspection at 10 Oclock. Devine
Serveace at 10½ Oclock. About 3½ Oclock pass'd Lands End. Now into the
Broad Atlantic running for St. George's Chanel. Hope to be in the port of
Queenstown to morrow.

MON. JUNE 19TH

At Daylight we were in sight of the Irish coast and about 7 bells we took on
board A Pilot and about 10½ Oclock we were at Anchor in the Harbor of
Queenstown. A verry fine Harbor. We were amediately beseiged by any
number of Boats in true Irish style.

TUESDAY JUNE 20TH

At Queenstown. Fine day. Many visitors on board. Several of our Offercers
went away to the Citty of Cork and Dublin.

WENS. JUNE 21ST

At Queenstown. Fine day. Many visitors on board. I went asshore in the
afternoon. The citty is small built on the slope of A Hill wich is verry tiresome
to ascend. The streets are thickly interspersed with Children and Beggars
innumerable. From the top of the Hill in the rear of the Citty you have a verry
fine view of the harbor of Queenstown.

THURS. JUNE 22ND

At Queenstown. Fine day. Several visitors on board. They are continualy
passing around the ship in steam Boats Cheering for the stars and stripes.

FRI. JUNE 23RD

At Queenstown. Many visitors on board. Gave some of our men Liberty that
have people here. Maild a letter to A.F.G. one to J.H.

SAT. JUNE 24TH

At Queenstown. Fine day. Full of visitors all day. Arrival of the "Persia" from
the States.

SUN. JUNE 25TH

At Queenstown. Fine day. We had Quarters and Inspection at 10 Oclock.
Devine serveace at 10½ Oclock. After 12 Oclock we were Ram'd, Jam'd and
Cram'd with visitors until 8 Oclock P.M. We had more visitors on board this
day than at any port that we have visited since we have been from home.
There was not A part of the ship but where there were some even Ladies into
the Fire Room. Arrival and departure of the "China" for New York.

MON. JUNE 26TH

At Queenstown. Verry fine day. Several of our men that were on liberty faild to
return and there was several deserted in the crowd yesterday. Went asshore.
Laid in sea stores. Returnd on board about 3 Oclock. Found all in readiness for
sea. At 5 Oclock we up Anchor and stood out for sea leaveing the "Saccramento" in Port. About 6 bells we discharged the Pilot. Made sail. Proceed
slowly. On our way we know not where we are bound. Ship'd seven Men.

> It turned out that the *Niagara* was going to visit both Britain and Flushing
> again. About the Queenstown visit, Craven had this to say in a communication
> to Welles on July 1 from Flushing Roads: "At Queenstown the people evinced
> great joy at receiving us and welcomed us most heartily, and had I consented
> to it would have made some public demonstration of their friendly sympathy
> toward us. During our stay there the ship was crowded with visitors from
> Cork and the neighboring towns."[149]

TUES. JUNE 27TH

We carried sail all night and until about 8½ Oclock A.M. when the wind
hauld ahead and we were obliged to furl sail and steam. We did not steam any
at all all night. Put down for cloathing. The Men Making white cap covers
about 4 bells P.M. land was reported (Lands End). Bear up for it.

WENS. JUNE 28TH

Running up the Chanel. Light winds. A little hazy. Evening quite cool. Pass'd
many sails on our way up. About 6 bells sent down Degallant and Royal yards.

THURS. JUNE 29TH

Running up Chanel. Quite hazey. About 7 Oclock we came to Anchor off
Deal. I went ashore. We took A North Sea Pilot about 6 Oclock A.M. About
9 Oclock we returnd on board.

FRI. JUNE 30TH

Off Deal. All hands were call'd about 4 Oclock bend sheet chains about
2 bells we up anchor and stood across the sea for the Scheldt. Made sail
about 4 bells. Making about 10½ knots. Shorten sail about 5 bells P.M.
arrived at Flushing at 6 bells. We received A Mail. I Received a letter from
S.S. Anvere.

SAT. JULY 1ST

At Flushing. Raining and Blowing all the day. Served out cloathing. The ship
presents the appearance of A Tailors ship as she do on every day that
cloathing is served out.

SUN. JULY 2ND

At Flushing. To day verry fine it haveing calm'd down. We had Quarters at 10
Oclock and inspection and Devine Serveace at 10½ Oclock. We received A
mail. I received A letter from my Sister and three papers from N.Y. All well at
home. Heard of many deaths among my people. Learnt of the marage of Mrs.
A.E.H. of Brook[lyn].

MON. JULY 3RD

At Flushing. Verry fine day. Exerciseing Boats. Wrote to my Sister and J.H.B.
Also to G.L.M. We received A Mail from the states.

TUES. JULY 4TH

At Flushing. Fine day this being the 89th aneversary of the United States.
We celebrated the day by Dressing the Ship and fireing A Nanational salute
at 8 Oclock a.m. 12 Oclock N and sunset. The Counsel gave A dinner to
which our Offercers were invited.

WENS. JULY 5TH

At Flushing. Fine day. We received an order from the Department forbiding
any of the American Ships from entering any English or French Ports or to
pay the customery respects to thair Flags. Heard from Antwerp.

THURS. JULY 6TH

At Flushing. Verry warm. Much warmer than we have felt it this season.

FRI. JULY 7TH

At Flushing. Rainy and warm. A little unwell. Yesterday we received news of the departure of Admiral Goldsborough. We have not yet heard from him.

SAT. JULY 8TH

At Flushing. Fine day. Nothing of importance goin on. Exerciseing Boats.

SUN. JULY 19TH [9TH]

At Flushing. Fine day. Quarters and Inspection at 10 Oclock and Devine Serveace at 10½ Oclock.

MON. JULY 10TH

At Flushing. Fine day. Received A letter from Cousin S.H. All well. Visited Middleburg.

TUES. JULY 11TH

At Flushing. Raining and cool. We are hourly looking for the "Colorado." Had some Corts De Visent takeen. Wrote to S.C. (anvere). We see that the Rebels are being pardon'd verry fast and that quiet will soon reighn throughout the states. Heard of the sailing of the Rebel ship Rappahnnock from Calis (France).

> In the wake of the Johnson amnesty, "Johnson gave 100 pardons a day to the Southerners exempted from his restoration plan, eventually pardoning 13,500 Southerners out of the 15,000 who applied."[150]
>
> Capt. Henry Walke of the *Sacramento* in a July 10 communication to Welles stated that he had been advised on July 6 that the *Rappahannock* had sailed for Liverpool, and that on July 5 he had seen a ship that seemed to him to look like her "steaming and sailing up the coast close to the shore, with English colors flying." However, Walke reported that, though the ship appeared to be in a "crippled condition, steering for Liverpool, when I left her," it was within three miles and he was thus unable to "molest her without violating the international laws of protection."[151]
>
> On July 11, Charles Francis Adams, U.S. minister to Great Britain, advised Capt. Walke that he had acted with "proper caution." Said Adams: "To have attempted to seize that vessel, even under a doubt about the British jurisdiction, would have merely run a hazard of raising a grave question which on all accounts it is prudent to avoid. There is another mode of proceeding in such a case which is safer and wiser. Should the vessel, however, be found outside of the jurisdiction and you are sure of her identity, it will be lawful for you under the authority of Mr. Seward's published dispatch, a copy of which was for-

warded to you, to take her. But you will take care not to stop or search any vessels with the British colors under the mere suspicion that it may be the *Beatrice*, for you are doubtless aware that that right of search has expired with the termination of the war."[152] The *Beatrice* was later known as the *Rappahannock*.

WENS. JULY 12TH

At Flushing. Cloudy and cool. Oh C. why do you not write. Our Men haveing liberty on A small scale.

THURS. JULY 13TH

At Flushing. Raining. Wrote to C.W.R. Nothing of importance goin on. Fine weather.

FRI. JULY 14TH

At Flushing. Quite warm. We are daily exerciseing sails and Boats.

SAT. JULY 15TH

At Flushing. Verry warm. The time passes verry heavaly here in this ancient country.

SUN. JULY 16TH

At Flushing. Inspection at 10 Oclock. Devine serveace at 10½ Oclock. We were visited by an Excursion party from Antwerp. Among them was Mr. and Mrs. Gillis. Quite well. They had A Band of Music with them.

MON. JULY 17TH

At Flushing. Last night we had verry heavy Thunder Showers and to day have been the hotest day of the season. In the Evening we had thunder showers. About 5½ Oclock A steamer appeard of the Port showing signals and to our great Joy it proved to be the U.S.S Frolic tender to the Frigate "Colorado." She saild from New York June the 21st she toutch'd at Halifax N.S. and Fayal Wst Isld and arrived here at 6 Oclock in advance of the Frigate. Oh! for the news for our return to the states.

TUES. JULY 18TH

At Flushing. Morning Rainy. Cleard off about 11 Oclock. Loos'd sails this Morning. Two Lieuts joind this ship. Messrs, Bach, and Batchelor. The "Frolic" saild for Antwerp. Furld sails about 3 Oclock. About 5½ Oclock the "Colorado" was reported comeing in. About 6½ Oclock we saluteed the Admiral. He return'd the salute. The Frigate came in and Anchord close to us. She saluted the Port. There was great crowds on the Quay. She braught us A mail but none for me.

WENS. JULY 19TH

At Flushing. Scrub'd Hammocks. We received A mail from the states. I received A letter from C.W.R. Also one from Sister. All quite well at home. They say that the Spotted Fever is verry fatal there and that many are dying.

THURS. JULY 20TH

At Flushing. Fine day. At 1 bells we loosd sails. About 4 bells we furld beating the Flag ship bad. Heard of the Execution of four of the Assassins viz. Payn, Harrold, Atzerott and Mrs. Surratt.

FRI. JULY 21ST

At Flushing. Cloudy. We hear the thrice glorious news that we are soon to be homeward bound. I received the Anglo. Return of three of our Offerecers.

SAT. JULY 22ND

At Flushing. Windy and Raining all day. Wrote to my Sister also to my cousin S.H. Yesterday Lieut Phoenix haveing resighnd took leave of us. Bound for the states the Crew were for bidden to cheer him but they watch'd thair chance and gave him three rouseing Cheers.

SUN. JULY 23RD

At Flushing. Rainy. Loos'd sails about 8 bells. We had Inspection at 4 bells. Devine serveace at 5 bells. Furld sail at 7 bells. We heard that soon we are to be off for the states. Wrote to C.W.R.

> However, there were to be some stops along the way. Rear-Adm. L. M. Goldsborough instructed Craven to "cruise around and about Ireland, in order to intercept in strictly neutral waters any vessels wearing the Confederate flag that may attempt reach the dominions of either England or France, until the middle of next month, at which time you will start for Boston, Mass."[153]

MON. JULY 24TH

At Flushing. Rainy. Departure of the Admiral for Antwerp. Also several of our Offercers. Maild A letter for Anveres and Received one from S.C.

TUES. JULY 25TH

At Flushing. Fine day. We hope soon to be on our way home. Coaling ship.

WENS. JULY 26TH

At Flushing. Fine day. Coaling ship. About 7 bells the "Kerasage" arrived. Some of our Offercers returnd from Antwerp.

THURS. JULY 27TH

At Flushing. Fine day. We are daily expecting to sail for the states. We received A Mail from the states. Heard of the Burning of Barnum's Museum.

FRI. JULY 28TH

At Flushing. Fine day. Nothing of importance goin on. Heard of the sale of the Georgia (our Prize) for a sum of ($42,000) What A prize.

SAT. JULY 29TH

At Flushing. Blowing quite hard all day. Received A letter from Anvere's. Wrote to S.S. Return of the Admiral.

SUN. JULY 30TH

At Flushing. Blowing quite fresh. We had Quarters and Inspection about 4 bells. Devine serveace about 5 bells. About 7 bells the Admiral signalzed to us to be off. We were soon all confusion and excitement. Started fires. Braught to on the Cable amediately thus everything stood untill about 6 bells when the welcom cry from the Boatswans Mates of All Hands Up Anchor for Home and soon the shrill sound of the Boatswains Pipe with the sharp notes of the fife and the tramp of the Men and clinking of the Capstain all told that we were soon to be plowing the deep Blue Sea on our homeward course. We passd Ostend about 6 bells P.M. and bid adue to the Scheldt.

> On the following day, H. S. Sanford, the U.S. minister to Belgium, advised Secretary of State William H. Seward that the *Niagara* "left the Scheldt yesterday on her return to the United States," and that she had made a "good impression" on Belgium. Sanford stated: "The presence of the Niagara in these waters has had an excellent effect. While in Antwerp she was visited by many thousand citizens, who came from all parts of the country for that purpose, and the courteous reception and kind attentions extended to them have done much, I doubt not, to stimulate the cordial good feeling which exists on the part of this Government and people for the people of the United States. Both ship and commander have done us credit and have left favorable impressions in Belgium."[154]

MON. JULY 31ST

This morning at sunrise we enterd the shails of Dover. We stop'd steaming and attempd to Beat down the Chanel but after makeing one or two tacks and did not gain any we about ship and stood up to the Downs where we Anchord off Deal the Comodore and several of the Offercers went asshore. I was on shore in the Evening. Returnd aboard about 8 Oclock. Raining alternately all day.

TUES. AUG. 1ST

Off Deal. Blowing quite fresh and cool. About 4 bells the Comodore returnd. We amediately began to up anchor where for we know not where. As soon as the Anchor was securd all Hands were calld to make sail. We laid our course down the Chanel under sail along. We have been tacking all day gaining but little headway.

WENS. AUG. 2ND

English Chanel. We tack'd all night and to day until about 12½ Oclock when we came to Anchor off Dungeness as we could not gain headway. Blowing quite fresh from the westward. We go along towards home verry slow.

THURS. AUG. 3RD

Off Dungeness. Still blowing quite strong from the westward. Last night we were visited by an Offercer of the Coast Guard who offerd to take letters asshore for us. We had General Quarters to day. About 11 Oclock we sent up Royal yards then up Anchor and make another trial to get down the Chanel. We stood away on our Port tack towards the Coast of France.

FRI. AUG. 4TH

English Chanel. We stood on our Port tack all night. This Morning about 3 bells we attempted to ship but she miss'd stays and we were obliged to square away on the same course. To day there was an auction selling off Mr. Yeatons things (he deserted last at Antwerp). We kept on our Port tack until about 3 bells when we tack'd and stood off on the starboard tack.

SAT. AUG. 5TH

Cruiseing in the Chanel. We have made several tacks during the day but yet is A long way from the Atlantic. Westerly winds are the rule nowadays. I feel verry unwell.

SUN. AUG. 6TH

English Chanel. Wind still ahead. Trying verry hard to get out into the Oceon but yet we are obliged to beat about in the Chanel. We had Inspection and Quarters at 4 bells and Devine serveace at 5 bells. We also have had several showers and apon the whole we can call it A wet day. One week have we been knocking about here and have not been able to get through but well we know that tis no fault of old Tom. It looks like we shall have A verry long pasage home. Oh! For the shores of the Etates Unis.

| "Old Tom" is presumably Comm. Thomas Craven.

MON. AUG. 7TH

English Chanel. Morning rainy with A continual west wind. It seems as if we are goin backwards for at noon to day we were opposite the same point on last evening. Oh! For A change of wind so so that we can reach our port of destenation this being our eighth day in the Chanel. We expects to reach home by the first of October.

TUES. AUG. 8TH

English Chanel. Still almost without A wind. We are just drifting down the Chanel. In the Afternoon we feel in with some fishing vessels off Plymouth (Edelynstone Light House being in sight). We procured A lot of Fish. We also discharged the Pilot who accompany'd us from Deal. We availed ourselves of the opportunity of sending off A Mail by him.

WENS. AUG. 9TH

English Chanel. We are making about 1½ knots. About sunset we were close up to the Lizards. To day we pass'd one of the Oceon Steamers. Goin up Chanel. Yesterday we heard that there was an accident of some kind happend to the Atlantic Cable. What the extent of the injuries we were unable to learn but there was no communication with the "Great Eastern" for several days. Oh for A good wind.

THURS. AUG. 10TH

Off the west coast of England. This morning we were close up to Lands End and about 5 bells we rounded the End and stood away for St. George's Chanel evedently bound for some part of Ireland where we hope soon to arrive haveing only been twelve days from Flushing. We carried full sail until about 5½ Oclock when we furld Royals and Degallant sails and took A reef in our Topsails. We are traveling verry slow. The Comodore is evidently not in A great hurry.

FRI. AUG. 11TH

St. George's Chanel. We made Land on the Irish coast about 9 bells A.M. we then stood the Chanel At short distance and turnd down again. Took on board A Cork Pilot 1½ Oclock and stood off and on all day. About 4 Oclock we Reef'd Topsails. We are just killing time. To day they scrub'd Paint work and began to paint ship. I suppose that we will try to make her look as well as we possible can. We had the report confirm'd to day that there is an accident to the Atlantic Cable. Being A little at leasure and nothing to read I amuse myself by overhauling my corospondancees.

SAT. AUG. 12TH

St. George's Chanel. Last night the Pilot told us that it was reported that President Johnston has been Assassinated and this morning the Comodore stood in for Queenstown to learn the truth of the report. We Anchord about the entrance of the Harbor. At 12½ Oclock we amediately sent ashore and glad we are to state that there is no truth in the report what ever. We heard of the loss of the Ocean Steamer "Citty of Glascow" by fire at sea on her passage from the states. We also heard again that there is something the matter with Telegraph cable as there have not had any communication with the "Great Eastern" for several days. The People were verry glad to see the ship return but quite sorry that we are not goin to remain. During the Evening we had several showers of Rain.

SUN. AUG. 13TH

Queenstown. All Hands were calld about 2 bells to up Anchor and by 3 bells we were steaming out of the Harbor. Raining and Blowing quite fresh we call'd all Hands to make sail and as soon as we were clear of the Harbor we quit steaming and began to knock about until about 10 Oclock. It began to blow quite fresh wish obliged us to seek A haven as we did not like to be caught in A blow about here. We then came to Anchor off Dungaveen about

12½ Oclock in the Evening it calm'd down and we were visited by several of the scions of the Emerald Isle.

MON. AUG 14TH

Off Dungaveen. All hands were call'd about 8 bells and after performing our morning Evolutions all hands were call'd to up Anchor. About 2 bells we then stood out to sea. We saw two Oceon Steamers at A distant we stood off and on all day until about 4 bells P.M. when we discharged the Pilot and stood down the Chanel. We struck sheet Cables below and we hope that we shall not have any further use for them this cruise.

TUES. AUG. 15TH

At Sea. Bound to the southard. We carried A couple of Reefs in our Topsails all night until about 11 Oclock to day when the wind hauld aft and all Hands were calld to make sail. We then shook out the reefs and sat Degallantsails. We then went along finely until about 5 Oclock when it began to blow quite fresh and we were obliged to take in our Topgallantsails and take A reef in our Topsails. While reefing Michel Murphy fell overboard from the Main Topsail Yard. We amediately (or at Least the Comodore did) let go of the life Bouy's. He got apon it and was pickd up by one of the Boats. He had a narrow escape but it is better to be luckey that rich. We now have A good breeze in our favor and we knock off our six and Eight knots quite easely. There have been A large steamer in sight all day. Steering the same course as we are goin.

> Later, after his return to Boston, Craven told Welles that he had left the Irish channel on the Aug. 15 because he had not heard of or seen "any vessels wearing the Confederate flag."[155]

WENS. AUG. 16TH

We are steering South West. Makeing between seven and eight knots. The ship mentioned in our last are still with us also. A Brig on our starboard Beam. About 1½ Oclock we shook out the reef from our Topsails and sat our Topgallantsails and all our Fore and Aft sails. The sea have moderated and we are quite steady. This evening the sun went down in splender and it is realy refreshing to be apon the spar deck enjoying the fresh sea Breeze provideing you posess A good segar to puff away the monotony of Sea Life.

THURS. AUG. 17TH

We are steering South west, half west with A good wind about three points
free. We carried all night our fore and aft sails, fore and main sails, Topsails
and Topgallantsails and about 6 Oclock we sat Royals. We carried them until
about 9 Oclock when we took in Royals and Degallantsails. As it began to
freshen up and come on thick the mist soon pass'd away when we again sat
Degallantsails. We have taken down our Fore Trysail and made preperation
to carry Staysails. They are paying good attention to Drill both before and
afternoon. It is drill, drill, drill. We are goin along quite well averageing about
8 knots. If we could only trice up our propeller we could make some speed.
The ship that have been in company with us for the last three days ran away
from us this evening but she is hastening to A market while we are only
roaming about.

FRI. AUG. 18TH

We are geting into warmer latitude. It is quite warm below decks. One
perspires with the least exertion and it was comfortable with an over Coat.
A day or two ago now we only reed that article at night we are nearing the
coast of Spain. We have lost the good wind that have befriend us for the last
four days and we were like A painted ship apon A painted Oceon. Towards
Evening it began to freshen up and we began to move slowly along. We have
seen A sail apon our Starboard Beam all day. To day we sat Main, Top and
Degallant Masts, Staysails which alter the looks of the ship A great deal. Oh
for A mail. It is now near three weeks since we had A Mail and we hope soon
to be able to take our thoughts to our loved ones without the Aid of the Mail
arangements.

SAT. AUG. 19TH

Off Cape Finesta. We have beend becalmd all day. Our sails hang idely from
the yards and only moves to flap against the Mast and hang to the motion of
the ship. We got up steam about 6 bells and steamd until 8 bell P.M. When
being clear of the Cape we again gave over ourselves to the motion of the sea.
All the afternoon the Highlands of Coruña were visible where we had the
adventure with the "Stonewall." By the By we have heard that the Stonewall
have beend surrenderd to the United States by Spain. There have been A

general cleaning all all day. It is quite warm and hazey. We think that we shall have wind enough soon. We may expect to fetch port some day or other. This is a long passage. Just killing time.

> The *Stonewall* arrived at Havana, Cuba, on May 11 and surrendered to the United States on May 19.[156]

SUN. AUG. 20TH

We have not gone far from our point of yesterday. We are just moveing throug[h] the watter trying to beat against A head wind which seems to be the rule since leaveing Flushing with three days exception. We had Quarters and Inspection at 10 Oclock and Devine serveace at 10½ Oclock. I[t] have been Rainy all day and on an Oil skin is quite comfortable. We have tack'd ship several times but appearantly we remain about the same point. If our passage home be against contrary winds as much as this from Flushing to Cadiz we may get there somewhere about the close of the year. What goes harder we have the power to go but cannot use it. Oh! for an accident.

MON. AUG. 21ST

We are still beating against head winds. This Morning about 4 bells A steamer signalized to us and pass'd us steering the same direction as we are goin. She was soon far ahead of us. They started the Engine and continued steaming all day. We are able to keep our cours. About 3½ Oclock we were able to set our Fore and Aft sails. We averaged about 7 knots the hour. There is some prospect now of geting into port at least during the week. The stroke of the Engine keeps us with hope. About sunset there was A Brig in sight on our weather beam and the steamer far in the distance ahead.

TUES. AUG. 22ND

We have been steadaly steaming all day but we we have not been able to make more than five knots the hour for we have A head wind blowing quite fresh and raining all day. We fear that we shall not be in port on the morrow as we have hope'd below decks. We are almost suffocated and on the spar deck. You must get wet from the rain but the rain is the most comfortable of the tow [two].

WENS. AUG. 23RD

We are off Lisbon. About four bells we could see the Citty. Runing close along shore. This morning we had Inspection of Bags and airing Hammocks. We expects to get into Port on the Morrow and right anxious are we at the prospect for we shall look anxiously for letters from home. Here we are still on this side and will remain for some time.

THURS. AUG. 24TH

We pass'd Cape St. Vincent last night in the last Dog watch. The wind veer'd around from ahead to Aft. We amediately sat all our sails that waffld draw carried them through the night. Yesterday and to day have been verry fine weather so warm that we will be able to wear white to day. The first time in six weeks. We made the Citty of Cadiz about 2 Oclock and came to anchor in the harbor. About 4½ Oclock we found here the Ship "Nanational Gaund." There were also in Port. Two Spanish Frigates and one sloop. Also an Italian Gun Boat. We received A Mail but not A line did I receive. No one favord me with A rememberance.

FRI. AUG. 25TH

Cadiz. Verry warm. This Morning as soon as all Hands were calld we out Boats and as soon as we had Breakfast we began to take our provissions from the store ship. We are also to take coal here. We sails from here direct to the states. To day we received A Mail. I received too papers dateed April 5th and 6th from C.W.R. Also an Anglo dated July 22nd.

SAT. AUG. 26TH

At Cadiz. Quite warm. Last night we made preperation to coal ship but the coal did not arrive. However this Morning the Coal came and we were soon hard at work coaling. We heard here that the "Colorado" have returnd to the states.

SUN. AUG. 27TH

At Cadiz. Verry warm. We coald ship all night and continued all day. We expected to sail this evening but not geting A supply of coal we were forced to remain one day longer. We had Prayers at 5 bells. There was great confusion. Geting everything ready and securd for sea. Raining lightly the Most of the day.

MON. AUG. 28TH

At Cadiz. Coald ship all night. The Pilot was on board last night but we were not ready to sail. We finishd coaling about 2 bells. We amediately up Anchor and stood out to sea. About 6 bells we discharged the Pilot and bid adue to Castiele and thair dark Eyed Beauties. About 4 bells P.M. we unbend Bow Cables and struck them below. That looks like crossing the great Western. About 6 bells we were able to set our Fore and Aft sails.

TUES. AUG. 29TH

At Sea. Homeward Bound. We were favord with A good Breeze wind. This Morning we sat squaresails and with steam. We went 10½ knots. About 9 Oclock we quit steaming and put on all the canvass that we could spread with Stunsails below and aloft. About 8 bells afternoon it began to blow quite fresh when we took in our stunsails as A precautionary Measure. We are goin about 8½ knots the hour and only hope for A continued wind and we soon shall meet our Friends at Home.

WENS. AUG. 30TH

At Sea. Fine weather. We still have A fair wind and are goin about 8 knots. We are not steaming at all. So far all well.

THURS. AUG. 31ST

At Sea. Fine weather. Verry warm. The sky is full of flying clouds but we hope the winds will not leave us yet. At 11 Oclock we were goin 10 knots the Hour. To day we set stunsails. Last night about 7 bells first watch we came verry near being down by A Clipper Ship all on the account of the incompetancy of the Offercer in charge of the Deck.

FRI. SEPT. 1ST

Still we have fair wind but it is geting verry light and consequently the ship rools verry much. This Morning warm and cloudy. We carried away our stunsail Halyards. Another was soon rove and again the sail was set to assist us on our way. We carried away Royals and Stunsails all night. When day dawn'd we could make out A ship on our lee beam bearing on the same course as we are goin. To day we carried all the sails that we could put on her, studinsails below and Aloft. Then we were only able to make about 4½ knots we continued this.

About 6.30 when we started the Engine which soon put us ahead. The power of steam is of great importance but for that we should now be plunging about these watters in comparitively idleness but thanks to that power we are able to keep on our course with A little speed. Served out Cloathing.

SAT. SEPT. 2ND

We are steering N.W. half N. Quite warm and not A breath of wind and below decks the heat is almost suffocateing. Many slept apon the spar Deck all night. Last night was was A beautiful night. The Moon shone forth in its splendor and one could sit for hours and medetate apon the works of nature. Myself I devideed my thoughts between Nature and the loved ones at Home and longs for the hour of our meeting wich we all cincerely hope will be soon. We have got the ship looking quite neat again for on each time that we coal ship we look A coal hunk. Served out clean Hammocks.

SUN. SEP. 3RD

At Noon. We were (1030) one thousand and thirty miles on our way being more than one third on our sixth day out. Quite warm. About 9 Oclock the wind hauld aft and we were able to set our Fore and Aft sails and by 4 bells we sat all of the squaresails. The wind is light but helps us on. We averaged about 8 knots the hour. We had Quaters and Inspection at 10 and Devine serveace at 10½ Oclock. We are steering N.W. by W. About 2 bells we made the Island (Western). We changed our course to the N.W. by W. half W. This braught the wind ahead when it became necessary to furl sail. Oh! for A continuance of good weather. Several Whales were seen this morning.

MON. SEPT. 4TH

Homeward bound. Fine day. Verry warm. We were able to set Fore and Aft sails. We wer[e] then goin six knots. About 4 bells we set all of our square sails. We are steering N.W. by W. half W. Should this weather last about two weeks we will be near our haven.

TUES. SEPT. 5TH

We are steering the same course as yesterday. We are goin about 4 knots with no wind at all. Of consequence were are goin to have A long passage. We are now none days out and not half way to our port.

WENS. SEPT. 6TH

This Morning the wind is dead ahead and we are oblige to tack ship. Verry warm. About 8 bells Afternoon watch the wind hauld in our favor. We amediately set our squaresails and laid our course once more for home.

THURS. SEPT. 7TH

We steamd last night enough to keep the ship from goin astern for we had no wind and this morning we are just rooling about in perfect idleness. We have the power to go but they will not use it. About 4 Oclock we quited steaming. Then at 8½ we again put the Engine in motion. We were obliged to Furl sail, the wind being right ahead. We are now 1000 Miles from our port. We are roolling along about 5 knots the hour.

FRI. SEPT. 8TH

Still the wind blows ahead. We continue to steam. We hope soon to enter the Gulf steam. Once across the steam our distance seems short. We begins to see the Grass from the stream and hope soon to be able to cross that mysterious stream. About 11½ Oclock we set the Foresail and about 1½ we sat all our squaresails and we began to go along quite free until about 5 bells when A squal arose from the Westward and we were obliged to take in our Degallantsails. The squal was soon over and we again spread them to the Breeze. This is quite A long passage for A steamer of the class of this ship.

SEPT. 9TH

We are hardly holding our own. We have A head wind and have been trying to work up A little but we go about 1½ knots ahead and about 3 knots to the Seeward. We were under single reef'd Topsails until about 11 Oclock when we shook out the reef and set the Degallantsails. It have been quite threatening to day, alternately sunshine and rain. About 7 Oclock we about ship and stood on the Port Tack bearing W. by South. We stood on this course until about 4 bells first watch when we stood N. by W. half W. being our course.

SUN. SEPT. 10TH

Blowing quite fresh. We were obliged to take in our Degallantsails and took A reef in our Topsails. We are steering on our course N.W.N. being A verry bad day. We did not have Quarters or Inspection. At 5 bells we had Devine

Serveace. It continued to Blow and by 12 N. all hands were call'd to make sail. Also took another reef in the Topsails. We are goin about 8 knots. About 3 bells A sail was reported from the Mast head about 4 points on the weather Bow. We made her out to be A ship steering on the same course as we are but she was too far to the windward to speak her. About 7 bells P.M. stopd the Engine. Rooling quite heavely. We only stop'd steaming about half an hour when we struck up again and continued all night.

MON. SEPT. 11TH

We are goin about 8 knots the hour under double reef'd Topsails and steam. About 9 Oclock we shook out the reefs stop'd the Engine. Afternoon we took off the Staysails and bend the Trysails again. Set Degallant and Royals about 4 bells P.M. we exchanged signals with A Chillanian Merchantman. Our Latetude 46.13. Hers 47.13. We have A good breeze this evening but do not expect it to last long. Last Night the Jack of the dust was caught in the fore Hold with A naked Light by the Master At Arms was reported that braught down strict orders regarding lights. So much for being careless. Well the Inocent must suffer alike with the Guilty. To day one of the Boatswain Mates was disrated for strikeing one of the Quarter Gunners.

TUES. SEPT. 12TH

The watter has become quite warm as we approach the Gulf. Goin along slowly. We neaver have A fair wind. We are now A Thousand Miles away from where we expected to be at this time. The wind hauld fair and we set all our square sails and under steam. Makeing about 8 knots the hour. Nothing of importance goin on except all hands wants to get home.

WENS. SEPT. 13TH

This Morning we are goin along quite easlay but not on our course. We entered the Gulf stream about 4 P.M. yesterday. About 9 Oclock we stop'd stop'd steaming or the wind was driveing us too far off of our course and they wants to save coal as it looks squaly. Took in all the sail excepting Fore and Main Topsails and Fore and Mainsails. Took A reef in the Topsails. We are also carrying Fore and Aft sails. About 11 Oclock all hands were call'd to muster. Read the articles of War. About 4 bells P.M. all Hands were calld to

Reef Topsails when we took A double Reef in the Fore and Main Topsails. We carried double reefd Topsails all night.

THURS. SEPT. 14TH

This morning we have A little Breeze. We shook out the Reefs and set Degallant sails. Wind verry light. Makeing about 4½ knots the hour. About Noon sat Royals. About 5 bells A sail was reported on our weather beam. We made her out to be A Brig bound to the Eastward. About 2 bells we had surprise Fire Quarters. We continued with all sail set until about 4 bells first watch they started the Engine.

FRI. SEPT. 15TH

We are wending our way slowly. We have steam all night and all day. Makeing about 8 knots at noon to day we were about 650 Miles from Boston. We hope to run that by Tuesday. At 4 bells we had Fire Quarters then Drilling with small Arms. About 3 bells P.M. stop'd the Engine. We saild all night. About 6 bells Mid watch whe had quite A rain storm. It blowd awful hard for about an hour and the rain in perfect Torrents. We took in all sail excepting Topsails. Those we double reef'd. About 1 Bell ceased raining.

SAT. SEPT. 16TH

About 5 bells started Engine and about 7 bells set Fore and Aft sails and about 6 bells we set all our Square sails. Makeing about 8 knots. We had a general Holystoneing to day. We steamd until 2½ Oclock when we stop'd the Engine. About 7 bells there came up A squal when we took in our Degallant and Royals. The squal did not last long and we sat our Degallant sails again. At 8 Oclock we were goin 9 knots. That is quite A fair rate of speed with the Propeller down. Oh! for A sight at the Cape. This Evening there was three Men caught (Playing Cards in the Fore Hold) by the First Lieut. They were put into the Brig. Also the Act. Capt. of the Hold. The ships Corporal of that Deck was Disrateed.

SUN. SEPT. 17TH

How slowly the time passes or that we in our anxiety are unconcious of its flight. We have been under both steam and sail all day. Weather fine. Devine serveace at 4 bells and before serveace we had Inspection and Quarters. We have been in sight of A Brig all day.

MON. SEPT. 18TH

Fine weather. Quite warm. Under both steam and sail last night in the Mid Watch she made 10½ knotss to day at Noon was 260 miles from the cape. We shall expect to reach Port on Wensday and wont that be Joyfull when we get thare. To day at ten Oclock A summary Court Martial conviend to try three Men for gambling and the first and second Captain's of the Hold for allowing gambling to be carried on in the hold without reporting it. As Night approachd it began to show signs of bad weather. Verry cloudy. Looks like storm is comeing on. Oh for that cry of *Land ho.*

TUES. SEPT. 19TH

Rooling heavaly. We feard A storm and one we have about 9 Oclock we took in Degallant sails and during the mid watch reef'd Topsails steaming all the time during the first watch. We took soundings. Braught bottom 80 Fatham's. Blowing quite fresh from the S.E. Makeing about 10½ knots. The hour about 6 bells made preperation to Rouse up Cable for Bow anchors and to bend them. To day there is A great deal of tumbling about at 640 have the Lead 45 fathoms.

WENS. SEPT. 20TH

About 8 Oclock A light was reported on our Port Bow which we took for Cape Cod but on sounding we found it to be A mistake. At Daylight the Island of Nantucket was in sight. We changed our course for the Cape. Morning verry fine. Oh! Beautiful. We made the Light about 9.30 and pass'd the Cape about 11 Oclock. We signalized as we pass'd. Took A Pilot from Boat No. 9 about 4 bells when about 25 miles from Boston about 6 bells all hands were call'd to shorten sail. We having been under full sail all day. We came to Anchor about one mile from Boston Light at 4.45 being about ten miles from the Citty. We received papers from the Pilot but there was no exciteing news. The sight of the shores of New England is A verry pleasant sight to one anxious as I am to get ashore as soon as we were safe at Anchor. We got supper then it was all Hands to Paint ship and soon the sides were alive with the men blacking her anew. While the Comodore and some of the Offercers tried thair luck at fishing but without success. We shall expect to make an earley start for the Citty where we hope that we shall all feel releived from our anxiety to get once more in the Dominions of Uncle Samuel.

THURS. SEPT. 21ST

Light House Chanel. This Morning all Hands were call'd quite early. We cleand ship Fore and Aft. A Brim Boat came alongside. We heard of the "Saccramento's" arriveal. We got up steam and about 11 Oclock we weigh'd anchor and started for the Citty. We were saluted by the Forts as we pass'd up. When near East Boston we saluted the Admiral (he returning the salute) and came to anchor of Lincoln's warf. There soon were several persons on board. Went asshore. Visited My Aunt. Also Mrs. Vaught, Mrs. Kellogg, Mrs. R. Found every boddy well and every thing statu[s] quo. Maild A Letter to C.W.R. one to Mr. R.H.

FRI. SEPT. 22ND

I returnd on board this Morning. Got scolded for remaining on shore. Met E.A.M. Met W.S. and Many of our old Boys. We soon will be out of Commission. There were about one hundred and fifty Men discharged to day which Makes quite A change in affairs aboard ship. Several of my asociates among them.

SAT. SEPT. 23RD

Boston Harbor. We have not received A Mail as yet. It seems that our ship was reported at New York and our Mail was sent there. We received A Mail this Evening. I received A letter from C.W.R. Discharged more men.

SUN. SEPT. 24TH

Boston. Went asshore to Market but could get nothing but Baked Beanes. Went asshore again during the Afternoon but without success. We received A Mail. I received A Letter from C.W.R. one from Sister and one from Mr. Robt. Hamilton. The Money sent to him in May Last was received and acknowledged in the Issue of July 26. we had General Muster at 4 bells and Devine serveace at 10½ Oclock.

> The reference to Hamilton has to do with the money sent to *The Anglo-African* and acknowledged in the letter published under the title "Our Noble Tars Speak." (The text is printed in Chap. 4.)

MON. SEPT. 25TH

Boston. Still where we anchord. To day the Chaplain and Comodore's Secetary were detachd. We expects to go to the Yard on to Morrow. It is now growing quite cool. Unbend sails.

TUES. SEPT. 26TH

At Anchor. Still waiting for the "Phowhattan" to haul out then we shall haul in. to day met Bill Briggs. Heard from Home.

WENS. SEPT. 27TH

Yet in the Stream. Oh! when shall we get in. We have been A long time geting home and now it seems as if we shall be for ever geting into the dock. Yesterday we sent down Degallantmast and all Runing Rigging. About 3 Oclock the "Phowhattan" hauld out. She pass'd us and Anchord off South Boston. We have made preperation to haul in Tomorrow and I hope we shall succeed.

THURSDAY SEPT. 28TH

Hauld into the Yard. A part of the Crew were discharged and they left in great joy.

FRIDAY SEPT. 29TH

At the Navy Yard Charlestown. At five Oclock I received my Discharge being three Years and nine days in the serveace of Uncle Sam and glad am I to receive it paid of $4.24.00. So end my serveace in the Navy of the United States of America.

William Benjamin Gould, in about the late 1870s or early 1880s.

Cornelia Williams Read Gould, around 1890.

WBG and Cornelia Williams Read Gould with their children in the late 1880s. Back row: Lawrence Wheeler Gould, Herbert Richardson Gould, William B. Gould Jr., Frederick Crawford Gould, Medora Williams Gould. Front row: Luetta Ball Gould, James Edward Gould, Cornelia Williams Read Gould, William B. Gould, Ernest Moore Gould.

Top, *left*, plaque on the pew dedicated to WBG and his wife in Church of the Good Shepherd's Chapel of All Saints. The chapel is dedicated to Father William F. Cheney, the church's first Rector. (Photograph by Elliot Foulds)

Top, *right*, the African Baptist Church, Nantucket, Massachusetts. WBG and Cornelia Williams Read were married there by its pastor, the Rev. James E. Crawford, who was instrumental in purchasing her out of slavery. (Photograph by Claudia Kronenberg)

Bottom, the Episcopal Church of the Good Shepherd in Dedham, Massachusetts. WBG was one of its founders in the 1870s. (Photograph by Beverly Mayne Kienzle)

Cornelia Williams Read Gould and William Benjamin Gould by the fireplace in their home on Milton Street in Dedham, Mass., circa 1880s or 1890s.

Above, WBG with other GAR members at the 250th anniversary of the settlement of Dedham. WBG is fifth from the left in the first row. The photograph, taken in September 1886, was published in the *Dedham Transcript* on May 21, 1921.

Right, two of the many documents issued under WBG's name as an official of the GAR post (both as commander and adjutant).

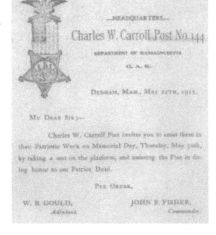

WBG with his six sons in service. This photograph of all of the Gould veterans originally appeared in the NAACP's magazine, *Crisis*, in December 1917. All of the sons are veterans of World War I except WBG Jr., a Spanish-American War veteran. Standing behind WBG are, from left to right:, Lawrence Wheeler Gould, James Edward Gould, William Benjamin Gould Jr., Ernest Moore Gould, Herbert Richardson Gould, and Frederick Crawford Gould.

Above, a reception for Company L on the Boston Common in 1898 on its return from Puerto Rico. The men are greeted by Mayor Josiah Quincy of Boston.

Left, William B. Gould Jr. of Company L, Sixth Massachusetts Infantry, United States Volunteers, in the service of his country during the Spanish-American War.

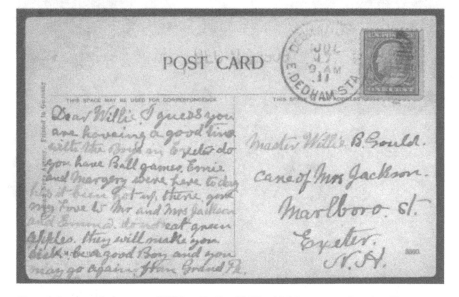

Top, right, a patriotic young William B. Gould III with his younger brother Ernest, in 1906.

Below, a postcard sent from Dedham by WBG, then 73, to William B. Gould III, then 9, on July 17, 1911. It says: "Dear Willie, I guess you are haveing a good time with the Boys in Exeter do you have Ball games. Ernie and Margery were here today has it been hot up there. give my love to Mr and Mrs Jackson and Emma. do not eat green apples. they will make you sick. be a good boy and you may go again. from Grand Pa." The front of the postcard (*top, left*) depicts the Dedham Boat Club houses on the Charles River, frequented by the author's parents both prior to and during their marriage.

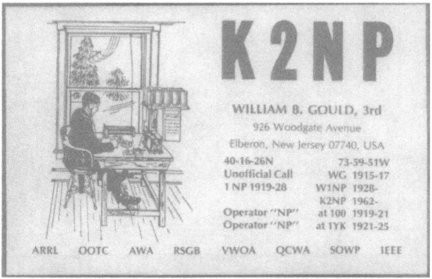

Top, WBG III (*fourth row, far left*) and his brother Ernest (*first row, right*) as acolytes at the Church of the Good Shepherd with Father Cheney, 1914.

Bottom, WBG III becomes a ham radio operator in 1915 at the age of thirteen, and obtains one of the earliest licenses issued in the United States.

Top, in the 1930s, WBG III (far right) serves as a member of the U.S. Naval Reserve.

Bottom, William B. Gould III with his wife, Leah Felts Gould, and their children, Dorothy and WBG IV, 1940.

Epilogue

𝒜s the New York Times recently noted, "the years now passing resemble for [the veterans of World War II] what the 1920s were for Civil War veterans . . . a final farewell."[1] On May 26, 1923, this headline appeared in the *Dedham Transcript*: EAST DEDHAM MOURNS FAITHFUL SOLDIER AND ALWAYS LOYAL CITIZEN: DEATH CAME VERY SUDDENLY TO WILLIAM B. GOULD, VETERAN OF THE CIVIL WAR.[2]

The second week of July 1999 provides a partial respite from the series of torrid heat waves and humidity the East Coast has been enduring. I drive to Dedham in a rental car after my plane arrives at Boston's Logan Airport. Undertaken periodically and sporadically since a visiting academic assignment in Cambridge, Massachusetts, three decades ago, a new round of examination of *Dedham Transcripts* and other materials at the Dedham Historical Society and the Dedham Public Library begins.

But important though it is, I experience much more than library research in Dedham. I drive down High Street past cathedral-like Saint Mary's Roman Catholic Church, which my great-grandfather helped to construct, and I turn left toward the Brookdale Cemetery, where I proceed to the gravesite to kneel in prayer. The graves of the first three William Benjamin Goulds are side by side, and I pray that my father would approve of my efforts to reconstruct the past, among other things. And then it is on to the Episcopal Church of the Good Shepherd, where I and three other William Benjamin Goulds were all baptized, and where the first three were confirmed. (My family's move to New Jersey when I was four years old—it was triggered by my father's employment with the U.S. Army Signal Corps at Fort Monmouth—meant that I would be confirmed there.)

The first William B. Gould was one of the founders of the Church of the Good Shepherd parish in the 1870s. The current rector, Father Edward Kienzle, shows me the old diagrams identifying the family pews of all the members, and we are able to locate where the Gould family sat from the founding of the parish. In the chapel, we discover a pew that, by a long-unnoticed plaque, identifies it as dedicated in memory of both William Benjamin and Cornelia Williams.

Then I drive on and stop at Milton Street near the Boston boundary line and look at 303 and 307, where I spent many a summer as a small child on our visits from our family home in Long Branch, New Jersey. I want to knock on the door and look at the backyard where I walked back and forth between the two houses; where I tipped the birdbath over; where I watched with fascination the locomotives moving up and down the train tracks. But I resist the impulse. I dare not give in to it, fearing that this effort would be viewed as an intrusive invasion of an unknown person's privacy.

⌐

As I have returned to Dedham in more recent years I have reflected upon those many visits, and the fact that never once did I hear anything said about my great-grandfather's service in the Civil War, let alone his origins in Wilmington, North Carolina. According to my mother, my father and his uncle Lawrence often discussed the first William B. Gould's naval career in both the states and Europe, but I do not personally recall any discussion of him whatsoever, a fact that, in retrospect, I find particularly ironic, given both my father's intellectual curiosity and considerable pride in his family and their achievements, and the fact that he and I often discussed and argued about politics with my great-uncles during our visits there. There, we discussed matters of substance and lamented my great-uncles' anachronistic allegiance to a Republican Party that had turned against or become indifferent to the principles of racial equality and civil rights, the cause that it had championed in the middle of the nineteenth century.

All six of my great-grandfather's sons were military veterans. Upon William Benjamin Jr.'s return to Dedham at the end of the Spanish-American War, the *Dedham Transcript* described his welcome home:

Sergeant William B. Gould, Jr., and private Charles S. Smith, both of Co. L., 6th Mass. regiment of volunteers were tendered a public reception by the citizens of the town and the officers and members of Gen. Stephen M. Weld Camp 75. S.O.V., in Memorial Hall last Saturday evening. The hall was well filled and members of Charles W. Carroll Post 144, G.A.R., the S.O.V. Camp and leading citizens of the town had seats on the platform. . . . Messrs. Gould and Smith have reason to feel proud of the welcome home tendered them. They did their duty on the battlefield and their townspeople respect and honor them for so doing.[3]

My five great-uncles served as officers and enlisted men in World War I. Values involved in this association with the military shaped the thinking of our entire family, particularly that of my father and ultimately mine. Indeed, my father, William B. Gould III, was to serve in the U.S. Naval Reserve between 1925 and 1939 and on active duty on numerous occasions. My great-grandfather's service was in the U.S. Navy, the less discriminatory institution in the armed services in the War of the Rebellion. Eventually, my father resigned from the Naval Reserve because of its color bar, which continued well into World War II.

In retrospect, it is apparent to me how deeply I was affected in my childhood and upbringing by those values. My father was to point out to me the inaccuracy of the school texts with which we were provided regarding Reconstruction. And long before it became more popularly known, he emphasized the role of Woodrow Wilson—who had come to be so highly regarded for failed foreign policy initiatives—in subordinating the role of blacks in the Civil War and, equally important, promoting racial discrimination in the federal government and throughout American society.

Many of the songs that my father sang to me during many illnesses as a child had been brought home from the Civil and First World wars by my Gould forebears. "The Battle Hymn of the Republic" was a cherished anthem, assuming religious dimensions for us. And on countless occasions my father sang "Marching Through Georgia" to me, noting wryly the angry reaction of contemporary southerners when they heard the song.

The naval tradition ran strong in my early years. My father would rouse my sister and me from early morning slumber when we were about to drive from New Jersey to Massachusetts with the exhortation, "Rise and shine you lazy loafers, hit the deck." And the morning call before those long trips would invariably conclude with a long shrill boatswain's whistle. I am not sure whether this stemmed from my father's service in the Naval Reserve or was based on what he had heard as a boy living next to my great-grandfather.

Beyond both the music and the cadence of the Civil War and World War I that I heard so frequently as a child in the 1940s, there was the legacy of the Episcopal Church. I was a choir boy for almost six years at Saint James's Episcopal Church in Long Branch, where I was confirmed in 1949 and subsequently served as an acolyte. The liturgy of the church, the vestments, the incense, the Sanctus bell, and the language of the Book of Common Prayer are in my bones as the result of this heritage.

The Episcopal Church, its liturgy and the language of its beautiful Book of Common Prayer, were very much a part of my upbringing. I think that all of this—language and values—comes from the first William Benjamin Gould and the Church of the Good Shepherd in Dedham. He was a signer of the Articles of Incorporation for that church and therefore one of the founders of the parish. The name of its first rector, the Rev. Father William F. Cheney, who presided over the parish until 1920, was spoken of in reverential terms in our house. And the Chapel of All Saints is dedicated to his memory.

The values and viewpoints of my great-grandfather affected our household in other respects as well. His passionate commitment to the cause of the War of the Rebellion and the principles of what he called "Right and Equality" in his diary were animating factors in his life.[4] William B. Gould's condemnation of the racist behavior of "scoundrels" in the navy is illustrative of the passion and depths of his commitment.[5] The same is true of his outspoken opposition to the proposal to colonize blacks in Africa that was aired by President Lincoln during the war and still bandied about for many years thereafter.

Of course, in the nineteenth and early twentieth centuries, those causes and values translated into support for the Republican Party. This most assuredly was the allegiance of my great-grandfather and also of my grandfather, whose membership in the local Republican caucus is recorded in the *Dedham Transcript*. (Indeed, my great-grandfather, in his capacity as commander of the Charles W. Carroll Post 144, wrote a special statement sorrowfully lamenting the assassination of the last of the Civil War soldier-Presidents, William McKinley, in 1901.) As I have noted, my great-uncles continued this allegiance well into the twentieth century, to the great dismay of me and my father.

Nonetheless, my family arranged for Mayor James Michael Curley of Boston (one of the leading Democratic Party bosses of the first half of the twentieth century) to speak to the Dedham Sons of Union Veterans of the Civil War, a function in which both William B. Gould Jr. and the great-uncles were involved. And Mayor Curley employed my father in the desperate circumstances of the Great Depression. Some of my father's functions were not only the professional work of a draftsman but also of the ward-heeling variety for the Curley machine, and he spoke of the mayor with considerable fondness, characterizing him as a kind of Robin Hood figure who helped both the poor and sometimes himself. (My father always took care to point out the mayor's shamrock-studded home in Jamaica Plains as we drove by on one of our summer Massachusetts visits.)[6]

Still, in my father's view, the Massachusetts Republican Party in the 1940s and 1950s tended to be more directly tied to the state's abolitionist tradition than the Irish-dominated Democratic Party in Boston. For him, Senator Leverett Saltonstall represented the kind of Republican moderate who was more likely to give a fair shake to blacks than the Democrats. But my father loved Mayor Curley, and he enthusiastically described the speeches with which he enthralled so wide a variety of audiences. Curley would gain the support of the most hostile crowd, my father said, by telling them basic facts about their own organization and thus flattering them in the most effective manner possible.

The Boston mayor (who served time in jail while in office on more than one occasion) helped the Gould family when it needed help. My father would speak of his distribution of Curley campaign literature in the Irish sections of Boston, and in a fine imitation of the language, he would relate how the Irish ladies would ask him, in a thick brogue, "Are you a good Catholic bye [boy]?" "Oh yes, ma'am," Episcopalian WBG III would quickly answer, knowing full well that the inevitable response would be, "Well come right in then, me bye."

The positions of the political parties on blacks in my great-grandfather's time, with the Democratic Party opposed to abolition and generally inclined to appease the Confederacy, and the Republican Party opposed to slavery in the territories and ultimately in any part of the country, were reversed in the century to follow. But the change was slow to come. Triggered by the lure of World War I and postwar jobs, the great migration from South to North gave the black masses their first franchise in the large urban centers above the Mason-Dixon line. Fre-

quent opponents of President Lincoln's war effort and post–Civil War expo-
nents of white supremacy, Democrats remained hostile to civil rights through the
Woodrow Wilson administration. Even the Franklin D. Roosevelt administration refused to support anti-lynching legislation in the 1930s and 1940s to avoid
antagonizing its "solid South" base. Only under President Harry Truman did
the party move in a more pro–civil rights direction. Thanks to FDR's New Deal
policies promoting the interests of workers and the unemployed and HST's Fair
Deal emphasis on civil rights, the majority of black Americans shifted their allegiance from the Republicans to the Democrats. That support became over-
whelming with the Democratic Party's solid backing of the landmark civil rights
legislation of the 1960s. The Republican Party, meanwhile, moved rightward, a
trend that was embodied in the "southern strategy," heralded by Barry Goldwa-
ter, who went down to a landslide defeat in 1964, and adopted more successfully
by Richard Nixon in the 1970s, Ronald Reagan in the 1980s, and the Congressional Republicans in the 1990s.

My father's last vote for the Republicans in any national election was in 1928.
From that point on, notwithstanding his respect for Stanford's Herbert Hoover,
he was unwavering in his promise to "never again" vote for the Republican
Party. And, like him, I have been faithful to the Democratic Party from the first
time that I cast a ballot. In our view, there was no inconsistency—and indeed
there was a very strong *consistency*—between our support of the Democratic
Party's civil rights and economic legislation and the Republican policies that
had won the support of both my great-grandfather and my grandfather.

There was another family ideal that cut through the generations and across
party lines. This was the attitude toward the military. Time and time again at
discussions at the dinner table and in our living room, my father's constant refrain was, "You wouldn't have any freedoms in this country if we didn't have a
strong military that was willing to defend them." In 1991, I wrote in *the New York
Times* that my great-grandfather and those who succeeded him in serving their
country in its later wars were the "backbone of this nation."[7] I am sure that this
view was shaped by my family's willing engagement in military service from the
Civil War onward.

July Fourth was always a great day in our family, a time when my father, even
beyond middle age, was prone to set off firecrackers in celebration of the coun-

try's independence on the steps outside our New Jersey home, and when the flag was flown, as it so often was also on Memorial Day and Armistice Day. And I can still hear my father speak of hundreds of Civil War veterans marching through the streets of Boston, and his reminiscences of my great-grandfather coming to the public schools on Memorial Day to tell the students of his experiences in and the lessons of the Civil War. (My father's Dedham boyhood chum, Benjamin Brewster, also recalled those speeches anew in a 1985 Copley Plaza Hotel tête-à-tête after my father's death.)

My father would often tell the story of a gruff old Civil War veteran calling and asking, "Is Bill Gould there?" "Yes, speaking," came the ready answer from my father. "The hell it is," said the caller. Three William Benjamin Goulds lived adjacent to one another in those early years of the twentieth century.

One of my father's stories that I remember most vividly had to do with my great-grandfather's work as a contractor on the Saint Mary's church project. According to my father, some of the workmen in his employ fell asleep at a critical time in the process, but the defects that occurred as a result had not been detected, and thus could have been easily covered up with no one knowing the better until years later. It was just about then that it was becoming clear that cement was a critical bonding agent in the preparation of mortar, and most probably, his workers added only lime to the mix. Although the absence of cement could not be discerned by even the best-trained eye,[8] my great-grandfather had all the plaster ripped out of the church and had the work done again at such great expense that he was nearly bankrupted. From this moment on, his stature in Dedham was enhanced, as was the name Gould.

⤸

Shortly after the war, perhaps in late October 1865, William B. Gould returned to Wilmington and sent a report (as "Oley") to *The Anglo-African* describing how the conflict had affected the city:

> We found the old Town anything but what we left it. Her streets are entirely deserted. Her wharves that used to groan under million of barrels and thousands of bales are entirely bare. Her stores are all closed with few exceptions, and her workshops are silent. The river glides noiselessly by, and not a ship there to break the current. The grass is growing unmolested in her streets.[9]

But he went on to point out that there was a "greater change for the better": from the site of the old slave auction block in Market Square, the "former Lords of the soil" were viewing passers-by "from a commanding position." He was pleased to find "colored citizens" involved in trade and expecting to do business—but regretted that "our people" were "so backward in regard to the most important questions of the day." He was worried about the "bad condition" of the freedmen for the coming winter and troubled that several even now were supported by public welfare.

The next month found William B. Gould back in the Bay State, in Nantucket, where he married my great-grandmother, Cornelia Williams Read, on November 22. Here he stayed for a year, during which Medora Williams Gould (Aunt Dora to me and my sister) was born. And he supported his small but growing family by practicing the trade that he learned in Wilmington. Masonry is a highly skilled, physically demanding, and difficult craft, and perhaps in part for that reason, only one of his six sons, Lawrence, chose to pursue it. As a modern commentator puts it, "Turning blobs of liquid plaster into long, die-crisp mouldings of stunning beauty and complexity is one of the most amazing techniques of the plasterers' art."[10]

But the elder Gould must have found the work rewarding beyond just financial security, judging by the beautiful craftsmanship he displayed in his North Carolina and Massachusetts projects. The plastering work he did on the Bellamy Mansion in Wilmington, in particular, reflects the quality of the workmanship that William B. Gould brought to Dedham, where it not only provided his wife and eight children with a measure of security, but also earned him acclaim and respect. Saint Mary's church was far from the only large project where he played the role of employer. The official reports are full of contracts that he was awarded for public buildings, including several schools.[11]

As for his outside activities, the most important by far centered on the Grand Army of the Republic's Charles W. Carroll Post 144, which he joined in 1882. The "camp-fire" and encampments where members could meet and sing old war songs were something that he participated in frequently. His unit was not formed until 1873, but black veterans were prominent in the Massachusetts organization from its inception, in 1867.

As Lisa King tells us:

To promote loyalty, especially among the growing immigrant population and the young who did not experience the war, the G.A.R. initiated many memorial reminders, such as monuments, fountains, statues of Union war heroes, and advocated for the preservation of Civil War sites and relics. The organization's lasting legacy was the creation of Memorial Day, observed May 30th. This observance started in 1868 as a day of remembrance for fallen comrades.

By the 1880s and 1890s the G.A.R. assumed a prominent place in national debates for the advocacy of patriotism in school textbooks, and most importantly, generous and inclusive pensions for veterans of the U.S. armed forces. As the Civil War veteran population aged, interest in pensions escalated and G.A.R. members began discussing national politics in local meetings.[12]

William B. Gould held virtually every position that it was possible to hold in the GAR from the time he joined until his death in 1923, including the highest post, commander, in 1900 and 1901. But it is not clear whether he was involved in the full range of activities that David Blight describes:

During 1883, black GAR posts held marches and public meetings from Massachusetts to Ohio, sometimes joining with white veterans in integrated gatherings. In Ohio, black GAR posts, which mobilized veterans of three regiments and booked special excursion trains, planned the largest gathering ever of their members for August in the town of Chillicothe. In New York, the Thaddeus Stevens post met in lower Manhattan in January 1883 for speeches and glee club entertainment. The following month, the William Lloyd Garrison post welcomed several other black posts from as far away as Hartford, Connecticut, and mixed with white veterans at the Bridge Street AME Church in Brooklyn for a full dress march and choir performance. The Shaw Guards (named for Colonel Robert Gould Shaw) in Boston held frequent meetings, bringing together the surviving black rank and file with white officers of the Fifty-fourth Massachusetts regiments. On Memorial Day, 1883, at Rainsford Island, Massachusetts, Julius C. Chappelle, the lone black member of that state's legislature, addressed a public ceremony conducted by black veterans.[13]

Still, he clearly did participate in many GAR functions at the state and regional level. For instance, in 1918, "as a 'past Commander,' he represented [post 144] at the 52nd annual encampment of the department of Massachusetts GAR at Faneuil Hall, Boston."[14] Similarly, the year before, the GAR association of

Dedham's home county, Norfolk County, elected him as the commander of the county group at its annual meeting at Weymouth.[15] But local affairs took up most of his time. For example, he often spoke at the Dedham schools on Memorial Day and at GAR and Sons of Union Veterans meetings. (Several of his sons, as well as my great-uncles and my grandfather, were members and officers of the latter organization.) Almost to the end of his life, he continued to participate in parades on Memorial Day and Armistice Day and to acknowledge the cheering of the crowds as he passed by in his red-, white-, and blue-festooned car.[16] He was forty-nine and a member of the General Staff when he posed for a GAR group photograph during the commemoration of Dedham's 250th anniversary. As the *Dedham Transcript* remarked when it ran the photograph in 1921, two years before William B. Gould's death, "Only a few in the group are now living."[17]

In earlier days, he and a fellow GAR member, Cornelius Taft, prepared a report for the *Dedham Transcript* on GAR monuments and memorials. The report, which was published in May 1909, noted that Dedham had "remember[ed] its heroic dead of the Civil War" by erecting the monument known as the Memorial Hall. It went on to say:

> There are fourteen comrades buried at this time in this lot and there is room for as many more. The shell that surmounts the shaft has a little history of its own. It was fired across the Potomac near Aquia Creek, where the confederates had a battery of four 100 lb. Blakely breech-loading rifled guns (these were English guns) to blockade the river to prevent vessels from carrying supplies to Washington.[18]

In 1900, in his capacity as commander of the GAR, he was the concluding speaker at a meeting, where, in the *Dedham Transcript*'s description, "his remarks were of a facetious nature." But in a more serious vein, "he thought a series of alternating entertainments by the Post and Camp [General Stephen M. Weld Camp 75, Sons of the Veterans] a good thing intending to cement more strongly the friendship between the two organizations."[19]

A few months later, he presided at the Memorial Day observances in Memorial Hall, where, at the conclusion of the services, his son "William B. Gould, Jr., acting captain, headed by the band, escorting the members of the Post and a visiting delegation, . . . proceed[ed] to the old village cemetery, where after selections by the band, a prayer . . . and the singing of 'America' by one and all present, the graves of comrades and the State monument were decorated."[20] He took the podium again the following year, to preside over the 1901 observances.[21]

My father, as well as my grandfather, participated in some of these events. Among the most memorable was a ceremony honoring the members of the National Guard who went to the Mexican border in June 1916, an affair that, according to the *Transcript*, was "largely attended," and where "the brave boys were right royally received and entertained."[22] So were the invited guests, the veterans of the Civil War, including my great-grandfather. To the reporter, "the blue-coated veterans of 1861–1865 and the grey-uniformed youngsters of 1916 made a picture of strong contrast as they were seated side by side—the nation's defenders of the olden days and those of the newer times." The paper found it worthy of note that when the doors of the hall were thrown open to the public and men and women began to file in, "William Gould 3rd" was one of them.

Generally, the content of William B. Gould's speeches is not recorded. For instance, in 1911 a reporter noted only that he gave "a short patriotic address."[23] In 1920 he co-authored a memorial statement about his colleague Cornelius Taft, the man who had joined him in preparing the report on the GAR's monuments:

> [He] could not be tempted from the simplicity and purity of living which march him to the end. Above all his dauntless independence shines forth. . . .
>
> He worked hard all his life and never wanted more for his labor than it was worth. [He possessed] the ardor of the generous contention for freedom and a broader national life, the common impulse furling from man to man . . . when in the Civil War he stood side by side with his comrades in the ranks, more eager for the victory of truth and of right than the glory of the spoils of conquest. . . .
>
> He had signally an honest mind. There was no sham in his make-up.[24]

These remarks apply equally to William B. Gould and the legacy that he has left for future generations. Truly, he was a most extraordinary man, not only in the years of his service to Uncle Samuel, but in all the years that followed.

Reference Matter

Glossary of Naval Terms

Awnings. Temporary canvas coverings spread over a deck as protection from the sun.

Battens. [WBG: seized on Battins] Thin strips of wood used for various purposes—for example, they are put around hatches to hold down a tarp (hence the phrase "batten down hatches") or inserted in sails to keep them flat.

Bend. To fasten with a bend or a knot. To unbend is to untie a rope or otherwise unfasten and remove sails or other gear. To bend a sail is to fasten it.

Boom. A general name for the spar or pole that provides an outreach for extending the foot of sails. *Jibboom*, *studding sail boom*, and *spanker boom* are all types that WBG referred to.

Cable. Generally used to indicate the wire, rope, or chain that connects the ship to its anchor.

Capstan. A mechanism used for raising anchors, hoisting *yards*, or otherwise lifting heavy weights. The lever that is used when the capstan is hand-operated is called the *capstan bar*.

Clew [WBG: clew'd up]. To hoist a square sail up a *yard* before furling. To "clew up" is to raise the lower corners of the sail up to the yard.

Cutter. A one-masted ship.

Davit [WBG: Davidts]. A small crane used to hoist boats, anchors, or other heavy items.

Furl. To roll up or take in a sail and secure it to its *yard*, *stay*, or *boom*.

Give chase. To pursue a vessel or fleet.

Halyard.   A line used to raise or lower sails, *yards*, or *spars*. The *halyard rack* is a wooden frame through which the halyard is coiled.

Heave.   1. To raise or hoist; 2. To cause to move or force into position; 3. [WBG: Hove the lead] To throw or cast; 4. [WBG: Hove to] To put a vessel into the position of "lying to"; to check the vessel's movement by causing the sails to counteract each other.

Holystone [WBG: Holy-stoned decks].   The soft white sandstone used with water and sand for scrubbing decks.

Jib.   A triangular sail set on a stay between the foremast and the *jibboom* (at the bow).

Jibboom.   The outermost extension of the post or stem at the bow (front end) of the vessel.

Masts.   Vertical poles that support the *yards, booms*, etc. In large vessels they are composed of several parts, from bottom to top: *lower mast, top mast, topgallant mast*, and *royal mast*. WBG refers to the *Degallant mast*, which must be the name of an additional segment of the mast. Depending on the number of masts on a vessel, they have different names. The masts from front to back on a four-masted vessel would be the *fore mast, main mast, mizzen mast*, and *spanker mast*.

Mizzen.   Refers to the *yards*, sails, and *rigging* for the *mizzen mast*, the third mast from the front in a vessel with more than three masts.

Moor.   To secure a ship in place with ropes, chains, or anchors.

Quarters.   The crew is "at quarters" when all men are manning their designated stations.

Reef.   One of the horizontal portions of a sail that can be rolled or folded up to expose less area to the wind. To reef is to fold or roll a sail to reduce its size.

Rigging.   A general term for all ropes, chains, and gear used to support and operate *masts, yards, booms*, sails, etc.

Sails.   Sails generally take their names from the *mast, yard*, or *stay* on which they are set. For example, the main topsail is the sail that is set on the main top mast.

Sheet.   A rope or chain that fastens to the lower corners of a sail. The sheets are used to extend the sail or change its direction.

Spanker.   A triangular or quadrilateral sail usually set on the mast at the rear of the vessel. On a four-masted vessel, this mast is called the *spanker mast.*

Spar.   A general term for the poles used for *masts, yards, booms,* etc.

Spar deck.   An upper deck.

Square sails.   Rectangular sails set from *yards* that can pivot at their middle point.

Stays.   The lines that form part of the *rigging* used to support the *spars* and *masts.* They extend diagonally from the head of a mast down to another mast or to the deck.

Staysail.   A triangular or trapezoidal sail hoisted on a *stay.*

Storm sail.   A sail made of heavy canvas used in bad weather. Storm sails are generally smaller than the corresponding sail used in normal weather.

Studding sail [WBG: Studinsail].   A light sail that attaches at its foot to a *studding sail boom.* Also called a stunsail.

Studding sail boom.   An adjustable *spar* that acts as an extension for some types of *yards.*

Topping lifts.   Lines used to bear the weight of a *yard* when adjusting it to the desired angle. WBG says "putting top liffts to the Davidts," which probably means they are using *davits* to manipulate these wires.

Trysail.   A quadrilateral sail that attaches to the *trysail mast,* a small mast to the rear of the main mast.

Wardroom.   Officers' dining area.

Weigh anchor.   To pull up the anchor from the bottom.

Yards.   The long horizontal poles above the sails used to support and extend them. The names of yards, like the names of sails, generally reflect their position on the mast. For example, a *royal yard* would be located on the top segment of the mast, the *royal mast.*

SOURCES: Basil W. Bath, *The Visual Encyclopedia of Nautical Terms Under Sail* (1978); René de Kerchove, *International Maritime Dictionary* (1948).

Correspondents of William B. Gould

Date	Initials or Name Used by WBG	Location	Comments by WBG

CORNELIA WILLIAMS READ

Date	Initials or Name Used by WBG	Location	Comments by WBG
25-Mar-63	C.W.R.		First mention of correspondence to C.W.R.
25-May-63	Miss C.W.R.	Boston	"Meet Miss C.W.R. also had quite A good time in Boston and vicinety. Saw many of my aquaintances."
29-Oct-63	C.W.R.		"Sent A Picture to C.W.R."
7-Mar-65	C		"C is quite well."
28-May-65	C.W.R.		"I received A letter from C.W.R. Quite well. She spoke of the Death of my Mother. Also of Abram Price."
12-Jul-65	C.		"Oh C. why do you not write"

NOTE: List of Dates where C.W.R. is mentioned: 25-Mar-63; 25-May-63; 15-Oct-63; 23-Oct-63; 29-Oct-63; 2-Nov-63; 16-Nov-63; 7-Dec-63; 23-Dec-63; 28-Dec-63; 3-Jan-64; 7-Jan-64; 14-Jan-64; 16-Jan-64; 20-Jan-64; 29-Jan-64; 3-Feb-64; 5-Feb-64; 10-Feb-64; 13-Feb-64; 18-Feb-64; 19-Feb-64; 22-Feb-64; 26-Feb-64; 28-Feb-64; 4-Mar-64; 6-Mar-64; 16-Mar-64; 17-Mar-64; 2-Apr-64; 8-Apr-64; 10-Apr-64; 13-Apr-64; 14-Apr-64; 17-Apr-64; 4-May-64; 6-May-64; 9-May-64; 13-May-64; 16-May-64; 20-May-64; 22-May-64; 24-May-64; 26-May-64; 30-May-64; 1-Jun-64; 27-Jun-64; 15-Aug-64; 30-Aug-64; 25-Feb-65; 7-Mar-65; 20-Mar-65; 21-Apr-65; 1-May-65; 23-May-65; 28-May-65; 15-Jun-65; 16-Jun-65; 12-Jul-65; 13-Jul-65; 25-Aug-65; 21-Sep-65; 23-Sep-65; 24-Sep-65

Date	Initials or Name Used by WBG	Location	Comments by WBG

GEORGE L. MABSON

Date	Initials or Name Used by WBG	Location	Comments by WBG
30-Oct-62	G.L.M.		"received two papers from my Nephew G.L.M"
21-Nov-63	G.L.M.		
18-Feb-64	George L. M.		"Heard that George L.M. has joined the 5th Mass Cav."
19-Feb-64	Nephew		
2-Mar-64	G.L.M.		"Received A letter from G.L.M. containing one from home bearing date Jan 16th."
13-Apr-64	G.L.M.		
24-Apr-64	G.L.M.		
29-Apr-64	G.L.M.		"Received A letter from G.L.M. and Picture."
21-Mar-65	G.L.M.		
30-Mar-65	G.L.M.		
5-Apr-65	G.L.M.		
30-Apr-64	G.L.M.		
11-May-64	G.L.M.		
16-May-64	G.L.M.		
3-Jul-65	G.L.M.		

HOME

Date	Initials or Name Used by WBG	Location	Comments by WBG
5-Dec-63	home		"write home"
7-Dec-63	home		"Maild A letter for home"
5-Jan-64	home		
8-Jan-64	home		
18-Jan-64	home		"Heard from home."
2-Mar-64	home		"Received A letter from G.L.M. containing one from home bearing date Jan. 16th. All well. They received one from me. This is the second one that I have received."
10-Apr-64	mother		

NOTE: Presumably, letters home are to his mother, Elizabeth Moore, and/or sister, Eliza Mabson in Wilmington.

Date	Initials or Name Used by WBG	Location	Comments by WBG

ELIZA MABSON

Date	Initials or Name Used by WBG	Location	Comments by WBG
25-Mar-65	sister		sent letter
24-May-65			"I recei[ved] A letter from my Sister bring[ing] me the sad news of the death of [my] Mother. She died March the 13th. —— sad news for me. The first lett[er] that I receive from my Sister s[hould] contain such news. Wrote to my Sister."
2-Jul-65	sister		"All well at home."
3-Jul-65	sister		
19-Jul-65	sister		"All quite well at home. They say that the Spotted Fever is verry fatal there and that many are dying."
22-Jul-65	sister		
24-Sep-65	sister		

ABRAHAM H. GALLOWAY

Date	Initials or Name Used by WBG	Location	Comments by WBG
23-Feb-64	A.H.G.		
5-May-64	A.H. Galloway	New York	"heard that A.H. Galloway is in the Citty"
11-May-64	A.H. Galloway		"Meet A.H. Galloway." Attends meeting of North Carolina Delegates at Sulivan Street Church at which Galloway speaks.

GEORGE W. PRICE

Date	Initials or Name Used by WBG	Location	Comments by WBG
10-Nov-62	George P—e		"Three Men Deserted. One of them George P—e. I am verry sorry for it."
19-Jan-64	G.W.P.		
13-Feb-64	G.W.P.		
21-Apr-64	George Price		
24-Jan-64	G.W.P.		

NOTE: Sails to *Cambridge* with WBG. Owned by William Benticott.

Date	Initials or Name Used by WBG	Location	Comments by WBG

WILLIAM McLAURIN

Date	Initials or Name Used by WBG	Location	Comments by WBG
17-Jan-64	William McLauren	New York	"Saw Benjamin Grier and William McLauren."
29-Feb-64	Wm McLauren	New York	"Visited Benjamin Grair and Wm McLauren."
3-Apr-64	Wm. McL		"visited Wm. McL at New York"

ROBERT HAMILTON

Date	Initials or Name Used by WBG	Location	Comments by WBG
28-Jul-64	R.H.		
21-Sep-65	Mr. R.H.		
24-Sep-65	Mr. Robt. Hamilton		"Money sent to him in May Last was received and acknowledged in the Issue of July 26."

CHARLES MALLETT

Date	Initials or Name Used by WBG	Location	Comments by WBG
12-Jan-64	Mr. C. Mallett		
15-Jan-64	C.M.		

NOTE: Born: Wilmington & lives there after the War; Occupation: carpenter; Prominent black Republican, frequently nominated for office; Service: *Monticello*, *Pequot*; *Vicksburg*.

MARY MOORE; MRS. THOMAS H. JONES

Date	Initials or Name Used by WBG	Location	Comments by WBG
30-Mar-63	Aunt		
31-Mar-63	Mary	Boston	"Heard from my Aunt in the afternoon she with her Daughter. Mary came on board."
15-Oct-63	Aunt		
14-Nov-63	Aunt		
14-Jan-64	Aunt		
11-Aug-64	Aunt Jones	Boston	"Write to Aunt Jones (No. 2 Sears Place Boston Mass)."
15-Aug-64	Aunt		
21-Sept-65	Aunt	Boston	"Visited My Aunt."

WILLIAM H. MOORE

NOTE: Son of Thomas H. Jones. A William H. Moore, Esq. is listed as one of the directors of the African Civilization Society in *The Anglo-African* in Jan. 1863. His address is given at 147 Mott St., NY. Unclear if this is the same individual.

Date	Initials or Name Used by WBG	Location	Comments by WBG
		JOHN JONES	
25-May-63	Cousin John J—s	Chelsea Hospital	"one instant while sick one of Cousins John J—s came to the Hospital on buisiness. He came as near as the door of the ward that I was in and askd me how I was and amediately left. I did not know what to think of this treatment but on recovery I learnt that it had been reported that I had the Small Pox."
		A. A. JONES	
4-Dec-63	A.A. Jones		
28-Dec-63	A.A. Jones		
29-Dec-63	A.A. Jones		
1-Feb-64	A.A.J.		
2-Feb-64	A.A.J.		
18-Feb-64	A.A.Jo.		
28-Feb-64	A.A.J.		
5-Mar-64	A.A.J.		
		JOSEPH HALL	
9-Feb-64	J. Hall		"Received A letter from J. Hall on board of the Receiving Ship Alegahny at Baltimore."
14-Mar-64	Mr. & Mrs. Hall		
2-Apr-64	J.H.		
23-Jun-65	J.H.		

NOTE: Sails to *Cambridge* with WBG. Owned by Wm. Benticott. Born: Wilmington; Occupation: carpenter; Father: Andrew Hall (born slave); Mother: Isabella Stowe (born free); Serves on *Cambridge* 1 year, then transfers to *Sacramento* for 5–6 weeks and then to *Victoria* where he remains for 15–18 months. He transfers to a receiving ship at Baltimore and remains on it from Nov.-Mar. (1864), then transfers to the *Winona* at Baltimore. Discharged from the *Winona* June 10, 1865. According to his pension, he and his wife, Lucilla Moseley, reside in Old Port Comfort, VA, after the war.

Date	Initials or Name Used by WBG	Location	Comments by WBG

LUCILLA MOSELEY (HALL)

Date	Initials or Name Used by WBG	Location	Comments by WBG
5-Nov-62	L. M—ly		"The Mystic returnd from the shoals with the Mails of the Fleet. . . . She had also thirteen Rebel deserters and several colard Reffugees among them several of My Aquaintances. Heard from my people. Mrs. L.M—ly was among the many that I saw. She saild about sun set for Hampton Roads."
19-Mar-63	Mrs. Hall	Newport News, VA	"Saw Mrs. Hall."
21-Mar-63	Mrs. H	Newport News, VA	"received some Delecacies from Mrs. H for which that Lady have my thanks."
20-Feb-64	Mrs. H		
22-Feb-64	Mrs. H		
14-Mar-64	Mr. & Mrs. Hall		

NOTE: Wife of Joseph Hall. See "An Interesting and Romantic Narrative" in Chapter four. According to the narrative Lucilla Moseley and Joseph Hall were married at Hampton Roads, Va. 20-Dec-62. (Hall's pension papers say they married 19-Dec-62). WBG visits Mrs. Hall (Lucilla) while she is in Virginia in '63. Mr. & Mrs. Hall were both in Baltimore (Hall's pension file confirms that his ship was in Baltimore) in Mar. '64 when they wrote to WBG. In June of '64, when WBG recounted their story, she was living in Baltimore, MD, and Joseph Hall was on the *Winona*. Note that there are two Mrs. H's: Mrs. Lucilla (Moseley) Hall and Mrs. Ann E. Hoagland of Brooklyn.

ANDREW C. HALL

Date	Initials or Name Used by WBG	Location	Comments by WBG
15-Aug-64	A.C.H.		letter

NOTE: Sailed to *Cambridge* with WBG; owned by Wm. Benticott. Born: Wilmington; testified in William Schenck and John Mackey's pension applications. At time of testimony, resided in Cambridge, MA.

EDGER MILLER

Date	Initials or Name Used by WBG	Location	Comments by WBG
4-Mar-64		Cambridge	"Heard of the arrival at Cambridge of Edger Miller."

NOTE: There is an Edgar Miller in Wilmington who was: (1) among the speakers (Geo. W. Price also a speaker) at a Republican Party rally at the 1869 Convention in Wilmington; (2) a waiter, in 1866–67 Wilmington directory; (3) a Wilmington policeman 1875–76.

Date	Initials or Name Used by WBG	Location	Comments by WBG

ABRAHAM PRICE

Date	Initials or Name Used by WBG	Location	Comments by WBG
28-May-65	Abram Price		"I received A letter from C.W.R. Quite well. She spoke of the Death of my Mother. Also of Abram Price."

NOTE: Abraham Price is listed among the men picked up by the *Cambridge* on 4-Oct-62. Owned by Wm. Benticott. Perhaps related to George Price, also owned by Wm. Benticott. Born: North Carolina; enlists off Wilmington, N.C. 8-Oct-62; serves on *Cambridge* until 31-Mar-63.

CHARLES GILES

Date	Initials or Name Used by WBG	Location	Comments by WBG
18-Nov-63	C. Giles		
24-Dec-63	Giles		
14-Jan-64	C. G.		
15-Jan-64	C. G.		
13-Feb-64	C. G.		

NOTE: Born: North Carolina; Service: *Cambridge*; sailed to Cambridge with WBG; owned by Dan Russell.

J. M.

Date	Initials or Name Used by WBG	Location	Comments by WBG
4-Jan-64	J.M.		
11-Jan-64	J.M.		
16-Jan-64	J.M.		
22-Jan-64	J.M.		
28-Jan-64	J.M.		
28-Feb-64	J.M.		
10-Apr-64	J.M.		
30-Apr-64	J.M.		
24-May-65	J.M.		"I re[ceived] A letter from J.M. _____ he had visited Wilmington. Saw m[any] people all well. I felt verry much releived but my joy was of short duration, for this evening I re-cei[ved] A letter from my Sister bring[ing] me the sad news of the death of [my] Mother."

NOTE: Perhaps John Mackey. Born: Wilmington; Occupation: carpenter's mate; Sailed to Cambridge with WBG; Service: U.S.S. *Cambridge* until 6-Jun-63 when marked as deserted at Boston Navy Yard; appears again on rolls of *Ohio* where he remains from 31-Aug-63 to 15-Jan-64; served on *Pequot* to 2-Jun-65; discharged from the *North Carolina* 7-Jun-65. John Mackey was aboard the *Pequot* in the vicinity of Wilmington when news from there was sent; Andrew C. Hall testifies on his pension application; Resides in Cambridge, MA after the war. John Mitchell, also on the small boat with WBG, is another possibility.

Date	Initials or Name Used by WBG	Location	Comments by WBG

WILLIAM H. SCHENCK

Date	Initials or Name Used by WBG	Location	Comments by WBG
18-Nov-63	W.H. Schenck		
28-Feb-64	W.H.S.		
2-Apr-64	W.H.S.		
14-Apr-64	W.H.S.		
4-May-64	W.H.S.		
22-Sep-65	W.S.	Boston	"Met W.S. and Many of our old Boys."

NOTE: Born: New York; Resides in Boston after War; Service: *Cambridge* (Nov '61–Sept. '64), *Ohio* (Oct. '64–Sept. '65), *Savannah*; Andrew Hall provides testimony in his pension application

SCIPIO A. SPICER

Date	Initials or Name Used by WBG	Location	Comments by WBG
27-Jan-64	S. Spicer		"Heard that S. Spicer was on board of the Colorado."

NOTE: Born: Wilmington; Occupation: carpenter; Service: *State of Georgia, Colorodo* (until 17-Apr-63), *Lockawanna*; Resides in "Spanish Honduras" after war, returns to Wilmington in 1905.

THOMAS COWAN

Date	Initials or Name Used by WBG	Location	Comments by WBG
18-Nov-63	T. Cowan		

NOTE: Born: Wilmington; Occupation: Brickmaker, mason; Service: *Monticello, Comm. Mc.Donough*.

CHARLES BROOKS

Date	Initials or Name Used by WBG	Location	Comments by WBG
18-Nov-63	C. Brooks		
2-Apr-64	C.H.B.		
14-Apr-64	C.B.		
10-May-64	C.B.		

NOTE: Born: Washington, D.C.; Occupation: cook, waiter, carpenter; Service: *Cambridge*.

C. L. SMITH

Date	Initials or Name Used by WBG	Location	Comments by WBG
26-Oct-63	C.L.S.; Smith		"Received A letter from A.M. Jose. Also one from C.L.S. containing the good news that I drew A Pitcher at Chelsea which I took A chance for before I left the Hospital. Verry cold all day. Write A letter to Jose and one to Smith."

(continued next page)

Date	Initials or Name Used by WBG	Location	Comments by WBG

C. L. SMITH *(continued)*

Date	Initials or Name Used by WBG	Location	Comments by WBG
29-Oct-63	C.L.S.		
3-Nov-63	C.L.S.		
7-Nov-63	C.L. Smith		

ANTONIO M. JOSE

Date	Initials or Name Used by WBG	Location	Comments by WBG
26-Oct-63	A.M. Jose		

NOTE: Born: Cape Verde; Enlists: Boston; Service: *Susquehanna* (Dec. '62–May '63); *Nipsic* (Oct. '63–Mar '64); *Monticello* (Jul. '65–Jun '65).

WILLIAM MORRIS

Date	Initials or Name Used by WBG	Location	Comments by WBG
6-May-65	Wm Morriss		"I received a note from Wm Morriss who left this ship last December. He is now Ward Room ____ "

NOTE: From New Bedford, Ma; cook; U.S.S. *Niagara*

HENRY L. BRISON

Date	Initials or Name Used by WBG	Location	Comments by WBG
21-Jan-64	H.L. Brissar; H.L.B.		"Received A letter from H.L. Brissar. . . . H.L.B. co A 5th Regmt. Mass Cavalry."
22-Jan-64	H.L.B.		
26-Jan-64	H.L.B.		
29-Jan-64	H.L.B.		
28-Feb-64	H.L.B.		
5-Mar-64	H.L.B.		
2-Apr-64	H.L. Brisar		"With mutch regret I heard of the death of H.L. Brisar. He died on the 26th of March of Consumption at Camp Meigs, Readville Mass., he being A priveate Co. A. 5th Regmt Mass. Cavalry."

NOTE: There is no service record for H.L. Brissar but there is an H.L. Brison of Co. A of the 5th Mass. Cavalry in CW Sailor System.

Date	Initials or Name Used by WBG	Location	Comments by WBG

ANN E. HOAGLAND

Date	Initials or Name Used by WBG	Location	Comments by WBG
8-Jan-64	Mrs. Hoagland	Brooklyn	"Call'd on Mrs. Culbreth and Mrs. Hoagland."
15-Jan-64	Mrs. A.E.H.	Brooklyn	visits
17-Jan-64	Mrs. A.E.H.	Brooklyn	"Went to Flett St. M.E. Church in company with Mrs. A.E.H. Saw in church M.E.W. much to my surprise."
18-Jan-64	Mrs. A.E.H.	Brooklyn	"Calld on Mrs. A.E.H. and went in company with her to Mrs. W."
13-Feb-64	A.E.H.	Brooklyn	visits
5-Mar-64	A.E.H.	Brooklyn	letter
14-Mar-64	Mrs. A.E.H.	Brooklyn	visits
15-Mar-64	Mrs. H	Brooklyn	" . . . went to A concert . . . by Maddam Greenfeild (the Black Swan). I visited Mrs. C. and Mrs. L. I accompany'd Mrs. H from the Concert."
15-Apr-64	Mrs. H.	Brooklyn	visits
29-Apr-64	Mrs. H.	Brooklyn	"Visited Mrs. C and Mrs. W and Mrs. H."
12-Apr-64	A.E.H.		"Received A letter from A.E.H. Quite unwell."
14-Apr-64	A.E.H.	Brooklyn	visits
17-Apr-64	A.E.H.		letter
5-May-64	A.E.H.		letter/visits
7-May-64	A.E.H.	Brooklyn	visits
24-May-64	A.E.H.	Brooklyn	visits
31-May-64	A.E.H.	Brooklyn	visits
1-June-64	A.E.H.		letter
23-May-65	A.E.[H.]		letter
2-Jul-65	Mrs. A.E.H.		"Learnt of the marage of Mrs. A.E.H. of Brook[lyn]."

NOTE: According to the Mar. 18, 1865, *Anglo-African*, a Mrs. Ann E. Hoagland of Brooklyn was married to Cyprian J. Roach of New York on March 9, 1865, in Brooklyn by Rev. R. H. Cain.

Date	Initials or Name Used by WBG	Location	Comments by WBG

LOUIS B. HOAGLAND

Date	Initials or Name Used by WBG	Location	Comments by WBG
25-May-63	Lewis B. Hoagland	Chelsea Hospital	"While at the Hospital I acted as A nurse. There were two of my Patients Died there names are respectfully Henry Burrow of Hamilton Canada west and Louis B. Hoagland Brooklyn N.Y."

NOTE: *The Anglo-African* for October 3, 1863 lists under deaths: "In Chelsea Hospital, Sept. 17th, of consumption, Lewis B. Hoagland, a resident of New York, aged 31 years."

MATILDA CULBRETH

Date	Initials or Name Used by WBG	Location	Comments by WBG
4-Jan-64	Mrs. Culbreth	Brooklyn	"I went ashore in Brooklyn and call'd on Mrs. Culbreth."
8-Jan-64	Mrs. Culbreth	Brooklyn	"Call'd on Mrs. Culbreth and Mrs. Hoagland."
20-Feb-64	Mrs. Culbreth	Brooklyn	"Visited Mrs. Culbreth."
11-Mar-64	Mrs. C.		"I calld apon Mrs. C then I went to Plymouth Church (Rev. H.W. Beecher)."
15-Mar-64	Mrs. C.	Brooklyn	" . . . went to A concert . . . by Maddam Greenfeild (the Black Swan). I visited Mrs. C. and Mrs. L. I accompany'd Mrs. H from the Concert."
29-Apr-64	Mrs. C		"Visited Mrs. C and Mrs. W and Mrs. H."
17-May-64	Mrs. Culbreth	Brooklyn	"Visited Mrs. Culbreth."

NOTE: In the obituary for Mrs. Matilda Culbreth in the Aug. 12, 1865, *Anglo-African* there is a note from the editor which reads: "It was our pleasure to be long aquainted with Mrs. Culbreth. She was born in Maryland but at an early age became a victim of the domestic slave trade, having been sold away to South Carolina and thus separated from some members of her family. She made great efforts to release all the enslaved members of her family. She was a woman of singular earnestness in the cause of our race. . . . She was widely familiar with the views of public persons in regard to the cause of the race, and was bold and clear in her criticisms of their views and actions. Her house was the welcome home of strangers and friends whom she always made happy and comfortable." She died on Jul. 16 at the age of 74. Her husband, Louis Culbreth, is listed in the Brooklyn Directory for 1863–65 (Lewis Culbreth/Louis Culbrath) as a laborer in a house on 102 Washington St.

Date	Initials or Name Used by WBG	Location	Comments by WBG

M. E. WHITE

Date	Initials or Name Used by WBG	Location	Comments by WBG
17-Jan-64	M.E.W.	Brooklyn	"Saw in church M.E.W. much to my surprise."
18-Jan-64	Mrs. W.	Brooklyn	"Calld on Mrs. A.E.H. and went in company with her to Mrs. W."
29-Apr-64	Mrs. W.	Brooklyn	"Visited Mrs. C and Mrs. W and Mrs. H."
5-May-64	Mrs White	Brooklyn	visits
25-Aug-64	Mrs. White		"Heard of the Death of Mrs. White."

NOTE: No reference to the death of Mrs. White in the *Anglo*.

MRS. M. E. L.

Date	Initials or Name Used by WBG	Location	Comments by WBG
25-Jan-64	Mrs. L.	Brooklyn	visits
27-Jan-64	M.E.L.	Brooklyn	"Heard from home through M.E.L. Heard that S.Spicer was on board of the Colorado."
8-Feb-64	M.E.L.	Brooklyn	visits
11-Feb-64	M.E.L.	Brooklyn	visits
15-Feb-64	M.E.L.	NewYork	"Met M.E.L. on Broadway. Draw'd ($10.00)"
3-Apr-64	M.E.L.	Brooklyn	visits
31-May-64	M.E.L.	Brooklyn	visits

BENJAMIN BROWN

Date	Initials or Name Used by WBG	Location	Comments by WBG
5-May-64	Mr. Benjamin Brown	Brooklyn	"Learnt of the whereabouts of Mr. Benjamin Brown."
7-May-64	Mr. Brown	Brooklyn	visits

NOTE: (1) There is a Benj. Brown listed as a representative from Baltimore, MD, to the Colored Citizens Convention. (Galloway and Robt. Hamilton were also reps.) (2) A Benjamin L. Brown, Esq. of NY, is married by H. H. Garnet in Brooklyn in Mar. 63 (*Anglo*, 21-Mar-63) (3) Many Benj. Browns are in the Brooklyn Directory, but only one, a seaman in a house on 187 S. 5th St., is listed as black.

BENJAMIN GREER

Date	Initials or Name Used by WBG	Location	Comments by WBG
17-Jan-64	Benjamin Grier	New York	"Saw Benjamin Grier and William McLauren."
29-Feb-64	Benjamin Grair	New York	"Visited Benjamin Grair and Wm McLauren."

NOTE: Ben Greer, Born: Wilmington NC, *Penobscot*, Enlists: September 23, 1862.

Date	Initials or Name Used by WBG	Location	Comments by WBG
ABRAM DAVIS			
23-Jan-64		New York	"Saw Abram Davis of Wilmington, now of the U.S.S. Vanderbilt."

NOTE: On Jan 17, WBG notes the arrival of the *Vanderbilt* in the Brooklyn Navy Yard. No service record in CW Sailor System.

WASHINGTON MORLLET			
21-May-64		New York	visits

O. S. BALDWIN			
12-Jan-64	O.S. Baldwin	New York	hears of his arrival in NY

JOHN HOWE			
7-Feb-64		New York	visits

NOTE: A. How, John Howe, and maybe even W.H.H. could be members of the Howe family of Wilmington. Many members of this family were carpenters/contractors and public servants. The Howes and Moores were connected by the marriage of Mary Howe and William H. Moore. Their son, William Henry Howe, was born in Wilmington, but raised in Brooklyn. (If he was W.H.H. he would have been 14 years old in 1865.) Mary Howe's brothers Anthony Jr. (A. How) and John Harris Howe (John Howe) were both carpenters in Wilmington.

A. HOWE			
7-Jun-65	A. How		

W. H. H.			
5-Mar-65	Mr. W.H.H.		
17-May-65	W.H.H.		
21-May-65	W.H.H.		

JAMES E. CRAWFORD			
19-Oct-63	Mr. C.		
4-May-64	Mr. C.		"Received A letter from W.H.S. and one from C.W.R. and a Photograph of Mr. C."
20-Mar-65	J.E.C.		"received A speech of senitor Kassion from Mr. J.E.C."

NOTE: Probably James E. Crawford whom WBG could have met while visiting Cornelia on Nantucket in May of '63. Cornelia resided at Crawford's home at this time.

Date	Initials or Name Used by WBG	Location	Comments by WBG

VIRGIL RICHARDSON

Date	Initials or Name Used by WBG	Location	Comments by WBG
25-Aug-64	Virgil Richardson		"Heard . . . that Virgil Richardson is engaged to Miss R.K."
21-Apr-65	V.R.		"hear[d] of the marrage of Miss R.K. to V.R."

MISS R. K.

Date	Initials or Name Used by WBG	Location	Comments by WBG
25-Aug-64	Miss R.K.		see above
21-Apr-65	Miss R.K.		see above

MRS. R.

Date	Initials or Name Used by WBG	Location	Comments by WBG
21-Sep-65	Mrs. R.	Boston	visits

NOTE: Mrs. Virgil Richardson?

THOMAS TAYLOR

Date	Initials or Name Used by WBG	Location	Comments by WBG
27-Mar-63		Boston	visits

FRED MYRICK

Date	Initials or Name Used by WBG	Location	Comments by WBG
27-Mar-63		Boston	visits

MRS. VAUGHT

Date	Initials or Name Used by WBG	Location	Comments by WBG
21-Sep-65		Boston	visits

NOTE: Perhaps Clara Vaught of the Boston Vigilance Committee.

MRS. KELLOGG

Date	Initials or Name Used by WBG	Location	Comments by WBG
21-Sep-65		Boston	visits

J. KELLOGG

Date	Initials or Name Used by WBG	Location	Comments by WBG
25-Aug-64			"Heard of the Death of Mrs. White. Also of the Wounding of J. Kellogg"

J. FUCHER

Date	Initials or Name Used by WBG	Location	Comments by WBG
2-Nov-63		Boston	"Maild A letter to J. Fucher to Boston."

Date	Initials or Name Used by WBG	Location	Comments by WBG
	E. A. M.		
22-May-64	E.A.M.		
24-May-64	E.A.M.		
22-Sep-65	E.A.M.	Boston	visits
	MISS S. SCOTT		
17-Jan-64	Miss S.S.	Antwerp	"received A letter from Miss S.S. from Antwerp"
6-Jun-65	Miss Scott	Flushing	"Call'd on Miss Scott from Antwerp. Found her well."
9-Jun-65	Miss S	Flushing	"When goin off to the ship I saw Miss S. Bade her good bye"
30-Jun-65	S.S. Anvere	Antwerp/Anvers	
	S.S.	Antwerp/Anvers	"Received A letter from Anvere's. Wrote to S.S."
	S. C.		
23-May-65	S.C.		
11-Jul-65	S.C.	Antwerp/Anvers	"Wrote to S.C. (anvere)."
24-Jul-65	S.C.		
	G. P. R.		
4-Mar-64	G.P.R.		see above
10-Mar-64	G.P.R.		see above
	J. H. B.		
3-Jul-65	J.H.B.		
	F. C.		
15-Oct-63	F. C.		
	J. R.		
14-Apr-64	J.R.		

Date	Initials or Name Used by WBG	Location	Comments by WBG

G. W. T.

Date	Initials or Name Used by WBG	Location	Comments by WBG
27-Feb-64	G.W.T.		from Wilmington

J. L. H.

Date	Initials or Name Used by WBG	Location	Comments by WBG
25-Mar-63	J.L.H.		

A. F. G.

Date	Initials or Name Used by WBG	Location	Comments by WBG
23-Jun-65	A.F.G.		

COUSIN M. C. G.

Date	Initials or Name Used by WBG	Location	Comments by WBG
29-Jan-64	Cousin M.C.G.		
10-Feb-64	cousin M.C.G.		
21-May-65	M.C.G.		

NOTE: Unidentified relative.

COUSIN S. H.

Date	Initials or Name Used by WBG	Location	Comments by WBG
10-Jul-65	Cousin S.H.		see above
22-Jul-65	cousin S.H.		see above

NOTE: Unidentified relative.

AUNT ELSIE

Date	Initials or Name Used by WBG	Location	Comments by WBG
24-Jan-64	Aunt Elsie		

SOURCES: William M. Reaves, *Strength Through Struggle: The Chronological and Historical Record of the African-American Community in Wilmington, North Carolina 1865–1950 (1998)*; The National Park Service Civil War Soldiers and Sailors System (The database of sailors, created by the Howard University Black Sailors Research Project, is available at http://www.itd.nps.gov/cwss/); United States City Directories for Boston, Brooklyn, and New York; Pension files of Joseph Hall, William Schenck, Scipio Spicer, John Mackey, and Charles Mallett; *The Anglo-African*, 1862–1865.

Three Speeches by William B. Gould IV

These three speeches, delivered in 1995 and 1998, are unedited and reflect the author's knowledge of William B. Gould's career at the time that they were given.

Lincoln, Labor and the Black Military: The Legacy Provided

This speech was delivered at the Officers' Club at the Washington Navy Yard, Washington, D.C., on February 11, 1995, to members of the Military Order of the Loyal Legion of the United States.

I heard the glad tidings that the Stars and Stripes have been planted over the Capitol of the Confederacy by the invincible Grant. While we honor the living soldiers who have done so much we must not forget to whisper for fear of disturbing the glorious sleep of the men who have fallen. Martyrs to the cause of Right and Equality.
—*Diary of William B. Gould, April 15, 1865.*

These are the words of my great-grandfather written 130 years ago at the time of Appomattox. They reflect the thoughts and passion of one of our country's black naval veterans of the Civil War and his commitment to the military initiatives waged by President Lincoln.

It is meet and right that we come here this evening to honor the memory of Abraham Lincoln, the sixteenth President of the United States, properly known throughout the world as the Great Emancipator. The New World's central political and social achievement, the Emancipation Proclamation which President Lincoln authored, transcends the ages and future generations. And his ideas about democracy and the rights of all people constitute the central vision of the American democratic system today.

As the sons of Union officers who fought in the Civil War, you know better than most that this 186th anniversary of Lincoln's birthday marks anew the ongoing struggle to free our country from the legacy of the odious institution of slavery so that all people may live out their lives and fulfill their aspirations without the actuality or fear of arbitrary limitation.

One of my law professors used to say that the "greatest constitutional decision ever rendered occurred when Pickett's charge failed at Gettysburg." The legacy of Appomattox and all that led to it resonates throughout our society to this evening here in Washington as part of the unceasing struggle against all arbitrary barriers which afflict mankind.

And both Gettysburg and Appomattox produced the great Civil War amendments to the Constitution, which reversed the infamous *Dred Scott* decision in which the Supreme Court declared blacks to be property constitutionally. The amendments, in turn, have provided our country with the historical framework for both the Supreme Court's great *Brown v. Board of Education*, 1954 ruling condemning separate but equal as a denial of equal protection and also the modern civil rights movement as well as the legislation that it produced. Similarly, Title VII of the Civil Rights Act of 1964, our most comprehensive anti-discrimination legislation relating to the workplace, is a lineal descendant of the previous century's developments.

I am not a Lincoln or Civil War scholar. Indeed, I find the amount of literature about both subjects to be daunting and, accordingly, I know that you do not expect a scholarly examination of President Lincoln from me. But there are matters which have and do involve me both practically and professionally with Lincoln and his times.

The first is that I am the fourteenth Chairman of the National Labor Relations Board and, as such, administer an agency and interpret a statute which both seek to implement some of Lincoln's most basic views on labor.

The second is that I am the great-grandson of the first William Benjamin Gould who, along with seven other "contraband" (seized property—the appellation which General Benjamin Butler gave to escaped slaves) set sail in a small boat from Cape Fear, North Carolina and boarded the U.S.S. *Cambridge* on September 22, 1862, the day that President Lincoln announced his intent to issue the Emancipation Proclamation. You will know that the Proclamation states in relevant part: "And I further declare and make known, that such persons of suitable condition [the freed slaves held by those in rebellion], will be received into the armed service of the United States to garrison forts, positions, stations, and other places, and to man vessels of all sorts in said service."

And thus it was that William B. Gould joined the United States Navy and served as landsman and steward on the North Atlantic Blockade and subsequently served on vessels visiting Britain, France, Belgium, Portugal and Spain, chasing the Confederate ships which were built by their undercover allies.

In 1864 the American Minister Charles Francis Adams had notified the British government that if the *Alabama* and the *Georgia*—two iron clad "rams" built by the British for the Confederacy—were allowed to go to sea, this would be construed by the United States as a declaration of war. William B. Gould sailed with the steam frigate *Niagara* for the European station to join other vessels such as the *Kearsarge* to keep, in my great-grandfather's words, a "sharp lookout" for these vessels. The *Niagara*'s destination was the Bay of Biscay where she eventually engaged in battle.

William B. Gould's service ended on September 29, 1865 when he made the following entry in his diary: "At the Navy Yard [Charlestown, Massachusetts] at five Oclock I received my Discharge being three years and nine days in the service of Uncle Samuel and glad am I to receive it . . . [pay] of four hundred and twenty four dollars. So end my service in the Navy of the United States of America."

I did not know the first William B. Gould for he died—in Dedham, Massachusetts where he resided from 1871 onward—thirteen years before my birth. I did not know my grandfather, William B. Gould, Jr., a Spanish-American War veteran, for he was to die nine years later in 1932. But the third William B. Gould was my greatest inspiration in my most formative years—and my belief is that the values and culture which he attempted to transmit to me were very much a part of the lives of the first two gentlemen to whom I have referred.

Truly then, President Lincoln's views and policies have had a major impact upon my own life.

As Chairman of the National Labor Relations Board, I have a responsibility to implement a statute which promotes the right of employees to band together for the purpose of protecting or improving their own working conditions, to join unions, to engage in collective bargaining and to be free from various forms of discrimination. This statute, enacted as part of President Franklin D. Roosevelt's New Deal in 1935, is one of the country's proudest achievements, expressing the policy that the protection of "the exercise by workers of full freedom of association, self-organization, and designation of representatives of their own choosing, for the purpose of negotiating the terms and conditions of their employment or other mutual aid or protection" should be encouraged.

In recent years, a number of scholars and critics, like myself, took note of the fact that the statute has not been working well in implementing these objectives because of poor administrative processes and ineffective remedies. Some of these matters can be and are being cured by us at the Board and some can be only addressed by

Congress. I hope to do what I can to make continued progress in the former category before I depart from Washington and return to California a few years down the road when my term ends.

I enthusiastically support the views contained in the preamble and have made my position known in books, articles, and speeches. In many respects, the fundamentally similar views of President Lincoln were a precursor of our own 1935 legislation.

Recall what Lincoln said to the New York Workingmen's Democratic Republican Association on March 21, 1864: "The strongest bond of human sympathy, outside of the family relation, should be one uniting all working people, of all nations, and tongues and kindreds."[1]

As the Presidential campaign of 1860 unfolded, Lincoln stated his philosophy in these terms: "When one starts poor, as most do in the race of life, free society is such that he knows he can better his condition; he knows that there is no fixed condition of labor for his whole life. . . . I want every man to have the chance—and I believe a black man is entitled to it—in which he *can* better his condition—when he may look forward and hope to be a hired laborer this year and the next, work for himself afterward, and finally to hire men to work for him! That is the true system."[2]

In the same speech, Lincoln makes clear that the right to strike is integral to a democratic society, a policy reflected in the language of Sections 7 and 13 of the National Labor Relations Act and in the Norris-LaGuardia Act of 1932 which preceded it. Just a few weeks ago, President Clinton took note of one of our law's limitations in his statement criticizing the Bridgestone/Firestone Company's use of permanent striker replacements, noting that such tactics show the need to enact legislation prohibiting such a denial of the fundamental right to strike.

It bears note that Lincoln's view of labor and the right to strike ran against the tide of laissez-faire thinking which predominated in the previous century—thinking which has reared its head again toward the close of this century, one of its forms being the repressive striker replacement weapon of which President Clinton spoke. President Lincoln supported the right to strike and spoke out in the spring of 1860 in support of a well-organized strike conducted by the boot and shoe workers in New England. Lincoln regarded the right to strike by free labor as a "virtue, not a failing, of free society," as G.S. Boritt has written in *Lincoln and the Economics of the American Dream*.[3]

Boritt also notes that during the Civil War several delegations of strikers from the Machinists and Blacksmiths Union of New York visited the White House and spoke to the President about their position. States Boritt: "The labor representatives took great comfort from their interview, reasoning that although their employers refused to deal with them, Lincoln received them. 'If any man should again say that combinations of working men are not good,' they concluded, 'let them point to the Chief Magistrate.' They even quoted the President as saying 'I know that in almost every case of strikes, the men have just cause for complaint.' It is rather likely that the union men quoted Lincoln correctly."[4]

Of course, Lincoln's view of labor was closely related to his view of slavery. Again, in 1860 he said: "'Owned labor' would compete with free labor so as to 'degrade' the latter." And, in an earlier and lengthy speech to the Wisconsin State Agricultural Society in Milwaukee on September 30, 1859, he noted that the so-called "mud-sill" theory was that a hired laborer is "fatally fixed in that condition for life" and thus his condition is the same as that of a slave.[5]

But as Lincoln noted, this theory proceeded upon the assumption that labor and education were incompatible and that one could not improve oneself and one's family through free labor. Lincoln's view was antithetical to all of this. He held the view that workers should be able to rise to new horizons.

And this view is closely related to another held by the President which has similar contemporary implications. Because Lincoln believed that all people could improve themselves and thus rise out of their station if opportunity were afforded them, unlike other proponents of the rights of labor, he did not see the working class as a well-defined unit, notwithstanding his endorsement of its use of the strike to defend its interests and act jointly in its dealings with employers. To some extent, said Professor Boritt, Lincoln shared the view that there was a harmony between the capital and labor and that it ought to be promoted so as to enhance the ability of workers to rise out of their class.

Again, these views resonate with us today as Congress considers proposals to enhance employee participation and proposed amendments to the National Labor Relations Act which will achieve this goal. I believe that President Lincoln would be sympathetic with contemporary efforts to promote employee involvement in the workplace and thus enhance our industry's global competitiveness—so long as such reforms do not interfere with the ability of the workers and unions to defend their own positions, a proposition that I have long advanced.[6]

The view that an individual was not "fatally fixed" in a particular condition forever constitutes the philosophy which prevailed in the Civil War and through the Emancipation Proclamation and the enactment of the Thirteenth Amendment which Lincoln sponsored before his assassination. Again, this is reflected anew in last month's State of the Union address by President Clinton when, in advocating new minimum wage legislation, he said that the worker who works must have his "reward" and that the job of government is to "expand opportunity . . . to em-power people to make the most of their own lives."

This is what is at the heart of modern democracy and the Bill of Rights for workers in the private sector which are contained in the National Labor Relations Act and similar statutes. And this has been the assumption behind the struggle for equality which has attempted to make good on the promise of emancipation in the previous century.

My great-grandfather, a mason who worked with his mind and hands and es-tablished a business as a contractor, employing other workers in Dedham, Massa-chusetts, benefited from the above-noted philosophy and the quoted portions of the Emancipation Proclamation. Said William B. Gould on March 8, 1863, two months after its issuance: "Read . . . the Proclamation of Emancipation . . . verry [sic] good."

The policy, of course, had evolved in fits and starts. As Benjamin Quarles has noted in *The Negro in the Civil War*, General Butler was the first to devise a policy of acceptance of blacks who wanted to fight with the North.[7] This was, as Quarles noted, the most "insistent" problem faced by the Lincoln Administration in 1861 and 1862. It emerged, as he has noted, after the Union defeat at Bull Run which was attributable "in part to the Confederate military defenses constructed by slaves."

Congress enacted legislation which provided for the forfeiture of all slaves whose masters had permitted them to be used in the military or naval service of the Confederacy. Quarles notes that the 1861 legislation "strengthened the hand of the small band of Union officers who from the beginning had been in favor of freeing the slaves." Two military initiatives—one designed by John C. Frémont in July 1861, "The Pathfinder," and the other undertaken by Major General Dave Hunter in the summer of 1862—were both rescinded by Lincoln out of his concern with preserv-ing the allegiance of the border states.

The Confiscation Act enacted on July 17, 1862, declaring free all slaves who were owned by those in rebellion was the next step in the process. This had the effect of increasing the number of fugitives in whom the United States Navy expressed a particular interest so as to make use of the information that they could provide about enemy locations and movements. As summer became fall the problem be-came more "insistent."

Three days after my great-grandfather boarded the U.S.S. *Cambridge* came this report of Commander G. H. Scott regarding the blockade of Wilmington: "Four-teen contrabands have reached the 'Monticello' and 'Penobscot' and several the 'Cambridge' within a few days, and as the vessels have not room for them, will you please direct what disposition shall be made of them?"

We know what disposition was made of William B. Gould. On October 3, 1862, he said: "All of us shipped today for three years, first taking the Oath of Allegiance to the Government of Uncle Samuel."

Thus he, and eventually I, benefited from both the Confiscation Act and the new policy expressed in the Emancipation Proclamation which was not to be effective for another three months. His service was made possible because of it. This was then his opportunity—and his observations, hopes and views are chronicled in the diary which he kept between 1862 and 1865.

On the perils of the seas and their storminess, he says:

[T]he gale still blows fresh and the seas running verry [sic] high. We shipped several through the night and one—fill'd the Ward Room with Water. I have got ducked awfully last night. It was worth something to be upon the Deck. Although there is much danger in a storm there is something very sublime to hear the roar of the storm. The hissing of the Waves, the whistling of the Rigging and the Cannon like report of the torn sail and above all the stern word of the commander and the sound of the boatswain's pipe all adds to the grandeur of the scene. For there is something grand in a storm. Allnight with eager eyes both Officers and Men paced the deck watching our Foretopsail, feeling in a measure secure as long as we could sail at all. It has it stood through the night. There was no sign of the storm abateing [sic]. All the galley fire is out and nothing to eat is the cry and almost nothing to wear on account of the Water. Shine out fair sun and smote the Waves that we may proceed on our course and all be saved.

And on December 25 and December 27 of 1862, he had this to say about the loneliness of his work off New Inlet: "This being Christmas I think of the table at home . . . cruised around as usual. Fine weather but very lonesome in the absence of news and we all had the Blues."

While on the North Atlantic Blockade with the U.S.S. *Cambridge* he says on November 17, 1862: "A sail was reported close under the land right ahead. We gave chase. When within range of our boat we told them good morning in the shape of a shot for her to heave to."

But then he describes the difficulties that arose: "To this [the shot] they took no notice. We sent another which fell under her stern . . . the ship stood for the Beach. Shot after shot was set after her but they heeded not . . . we immediately manned the first cutter and sent her . . . to board and destroy her. We also sent two other boats to lend assistance . . . [after sending a line to these boats so that they could return to the main ship] . . . they got the Boat all ready to come out when a body of Rebel Solders dashed over the hill at the double quick and all were prisoners. We could see them from the ship marching off our men and dragging the boats after them. We lost eleven men and three officers. Rather a bad day's work."

But the fortunes of war were not all negative as testified to by him in this entry in the summer of 1864 off Portugal: "[W]e made a steamer and stood for her. She kept on her course without any until we got within 5 miles of her when she suddenly changed her course. We beat to Quarters and Fired a shot. She showed the English collors [sic]. We Fired another. When she came to be boarded her and found her to be the Rebel Privateer 'Georgia' from Liverpool on her way to refit a cruiser. But the next cruise that she makes will be for Uncle Samuel . . . this capture makes a crew feel verry [sic] proud."

While in the English Channel: "[W]e took on board an English Pilot who brought the thrice glorious news of the sinking of the 'Alabama' by 'Kearsarge' off Cherbough. . . . [A]lthough we have been disappointment to us in not getting a shot at the 'Alabama' we are satisfied that she is out of the way."

And in 1864 while serving on the Niagara he said about the people that he saw in Spain: "[I]t looks very strange in this country which nature have lavished with riches that there should be so many Poor People."

And again on the shameful treatment of black soldiers on his ship: "Yesterday about 900 men of the Maryland (colored) regiment came on board (they being transfered to the Navy) and took dinner then departed for Portsmouth, New Hampshire. They were treated very rough by the crew. They refused to let them eat out of the mess pans and call them all kinds of names. One man [had] his watch stolen from him by these scoundrels. In all they were treated shamefully."

On the proposed colonization of blacks to Africa or the Caribbean: "We see by the papers that President [Johnson] intimates colonization for the colored people of the United States. This move of his must and shall be resisted. We were born under the Flag of the union and never will we know no other. My sentiment is the sentiment of the people of the States."[8]

All of this ended in 1865 and provided William B. Gould with his chance at life. Sometimes I think about his thoughts as he walked the streets of Wilmington a young man and what would have been had he stayed in North Carolina and the events of those four critical years had not taken place. Most certainly his great-grandson would not be here today addressing you as Chairman of the National Labor Relations Board.

I am privileged to have this opportunity in 1995 to contribute to the public good in the most inspirational and progressive Administration in Washington since the 1960s—one which is unabashedly committed to the principles of those who fell 130 years ago.

My hope is that I can reflect well upon the first William B. Gould and the chance that he made for me by rising out of his "fixed station," to use Lincoln's words, and I am all too aware of the limitations of time as we move rapidly toward a new millennium.

As William B. Gould said on December 31, 1863, in New York harbor: "We are obliged knock off on the account of the storm. It blew very hard from South East. The old year of '1863' went out furiously as if it was angry with all the world because it had finished the time allotted to it. Sooner or later we must follow."

My first major impression during my first trip outside of the United States in 1962, as a student at the London School of Economics, is of the grand and majestic statue of President Lincoln which sits in Parliament Square today. Now I live in Washington within a mile of the great Lincoln Memorial in which his brooding historical omnipresence is made so manifest.

You and I, the entire nation and the world honor President Lincoln and his policies tonight. Both personally and professionally they are with me always as is the legacy provided by him and so many others in what my great-grandfather called "[T]he holiest of all causes, Liberty and Union."[9]

A Memoir of the Sea, Freedom and Love

This speech was delivered on May 25, 1998, at Coffin School, Nantucket, in a program jointly sponsored by Friends of the African Meeting House and the Egan Institute of Maritime Studies.

It is good to be back here in Nantucket where I first came as a child with my parents many years ago. This is my third visit to the island since being appointed by President Clinton to be Chairman of the National Labor Relations Board. The first was a private trip in 1995 to continue the quest of which I am going to speak to you today, and the second was last fall to address a conference of labor lawyers when, with my Nantucket guide and good friend, Helen Seager, I was pleased to see and stand inside the restored African Baptist Church where my great-grandparents exchanged vows so many years ago.

My visits to Nantucket have been inspired by the fact that my great-grandfather, William Benjamin Gould, shortly after his discharge from the United States Navy on September 29, 1865 at the Charlestown Navy Shipyard, came to Nantucket and

married my great-grandmother, Cornelia Read on November 22, 1865. The following year, the first of their eight children, Medora (whom I knew when I was a small
child), was born here in Nantucket.

My interest in my great-grandparents and Nantucket is enhanced by the fact that
my great-grandfather kept a diary while serving in the United States Navy beginning on September 22, 1862—the diary commences five days later—until the last
entry on September 29, 1865, his last day of service for "Uncle Samuel," as he so
frequently referred to our country.

The diary was bequeathed to my late father, William B. Gould III—and the only
gaps are from May through October 1863 when the first William Benjamin Gould
was in the Chelsea Naval Hospital with measles—and from October 1864 through
January 1865 because that portion was apparently thrown out before my father retrieved the balance of it in my late great-uncle Lawrence's attic. I expect to complete
an annotated version of that diary when I return to California, after completing my
own service to the United States Government this summer.

My great-grandparents had been slaves in Wilmington, North Carolina. And the
road that they each took to Nantucket was a very different one.

When I spoke three years ago in Washington on the occasion of President Lincoln's birthday, I drew upon some of the themes of the first William Benjamin's life
and diary which unite our lives.[10] Most important, as I noted at that time, had not
the struggle in which he participated prevailed at Appomattox and its immediate aftermath in 1865, my own work as Chairman of the National Labor Relations Board
would have been impossible. Not only could I personally never have become a
lawyer, law professor and Chairman of one of the country's most important quasi-
judicial administrative agencies, but also it is unlikely that the National Labor Relations Act itself would have emerged.

For as I suggested, that February evening at the Washington Navy Shipyard, the
National Labor Relations Act, providing for the right of employees to organize and
to engage in the collective bargaining process and promoting stability and the balanced and impartial resolution of disputes between labor and management is a direct descendent of the great changes wrought by the War of the Rebellion. The
Emancipation Proclamation, which my William Benjamin Gould commented on in
his diary when the word reached him on ship two months later,[11] the Thirteenth
Amendment to the Constitution (the passage of which he notes as well[12]) along
with the other great post-Civil War amendments which follow in its wake, guaran-
teed free labor in our country. The National Labor Relations Act, a product of President Roosevelt's New Deal and one which has outlasted the labor law framework

of every other industrialized country in the world except for the Scandinavian labor laws, is a mechanism through which achievements of the previous century of which my great-grandfather was associated are today realized.

Yet there is a third connection which was not as apparent to me in early 1995 as it is now. My commitment to the Act's principles is controversial and sometimes dangerous to express in an era of polarization between labor and management when autonomous and balanced relationships between workers and management are imperiled. Indeed, as the recent Civil War debate in Virginia vividly dramatizes, it appears that the question of whether slavery itself should be condemned is very much a matter of debate in some conservative circles.[13]

I confess that I frequently take comfort and derive new inspiration and energy in Washington as I read and re-read the pages of his diary and experience with him anew the struggle for freedom—a struggle in which he, at a much younger age, braved real live bullets from the Confederacy rather than the budget slashing, as disastrous as that is and would be to our law enforcement mission, as well as abusive verbal arrows and grenades aimed at me, designed as they are to tear apart a legal framework which I and so many others cherish.

The first that we know of William Benjamin Gould comes from the log of the U.S.S. *Cambridge* commanded by William A. Parker, Ensign on September 22, 1862 as it operates with the North Atlantic Blockade outside Cape Fear near Fort Fisher: "Saw a sail S.W. by S. and signaled same to other vessels. Stood for strange sail and at 10:30 picked up a boat with eight contrabands from Wilmington, N.C. . . . names and contrabands and their masters: . . . William B. Gould owned by Nicholas Nixon."

He quickly took the oath of allegiance to "Uncle Samuel" on October 3, 1862 and was mustered in as a "Boy," later a "Landsman" and "Wardroom Steward."

A few months after mustering in, while serving on the U.S.S. Cambridge, as it comes close to land, on February 16, 1863 my great-grandfather has this to say: "About 1 Oclock we passed Rich Inlet. Verry close in shore. Took a good look at the place that I left in 62."

A year ago I visited this area at Porter's Neck north of Wilmington and the surrounding area and stood immediately adjacent to Rich Inlet and looked towards the mainland. It was the Nixon Plantation.

The diary is filled with references to letters received and sent to C.W.R.—my great-grandmother, Cornelia Williams Read. She was born in Charleston, South Carolina in November 1837, the same month and year of William B. Gould's birth. [My later research showed that she was in fact about a half year older than he, born on May 30 of that year.] Said W.B.G. in his application for a war related pension from the Department of Interior, Bureau of Pensions: "I knew her from childhood."

I was puzzled as to how they could know one another as children given the fact that Wilmington and Charleston were more distant in the early part of the previous century. But three years ago, in my first of these three visits to Nantucket through Helen Seager, I was able to uncover a series of articles about Cornelia Read and to learn the circumstances of her purchase from slavery in late 1857 or early 1858. The Reverend J. E. Crawford, my great-grandmother's uncle by marriage, a Nantucket Baptist minister at the African Baptist Church was responsible. It was Crawford who arranged for the purchase of both my great-great-grandmother and my great-grandmother, who traveled to Wilmington from Nantucket on a perilous journey with the latter. As the Nantucket newspaper said, "Crawford . . . trembled for his safety in North Carolina, as free negroes are at a discount there, and Mr. Crawford is a free negro."

In February 1858 Crawford described his journey by railroad and the fact that Miss Read was not allowed to travel in the first class car but placed in the baggage car. Said the New Bedford Mercury: "on Sunday last, the same girl was in one of our churches among her friends, and the subject of the warmest congratulations by reason of her escape from the land of captivity, even if she was purchased for so much gold."

The story begins with an article on July 1, 1857 which states that the Reverend J. E. Crawford has ministered to the Pleasant St. Baptist Church for three years without "fee or reward" and has supported himself and his family by his own labor, collected $700 for his wife's sister. The article continues: "He has now relinquished his ministerial connection and his business here, and will soon engage in an effort to raise $1000 to purchase the liberty of a niece; the daughter of the sister-in-law who was rescued from slavery by his zealous labors. Such a man is deserving of encouragement; his industry, intelligence, ministerial devotion, and uprightness as a citizen, justly commend him to favorable considerations."

In a more detailed subsequent article entitled "A Card" J. E. Crawford and Family express their "deep gratitude to all who have aided in accomplishing an end [her 'ransom'] . . . so long and fervently desired by many anxious hearts." The article states that the amount demanded and paid was $1,000 " . . . nearly one-half of which was raised in England by the subscription and efforts of Henry and Anna Richardson, members of the Society of Friends in Newcastle-on-Tyne and a Miss Hilditch, of Shrewsbury." The article thanks Mr. Christopher Hussey of Nantucket who commenced the correspondence with Mrs. Richardson which led to payment of $500 as well as an additional $481 obtained through Mr. Lewis Tappan of New York. Numerous others from Wilmington, North Carolina, New Bedford, Portland, Maine, Hyannis, Fall River, Taunton and Nantucket are mentioned.[14]

As noted above, there are numerous communications between William Benjamin Gould and Cornelia Williams Read while he is in the Navy. His first letters to Boston are noted on February 17, 1863—and while his ship is docked in Boston he says on May 3: "While on liberty I visited Nantucket. Met Ms. C.W.R. also had quite a good time in Boston and vicinity. Saw many of my acquaintances."

The relationship with my great-grandmother seemed to have flowered once my great-grandfather was transferred to the U.S.S. *Niagara* in the fall of 1863. As he had anticipated, this duty was to be much more stimulating work than the occasionally explosive but sometimes dull, dreary duty of the North Atlantic Blockade.

As I have indicated, the diary is then interrupted, but it resumes in the fall and he says on October 15 that he mailed a letter to C.W.R. The first letter that he acknowledges receipt of from her in that fall is on October 22, 1863 when he is at anchor off Gloucester. On October 29 he says that he sent a picture to C.W.R. and he receives a letter from C.W.R. on November 2. Sometimes, as on November 16, he receives a letter and sends one back to her on the same day. There are entries indicating that approximately 60 letters were exchanged, at least in the portion of the diary that I possess.

But the North Atlantic Blockade on the U.S.S. *Cambridge* could be, in his words, "lonesome." Some of this can be best seen through the following entries:

January 2, 1864 in New York: "It is a shame to the country that we laying in the harbor of New York and have been three days without a mail. Such is the regulation of Uncle Samuel to his children. Oh for a mail. A mail. A kingdom for a mail."

On January 10 again at the Navy Yard in New York: "Indulge all day in thoughts of those far away and sighed for a letter. I hope some kind friend will send me one."

April 18, 1865 at Cadiz, Spain: "No news except by telegraph. Oh for a mail."

June 5, 1865 at Flushing, Netherlands: "We received a mail from the states. Nary [a] letter for me."

August 24, 1865 again in Cadiz: "We received a mail but not a line did I receive. No one favored me with a remembrance."

Note especially this entry on July 12, 1865 while at Flushing: "Oh C., why do you not write."

Three years ago in my Lincoln Birthday speech in Washington, D.C., I chronicled some of his ships' engagements. Beyond those that I spoke about that day here are some of the others:

On November 5, 1862, having described an engagement in which the *Daylight* and the *Mount Vernon* were destroying the Confederate *Sophia*, which had come in from Liverpool, my great-grandfather says: "Off New Inlet. We sent up our life boat and a lot of spare rope to try and get the men off but, when daylight dawned, low and behold the Rebs had nabbed them all and a battery on shore sent the boats word not to come near. There was 14 men from the 'Daylight' and 6 from the 'Mount Vernon.' The Rebs sent out a flag of truce to us informing us of the situation of our men. We sent them (from the 'Daylight') their clothes, bedding and some provisions. The 'Mystic' returned from the shoals with the mails of the fleet. She exchanged boats with us. One of our lieutenants went passenger in her. She had also thirteen Rebel deserters and several colored refugees. Among them several of my acquaintances. Heard from my people."

On January 14, 1863, he states that a sail was reported at 5 bells. He says: "Sent the 'Genesee' in chase. At 12 Oclock Fort Fisher fired a salute of (13) guns, about 2 bells we sent in a boat in charge of Act Ensign McGleney to put down some buoys and to see if the other buoys were in their places. The 'Mount Vernon' convoyed the boat when in about two miles off the Fort, they opened fire on the boat with shell and shot and done some verry close shooting. Showed that they knew their work."

And then he notes on January 15 that a boat from the "Columbia" was looking for assistance after going ashore on Masonboro and that the men were: "verry much used up having been rowing and exposed to wind and rain for eighteen hours." It is impossible to find the wreck off Masonboro after 1 o'clock, he states on January 16:

> We up anchor about 4 Oclock. Ran along the coast slowly with the first streak of dawn. Came the sound of artillery. We stood in for where we heard the firing. There we found the "Penobscot" trying to save the crew. The Rebels were firing upon the wreck who had refused to haul down the Flag of Right from the mast. They also fired upon the boats that were sent to pick up the crew if possible. The "Penobscot" succeeded in rescuing about 40 before we got up. Both ships ran in and opened fire on the Johnies but, it being verry rough, we hauled off and came to anchor.

On January 17 he states:

> Then we both stood in for the wreck (It having calmed down during the night the Rebs had boarded the wreck and took all prisoners. At daybreak we could see the boats filing to and from the ship with the booty.) and opened fire upon

the same. The "Penobscot" got her 11 inch gun disabled so that she was obliged to draw off. We kept up the fire for about 2 hours. When we discovered the wreck on fire we hauled off as we wanted to prevent the Rebs from getting any of her. The Rebels were replying to us all the time from six rifle field pieces, which they handled with much skill and accuracy, though they did not hit us once. Many a shot passed too close to us to be at all agreeable.

William B. Gould's service on the U.S.S. *Cambridge* came to an abrupt conclusion on May 29, 1863 for as he said:

> . . . measles broke out upon me and I was sent to the hospital (Chelsea). I arrived at the hospital on the 29th where I remained until the 13th of Oct. While there sick I was taken good care of by the surgeons, Fox and Gilbert. Also the steward and nurses were verry kind to me and when I was going to leave they insisted on my remaining, but I have spent a verry long time on shore and now desires to be afloat once more. There is nothing like the whistling wind and the danceing bark on the bounding billow bearing its precious treasure to the shores of some distant clime. . . .
>
> I remained at the hospital until the 13th day of October when having made an engagement with Dr. Fox who is ordered to the "Niagara." She being going on a cruise to Europe. Dr. Beale, Dr. Fox sincerely insisted on my remaining, but as this will be a good opportunity of visiting Europe, I will avail myself of this opportunity and go in. I will say good bye until you hear from me again.
> Etc. Wm.B.G.

So after going through the recciving ship *Ohio*, he was transferred to the steam Frigate *Niagara* which was under the command of Thomas T. Craven. Through the remainder of 1863 and early 1864 he was in Boston, Gloucester and New York. Some of the occasions are quite pleasant. On March 14, 1864 in New York he says: "As I was leaving the ship the band from the 'North Carolina' came on board. I returned about 12 Oclock to find quite a number of ladies assembled and dancing going on. We now made preparation for the luncheon which passed off finely. When dancing was again resumed, which lasted until four when the band left, the company remained later and the last did not get away until five. So ended our trouble of today."

On March 15 he went to New York at the Fleet Street Church to hear the singer Madam Greenfield known as "The Black Swan."[15]

On April 15, 1864 in New York: "A beautiful day. Spring commences to put forth in her beautiful dress of green."

I like his commentary while in Europe on other social conduct. June 6, 1865 at Flushing: "Went out to the farmers fair. Seemed to be the rule for everybody to drink as much gin as they could stand under and many, both male and female, could not stand but a verry short time."

On June 1 the 'Niagara' set forth on its expedition to find Confederate cruisers, particularly the 'Alabama' which were being fitted in Britain and harbored throughout Europe. The mission of the 'Niagara' was secret and the papers containing relevant instructions from the Secretary of Navy were not to be opened until the ship was at sea.

As the ship was embarking for Europe, my great-grandfather on June 1 said: "All our stores arrived and the pilot, being already on board, the shrill notes of the fife, and the regular tramp of the men together with the clank of the capstan, all told that we were soon to feel the motion of the swelling sea."

That evening, as he said, "we steamed out." He was "verry tired" from his "new occupation" in the day's events. As he had said earlier: "About eleven we found that a part of our stores were not on board. Here was trouble. However it was soon overcome. Then a draft of men came for us. All the men having less than three months to serve were transferred to the 'North Carolina.' Among them was . . . Hutcheson Allen (ward room cook). Here we were, left without a cook, but I attempted to get the dinners ready amid the greatest confusion imaginable by three Oclock." He said that he hoped that someone would fill the place of Mr. Allen.

By this time William B. Gould seemed to be a seaworthy veteran. Note his commentary on March 18, 1864 after leaving New York and passing Sandy Hook in New Jersey: "We now are once more on the boundless deep. Blowing quite fresh, the ship rolls heavily, the greater portion of our crew being landsman on their first cruise, there is a large number them sea sick. You can see them trying to get forward by crawling and helping each other. They do not like their first feeling of a seafaring."

He himself had already experienced some of the difficult mishaps involved in being a sailor on March 16 of that year in New York: "This morning I went to the supply store and got our stores then came down to the wharf to return on board. Here I took an unintentional bath. The ladder that we had placed alongside of the wharf for our convenience of getting in and out of our boats, the ladder had become coated with ice and as I descended the ladder to the boat I slipped from the ladder into the river. I was rescued by the boats crew. It was verry cold and my face and clothes became coated with ice. I soon got on board and changed my clothes. In the evening I felt quite unwell from the effect of my bath."

Now his ship moved on to Europe.[16] On June 16, 1864 at Flushing he says: "We all believe that we are on a course to some foreign port."

Then on June 22 the *Niagara* is in the Bay of Biscay. The following day he was "standing in for the English Channel and leaving the Bay of Biscay." And on June 24 from a British pilot comes the "thrice glorious news" of the *Alabama*'s sinking by the *Kearsarge*. Though the *Niagara* herself is seeking out the same *Alabama*, they rescue 72 of the *Alabama*'s crew and he says: "All honor to Captain Winslow and his brave crew of the 'Kearsarge.'"[17]

And now it is on to Dover and to the North Sea and on June 26 to arrive in Flushing. "The country presents beautiful scenery as we pass up the river. Beautiful cottages and farms looking verry beautiful. A plenty of shipping among them. Several American ships."

The ship reaches Antwerp on June 27. He observes in his diary entry after being in port two days that there are: "A great many visitors today of both sexes." On July 2 the *Niagara* departs from Antwerp and the following day sails back to Flushing. On July 4 his ship runs along the coast of England "with land in full view. Perfectly lovely in the channel. We can see a large city in the distance. Supposed to be Portsmouth."

More of the same throughout July except for a July 6 visit to Cherbourg: "This place Cherbourg is verry strongly fortified place. The 'Sacramento' is in the port. Also the 'Kerasage.' There is a great breakwater in front of the harbor and answers the double purpose of breakwater and fort."

On August 15 cruising off the coast of Portugal, the *Niagara* intercepted the rebel privateer *Georgia* from Liverpool and it was sent to Boston as a prize ship. Said William B. Gould: "We now take a look for some of the other cruisers of would be King Jeff."

Though he never complains of any unfair treatment towards himself, hear what he has to say about race during the war. On April 16, 1864: "Today we also heard of the capture of Fort Pillow by the rebels and the massacre of all the troops, both white and colored. Still the government do not retaliate."

April 26, 1864: "Heard of the capture of Plymouth by the rebels and a report of the massacre of both white and colored soldiers belonging to North Carolina."

May 25, 1864 while in New York: "At night there was a melee on deck between the white and colored men."

March 21, 1865 in Coruña, Spain: "This morning four or five white fellows beat Jerry Jones/colored. He was stabbed in his left shoulder verry bad."

On May 27, 1865: "One man deserted. The first colored man that left on this side of the water."

There are many public events which he chronicled, not the least of which is President Lincoln's assassination. On May 28, 1865, he says: "We hear that the conspirators are being tried at Washington. I hope that they shall reap their reward."

In my Lincoln speech I caught some of his passionate eloquence about the war's conclusion.[18] On June 16, 1865 he expresses his views as follows:

"We heard that Davis have been carried to Washington to be tried by court martial on the indictment of treason. We hope that the sour apple tree is all ready."[19]

And then there is this poignant note on May 24, 1865 at Flushing: "Fine day. I received a letter from J.M. _____ he had visited Wilmington. Saw my people all well. I felt verry much relieved, but my joy was of short duration, for this evening I received a letter from my sister bringing me the sad news of the death of mother. She died March the 13th. What sad news for me. The first letter that I receive from my sister contains such news."

After the long journey back from Europe on September 29 of that year, the day after the *Niagara* has been decommissioned in the Charlestown Navy Shipyard, he says: "I received my discharge being three years and nine days in the service of Uncle Samuel. . . . So ends my service in the Navy of the United States of America."

Thus begins a new life in Massachusetts for William and Cornelia—first here in Nantucket and then in Manchester, New Hampshire, Taunton, Massachusetts and ultimately Dedham, Massachusetts where he resided from 1871 until his death in 1923. Cornelia predeceased him in Dedham in 1906.

William B. Gould worked as a plasterer or mason, eventually as a contractor who employed other men. The diary indicates that he was a literate, well read man corresponding during the Civil War with friends and family in both the North and South. Notwithstanding his marriage in the Baptist Church, he was one of the founders of the Episcopal Church of the Good Shepherd in Dedham in the 1870s, the parish in which I was baptized in 1936.

Today, Memorial Day, is a particularly fitting one to remember him because, like so many other Civil War veterans, he would visit the public schools to recount the events and lessons of the War at this time of year.

Finally, amongst the offspring of the marriage between William and Cornelia were a Spanish-American War veteran, my grandfather—William B. Gould, Jr. — and four officers who served in Europe in World War I. They, along with the first

William B. Gould, were the backbone of the country. Their lives and mine owe much to this island, Nantucket.

The Unwinding Trail: Some Reflections on the Life and Times of William Benjamin Gould

This speech was delivered in Wilmington on December 15, 1998, under the sponsorship of the Bellamy Mansion Museum and the New Hanover Public Library.

Thank you Jonathan Noffke and Beverly Tetterton for bringing me here to speak about my great grandfather and his life and times. I am grateful to you and so many others for your help in this venture.

The first William Benjamin Gould was born here in Wilmington, North Carolina on November 18, 1837, the son of Alexander and Elizabeth (Betsy) Gould, nee Moore. As my life has progressed, my search for William Benjamin Gould has accelerated along a long and winding trail.

When my late father, William Benjamin Gould III, and I first began to focus upon this subject, we thought that we would work together on this project. And the pity is that we did not do it when he was alive and when many others were alive who could have told us so much more than we will ever glean from the written page.

The first William Benjamin Gould left Wilmington to board the U.S.S. *Cambridge* on September 22, 1862—the day that President Lincoln proclaimed his intention to promulgate an Emancipation Proclamation, five days after General Lee was stopped at Antietam.

The trail really begins in my own family homes in Massachusetts and New Jersey and in the values and lessons provided to me by my father. It begins with the music that I heard as a child and its military cadence, so often sung to us by my father—*Marching Through Georgia*, with my father's descriptions of the bitter reactions of the Southerners to General Sherman's great march to the sea, and *The Battle Hymn of the Republic* which always assumed a religious significance in our home. This, of course, was derived from my father's exposure to William Benjamin Gould whom he knew as a child and young man—my father being 21 years old when the first William Benjamin died. And my father sang to us the World War I songs of my great uncles with whom I became acquainted during our visits to Dedham, Massachusetts, my great grandfather's residence from 1871 to 1923 after we moved to New Jersey in 1940.

And there are so many other things that I think that my father transmitted to me from that William Benjamin Gould. As a child in New Jersey, I can recall an uneducated black laborer who was working with us, sitting at our table saying grace to himself before his meal—and my father emphasized afterwards how good and important this was, even more fundamental, he seemed to say, than formal education which we were taught to value.

William Benjamin Gould's commitment to the Union cause in the War of the Rebellion as a struggle for "Right and Equality," as he called it, and his reference to that struggle as "[T]he holiest of all causes, Liberty and Union" always had immediate relevance to me as a small child and young man. This commitment to equality, particularly as shaped during the civil rights desegregation litigation of this century as well as an uncompromising support for civil rights legislation in the time of FDR and Truman and beyond were part of the legacy that my great grandfather provided to the home in which I was raised.

And time and time again, at discussions at the dinner table and in our living room, my father's constant refrain was—particularly when he realized that I was moving toward the law—"You wouldn't have any freedoms in this country if we didn't have a strong military that was willing to defend them." I am sure that this view was derived from both the service of William Benjamin Gould in the War of the Rebellion, William Benjamin Gould, Jr. in the Spanish-American War and the rest of his sons in World War I. As I have said earlier, they were "the backbone of our country."

July 4th was always a great day in our family when my father, even beyond middle age, was prone to set off firecrackers, when the flag was so often flown as it was on Memorial Day and Armistice Day. And I can still hear my father speak of hundreds of Civil War veterans marching through the streets of Boston and his reminiscences of my great grandfather coming to the public schools on Memorial Day to tell the students of his experiences in and the lessons of the Civil War.

When my father was a young boy in Hyde Park in Boston, just across the line from Dedham, and my grandfather was living next door to my great grandfather, he told me of receiving a call from a gruff old Civil War veteran one day on the telephone: "Bill Gould?" the caller said. "Yes," my father answered, "Speaking." The caller retorted: "The hell it is." The three Bill Goulds were in close proximity, often fielding one another's calls.

One of the stories I remember most vividly was of my great grandfather's work as a tradesman—he was a plasterer or mason and apparently learned his trade here in Wilmington as we see by his work on the Bellamy Mansion. The story focused upon his work for the very large Roman Catholic Church in Dedham, St. Mary's.

At this point my great grandfather had become a contractor, employing other men. According to my father, some of the workmen fell asleep at a critical time in the process, but their deficiencies could not be observed and could have been easily covered up without the defects becoming apparent until years later. But my great grandfather had all the plaster ripped out of the church and had the work done again at such great expense that he was nearly bankrupted. From this moment on, his stature in Dedham was enhanced, as was the name Gould.

The most recent page in the story of his work is to be found in a telephone call that I received from the Curator of the Bellamy Mansion, Jonathan Noffke, here in Wilmington just three months ago, informing me of the fact that he had found my great grandfather's initials, along with that of other workmen, apparently both slave and free, in the plaster of the mansion itself. The fact that I had been in this very mansion at a reception just eighteen months earlier added to the waves of excitement that ran through me when I heard this news! In a number of major aspects, I feel close to this gentleman whose death preceded my birth by only 13 years.

In the 1960s, my great uncle Lawrence Gould died and bequeathed his property to my father. My father traveled to Dedham to discover that many papers and books were being thrown out. My father found a diary kept by the first William Benjamin Gould covering almost his entire service in the United States Navy in the Civil War, the diary commencing on September 27, 1862 and being completed on September 29, 1865 when my great grandfather received his honorable discharge in the Charlestown Naval Shipyard in Massachusetts. I well recall seeing my father read the diary in our living room in New Jersey and discussing it with him. My impression was that this written work gave my father a new and more profound appreciation for the greatness of William Benjamin Gould and his achievements under the most difficult of circumstances.

The diary covered his Civil War service in the North Atlantic Blockade on the U.S.S. *Cambridge* and also his service on the U.S.S. *Niagara* in 1864–1865 as it sought out Confederate cruisers in European waters. There are two gaps—one attributable to the fact that my great grandfather was in the Chelsea, Massachusetts Naval hospital in the summer of 1863 with measles and the second, between late 1864 and early 1865, which my father always believed was thrown out prior to his arrival in Dedham after Lawrence's death.

I began to follow the trail of William Benjamin Gould in the fall of 1971 when I commenced a year as Visiting Professor of Law at Harvard Law School in Cambridge, Massachusetts. The year before I had obtained copies of the pension papers filed with the United States Department of Interior in 1889, 1912 and 1915 by

William B. Gould, some of which had been retrieved by my father. My great grand-father had difficulty obtaining a pension, attributable to his rheumatoid condition, because he had no birth certificate—his home was destroyed during the Civil War and the Bible which recorded his birth was destroyed as well—and had to explain something about his life.

In these papers he wrote about his late wife Cornelia Williams Read—she had predeceased him in 1906—and stated that he had known her "since she was a child," though she was born in Charleston, South Carolina. How had they met, given the distance between these two cities—particularly if they were slaves and not free?

During that time I visited Dedham frequently and obtained documents from the Church of the Good Shepherd and whatever state records I could find. Four William Benjamin Goulds were baptized at the Episcopal Church of the Good Shepherd in Dedham and the first three were confirmed there. Though discussions with the church's rector in the early 1970s led me to believe that William Benjamin was one of its founders in the 1870s—and he may have been (this led me to look at St. James Episcopal Church in Wilmington and others in this area), it is quite possible that he became an Episcopalian in Dedham inasmuch as he was baptized there and was married to my great grandmother Cornelia Gould, nee Cornelia Williams Read, in the African Baptist Church in Nantucket, Massachusetts on November 22, 1865.

The Episcopal Church, its liturgy and the language of its beautiful Book of Common Prayer were very much a part of my upbringing. I count it as part of my heritage and I think that it comes from the first William Benjamin Gould and the Church of the Good Shepherd.

While at Harvard, I discovered at the Dedham Library a document taken down by someone else captioned: "A Portion of the Cruise of the U.S. Steam Frigate 'Niagara' In Foreign Waters: Compiled from the Journal of Wm. B. Gould." This summarized portions of the diary and spoke of the history of the period which, undoubtedly my great grandfather had an opportunity to reflect upon and read more about subsequent to his service.

Then, after I began my professorship at Stanford Law School in the fall of 1972, almost 3,000 miles from the East Coast, I allowed the trail to go cold and did not pursue him further. But, in the late 1980s I was able to convince Dr. John Hope Franklin of Duke University—for whom I had acted as a chauffeur when he was our commencement speaker at Stanford in 1977—to accept a visiting professorship at Stanford Law School. A fortunate byproduct of this visit was that Dr. Franklin kindly read the diary and provided a very detailed memo about it. Franklin noted that many of the papers referred to my great grandfather as a "contraband" and he was not sure whether my great grandfather was free or a slave. Franklin was skeptical of the idea that William B. Gould was a slave because the diary showed him to be not only extraordinarily literate but also in correspondence with other members of his family. Was William Benjamin Gould a slave or free?

In 1989 when I returned east to visit at Howard Law School in Washington, D.C., I began to find some answers to some of the obvious questions. Officials in the National Archives in Washington found the log of the U.S.S. *Cambridge* which showed the entry for the day that WBG came onboard. The entry reads as follows: "Saw a sail S.W. by S. and signaled same to other vessels. Stood for strange sail and at 10:30 picked up a boat with eight contrabands from Wilmington, North Carolina . . . names of contraband and their masters: William B. Gould owned by Nicholas Nixon." The others on this boat were Joseph Hall, George Price and Andrew Hall, all owned by William C. Benticott; John Mackey, owned by John Nash; Charles Giles, owned by Dan Russell; John Mitchell, owned by Killion P. Martin, and William Chance, owned by William Robbins. We have found the deposition of Joseph Hall, executed in September 1902 in Virginia, stating that he " . . . enlisted in the U.S. Navy at or off Wilmington, North Carolina October 1, 1862 . . . went aboard the U.S.S. *Cambridge* 22 September, 1862." (In his diary WBG states that "we took the Oath of Allegiance to the Government of Uncle Samuel" on Oct. 3.)

This was very big news and led me to the state archives in Raleigh, North Carolina where I began to look carefully through the records of Nicholas Nixon. The inventory of slaves did not include names of individuals and, though I could find one person whose sex and age seemed to fit that of the first William B. Gould, I could not prove it definitively. In the slave schedule of 1850 which was part of the census for Wilmington (recall that the Constitution gave the slave states three-fifths representation for slaves), it is set forth that Nixon owned 69 slaves, but they are not mentioned by name, though there is a black slave who is male and 12 years old at the time. William Benjamin Gould turned 13 in November 1850.

Meanwhile, prior to coming to North Carolina, I turned back toward Massachusetts, and looked at church records which showed baptism and confirmation dates for my great grandfather and his wife, Cornelia Williams Read, my great grandmother. Just as a matter of course, I ordered his death certificate and discovered that his father, Alexander Gould, had been born in England. Some of the pension papers had referred to WBG as "mulatto." But no one had ever said anything about this! The 1820 census showed that Alexander lived in Granville County, North Carolina. Now I felt that the trail was unfolding.

But I was soon to run up against roadblocks. As I drove back across the country,

I made my way through the southeast and stayed one night at the home of Dr. John Hope Franklin before venturing forth to both Raleigh and to Wilmington itself. Said Franklin to me as we had breakfast the morning of December 14: "I wish I could go with you! I wish I could walk the streets of Wilmington with you as you look for him!"

And so it was on to Raleigh and the examination of the Nixon records and the Census records for the previous century which turned up no Goulds in Wilmington itself. But I did find Goulds in the 1900 census in North Edenton, Mark's Creek, Hamlet Village, Red Springs, in Chowan, Richmond and Robeson Counties, respectively. Most of these Goulds are black. I also found Goulds in the 1989 telephone book in Hamlet and Rockingham, some of whose first names appear to suggest that they might be black.

After Raleigh, I drove over to Wilmington to simply, to use Dr. Franklin's words, walk the streets and reflect upon what my great grandfather must have thought as he walked those same streets as a young man. I attended the Sunday Eucharist at St. James Episcopal Church and wondered whether he had been there.

My next chance to return to Wilmington was in early 1997 in late February on a beautiful spring-like weekend when I drove down from Washington, D.C. But, again, before coming to North Carolina, I turned to Massachusetts—this time to the Island of Nantucket in the fall of 1995. Here I met Helen Seager who was actively involved in the restoration of the African Meeting House of Nantucket, which had been the African Baptist Church where my great grandparents were married. We had a mutual interest in retracing the steps of both William B. Gould and Cornelia W. Read.

Early on in my visit we went to the Nantucket Library and Ms. Seager, upon opening one of the volumes of old Nantucket newspapers, exclaimed! There were articles reciting the circumstances under which Cornelia Read had been purchased out of slavery from Wilmington in 1858, when she was owned by John N. Maffit. Now we could immediately speculate as to how William and Cornelia had met—it was most probably in Wilmington and not Charleston.

The articles described the circumstances of the purchase of both Cornelia Williams Read and her mother, my great great grandmother Diana Williams, by virtue of the intervention of James Crawford, the black minister at the Nantucket African Baptist Church, who was married to Cornelia Read's aunt. Moreover, the articles describe the people who contributed to the purchase price of $1,000 for Cornelia, $700 for Diana, and the involvement of the famous Abolitionist Lewis Tappan— and the perilous journey that Mr. Crawford made from North Carolina back to Nantucket. It was from here that Cornelia Read corresponded with William during the Civil War. When I made the third of three visits during my time in Washington, in May 1998, I chronicled the references to their correspondence (we do not have the letters themselves) and their first meeting in Nantucket in 1863.

A month prior to my May 1998 speech in Nantucket, I had traveled from Washington to the Charlestown Naval Shipyard in Boston where William Benjamin Gould was discharged from the United States Navy on September 29, 1865. I saw the structure where he received his papers and the dock where his ship in the European part of his service, the U.S.S. *Niagara*, had come for repairs.

Meanwhile, I had made the second of three journeys to Wilmington. One of the first things that I saw as I drove into North Carolina were the signs referring to Weldon. In his diary, William speaks of hearing that Union troops had occupied Weldon, although apparently this was not the case. The objective, of course, was to cut the Wilmington/Richmond railway and to cut off General Lee's supplies.

Last year during that second visit, I met here in Wilmington with Beverly Tetterton, George Stevenson and David Cecelski. I was the beneficiary of the generous hospitality of Michael Murchison at whose house I stayed—just a few blocks away from the former home of T. C. Worth, the only person from Wilmington who contributed to my great grandmother's purchase price.

During this visit, I was particularly curious about Rich Inlet from where William wrote in February 1863 that he was able to get a good look at the place he came from in 1862. It soon became apparent to me that he was looking at the Porter's Neck area where the Nixon Plantation was and, by gaining entry to Double Eight Island, I was able to walk out to nearly the point where his ship was anchored when he made this observation.

After Wilmington, I traveled down to Fort Fisher and Fort Caswell, both of which his ship traded much gunfire with, and near to Lockwood's Folly Inlet—and then on to other areas described in the diary, New Inlet, New Topsail Inlet and Masonboro Inlet. And then it was on to Beaufort where his ship frequently coaled and where he met General Burnside the first week of his enlistment on the U.S.S. *Cambridge*.

In Beaufort I lunched in a restaurant overlooking the waters where, I was told, the Union ships had arrived and anchored—and walked along the shore and visited Fort Macon as well. (A decade ago, I had done the same in Cadiz, Spain where he had docked during his European service in 1864–1865.) There again, as in Wilmington, I felt near this man and the practical problems that his old vessel experienced as it went through its many repairs in that port.

What was his life like here in North Carolina? How did he become such a literate man? How did he obtain his religion? (Nixon was a prominent Episcopalian in

Wilmington.) His trade? (Perhaps he was contracted out by Nixon to work on the Bellamy Mansion.)

What was his contact with his father as well as his mother? His diary records receipt of the "sad news" of his mother's death in 1865. Where are the descendants from the family that he left behind when he left Wilmington? Though I do not believe that he ever returned here from New England after the War [I later learned that WBG probably returned once, around October 1865], Beverly Tetterton has found a news account of him and his sons after World War I in the local newspaper. Someone here must have had some interest in him. These are some of the unanswered questions which I ponder.

I have found many answers with many friends both here and in Massachusetts and Washington. I still have much ground to cover. I thank Jonathan Noffke for making this opportunity available for me to come here and to speak to you, and I also am most grateful to Beverly Tetterton for her kind support.

I shall do the best that I can, consistent with my other duties, to write about the first William Benjamin Gould and the inspiration I have gained from the chronicle, albeit incomplete, of his service to his country and his legacy as my namesake.

Thank you very much.

Notes

The following short forms and abbreviations are used in the Notes:

Lee Papers: *Samuel P. Lee: A Register of his Papers in the Library of Congress.*
          In the Naval Historical Collection
ORN: *Official Records of the Union and Confederate Navies in the War of*
          the Rebellion, 1893–1922

Unless otherwise noted, all the ships' logs and navy pension files cited are in the National Archives, Washington, D.C.

Prologue

1. Diary of Charles B. Fisher, ed. Paul E. Sluby Sr., and Stanton L. Wormley (1983). The unpublished diary of John Cornelius Hart is held by David Hart of Detroit. Fisher was a freeman, and Hart a freedman.

2. Diary, Sept. 18, Aug. 18, 1865.

3. Diary, Sept. 2, 1865.

4. This reference to "Book 3" remains a mystery. I possess only two bound books; the unbound pages, which could comprise a third book, come after this entry.

5. I am indebted to Sarah Preston for her examination of the diary. She has added descriptive comments to this portion of the text.

6. *The Random House Dictionary of the English Language* (1967).

7. *Webster's New Collegiate Dictionary* (1979).

ONE: An Introduction to William B. Gould

1. WBG under the pen name Oley writes that the escape took place Sunday night, Sept. 20. Sunday night was Sept. 21. Either *The Anglo-African* misprinted the date or WBG was mistaken about it.

2. "An Interesting and Romantic Narrative," p. 1 (for the text of this item, see Chap. 4).

3. U.S.S. *Georgia* and *Cambridge* logs, Sept. 22, 1862. I am indebted to Rebecca Livingston of the National Archives for retrieving the various ship logs for me.

4. John Hope Franklin, *The Emancipation Proclamation*, p. 43 (1965).

5. "Interesting and Romantic Narrative."

6. Diary, undated entry, "Notes by W.B.G."

7. Diary, undated entry, "The Negro his Friends and Foes."

8. Diary, May 6, 1864.

9. James M. McPherson, *Drawn with the Sword: Reflections on the American Civil War*, p. 64 (1996).

10. Ibid., pp. 78–79.

11. Robert M. Browning Jr., "Defunct Strategy & Divergent Goals: The Role of the United States Navy along the Eastern Seaboard during the Civil War," *Prologue: Quarterly of the National Archives and Records Administration*, 33.3 (Fall 2001): 170.

12. Diary, March 22, 1863: "Genl. Burnside went on board."

13. Bruce Catton, *Terrible Swift Sword*, p. 365 (1963).

14. Stephen W. Sears, *Landscape Turned Red: The Battle of Antietam*, p. 62 (1983).

15. Shelby Foote, *The Civil War, A Narrative: Fort Sumter to Perryville*, p. 662 (1986).

16. Howard Jones, *Union in Peril: The Crisis over British Intervention in the Civil War* (1992).

17. Maj. Rufus Dawes, cited in Sears, *Landscape Turned Red*, p. 198.

18. Foote, *Civil War*, p. 704.

19. Ibid.

20. "Interesting and Romantic Narrative." According to Joseph Hall, he was "stripped and given a thorough physical examination" (Hall U.S. Navy pension file). Whether or not he was referring to this encounter or the day of his enlistment is unclear.

21. Report, Cmdr. G. H. Scott to Acting Rear-Adm. S. P. Lee, Sept. 25, 1862, *ORN*, 1.8: 87.

22. Letter, Cmdr. William A. Parker to Acting Rear-Adm. S. P. Lee, Sept. 17, 1862, *Lee Papers*.

23. Greg Marquis, *In Armageddon's Shadow: The Civil War and Canada's Maritime Provinces*, p. 166 (1998).

24. "Portion of the Cruise," pp. 226–29 (for this statement, see Chap. 4). WBG's description of the position of Charles Francis Adams is confirmed in Dean B. Mahin, *One War at a Time: The International Dimensions of the American Civil War*, p. 181 (1999).

25. Steven J. Ramold, *Slaves, Sailors, Citizens: African Americans in the Union Navy*, p. 178 (2002).

26. "Portion of the Cruise."

27. For further discussion of the exploits of the *Georgia*, see Hawley Stevens, "C.S.S. *Georgia*: Memory and History," *American Neptune: A Quarterly Journal of Maritime History*, 45.3 (1985).

28. Diary, Aug. 15, 1864.

29. Ibid.: "[W]e boarded her and found her to be the Rebel Privateer 'Georgia' from Liverpool on her way to refit as A cruiseer."

30. *The Steamship Georgia v. The United States*, 7 Wall. 32 (1869).

31. Thomas Willing Balch, *The Alabama Arbitration*, p. 13 (1900, reprinted 1969).

32. Balch (ibid., p. 11) notes: "American sentiment was well expressed in Lowell's *Jonathan to John*:—

We own the ocean, tu, John:
You mus'n take it hard,
Ef we can't think with you, John
It's jest your own back-yard.
Ole Uncle S. sez he, 'I guess,
Ef *thet's* his claim,' sez he,
'The fencin'-stuff'll cost enough
To bust up friend J.B.,
Ez wal ez you an' me!

Why talk so dreffle big, John,
Of honor when it meant
You did n't care a fig, John,
But jest for *ten per cent.?*
Ole Uncle S. sez he, 'I guess
He's like the rest,' sez he:
'When all is done, it's number one
Thet's nearest to J.B.,
Ez wal ez t' you an' me!"

33. Diary, Feb. 9, 1865.

34. Diary, Feb. 13, 1865.

35. Diary, March 21, 1865.

36. Diary, March 24, 1865. For more on the C.S.S. *Stonewall*, see Edwin Strong, Thomas Buckley, and Annetta St. Clair, "The Odyssey of the CSS Stonewall," *Civil War History*, 30.4 (1984).

37. "The Escape of the Ram Stonewall," *New York Times*, April 13, 1865, p. 4.

38. Some 135 years later, during the summer of 2000, I had a chance to retrace WBG's steps as his ship made its way along the Spanish coast. Here are some of the notes I made on the aptness of his comments. "July 14, 2000, A.M. La Coruña. Good conversation re diary with Jaime Martínez García [a local historian and tourism official] prior to El Ferrol departure. He discovers Gaberon which WBG mistakenly calls a Gallica—most maps don't have it. It is 'just rocks' he [MG] says. He says there are 2 lighthouses as WBG said. . . . There is another small one that I found yesterday at Saint Antoine fortress. The latter is one of six that WBG refers to—MG refers to at least four, Santa Cruz and San Diego that he mentions. [He subsequently wrote me to confirm the 6 forts to which WBG refers.] Re WBG's reference to the Pyrenees at El Ferrol, MG says that even though WBG is technically correct, they are so small that the Spanish don't refer to them that way. He notes that the *Niagara* couldn't dock at Coruña—it was too shallow—small boats required to reach land. Re El Ferrol, he says that there were often metal chains across the entrance. 12:10 we depart La Coruña for El Ferrol. . . . We pass San Antoine to the left. As we turn to El Ferrol it's clear how they could see anything coming out from Coruña to the South. At about 12:45 we move into Ria de Ferrol with *Bossa Nova* blaring on the ship PA system. This is the path taken by WBG when he was younger than any of my sons. . . . At about 1 p.m. we move into a narrow portion of the river that WBG described—the first fortification is on

left—then two fortifications up front on each side as river narrows more. Now in the harbor area at 1:15 we veer to the left. . . . Not able to ascertain precisely where ships lay, but I photograph the most likely places. [Returning to El Ferrol I can see what WBG saw as he approached it.] The river narrows and, as it does, the fortifications described by WBG appear on each side [he wrote on Feb. 14, 1865: "The passage is A verry narrow one bu(t) verry cold Watter. The whole passage for A mile in length is one continued line of Fortifacations]. Seemingly everything, La Coruña's "ancient" churches and the memorial to Peninsular War casualty John Moore (both described by WBG [on Feb. 23, 1865]), is exactly as it was then."

39. "Portion of the Cruise."

40. Ibid.

41. Diary, June 19, 1865.

42. I am grateful to Prof. Chris Fonvielle for bringing to my attention the concerted nature of WBG's escape.

43. Price may in fact have deserted from the *Cambridge*. WBG writes in his diary on Nov. 10, 1862: "Three Men Deserted. One of them George P—e. I am verry sorry for it."

44. William McKee Evans, *Ballots and Fence Rails: Reconstruction on the Lower Cape Fear*, p. 126 (1966).

45. William M. Reaves, *Strength Through Struggle: The Chronological and Historical Record of the African American Community in Wilmington, North Carolina, 1865–1950* (1998).

46. David Cecelski, "Abraham H. Galloway: Wilmington's Lost Prophet and the Rise of Black Radicalism in the American South," *Democracy Betrayed: The Wilmington Race Riot of 1898 and Its Legacy*, p. 51 (1998).

47. Diary, May 5, 1864: "heard that A.H. Galloway is in the Citty." A few days later, on May 11, 1864: "Meet A.H. Galoway. Went to Sulivan street Church where there was A meeting to receive the Delegates from North Carolina. The meeting was verry poorly attended. Speeches were deliverd by Messers Hill on behalf of the Church and by Miss Pierson & Galoway in behalf of the Delegation."

48. Reaves, *Strength Through Struggle*, p. 431, quoting from the *Wilmington Post*, March 31, 1876.

49. Diary, Feb. 18, 1864: "Heard that George L.M. has joined the 5th Mass Cav."

50. *Wilmington Weekly Journal*, cited in Evans, *Ballots and Fence Rails*, p. 139.

51. Cecelski, "Abraham H. Galloway."

52. "Items of Interest from Wilmington" (see text in Chap. 4).

53. Diary, Aug. 11, 1864. March 31, 1863: "Heard from my Aunt in the afternoon she with her Daughter. Mary came on board." He writes of visiting an aunt in Boston again on Sept. 21, 1865. (See Appendix B for other possible references to Aunt Jones.) In 2001, a visit to Boston reveals for me the probable location of 2 Sears Place, where Aunt Jones lived. Sears Place no longer exists as an official street. It is now an enclosed alley in the northwest corner of the city, near the State House, a section once disproportionately settled by blacks, some newly arrived in the 1850s. The African Meeting House still stands nearby.

54. According to the *Dedham Historical Register*, the town at one time had several black families: "The original home of the *Thompson* family is thought to have been on the 'Island,' near the Needham line. But, the writer knows little or nothing of the early history of this family, and can state nothing positively in regard to the generation that preceded the last. These, and the other people whom we have located to the best of our knowledge—namely, the John-

sons, the Freemans, the Gerrishes, the Harrisons, the Robinses, and the Nicholses—represented those branches of the colored race that a permanent residence in or near the First Parish in Dedham in 1830 and thereabouts. Some of the men folks had colonized here from New Jersey at the close of the Revolutionary War, and it was generally supposed by the town's people that those who had once been slaves constituted a majority of the whole number. There were, also, of course, many single colored individuals in domestic service throughout the town, and to an extent proportionately greater than at the present day." *Register*, 1.3 (July 1890): 101. I am indebted to Peg Bradner for calling this source to my attention.

55. Diary, May 24, 1865.

56. On Cornelia William Read's death, the *Dedham Transcript* of Dec. 29, 1906, commented: "She was an earnest and active worker in the church, charitable and grand army affairs."

57. William B. Gould pension file, March 18, 1915.

58. Edward Ball, *Slaves in the Family* (1998).

59. Martin B. Pasternak, *Rise Now and Fly to Arms: The Life of Henry Highland Garnet* (1995).

60. Diary, April 30, 1864: "Went to Fleet street church. Heard Rev. Mr. Garnet."

61. *Weekly Mirror* (Nantucket), March 13, 1858.

62. Ibid.

63. Unidentified newspaper clipping, July 1, 1857, in Grace Brown Gardener Scrapbook 34, Nantucket Historical Association Manuscript Collection 57.

64. J. E. Crawford & Family, "A Card," in ibid.

65. *New Bedford Mercury*, Feb. 26, 1858, in Gardener Scrapbook 34.

66. Ibid.

67. Anna H. Richardson, *Anti-Slavery Memoranda* (1860). The pamphlet is reprinted in William Still, *The Underground Railroad* (1968); the quote appears at p. 597.

68. Diary, Feb. 16, 1863.

69. Jenny Borune Wahl, "Legal Constraints Towards Slave Masters: The Problem of Social Cost," 41 *American Journal of Legal History*, 1.24 (1997).

70. Kenneth M. Stampp, *The Peculiar Institution: Slavery in the Ante-bellum South*, p. 361 (1956). On the subject of fugitive slaves, see John Hope Franklin and Loren Schweninger, *Runaway Slaves: Rebels on the Plantation* (1999).

71. Ibid., p. 372.

72. I am indebted to Beverly Tetterton for bringing this point about Wilmington to my attention.

73. Diary, April 15, 1865, Jan. 16, 1863.

TWO: William B. Gould's Worlds

1. Ginny Turner, "Exploring the Carolina Coast: Cities Offer Mix of Past and Present," *Orlando Sentinel Tribune*, Aug. 26, 1990.

2. Diary, June 24, 1864.

3. Erastus Worthington, *Proceedings at the celebration of the two hundred and fiftieth anniversary of the incorporation of the town of Dedham, Massachusetts, September 21, 1886*, p. 24 (1887).

4. See Chap. 1, n. 54, regarding black families in Dedham.

5. *Dedham Transcript*, Dec. 8, 1883.

6. Beverly Tetterton has pointed out to me that there were many black Americans in Wilmington named Richardson, including Willis Richardson, a famous African American playwright. It is possible that Herbert Richardson was named for one of these Richardsons. Also, Virgil Richardson, a friend and correspondent who escaped simultaneously with WBG.

7. See David Cecelski, *Democracy Betrayed: The Wilmington Race Riot of 1898 and Its Legacy* (1998).

8. *Wilmington Dispatch*, Dec. 16, 1917, p. 2.

9. *Dedham Transcript*, May 25, 1918, p. 1.

10. Ibid., June 1, 1918, p. 2.

11. WBG submitted a statement to a GAR scribe after the war in which he stated that he actually entered the service on Aug. 21, 1861, as a Landsman on board the *Cambridge*, was discharged on Oct. 20, 1862, and then reenlisted. He claimed to have taken part "in engagements with the Rebel Batteries along the Potomac and James Rivers the last of 61 and also 62. At Hampton Rhodes March 8th 1862. Pittsburg Landing July 1862." I do not know what to make of this; there is no doubt that he was picked up as a runaway by the *Cambridge* on Sept. 22, 1862, as her log indicated, and that he enlisted on Oct. 3, as he noted in his diary.

12. Annual message to Congress, Dec. 1, 1862, in Roy P. Basler, ed., *The Collected Works of Abraham Lincoln*, vol. 5, p. 537 (1953).

13. Diary, May 6, 1864.

14. Diary, April 15, 1865.

15. Diary, Aug. 15, 16, 1864.

16. Diary, May 28, June 16, 1865. On the "sour apple tree" usage, see the annotation for the June 16, 1865, diary entry. Davis was never actually tried for treason.

17. WBG would hardly have been receptive to Jay Winik's romanticized picture of Robert E. Lee in *April 1865: The Month That Saved America* (2001). But I suspect he would have subscribed to the hardheaded and factual description of Lee in Alan T. Nolan, *Lee Considered: General Robert E. Lee and Civil War History* (1991).

18. Diary, April 26, 1864.   19. Diary, June 14, 1865.

20. Diary, Jan. 17, 1863.   21. Diary, Jan. 14, 1863.

22. Diary, Nov. 17, 1862.   23. Diary, Jan. 30, 1863.

24. Diary, March 8, 1863.

25. Diary, May 18, 1864. The incident was also covered by the *Anglo-African in its May 28th issue*: "Shameful Treatment of Colored Soldiers: On Board the U.S. Steam Frigate Niagara, May 16th, 1864."

26. C. Peter Ripley, *The Black Abolitionist Papers*, vol. 5, pp. 27–28 (1986).

27. The letter was addressed from "On Board the U.S. Steam Frigate Niagara, Off New York, April 5, 1864."

28. The full title was "Our Noble Tars Speak—How They Feel For The Freedmen" (for the text, see Chap. 4).

29. "Interesting and Romantic Narrative" (see text in Chap. 4).

30. Diary, Nov. 5, 1862.

31. "Interesting and Romantic Narrative." In his pension application, Hall stated that he married Mosley on Dec. 19, 1862, not Dec. 20. Hall U.S. Navy pension file.

32. "Interesting and Romantic Narrative."

33. Diary, May 18, 1864.

34. "Shameful Treatment."

35. Letter, Fred White, U.S.S. *Niagara*, New York Harbor, to F. A. Belcher, May 22, 1864. *In* Naval War College, Naval Historical Collection. See the note for the May 22, 1864, diary entry.

36. Diary, Aug. 28, 1865.   37. Diary, March 14, 1864.

38. Diary, June 6, 1865.   39. Diary, Nov. 15, 1862.

40. Diary, June 1, 1864.   41. Diary, Feb. 15, 1865.

42. Diary, June 26, 1864.   43. Diary, June 27, 1864.

44. Diary, June 30, 1864.   45. Diary, July 21, 1864.

46. "Perilous Voyage of the Niagara," *New York Times*, April 5, 1864.

47. Diary, March 18, 1864.

48. "Perilous Voyage."

THREE: The Democratic Impulse and the Navy

1. David Brion Davis, "The Enduring Legacy of South's Civil War Victory," *New York Times*, Aug. 26, 2001, Sec. IV, p. 1.

2. Kinley J. Brauer, "Gabriel García y Tassara and the American Civil War: A Spanish Perspective," *Civil War History*, 21.1: 13.

3. *Dred Scott v. Sandford*, 60 U.S. 393 (1856).

4. 347 U.S. 483 (1954).

5. I have often spoken about this connection in my writings. See, for example, "Lincoln, Labor and the Black Military," in Appendix C.

6. *Bailey v. State of Alabama*, 219 U.S. 219, 241 (1911). The relationship between the Thirteenth Amendment and contemporary policies on free labor is set forth in Robert J. Steinfeld, "Changing Legal Conceptions of Free Labor," and David Brody, "Free Labor, Law and American Trade Unionism," both in Stanley L. Engerman, ed., *Terms of Labor: Slavery, Serfdom and Free Labor* (1999).

7. Roy P. Basler, ed., *The Collected Works of Abraham Lincoln*, vol. 4, pp. 24–25 (1953).

8. Ibid., vol. 3, p. 259.

9. Ibid., vol. 5, p. 52.

10. Gabor S. Boritt, *Lincoln and the Economics of the American Dream*, p. 18 (1978).

11. Ibid., p. 185.

12. Basler, ed., *Collected Works of Abraham Lincoln*, vol. 3, pp. 477–78.

13. See Michael Vorenberg, *Final Freedom: The Civil War, the Abolition of Slavery, and the Thirteenth Amendment* (2001), for the most extensive discussion of the Thirteenth Amendment.

14. Eric Foner, *Free Soil, Free Labor, and Free Men: The Ideology of the Republican Party Before the Civil War* (1970). Cf. David Montgomery, *Beyond Equality: Labor and the Radical Republicans 1863–1872* (1981).

15. Ibid., pp. 26–27.

16. See Chap. 4 for the text of this undated document.

17. Foner, *Free Soil*.

18. William M. Fowler Jr., *Under Two Flags. The American Navy in the Civil War*,

pp. 31–32 (1990). See, generally, Richard S. West Jr., *Mr. Lincoln's Navy* (1957); Dennis J. Ringle, *Life in Mr. Lincoln's Navy* (1998).

19. Stephen R. Wise, "The Union and Confederate Navies," p. 3. Paper presented at the symposium on "War on the Waters: Civil War Naval Operations," Chicago, Sept. 23, 2000.

20. Ivan Musicant, *Divided Waters: The Naval History of the Civil War*, pp. 1–2 (1995).

21. Frank Merli, *Great Britain and the Confederate Navy, 1861–1865*, pp. 7–9 (1965).

22. Wise, "Union and Confederate Navies," p. 4.

23. Ibid., p. 5.

24. J. deKay, *Monitor: The Story of the Legendary Civil War Ironclad and the Man Whose Invention Changed the Course of History* (1997).

25. Fowler, *Under Two Flags*, pp. 303–4.

26. Letter, Abraham Lincoln to James C. Conkling, Aug. 26, 1863, in Basler, ed., *Collected Works*, vol. 6, pp. 409–10.

27. Stephen J. Ramold, *Slaves, Sailors, Citizens: African Americans in the Union Navy*, p. 7 (2002).

28. Benjamin Quarles, *The Negro in the Civil War*, pp. 59–61 (1953), p. 64. On blacks in the U.S. Navy generally, see David L. Valuska, *The African American in the Union Navy: 1861–1865* (1993).

29. Quarles, *Negro in the Civil War*, p. 66.

30. Ibid.

31. Joseph P. Reidy, "Black Men in Navy Blue During the Civil War," *Prologue: Quarterly of the National Archives and Records Administration*, 33.3 (Fall 2001).

32. Valuska, *African American*, p. 22.

33. Michael J. Bennett, "'Frictions': Shipboard Relations Between White and Contraband Sailors," *Civil War History*, 47.2 (June 2001).

34. Reidy, "Black Men in Navy Blue." 35. Valuska, *African American*, p. 33.

36. Reidy, "Black Men in Navy Blue." 37. Ibid.

38. Herbert Aptheker, "The Negro in the Union Navy," *Journal of Negro History*, 32 (1947): 183–84.

39. Reidy, "Black Men in Navy Blue."

40. Ramold, *Slaves, Sailors*, p. 185.

41. Thus, WBG's reference to "the commission of A colard Man as Major" on March 24, 1865, seems to be erroneous.

42. Diary, May 25, 1864. 43. Diary, March 21, 1965.

44. Bennett, "Frictions." 45. Diary, May 30, 1865.

46. Diary, May 31, 1865. 47. Reidy, "Black Men in Navy Blue."

48. *Diary of Charles B. Fisher*, ed. Paul E. Sluby Sr., and Stanton L. Wormley, p. 24 (1983).

49. Ibid., pp. 37–38.

50. Ramold, *Slaves, Sailors*, p. 113.

51. Ibid., p. 154. On May 27, 1865, WBG writes: "One Man Deserted. The first Colord Man that left on this side of the watter."

52. Diary, June 5, 1864. 53. Diary, Nov. 18, 1863.

54. Diary, Oct. 23, 1863. 55. Diary, May 22, 1865.

56. Diary, Nov. 18, 1863. 57. Diary, May 27, 1864.

58. Diary, May 30, 1864. 59. Diary, Sept. 2, 1864.

60. Diary, Sept. 16, 1865.

61. Diary, Dec. 15, 1863: "I was put on watch for two hours from 8 to 10 P.M. for punishment for sewing in the Pantry."

62. Diary, May 18, 1864.

63. Valuska, *African American*, p. 19.

64. Ibid.; Aptheker, "Negro in the Union Navy"; W. Jeffrey Bolster, *Black Jacks: African American Seamen in the Age of Sail* (1997).

65. Valuska, *African American*, p. 20.

66. Reidy, "Black Men in Navy Blue."

67. Ibid.

68. Ibid.

The Diary

1. Navy Department, *Dictionary of American Naval Fighting Ships*, vol. 2, p. 20 (1963).

2. Ibid.

3. Robert M. Browning Jr., *From Cape Charles to Cape Fear: The North Atlantic Blockading Squadron During the Civil War*, pp. 143–44 (1993).

4. John G. Barrett, *The Civil War in North Carolina*, p. 134 (1963).

5. E. B. Long and Barbara Long, *The Civil War Day By Day: An Almanac, 1861–1865*, p. 269 (1971).

6. Ibid., p. 271.

7. Royce Shingleton, *High Seas Confederate: The Life and Times of John Newland Maffitt*, p. 52 (1994). Maffitt, it will be recalled, had been the owner of WBG's future wife.

8. As cited in *Cambridge* log, Oct. 16, 1862.

9. *Civil War Day by Day*, p. 271.

10. See Barrett, *Civil War in North Carolina*, pp. 139–48.

11. *Dictionary of American Naval Fighting Ships*, vol. 2, p. 20.

12. Report, Cmdr. William A. Parker to Cmdr. G. H. Scott, Nov. 17, 1862, *ORN*, 1.8: 214–15.

13. Report, Acting Mstr. William H. Maies to Secy. of the Navy Gideon Welles, Dec. 3, 1862, ibid., p. 215.

14. Report, Cmdr. William A. Parker to Rear-Adm. S. P. Lee, Nov. 20, 1862, *Lee Papers*.

15. *Civil War Day by Day*, p. 285.

16. Report, Acting Volunteer Lt. James Trathen to Rear-Adm. S. P. Lee, Dec. 3, 1862, *ORN*, 1.8: 254.

17. Report, Cmdr. William A. Parker to Rear-Adm. S. P. Lee, Dec. 3, 1862, *Lee Papers*.

18. *Dictionary of American Naval Fighting Ships*, vol. 2, p. 20.

19. Report, Cmdr. William A. Parker to Rear-Adm. S. P. Lee, Dec. 4, 1862, *ORN*, 1.8: 255.

20. See *Civil War Day by Day*, pp. 295–96.

21. Letter, Cmdr. William A. Parker to Maj.-Gen. J. C. Foster, Dec. 8, 1862, *Lee Papers*.

22. Report, Rear-Adm. S. P. Lee to Secy. of the Navy Gideon Welles, Dec. 23, 1862, *ORN*, 1.8: 313.

23. Report, Cmdr. William A. Parker to Rear-Adm. S. P. Lee, Dec. 26, 1862, *Lee Papers*.

24. See Robert M. Browning Jr., "Defunct Strategy & Divergent Goals: The Role of the United States Navy along the Eastern Seaboard during the Civil War," *Prologue: Quarterly of the National Archives and Records Administration*, 33.3 (Fall 2001).

25. *Civil War Naval Chronology, 1861–1865*, vol. 3, p. 16 (1971).

26. Report, Cmdr. William A. Parker to Rear-Adm. S. P. Lee, Jan. 24, 1863, *ORN*, 1.8: 471.

27. Report, Cmdr. William A. Parker to Rear-Adm. S. P. Lee, Jan. 31, 1863, *Lee Papers*.

28. Report, Cmdr. William A. Parker to Rear-Adm. S. P. Lee, Feb. 14, 1863, *Lee Papers*.

29. *Civil War Day by Day*, p. 317.

30. Report, Cmdr. William A. Parker to Rear-Adm. S. P. Lee, Feb. 23, 1863, *Lee Papers*.

31. Barrett, *Civil War in North Carolina*, pp. 151–52.

32. Mark Hayes of the Naval Historical Center, Washington, D.C., provided this information.

33. *Civil War Day by Day*, pp. 315, 331–32.

34. Donald L. Canney, *Lincoln's Navy: The Ships, Men and Organization, 1861–65*, p. 67 (1998).

35. Cited in Donald L. Canney, *The Old Steam Navy*, vol. 1, p. 57 (1990).

36. Canney, *Lincoln's Navy*, p. 121.

37. See "Seamen for the Navy," *Gloucester Telegraph*, Oct. 8, 1863.

38. "Men for the Navy," *Gloucester Telegraph*, Oct. 31, 1863.

39. Steven J. Ramold, "Valuable Men for Certain Kinds of Duty: African Americans in the Civil War Navy." Ph.D. dissertation, University of Nebraska, 1999.

40. Canney, *Lincoln's Navy*, p. 136.

41. *The Gloucester Telegraph*, Dec. 2, 1863.

42. Telegram, Secy. of the Navy Gideon Welles to Comm. T. T. Craven, Dec. 10, 1863, *ORN*, 1.2: 517.

43. Canney, *Old Steam Navy*, vol. 1, p. 57.

44. *Civil War Day by Day*, p. 445. For a further discussion of the *Chesapeake* incident, see p. 34.

45. Report, Cmdr. A. G. Clary to Comm. George F. Pearson, Dec. 18, 1863, *ORN*, 1.2: 529.

46. Report, Comm. T. T. Craven to Secy. of the Navy Gideon Welles, Dec. 23, 1863, ibid., p. 554.

47. *Gloucester Telegraph*, Dec. 12, 1863.

48. Report, Comm. T. T. Craven to Secy. of the Navy Gideon Welles, Dec. 23, 1863, *ORN*, 1.2: 554.

49. Ibid.

50. Report, Cmdr. A. G. Clary to Comm. George F. Pearson, Dec. 18, 1863, ibid., p. 529.

51. Telegram, Secy. of the Navy Gideon Welles to Comm. T. T. Craven, Dec. 20, 1863, ibid., p. 525.

52. Report, Comm. T. T. Craven to Secy. of the Navy Gideon Welles, Dec. 23, 1863, ibid., pp. 554–55. On the return of some of the "pirates," see Greg Marquis, *In Armageddon's Shadow: The Civil War and Canada's Maritime Provinces*, p. 172 (1998). The promise made to Commodore Craven by the provincial governor was never realized: "The *Chesapeake* was handed over to revenue officers to await adjudication in the colonial Admiralty

court. The American vessels, their mission accomplished, began to take their leave. Prior to departing, Commodore Craven of the *Niagara* paid his respects to the lieutenant-governor, who personally promised that the pirates would be arrested and brought to trial. But warrants issued in Nova Scotia, either because the suspects had left the colony or were sheltered by sympathizers, remained outstanding. As one Halifax journal pointed out, neither the colonial nor municipal government exerted themselves in tracking down the gang. No 'hue and cry' was issued and no reward was posted. From afar, this lack of official action appeared not as inefficiency or procrastination but pure ant-Yankee feeling, further indication of Bluenose support for the Rebels [Canadian and British]." Ibid., pp. 172–73. On the subsequent litigation, see pp. 176–210.

53. See "A Portion of the Cruise" in Chap. 4.

54. Canney, *Old Steam Navy*, p. 57.

55. Joseph T. Glatthaar, *Forged in Battle: The Civil War Alliance of Black Soldiers and White Officers*, p. 141 (1990).

56. "New York Redeemed!: Two Hundred Thousand of her Citizens doing honors to a Black Regiment: A Partial Atonement for the Outrages of July," *The Anglo-African*, March 12, 1864.

57. "Letter from Rollin Brown," *The Anglo-African*, Feb. 20, 1864.

58. See Harold C. Schonberg, "The Black Swan That Sang for the Nobility," *New York Times*, April 12, 1970. This article was discovered and read by William B. Gould III and inserted with the original of the diary at some point in the 1970s. See also "Miss E.T. Greenfield—The Black Swan," March 19, 1864, and "Personal," Jan. 2, 1864, both in *The Anglo-African* (the second describes her concerts in the Midwest).

59. "Perilous Voyage of the Niagara," *New York Times*, April 5, 1864.

60. Ibid.

61. Ibid.

62. Dudley Taylor Cornish, *The Sable Arm: Black Troops in the Union Army, 1861–1865*, pp. 174–76 (1987). See particularly the discussion in "The Massacre at Fort Pillow," *The Anglo-African*, April 23, 1864.

63. *Civil War Day by Day*, p. 487. See also Barrett, *Civil War in North Carolina*, pp. 213–20.

64. See *Civil War Day by Day*, pp. 488–89.

65. Barrett, *Civil War in North Carolina*, p. 220.

66. "War News: Surrender of Plymouth, N.C.," *The Anglo-African*, May 7, 1864.

67. *Civil War Day by Day*, p. 498.

68. Ibid., p. 493.

69. See "Reception of the North Carolina Delegation," *The Anglo-African*, May 14, 1864.

70. See "Shameful Treatment of Colored Soldiers," *The Anglo-African*, May 28, 1864.

71. Telegram, Secy. of the Navy Gideon Welles to Rear-Adm. Hiram Paulding, May 20, 1864, *ORN*, 1.3: 38.

72. Fred White to F. A. Belcher, May 22, 1864. In Naval War College, Naval Historical Collection.

73. Telegram, Secy. of the Navy Gideon Welles to Rear-Adm. Hiram Paulding, May 23, 1864, *ORN*, 1.3: 39.

74. Order, Secy. of the Navy Gideon Welles to Comm. T. T. Craven, May 30, 1864, ibid., p. 40.

75. Instructions, Secy. of the Navy Gideon Welles to Comm. T. T. Craven, May 30, 1864, ibid., p. 41.

76. "Portion of the Cruise."

77. Ibid.

78. Ibid.

79. W. Marvel, *The Alabama and the Kearsarge: The Sailor's Civil War*, p. 243 (1996).

80. Henry Smith, "Foreign Correspondence: U.S.S. Frigate Niagara, Antwerp, Belgium, June 29, 1864," *The Anglo-African*, July 30, 1864.

81. Warren F. Spencer, *The Confederate Navy in Europe*, p. 190 (1983).

82. Henry Smith, "Foreign Correspondence: U.S. Steamship Niagara, Flussing Roads, Holland, Sept. 16th, 1864," *The Anglo-African*, Oct. 8, 1864.

83. Report, Comm. T. T. Craven to Secy. of the Navy Gideon Welles, June 28, 1864, *ORN*, 1.3: 89.

84. Smith, Flussing Roads, Holland.

85. See note 83 above.

86. Letter, Asst. Secy. Benjamin Moran to Capt. John A. Winslow, Aug. 2, 1864, *ORN*, 1.3: 130.

87. Letter, Amb. C. F. Adams to Comm. T. T. Craven, July 27, 1864, ibid., p. 127.

88. Letter, Asst. Secy. Benjamin Moran to Capt. John A. Winslow, July 27, 1864, ibid., pp. 127–28.

89. On Aug. 4, Benjamin Moran of the London legation wrote the U.S. vice-consul at Liverpool about providing him with information to the effect that the Portuguese government chartered the steamer *Georgia*. Moran said: "I have told him [the Portuguese government official] that we still consider the vessel a pirate and will capture her at sea if possible. This may put an end to the charter party. As matters stand the depositions will not be used now, but Commodore Craven should not let the *Japan* escape." Letter, Asst. Secy. Benjamin Moran to Vice-Consul James Wilding, Aug. 4, 1864, ibid., p. 132.

90. Letter, Vice-Consul James Wilding to Comm. T. T. Craven, Aug. 8, 1864, ibid., p. 133.

91. Report, Comm. T. T. Craven to Secy. of the Navy Gideon Welles, Aug. 15, 1864, ibid., p. 186.

92. Order, Comm. T. T. Craven to Acting Mstr. Jacob Kimball, Aug. 15, 1864, ibid., pp. 187–88.

93. Smith, Flussing Roads.

94. Report, Comm. T. T. Craven to Secy. of the Navy Gideon Welles, Aug. 24, 1864, *ORN*, 1.3: 187–88.

95. *Law Times* (London), Sept. 3, 1864, p. 480.

96. Ibid., p. 492.

97. Ibid., Sept. 17, 1864, p. 499.

98. *The Georgia*, 1 Lowell, 96 (1866).

99. *The Steamship Georgia v. The United States*, 7 Wall. 32 (1869).

100. See *Civil War Day by Day*, pp. 551–52.

101. In a telegram to Capt. Henry Walke of the U.S.S. *Sacramento* on Oct. 11, Moran

alerted the *Niagara* to new difficulties with Semmes, previously of the *Alabama*: "Semmes [Waddell] with 8 officers and 100 men sailed from Liverpool on Sunday in screw steamer 'Laurel,' with six guns as cargo. She has one pipe, two masts, fore and aft schooner-rigged, plain stem, round stern, hull black. Report says he had gone to meet another vessel, chartered for Matamoras. Tell Commodore Craven." *ORN*, 1.3: 298. On the same day, both the legation in London and the consulate in Liverpool were in touch with Craven about the *Laurel*. Said Moran to Craven: "I sent you a telegram about the *Laurel*. The rebels bought her at Liverpool last Tuesday. Captain Semmes sailed in her on Sunday, with eight officers and about 100 men. Forty of them were of the crew of the No. 290, or *Alabama*. She cleared for Matamoras, via Havana and Nassau, which means that she will go anywhere. She took on board in cases six 68-pounders, with the requisite gun carriages, and also small arms. It is doubtless Semmes' purpose to meet and arm some other vells [vessels], as the *Laurel* is not large enough for all the guns, her tonnage being not more than 350. She is new, very strong, and very fast, and was built to carry passengers between Liverpool and Sligo, in Ireland. She has one funnel, two masts, is fore-and-aft schooner-rigged; has a plain stem, round stern, and black hull. Mr. Dudley, the consul at Liverpool, will take the responsibility of her capture anywhere at sea. I would take her wherever I could find her. I regret I can not tell where she went from Liverpool. Among the officers on board her are Armstrong, Howell, and O'Brien, all late of the *Alabama*. O'Brien is an engineer. She is a screw steamer and an excellent sea boat. Semmes has his steward with him, which looks as if he meant to keep afloat awhile." Ibid., p. 343. Thomas H. Dudley, the consul in Liverpool, sent a description of the *Laurel* as well. On Oct. 31, Moran advised Craven that both the *Sea King* and the *Laurel* had been operating in the area of Madeira, Spain. That same day Craven advised Welles that he had been unable to intercept the *Laurel*. In the same communication he spoke of a fruitless search for the Spanish steamer *Cicerone* of which Moran had previously noted his "strong suspicion."

Further discussion of the tactics of both the *Laurel* and the *Sea King* as relayed to Commodore Craven is set forth in Dudley's Nov. 13 letter to him: "Dear Sir: The *Laurel* went to Madeira, where she lay some three days. The steamer *Sea King*, that sailed from London on the 8th of October, went off the island and on the 18th signaled the '*Laurel*' to come out. She immediately got up steam and both steamers went to a small barren island within sight of Madeira, anchored alongside in 17 fathoms water, and the *Laurel* transferred to the *Sea King* the six guns and carriages, a large quantity of shot, shell, powder, etc. After this was done the captain of the *Sea King* called all the men back, told them he had sold the vessel to the Confederates, and that she was hereafter to be a privateer, the same as the *Alabama* but that she would not fight. He then did all he could to get the men to enlist. Some did so under the influence of liquor, which was served out in profusion. She is to be called the *Shenandoah*. My informant does not know Captain Semmes, but was told he was to be her commander. When they left her she had the Confederate flag flying. The *Sea King* is about 222 feet long, 32 feet beam, and draws some 13 or 14 feet of water; is shiprigged, three mast, bright, and heavily sparred. Her bulwarks are high. Her screw is so constructed that it can be taken up out of water. She is an excellent sailer [sic] and altogether a fine vessel for the business of privateering. A part of the guns are 68 and the others 32 pounders. She also has two 20 pounders, making eight in all. I much fear another vessel is to go either from England or France. Eleven guns, 68 pounders, with their carriages, are now lying in Liverpool ready to be embarked in some vessel. . . . (P.S.)—The *Laurel* went to Teneriffe and landed the men who would not join the *Shenandoah*. The latter vessel went in another direction, and is no doubt now burning and destroying vessels." Ibid., pp. 372–73.

102. Report, Comm. T. T. Craven to Secy. of the Navy Gideon Welles, Nov. 22, 1864, ibid., p. 378.

103. Spencer, *Confederate Navy in Europe*, pp. 149–50.

104. Ibid., pp. 168–69.

105. Letter, John Bigelow, U.S. chargé, Paris, to Horatio Perry, U.S. chargé, Madrid, Feb. 8, 1865, *ORN*, 1.3: 440.

106. Report, Comm. T. T. Craven to Secy. of the Navy Gideon Welles, Feb. 28, 1865, ibid., p. 434.

107. Letter, Capt. T. J. Page to Cmdr. James Bulloch, Feb. 12, 1865, ibid., p. 737.

108. Report, Comm. T. T. Craven to Asst. Secy. of the Navy Gideon Welles, Feb. 28, 1865, ibid., p. 434.

109. Margaret Clapp, *Forgotten First Citizen: John Bigelow* (1947).

110. *Civil War Day by Day*, p. 633.

111. Edward Stokes Muller, "The Dilemma of Commander Craven," *Civil War Times Illustrated*, Nov.–Dec. 1994, p. 34.

112. Letter, Comm. T. T. Craven to U.S. Chargé Horatio J. Perry, Feb. 28, 1865, *ORN*, 1.3: 439.

113. StreetSwing's Dance History Archives, "The Spanish Fandango," at www.streetswing.com

114. Letter, Vice-Consul James Wilding to U.S. Chargé Horatio J. Perry, March 14, 1865, *ORN*, 1.3: 458.

115. *Civil War Day by Day*, p. 624.

116. Ibid., p. 642.

117. Abstract log of U.S.S. *Niagara*, March 21–28, 1865, *ORN*, 1.3: 464.

118. Report, Comm. T. T. Craven to Secy. of the Navy Gideon Welles, March 29, 1865, ibid., p. 461.

119. Abstract log of *Niagara*, ibid., p. 464.

120. Report, Comm. T. T. Craven to Secy. of the Navy Gideon Welles, March 29, 1865, ibid., p. 461.

121. Letter, Capt. T. J. Page to Cmdr. John Bulloch, March 25, 1865, ibid., p. 741.

122. Abstract log *Niagara*, ibid., p. 465.

123. Report, Comm. T. T. Craven to Secy. of the Navy Gideon Welles, March 29, 1865, ibid., p. 461.

124. Letter, Capt. T. J. Page to Cmdr. John Bulloch, March 27, 1865, ibid., p. 745.

125. Abstract log *Niagara*, ibid., p. 465.

126. Letter, Comm. T. T. Craven to James E. Harvey, March 28, 1865, ibid., p. 477.

127. "The Escape of the Ram Stonewall," *New York Times*, April 13, 1865, p. 4. For a discussion of the entire *Stonewall* matter by a diplomatic participant, see John Bigelow, *France and the Confederate Navy 1863–1868: An International Episode* (1888). See also Le Roy Fischer and B. J. Chandler, "United States–Spanish Relations During the American Civil War," Lincoln *Herald*, 75.4 (Winter 1973): 142–44.

128. Report, Comm. T. T. Craven to Secy. of the Navy Gideon Welles, March 29, 1865, *ORN*, 1.3: 461.

129. General Order, No. 68, Relative to the court-martial of Commodore Thomas T. Craven, Navy Department, Dec. 6, 1865, ibid., p. 467.

130. *Record of the Testimony Taken in the Trial of Commodore T. T. Craven, United States Navy, Held in Washington, D.C., in November, 1865*, pp. 98, 100 (1866).

131. General Order 68, pp. 467–70.

132. Edward Stokes Miller, "The Dilemma of Commodore Craven," *Civil War Times Illustrated*, 33.5 (Nov.–Dec. 1994): 41, 99, 118 (the last cites the charges); Frank Merli, *Great Britain and the Confederate Navy, 1861–1865* (1965).

133. Miller, "Dilemma of Commodore Craven," p. 99.

134. Letter, Duke de Loulé, Minister and Secretary of State for Foreign Affairs, to James E. Harvey, U.S. minister to Portugal, March 31, 1865, *ORN*, 1.3: 481.

135. Report, Cmdr. A. D. Harrell to Secy. of the Navy Gideon Welles, May 2, 1865, ibid., p. 507.

136. See "Our Noble Tars Speak" in Chap. 4.

137. Order dated May 8, 1865, provided by Joaquim Alho Pereira Lina, Chefe do Arquivo Central, Biblioteca Central da Marinha, Lisbon. Translated by Osvaldo Agripino de Castro Jr., Visiting Scholar, Stanford Law School.

138. *Civil War Day by Day*, p. 687.

139. Report, Comm. T. T. Craven to Secy. of the Navy Gideon Welles, May 11, 1865, *ORN*, 1.3: 515.

140. Report, Craven to Welles, May 26, 1865, ibid., p. 529.

141. Michael J. Bennett, "'Frictions': Shipboard Relations Between White and Contraband Sailors," *Civil War History*, 47.2 (June 2001).

142. Letter, Acting Secy. of the Navy G. V. Fox to Rear-Adm. L. M. Goldsborough, June 6, 1865, *ORN*, 1.3: 542.

143. *Civil War Day by Day*, pp. 690–91.

144. Ibid., pp. 690, 692.

145. James M. McPherson, *The Negro's Civil War: How American Negroes Felt and Acted During the War for the Union*, p. 97 (1982).

146. Ibid., pp. 78, 84; Michael Vorenberg, *Final Freedom: The Civil War, the Abolition of Slavery, and the Thirteenth Amendment*, pp. 158–59 (2001). Vorenberg writes: "Unwilling to stand by idly as Republican leaders kept quiet on emancipation, African Americans in October called for a national convention of 'colored men' to meet in Syracuse, New York—the first national meeting of African Americans in nine years. About 150 men attended, including Frederick Douglass, who was elected president of the convention. . . . Another purpose [of the convention] was to drive the final stake into the idea of colonizing blacks abroad. Former proponents of colonization, including Henry Highland Garnet, now joined with old rivals in a pledge to improve the lives of the freed people at home rather than sending them away."

147. Philip Paul Bliss and James R. Murray, *The Songs of P. P. Bliss*, p. 54 (1877).

148. *Civil War Day by Day*, pp. 687, 689.

149. Report, Comm. T. T. Craven to Secy. of the Navy Gideon Welles, July 1, 1865, *ORN*, 1.3: 561.

150. Heather Cox Richardson, *The Death of Reconstruction*, p. 16 (2001).

151. Report, Capt. Henry Walke to Secy. of the Navy Gideon Welles, July 10, 1865, ibid., p. 563.

152. Letter, Amb. C. F. Adams to Capt. Henry Walke, July 11, 1865, ibid., p. 565.

153. Order, Rear-Adm. L. M. Goldsborough to Comm. T. T. Craven, July 23, 1865, ibid., p. 570.

154. Letter, U.S. minister to Belgium H. S. Sanford to Secy. of State William H. Seward, July 31, 1865, ibid., p. 513.

155. Report, Comm. T. T. Craven to Secy. of the Navy Gideon Welles, Sept. 21, 1865, ibid., p. 592.

156. *Civil War Day by Day*, pp. 688, 689.

Epilogue

1. "Stories from Silence," *New York Times*, May 28, 2001.

2. *Dedham Transcript*, May 26, 1923. The *Transcript* said: "William B. Gould, one of Dedham's best known citizens, died of heart trouble at his home on Milton street, East Dedham, May 23, 1923. He was the son of Alexander and Elizabeth (Moore) Gould and was born in Wilmington, N.C., Nov. 13, 1837. He came to Dedham in 1871 and established himself in business as a brick mason and contractor, a business from which he retired several years ago. He was a naval veteran of the Civil War and served as a petty officer on the U.S.S.S. Cambridge, Ohio, and Niagara of the fleet engaged in the European blockade. The deceased was a member of the Norfolk County Grand Army of the Republic Association, the U.S. Naval Veterans Association and of the Charles W. Carroll Post 144, G.A.R. Of the last named organization he was a past commander and had served it for many years as its adjutant."

3. *Dedham Transcript*, Nov. 11, 1898.

4. Diary, April 15, 1865.

5. Diary, May 18, 1864.

6. See Jack Beatty, *The Rascal King: The Life and Times of James Michael Curley (1874–1958)* (1992).

7. William B. Gould IV, "Equal Opportunity for Black Civilians," *New York Times*, March 7, 1991, p. A18.

8. I am indebted to Pete Wismann of Mountain View, Calif., an experienced mason (and a former center and linebacker for the San Francisco 49'ers football team), for this information.

9. See "Items of Interest from Wilmington" in Chap. 4.

10. Gordon Bock and Frank Mangione, "Mouldings on the Run: The Art of Bench-run Plaster Mouldings," *Old-House Journal*, Jan./Feb. 1999, p. 56.

11. I am indebted to Morris Rabinowitz, director of the Dedham Public Library, for bringing the records of so much of William B. Gould's craftsmanship to my attention.

12. Lisa Y. King, "Wounds That Bind: A Comparative Study of the Role Played by Civil War Veterans of African Descent in Community Formation in Massachusetts and South Carolina, 1865–1915," pp. 149–50. Ph.D. dissertation, Howard University, Washington, D.C., 1999. Because of the efforts of the GAR and political competition for the votes of northern veterans "the total cost of pensions doubled between 1880 and 1890 and rose by another third between 1890 and 1896, by which time veterans' pensions accounted for about forty-five percent of federal outlays." This led to the passage of the Sixteenth Amendment to the Constitution authorizing an income tax. Robert William Fogel, *The Fourth Great Awakening and the Future of Egalitarianism*, pp. 127–28 (2000).

13. David W. Blight, *Race and Reunion: The Civil War in American Memory*, pp. 304–5 (2001).

14. *Dedham Transcript*, April 13, 1918, p. 3.

15. Ibid., Sept. 22, 1917, p. 3.

16. Interview with the Chesnut family, July 1999.

17. *Dedham Transcript*, May 21, 1921, p. 4.

18. Ibid., May 29, 1909, pp. 4–5.   19. Ibid., Feb. 17, 1900.

20. Ibid., June 2, 1900.   21. Ibid., June 1, 1901.

22. Ibid., Jan. 27, 1917.   23. Ibid., July 8, 1911.

24. Ibid., Oct. 12, 1920, pp. 2, 5.

Appendix C

1. Roy P. Basler, ed., *The Collected Works of Abraham Lincoln*, vol.7, p. 259 (1953).

2. Ibid., vol.4, pp. 24–25.

3. Gabor S. Boritt, *Lincoln and the Economics of the American Dream*, p. 184 (1978).

4. Ibid., p. 185.

5. Basler, ed., *Collected Works of Abraham Lincoln*, vol. 3, pp. 477–78.

6. Of course, I advanced such ideas in the context of proposals for comprehensive labor law reform. See W. Gould, *Agenda for Reform: The Future of Employment Relationships and the Law*, pp. 109–50 (1993).

7. B. Quarles, *The Negro in the Civil War*, pp. 59–61, 64 (1953). On blacks in the U.S. Navy generally, see D. Valuska, *The African American in the Union Navy, 1861–1865* (1993).

8. Of course, President Lincoln had earlier proposed colonization within the context of compensated emancipation.

9. Diary May 6, 1864.

10. William B. Gould IV speech before the Loyal Legion of the United States, "Lincoln, Labor and the Black Military: The Legacy Provided" delivered on Feb. 11, 1995, in Washington, D.C.

11. Said William Benjamin Gould on March 8, 1863, two months after its issuance: "Read . . . the Proclamation of Emancipation . . . verry good."

12. On March 7, 1865: "We have an account of the passage of the amendment to the Constitution prohibiting slavery throughout the United States."

13. Spencer S. Hsu, "Slavery 'Abhorred,' Gilmore Says: Words Anger Confederate Defenders; Event Upsets Rights Groups," *Washington Post*, April 10, 1998, pp. C1, C7. See also an op-ed contribution by Thomas M. Boyd, "The Curse of Slavery," ibid., May 2, 1998, p. A19, which, while expressing disagreement with slavery's new apologists, erroneously characterizes General Lee as an opponent of slavery. See A. Nolan, *Lee Considered: General Robert E. Lee and Civil War History* (1996).

14. An expression of gratitude is conveyed to "Dr. T. C. Worth, of Wilmington, N.C., Joseph S. Tillinghast, Wm. C. Taber, Matthew and Rachel Howland, of New Bedford; Wm. Shaler, D.D. of Portland, Me., Rev. J. S. Bronson of Hyannis; to the Barnstable Baptist Association; Rev. Mr. Steer and others of the Free-Will Baptist denomination; Rev. Mr. Woodbury and others of the Unitarian denomination; Rev. Messrs. Wolcott and Edwards, also others of the Congregational denomination; Rev. Mr. Snow and others of the Methodist de-

nomination; Rev. Messrs. Eaton and Cook, also others of the Universalist denomination; Rev. Mr. Pollard and others of the Taunton Baptist Association; Col. Borden, of Fall River, and to the Honorable Selectmen and Mess. Wm. Hudwen, John W. Barrett, Francis M. Mitchell, and James F. Cobb of this town, for the part they have taken and the labor they have performed in raising the balance of the required sum."

15. My father has attached a commentary on her work to the diary. Schonberg, "The Black Swan That Sang for the Nobility," *New York Times*, April 12, 1970.

16. I have the diplomatic correspondence between the Secretary of Navy and Commodore Craven about this—as well as the court martial proceedings, subsequent to the war which grew out of the failure of Craven to confront the *Stonewall* in Ferrol and Coruña.

17. "The significance of the *Kearsarge-Alabama* struggle has less in the battle itself than it does in the location of the battle. The course of the war was affected not one whit by the battle. Had Semmes [of the *Alabama*] won, he would have had to face the U.S.S. *Niagara*, which was then en route to Europe and more powerful still than the *Kearsarge*." W. Spencer, *The Confederate Navy in Europe*, p. 190 (1983).

18. In particular, I like his April 15, 1865 entry: "I heard the glad tidings that the stars and stripes had been planted over the capital of the confederacy by the invincible Grant. While we honor the living soldiers who have done so much, we must not forget to whisper for fear of disturbing the glorious sleep of the many who have fallen. Martyrs to the cause of right and equality."

19. This expression is apparently based upon the song "Good Bye, Jeff" by Philip Bliss, which concludes:

But the soul of famous Old John Brown has not stop'd marching, Jeff,
And the last of Southern chivalry we'll see,
When the echo of the "Hallelujah Chorus," Jeff,
Finds you hanging on a "sour apple tree."

Index

Other Books by William B. Gould IV

Black Workers in White Unions: Job Discrimination in the United States
    Cornell University Press, 1977

Japan's Reshaping of American Labor Law
    MIT Press, 1984

Strikes, Dispute Procedures, and Arbitration: Essays on Labor Law
    Greenwood Press, 1985

Labor Relations in Professional Sports (with Robert C. Berry and Paul D. Staudohar)
    Auburn House, 1986

A Primer on American Labor Law
    MIT Press; Third Edition, 1993

Agenda for Reform: The Future of Employment Relationships and the Law
    MIT Press, 1993

Labored Relations: Law, Politics, and the NLRB—A Memoir
    MIT Press, 2000

CPSIA information can be obtained
at www.ICGtesting.com
Printed in the USA
JSHW030011060721
16604JS00002B/2

31901068021650